HILL FOLKS

HILL FOLKS

A HISTORY OF

ARKANSAS OZARKERS & THEIR IMAGE

BROOKS BLEVINS

THE UNIVERSITY OF NORTH CAROLINA PRESS

CHAPEL HILL AND LONDON

© 2002 The University of North Carolina Press
All rights reserved
Manufactured in the United States of America
Designed by April Leidig-Higgins
Set in Minion by Copperline Book Services, Inc.

The paper in this book meets the guidelines for permanence and
durability of the Committee on Production Guidelines for Book
Longevity of the Council on Library Resources.

Portions of this work have been reprinted in revised form from
the following works: "Heading to the Hill: Population Replacement
in the Arkansas Ozarks," *Agricultural History* 74, no. 2 (2000),
© 2000 by Agricultural History Society, reprinted by permission of
the University of California Press, and "Wretched and Innocent:
Two Highland Regions in the National Consciousness," *Journal
of Appalachian Studies* 7, no. 2 (2001), © 2001 by Journal of
Appalachian Studies, reprinted by permission.

Photo on page iii: Ozark hill folks, Izard County, date unknown.
Courtesy of Betty Brunson.

Library of Congress Cataloging-in-Publication Data
Blevins, Brooks, 1969–   Hill folks: a history of Arkansas Ozarkers
and their image / Brooks Blevins.
p. cm.   Includes bibliographical references and index.
ISBN 0-8078-2675-8 (cloth: alk. paper)
ISBN 0-8078-5342-9 (pbk.: alk. paper)
1. Ozark Mountains Region—History. 2. Arkansas—History.
3. Ozark Mountains Region—Social conditions. 4. Arkansas—
Social conditions. 5. Mountain whites (Southern States)—Ozark
Mountains Region—History. 6. Mountain whites (Southern
States)—Arkansas—History. I. Title.
F417.09 B63 2002   976.7′1—dc21   2001049160

CLOTH 06 05 04 03 02   5 4 3 2 1
PAPER 06 05 04 03 02   5 4 3 2 1

For Sharon and B.

CONTENTS

ILLUSTRATIONS, MAPS, AND TABLE

MAPS

TABLE

PREFACE

I BEGAN THIS WORK more than a decade ago as an undergraduate student at Arkansas (now Lyon) College, driven by a desire to better understand the history of a region that, as I was to discover, had been unsatisfactorily documented. Much has been written about the Ozarks, of course, but only a small fraction of it has been of a scholarly, historical nature. Folklorists and travel writers discovered this mid-American highland region in the early twentieth century. Perhaps this helps explain the paucity of historical treatment. Folklorist Vance Randolph, travel writer Otto Ernest Rayburn, and their successors have so dominated the image of the Ozarks that social scientists and historians have for the most part left the region to vacationers and folk song gatherers. Or perhaps the difficulty of identifying the Ozarks with some larger American region has been the stumbling block. The Ozark region, in fact, often seems a hybrid of the South, the Midwest, and the West. Maybe the historical oversight stems from the misconception that, as Randolph himself claimed, the Ozark region is simply a "small edition" of the Appalachian highlands.

Whatever the reasons have been, the Ozark region has largely been denied a scholarly, historical record. The ingredients for an engaging study are evident: the aforementioned disparate regional affiliations, image versus reality, and paradox. How could a region simultaneously produce a J. William Fulbright and an Orval Faubus, provide the setting for a young Bill Clinton's first political race, spawn Fortune 500 companies such as Wal-Mart and Tyson Foods, and still be saddled with an image of static backwardness, of immunity from the march of time and historical progression? What follows is an attempt to take the first step in the journey to discover the story of an American region. It is my hope that this work will spark the interest of other students and potential students of Ozark history and of regional American history.

A few things about the book, its structure, and its underlying geography deserve mentioning. Geographers have long disagreed over the boundaries of the Ozark region. Fortunately for this study, most of their disagreements concern borders outside the state of Arkansas. For the purposes of this book the Ozark region comprises roughly the north-western and north central one-quarter of the state. For statistical purposes I have limited the region to fifteen counties lying wholly within the upland region: Benton, Washington, Madison, Carroll, Boone, Newton, Van Buren, Searcy, Marion, Baxter, Stone, Cleburne, Izard, Fulton, and Sharp. In addition, the text includes references to and examples from Ozark areas in adjoining counties: Independence, Lawrence, Randolph, Johnson, Pope, and others.

The structure and style of the book may be described as narrative within the framework of chronologically organized sections. As the title suggests, *Hill Folks: A History of Arkansas Ozarkers and Their Image* is about a people and an image. As such it is social history, not in the sense of conforming to a certain set of methodologies, philosophies, or presuppositions but in the sense that it conveys the stories and common experiences of an identifiable group of people. Where possible I have tried to relate this story in the voices and through the experiences of the participants themselves. These Ozarkers can be as extraordinary as John Quincy Wolf Sr. and Jimmy Driftwood or as unheralded as Tom Ross and Beulah Billingsley. Finally, in an attempt to present this material as a foundation work of sorts, I have absorbed into the narrative a wide range of topics, including settlement patterns, mining, migratory labor, and travel writing. Consequently, no single topic, with the possible exception of certain agricultural activities, undergoes an exhaustive exploration. It is my sincere desire that these many threads will be pursued fully by subsequent historians and by myself in the coming years.

The aid and advice of many people have contributed invaluably to this work over the past decade. To the many Ozarkers who openly and gladly revealed to me their life stories through oral history, I offer my sincerest gratitude. Among the people who offered valuable critical readings of sections of this work at various stages are Jane B. Fagg, Charles Kimball, W. David Lewis, Joe Molnar, Conner Bailey, Guy Beckwith, Ruth Crocker, Anthony Gene Carey, W. K. McNeil, David E. Harrell, Richard Starnes, Lynn Morrow, and Robert Cochran. Jason White provided valuable assistance and advice in the making of maps for the book. The excellent staff members at the University of North Carolina Press have devoted their time and energy to make this a better book than it otherwise would have been; I especially appreciate Sian Hunter, Paula Wald, and Cornelia Wright.

I thank all of the teachers who have encouraged me to write and who have communicated to me an appreciation for the study of history. Among these are Shelia Dinnella, Sandy Evans, Sally Adkisson, Shelby Qualls, Don Weatherman, Jane Fagg, and the late Dan Fagg. To Elizabeth Jacoway I will forever be thankful for sharing her passion for southern history and inspiring me to pursue my love for the same. I thank Lynn Morrow, Tom Dillard, and Gene Hyde for introducing me to crucial works I might otherwise have overlooked; I also thank Gene for his camaraderie, enthusiasm, and unflagging support. I am indebted to Vance Randolph, Otto Ernest Rayburn, Charles Morrow Wilson, W. K. McNeil, Milton Rafferty, and the others who have written about the Ozarks and have sparked our interest with their passion for the region. I am grateful for Donald Harington, a historian at heart who brings the Ozarks' past to life with unsurpassed beauty and insight. I deeply appreciate two Ozarkers who also happen to be old friends and former college roommates: Brien Hall, whose energy and love of community constantly inspire me, and Chris Cochran, whose insights I envy and whose earnestness I value above all.

I have received gracious and expert assistance at archives, in local libraries, and in courthouse vaults across the Ozark region and beyond. Among those whose help I could not have done without were Michael Debrishus, Andrea Cantrell, and the staff at the University of Arkansas Special Collections in Fayetteville; Tom Dillard, Brian Robertson, and Timothy Nutt at the Butler Center for Arkansas Studies in Little Rock; Russell Baker and the staff at the Arkansas History Commission in Little Rock; Jimmy Bryant at the University of Central Arkansas Archives in Conway; Pete Scholls at the National Archives and Records Administration, Southwest Region, in Fort Worth; Manon Wilson and Susan Young at the Shiloh Museum of Ozark History in Springdale; Jo Blatti at the Old Independence Regional Museum in Batesville; Cathy Whittenton and Nancy Griffith at Lyon College; Joan Mabry and Zennie Pollard at the Izard County Library in Melbourne; Bonnie Rush at the Izard County courthouse in Melbourne; and all the other librarians and vault keepers I met across the region.

I thank Wayne Flynt for never doubting the too-often-opaque intentions of an Arkansas country boy and for always demanding excellence and effort. Without his guidance, this book would not exist. As always I owe the biggest debt of gratitude to my wife Sharon for her constant support and faith and for bringing into the world Bryan, my inspiration. Finally, I acknowledge the two Ozarkers I most admire: Mom, for taking the time to read to her children and for instilling in me a love for learning and a desire to reach my goals, and Dad, for teaching me by example to love a hilly, rocky land, to act with integrity and decency, and to always stay true to myself.

HILL FOLKS

INTRODUCTION

IN THE INTRODUCTION to his 1931 book, *The Ozarks: An American Survival of Primitive Society*, Vance Randolph warned the reader that his subjects were not the "progressive element in the Ozark towns, nor . . . the prosperous valley farmers" but the "diverting and picturesque" residents of the backwoods, the "hill-billy" and the "ridge-runner." Randolph had fired one of the first volleys in what would become a barrage of nonfiction treatments of "the most backward and deliberately unprogressive region in the United States." He, along with many other midwesterners, had found a place "practically unknown to the readers of guide-books" and a people differing "so widely from the average urban American that when the latter visits the hill country he feels himself among an alien people."[1]

Subsequent chroniclers of Ozark life and culture were less forthright in their approaches to their subjects and in their relationships with their readers. The disclaimer Randolph boldly asserted throughout half a century of roaming the hills, recording stories and songs, and writing books and articles gradually faded into the background in succeeding decades. The "diverting and picturesque" became the norm. Randolph assured the reader that "the most picturesque of the Ozark natives are seldom seen by the casual summer visitor." He was not mistaken, and the observation has almost universally remained true to this day. But the efforts of Randolph and dozens of other writers in the coming years revealed these hillbillies in all their homespun, rustic quaintness or wretched backwardness; they etched into the American consciousness images of contrast and paradox while they obscured the history, diversity, and complexity of the Ozark region.[2]

These conflicting depictions of a region and its people served America well throughout much of the twentieth century. As Henry Shapiro discovered, Americans have long been adept at utilizing their southern mountains and mountaineers for purposes both physical and psychological. In *Appalachia on Our Mind,* Shapiro examines the American (generally northeastern) image of a backward region in the late nineteenth and early twentieth centuries. Shapiro's Appalachia, the Ozarks' mother region, served as a living gauge by which "progressive" America could measure its advancement. This peculiar region of centuries-old culture proved to be both a cause for continued faith in modernization and a burden on the minds of all who desired to modernize the mountaineer. But as progressivism and the spirit of social missionary activity waned after World War I, so too did the missionary's social and moral concern for the salvation of Appalachia.[3]

Faced with the burdens of the modern age that took shape after World War I, many Americans sought an arcadian region of innocence and beauty. To a country racked by depression, war, and the anxieties of the nuclear age, the Ozarker embodied the frontierlike individualism that pervades American tradition, a trait quite removed from modern society. And the region's rural, isolated characteristics proved both aesthetically pleasing and nostalgically reassuring. Furthermore, as mechanization and New Deal agricultural relief programs transformed the rural landscape, and as the nuclear age brought into question the intrinsic value of change and the inevitability of technological progress, Americans searched for a region untouched by the modern world and indicative of a more innocent time. Many of them discovered the Ozarks, which, ironically, was a region well advanced into the process of rural transformation and decline. Simultaneously, the degraded and backward state of the hillbilly helped expel, or at least soften, any doubts that depression-era and Cold War Americans might harbor concerning the innate goodness of science and "progress."[4]

Perhaps the quilting, folk song–humming grandma shared a leaky log cabin with the barefooted, black floppy hat–wearing moonshiner. The conflicting images both had their appeal to post–World War II generations. To urban and small-town Americans burdened by the Cold War and their own attempts to adjust to a rapidly mechanizing and modernizing society, the Ozarks offered a haven, both physically and mentally. Urban midwesterners flocked to the region's lake shores, river banks, and hiking trails in ever-increasing numbers to escape, if only for a brief time, the rigors of fast-paced life. Even more therapeutic was the region's developing image. Many Americans, separated from a rural past, yearned with foggy-eyed nostalgia for the bucolic countryside, the homestead of American lore. Through the ink of the travel writer the Ozarks could supply this need. More important, the Ozarks, like its parent to the east, seemed to provide a direct link with the American past, especially in the Anglocentric days surrounding World War II. Some sort of pure "Anglo-Saxon" culture had been carefully preserved there by "contemporary ancestors." Lest Americans become too overburdened by a sense of guilt over the loss of heritage and frontier survival skills, however, the bare-footed moonshiner stared out from comic strips and postcards to sober the nostalgic spirit and reaffirm the resolve toward progress and modernization. As one New York writer wrote in 1949: "Even more than most places, the Ozark Mountains are all things to all people."[5]

The Ozarks attracted few missionaries and entrepreneurs of the type who had traveled into the Appalachian Mountains before the turn of the century. The Ozark region did, however, summon other kinds of seekers similar to the ones who explored Appalachia and its culture in the early twentieth century. Many came to record and preserve a soon-to-be obsolete way of life in books of photographs and stories of the last mountaineers. Others sought to preserve disappearing arts and handicrafts once widely practiced by America's frontier families. The most famous simply recorded the wealth of folklore, oral traditions, and mountain ballads. The focus had changed since reformers first entered Appalachia. The Progressive Era spirit of reform and conformity had passed, and in its place thrived an appreciation for nostalgia and a yearning to preserve some vestiges of a bygone era, some physical and spiritual connection to a frontier long vanished. The Ozarks would be rediscovered in the 1960s, but its image would not undergo the fundamental revision experienced by Appalachia during that decade. The American spirit of nostalgia and the actions of a group of non-Ozarkers and natives concerned with tourism promotion and folk culture preservation would maintain the region's static, contemporary ancestor image into the late twentieth century.

The entrepreneurs who entered the Ozarks in growing numbers after 1945 were not the coal and timber barons who had come to rule the remote hollows of Appalachia years earlier. These businessmen came to capitalize on the region's scenic beauty and the nation's growing prosperity and culture of leisure, factors that led to the emergence of widespread tourism. Although the region's best timber resources had been harvested early in the century, the smaller scale of the Ozark operation (when compared to Appalachia) left fewer visible scars. Furthermore, mining activity, primarily zinc and manganese ore extraction, proved relatively minuscule and less damaging to the aesthetic qualities of the environment. These tourism entrepreneurs would eventually capitalize on everything from scenic river canoeing to mountain music to theme parks perpetuating Ozark stereotypes, sometimes with the assistance of Ozark natives.

Despite the conflicting images of rustic isolation and uncultured backwardness promoted by Ozark boosters, the Ozarkers and their lands were in the midst of a transformation in the years following World War II. The forces effecting the modernization of the United States and the demise of rural communities—the same technological, political, and institutional forces breeding and cultivating the increasing interest in the Ozark region—were at work in even the most remote northern Arkansas hollow and had been for half a century or more. The region of traditional rural communities and families popularized and romanticized in the nation's imagination stared beyond the darkening horizon of its last sunset. In reality the Ozarks that survived in the minds of post–World War II Americans had long since disappeared, if indeed it ever had existed.[6]

The purpose of this study, then, is to reveal the Ozark region and the Ozarkers that did exist, to look beyond picturesque diversions into a region almost wholly unexplored by the historian. In so doing, I hope not only to shed light on a region long darkened by misunderstanding and misrepresentation but also to chronicle the chroniclers of the Ozark image.

The Arkansas Ozark region of the post–World War II era was, for a brief moment, still the domain of the small farmer. But it was also a land of flux and outmigration, and the home of a people experiencing the effects of modern science and technology, government intervention, and Cold War American affluence at a level heretofore unimaginable in much of the relatively isolated countryside. The Ozarkers of the foothills, creek bottoms, and mountain hollows had never been as isolated and as unconsciously immune or consciously resistant to modernizing influences and brushes with the outside world as folklorists and travel writers had suggested.

This observation pushes the beginning of this study back almost a century and a half before World War II, back into the sparsely settled wilderness that was the Ozark region at the beginning of the nineteenth century, in order to reveal the historical forces, the complexities, and the nuances that comprised the past and explained the present of the region and its inhabitants discovered by tourists and folklorists in the middle of the twentieth century. Therefore, although the jumping-off point for this study is the interplay of image and reality in the post–World War II era, what follows is a dual effort. It is an exploration of the development and perpetuation of the Ozark image as well as the first treatment of the re-

MAP I.1. Counties in the Ozarks. From Milton D. Rafferty, *The Ozarks: Land and Life* (Fayetteville: University of Arkansas Press, 2001).

gion's social history, the reality behind the image. It seems only natural that the initial scholarly study of a region long obscured, even eclipsed, by myth and stereotype should proceed in such a dichotomous fashion.

In the decades after the first white settlers pushed into northern Arkansas after the War of 1812, Ozark settlers and their descendants, although certainly more isolated than the vast majority of Americans, witnessed the coming of the steamboat, the introduction of cash crops, the construction of railroads, and the harvesting of hundreds of thousands of acres of virgin timber. Yet the diversity of topographic conditions, soil qualities, and water resources prevented uniformity in the Ozarkers' experiences with change and modernization. Whereas the fertile plains of extreme northwestern Arkansas and the rich bottomlands along the White and other Ozark rivers brought prosperity to many agriculturists, the comparative barrenness of the vast interior of rocky hillsides and rugged mountains left other generations of Ozarkers the unenviable task of providing food and shelter within a harsh and unforgiving country. This intraregional diversity has been a key feature in the history and development of the Arkansas Ozarks.[7]

Until a couple of generations ago, the vast majority of Ozarkers scratched out their livings on hillside and creek bottom farms. Consequently, any historical study of the region must necessarily begin with agriculture and rural life. Farming in the Ozarks has in no way been a stagnant occupation. While photographers who combed the most remote recesses of the region in the 1940s and 1950s could on occasion find old men and women on isolated farmsteads whose practices varied little from those of their grandparents, such models of contemporary ancestors were nearing extinction. Although less picturesque and interesting to journalists and folklorists, the small farmers whose cotton and corn patches speckled the hillsides, whose dairies supplied the expanding milk markets, and whose poultry flocks and cattle herds fed the changing appetites of postwar Americans dominated the Ozark region. That is not to say the Ozarks was simply another rural region quite like any other in most regards. It certainly was different from other regions but not as monumentally as its chroniclers have had us believe. Agricultural mechanization arrived belatedly in northern Arkansas, and in most cases the Ozarker's clinging to the tradition of animal and man power was a decision made of economic necessity, not from a stubborn disregard for modernity. And when the modern world of technology did visit the hillside farm, it often did so with striking and incongruous results. Not only did sons mount small, one- and two-row tractors in fields beside their father with his team of mules, but electric milking machines and tractor-drawn hay balers coexisted alongside smokehouses and mule-powered sorghum mills.

In a century and a half, technological, governmental, and institutional forces effected the transformation of the region from an isolated, subsistence farming culture to, first, one of scattered row crops and general farming (not unlike other parts of the Upper South and lower Midwest) and then to one of fewer and larger farms specializing in livestock and poultry. The factors spurring the transformation of farming practices also affected every facet of rural life—churches, schools, local institutions, traditions, and crossroads businesses.

The region's past and present are riddled with paradox. The three decades following the Great Depression witnessed a mass exodus from the Ozarks as mechanized, large-scale farming on more arable soils left the small hillside farmer unable to compete, and the spread of technological innovation to the countryside scattered rural communities. As the last of the migrant families left their homes for work elsewhere, retired northerners—beneficiaries of Cold War America's affluence—flocked southward in search of quieter, cleaner, warmer environments in which to spend their golden years. They spurred Ozark tourism and construction activity in the process. In true twentieth-century irony, the very forces of modernization that transformed agriculture and drove thousands of rural families from their communities in search of work also provided the only available livelihoods for the many who remained on the land of their grandfathers and in the company of family.

The study that follows is more than a refutation or qualification of long-held misconceptions and exaggerations of a region and its people. The Ozarks merits examination not only in response to decades of criticism, distortion, and uninformed appraisal by outsiders, but in its own right. Therefore, first and foremost, my research reflects an attempt to fight through the thicket of myth, nostalgia, and stereotype. In the clearing beyond we will discover the story of the Ozarks, a region's transformation and a people's perseverance. Such a treatment will likely lend nuance to our understanding of cultural transformation and rural modernization and perhaps reveal a region long subjugated by the American preference for image over substance. At the very least it will offer a first, in-depth study of a region long ignored by historians and quite worthy of their attention.

PART ONE

Beginnings

IN THE HISTORY of the Ozark region of Arkansas, the nineteenth century is more than an arbitrary succession of decades and years extracted from human experience. The century instead quite neatly encapsulates an era dominated by the settlement of a frontier and the development of a society. In 1800 the Ozark region was home to no white settlers and served as little more than a seasonal hunting ground for the Osage, whose more permanent dwellings lay many miles to the north. By the end of the nineteenth century, the Arkansas Ozarks was home to approximately a quarter of a million American settlers; the region had been fully settled and had reached the capacity of people the land could support.

Although most of the Ozark region remained quite rural and even isolated by American standards in 1900, the forces of modernization synonymous with the nineteenth century had not eluded Ozarkers. By mid-century, steamboats plied the swift waters of the White River above Batesville, penetrating the rugged hills and exposing to the outside world the narrow bottoms of small settlements and small farms. In the decades following the Civil War, large numbers of Ozark farmers entered the staple-crop economy, and general stores sprang up in small towns and at rural crossroads to serve a burgeoning population. In the 1880s railroads skirted the region, bringing prosperity or at least opportunity to a limited number of Ozark residents and revealing a taste of things to come in the early twentieth century.

The three chapters that follow explore developments in the region from the beginnings of white settlement around the time of the War of 1812 to the end of the century. Chapter 1 establishes the geographical diversity of the Arkansas Ozarks, traces the waves of pre–Civil War settlement, and charts the agricultural development of a yeoman-dominated society. Chapter 2 carries the discussion of farming in the region to the end of the nineteenth century, revealing an increasingly diverse agricultural economy of cotton growers, orchardists, general farmers, and isolated semisubsistence farmers. Chapter 3 explores social life—education, family life, religion, and community and social activity—in the region during the first century of white settlement.

The Other Southern Highlands

IN EARLY NOVEMBER 1818 a twenty-five-year-old New Yorker and his companion set out on a three-month journey through a rugged, sparsely settled land west of the Mississippi known as the Ozarks. Leaving Potosi, a small Missouri outpost some sixty miles southwest of St. Louis, the duo traveled hundreds of miles on foot and by horseback through a wild frontier in which they found bear, deer, elk, buffalo, the remnants of Osage hunting camps, and the freshly built cabins of white settlers. They found a country diverse beyond their expectations—a land of sterile hills and fertile prairies, of wooded valleys and treeless balds, of great virgin forests and rivers so clear no fish could escape the canoeists' gaze.

The young New Yorker was Henry Rowe Schoolcraft, a mineralogist who would later build a reputation as an expert on Native American customs and affairs in the Old Northwest. Schoolcraft's journal, published in London two years after his journey, reveals his acute awareness of topographical and geological variations within the region, foreshadowing variations of Ozark development based on subregional characteristics. The Arkansas Ozarks can be broadly divided into four geographic subregions: the Salem Plateau, White River Hills, Springfield Plain, and Boston Mountains. Approaching the area from the northeast, Schoolcraft and his companion Levi Pettibone first entered the Salem, or Central, Plateau, a wide swath of gently undulating upland stretching from the southeastern border of the Ozarks through southern and central Missouri to the region's northeastern edge. Composed of generally infertile, rocky soils, the Salem Plateau comprises only the northeastern corner of the Arkansas Ozarks, or the upland counties east of the White River.

Schoolcraft, having been raised in the prosperous Hudson Valley, found nothing to recommend the Salem Plateau to prospective settlers.

He discovered a "sterile soil, destitute of wood, with gentle elevations, but no hills or cliffs, and no water." After one difficult hike through the wilderness east of the Great North Fork (North Fork) of the White River, Schoolcraft sighed in his journal: "Nothing can exceed the roughness and sterility of the country we have today traversed." The young travelers found bluffs lined with pine, rocky hillsides, and forests of post oak and gnarled black oak, not the coveted majestic white oak found farther west. The subregion's relative barrenness was represented most conspicuously by cedar glades, outcroppings of exposed bedrock fit only for the growth of cedars and greenbriers. Despite its manageable terrain and tempting location at the southeastern edge of the region, settlers would avoid the rocky, infertile interior of the Salem Plateau for decades, choosing instead to settle the fertile plains of the western Ozarks and the river bottoms of the east.[1]

"The country passed over yesterday, after leaving the valley of the White River, presented a character of unvaried sterility, consisting of a succession of lime-stone ridges, skirted with a feeble growth of oaks, with no depth of soil, often bare rocks upon the surface, and covered with coarse wild grass." Such was Schoolcraft's observation after having traversed the White River Hills, a steep and rugged range that follows the White River on its circuitous route from northwestern Arkansas up into Missouri and back down through north central Arkansas almost as far as Batesville. Extending sometimes for fifteen or twenty miles on either side of the river, these hills present the traveler or settler with as daunting a sight as is found in the Ozarks.[2]

Nestled within their protective embrace is the White River, the life-blood of the Ozark region and the destination of northern Arkansas's streams and branches. Schoolcraft marveled as he floated along the clear river: "Every pebble, rock, fish, or floating body, either animate or inanimate, which occupies the bottom of the stream, is seen while passing over it with the most perfect accuracy; and our canoe often seemed as if suspended in the air, such is the remarkable transparency of the water." The valley of the White River had attracted the first white settlers to the Arkansas Ozarks a few years before Schoolcraft's arrival, though it continued to serve as a prime spring and fall hunting ground for the Osage. The White River would connect large sections of the interior Ozarks with the outside world until the early twentieth century, when the railroad replaced the steamboat as exporter of cotton and hides and purveyor of manufactured goods from such places as New Orleans and St. Louis. But the White River Hills also separated the inhabitants of the interior plateaus from the river valley and denied them access to river trade, thus isolating pioneers for many years in the vast open lands beyond these protective hills.[3]

To the west and northwest of the White River Hills lies a fertile, gently sloping prairie, the Springfield Plain. Blessed with the richest soils of the Ozarks, the Springfield Plain occupies a meandering corridor between the White River Hills and the Boston Mountains, extending from Batesville in the east to the border of the Great Plains in the west. The Springfield Plain impressed the discriminating Schoolcraft. Having escaped the inhospitable White River Hills, he and Pettibone discovered the plain's "prairies, which . . . are the most extensive, rich, and beautiful, of any which I have seen west of the Mississippi River. They are covered by a coarse wild grass, which attains so great a height that it completely hides a man on horseback in riding through it."[4]

Thousands of pioneers shared Schoolcraft's estimation of the Springfield Plain. By the time Arkansas achieved statehood almost two decades later, in 1836, the fertile prairies would rank among the most populous and prosperous areas of the state. Just as the Salem Plateau's thin soils and rocky hills hindered settlement and agricultural production, the Springfield Plain's fertility invited immigrants and rewarded their labors. The development of both areas would depend heavily on their differing topographies and soil qualities.

Schoolcraft and Pettibone avoided the Ozarks' highest and most rugged elevations, as would at least a generation of settlers. The Boston Mountains make up the entire southern boundary of the Ozark region, extending from eastern Oklahoma to the escarpment south of Batesville. Though the subregion is generally characterized by relatively smooth wooded slopes that rise up to 1,200 feet above the valley floor, the Boston Mountains area is home to a few lowland basins, such as the Richwoods of present-day Stone County, that attracted early pioneers into the isolated upland ranges. The mountains' most prized resource was timber, especially the mammoth white oaks that canopied the western and southern slopes of ridges. These stands of virgin timber would eventually attract lumber companies and influence the routing of railroads into some of the region's most remote mountain coves and hollows.[5]

When Schoolcraft arrived in the Arkansas Ozarks, most of the settlers he encountered had been there only a short time, and many lived isolated lives miles from another human. These settlers harbored the white pioneer's fear and resentment of the Native American, in this case mainly the Cherokee, to whom an 1817 treaty had granted thousands of acres lying

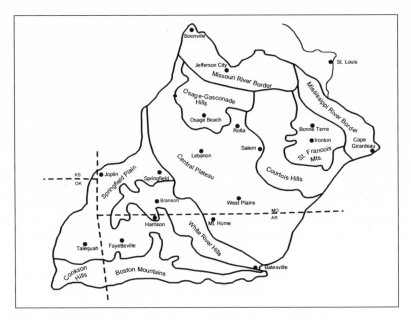

MAP 1.1. Geographic Regions of the Ozarks. From Milton D. Rafferty, *The Ozarks: Land and Life* (Fayetteville: University of Arkansas Press, 2001).

south and west of the White River. Even the Cherokee were newcomers. The Ozark region had historically been the domain of the Osage, who seasonally swept down into the White River country from their villages in western Missouri to hunt buffalo and deer, leaving in their wake abandoned camps of "inverted bird's nest" huts made of flexible green poles (perhaps the saplings of the Osage orange or hedge apple tree, known in the Ozarks as bois d'arc or "bodark"). In 1808 the Osage had given up their lands between the Missouri and Arkansas Rivers east of a line drawn due south from Fort Osage, on the Missouri about twenty miles east of the present site of Kansas City, to the Arkansas. Even before the Osage signed away the region, the Cherokee, along with smaller numbers of Delaware and Shawnee, had begun to settle the Ozarks. The Cherokee would retain title until 1828, when they exchanged their Arkansas lands for 7 million acres in the Indian Territory (Oklahoma).[6]

The earliest white settlers of the Arkansas Ozarks entered the region from the southeast by way of the White River. In the first decade of the nineteenth century, a middle-aged Ulster Irishman left his home in Tennessee and settled his family in a log cabin on a rise above the west bank of the White River in what today is Stone County. John Lafferty, the first recorded white settler in the Arkansas Ozarks, was a veteran of the American Revolution and a professional keelboat operator who had explored the upper White River country as early as 1802. In late 1810 Lafferty and his son-in-law Charles Kelly permanently relocated their families in the wilderness, which was teeming with bear, deer, and panthers. Shortly after Lafferty's arrival, Dan Wilson and his three sons settled at the mouth of Rocky Bayou (Izard County), farther up the river. Within a few years other settlers made their way up Rocky Bayou and other tributaries, prompting Poke Bayou merchant Robert Bean to ascend the river by keelboat with salt, whiskey, powder, and lead to exchange for buffalo hides, bear skins, and chickens.[7]

Poke Bayou, settled in 1812 by Missourian John Reed, quickly became the region's largest settlement and trading center. Today known as Batesville, Poke Bayou lay some thirty miles downstream from Lafferty's place, and its position at the fall line just a few miles above the Ozark escarpment assured its continued prominence. Poke Bayou became the center of operations for the upper White's busiest keelboatman before 1819. John Luttig, an agent for St. Louis merchant Christian Wilt, bartered for pelts, hides, tallow, buffalo tongues, beef, turkeys, ham, and venison by supplying the frontiersmen whiskey, silk, corn, and other goods. He also carried on a brisk trade with the various resettled Native American groups living west and south of the river. By the early 1820s, the combined population of Weas, Peorias, Kickapoos, Shawnee, and Piankashaws numbered approximately 10,000. In January 1819 Schoolcraft encountered Lafferty's widow, who, like the other white settlers on the right bank of the river, was anxious over the recent treaty ceding her lands to the Cherokee. By the time of Schoolcraft's visit, the widow Lafferty still lived an isolated existence, but the village of Poke Bayou had grown to a dozen houses, including Robert Bean's permanent trading post.[8]

In 1815 North Carolinian Jehoida Jeffery left southern Illinois with a large stock of cattle and horses and settled the following year upriver from Rocky Bayou, two miles above what would become the Mount Olive community. Jeffery, with whom Schoolcraft and his partner spent a January night, would soon become prominent in local politics, once enough people entered the hills to make the effort worthwhile. As a member of the territorial legislature in 1824, he would prove influential in the creation of a new county, Izard, which he would serve as judge for more than a decade.[9]

Another immigrant with political aspirations settled about twenty-five miles above Mount Olive at the mouth of the North Fork of the White River. Jacob Wolf, a Kentuckian of German ancestry born in western

North Carolina, joined members of his extended family there around 1820. When Schoolcraft had visited the area in 1819, he found only a man named Matney who operated a small trading post a half-mile above the mouth of the North Fork. In 1824 Wolf purchased a plot of land just below this junction, on the heights overlooking the White River, and later constructed a large, two-story dog-trot house of hewn pine logs. The house, which served at times as a trading post, inn, and post office, became the seat of justice for Jeffery's new Izard County. Wolf's brother-in-law, John Adams, became Izard's first county judge, and four years later a neighbor, Matthew Adams, was elected sheriff. Wolf gained appointment as Izard County's representative to the territorial council (upper house) in 1827, a seat that he would retain until Arkansas's statehood in 1836; he would later serve as postmaster of North Fork (Norfork) from 1844 until his death in 1863.[10]

On his journey up the White River, Schoolcraft encountered two families at the mouth of Beaver Creek in present-day Taney County, Missouri. The Holt and Fisher families had located there only months earlier and represented the farthest advance of white settlement up the valley by the end of 1818. The previous year's advance had been marked by the extended settlement of the Coker family. Joe Coker and his Native American wife Ainey left Alabama for the White River valley in 1814, settling on the Sugar Loaf Prairie of Boone County. In January 1815 Joe's father Buck settled in a bend of the river near his son. By December 1818 a total of four families lived along an eight-mile stretch of the river in the vicinity of Sugar Loaf Prairie.[11]

Following the tributaries of the White River, settlers eventually pushed into the Ozarks' most remote Boston Mountain valleys and hollows. In the early 1820s Kentuckian Robert Adams ventured up the Buffalo River and settled on Bear Creek. In 1825 Tennesseans John Brisco and Solomon Cecil settled even farther up the valley near the present-day Newton County communities of Jasper and Compton, respectively.[12]

The southern section of the Boston Mountains was settled by pioneers who came up tributaries of the White and Arkansas Rivers and by others who traveled by land across the Ozark wilderness. In 1811, after the New Madrid earthquake had decimated their fortunes, John Benedict, a young New Yorker, and his three brothers-in-law traveled by land from southeastern Missouri into the Arkansas backwoods, where they settled on the Little Red River in what is now Cleburne County. Subsisting on the plentiful game of the area, the four young men cleared thirty acres and built three small cabins. Two and a half years later Benedict's father-in-law

John Standlee brought his family, slaves, and livestock to join them. The last of the Standlees left the area in 1821, and a few years later John Lindsey Lafferty, son of the original Ozark pioneer, purchased part of the Standlee land. Lafferty, like Jehoida Jeffery and Jacob Wolf before him, parlayed his pioneer status into political power, helping to organize the new county of Van Buren in 1833 and serving intermittently as county judge and state legislator over the following thirty years.[13]

The Black River and its tributaries, the Strawberry and the Spring Rivers, deposited settlers along the eastern rim of the Ozarks. On his return trip to Potosi in early 1819, Schoolcraft passed through a "country wear[ing] a look of agriculture, industry and increasing population" in the environs northeast of Poke Bayou. The traveler covered more than thirty miles along the eastern rim of the Salem Plateau before encountering a village of fifteen buildings—including a gristmill, whiskey distillery, blacksmith shop, and tavern—on a tributary of the Strawberry River. To the northeast, on a height overlooking the confluence of the Black and Spring Rivers, lay Davidsonville, site of Arkansas's first post office and the original seat of justice for Lawrence County (which covered almost the entire Ozark section of Arkansas at one time).[14]

While explorers and settlers infiltrated the eastern Ozarks in the early nineteenth century, the majority of northwestern Arkansas lands remained in the possession of the Cherokee until 1828. Consequently, the area was legally off-limits to white settlers for almost two decades after settlement began on the White River, but some white families did make their way into the region before 1828. One history of Washington County reports that six white families settled there as early as 1826 and had their corn crops decimated by soldiers' swords for their trespassing. With the signing of the 1828 treaty removing the Cherokee westward beyond the Arkansas border, the floodgates were opened. Especially appealing to settlers were the rolling prairie lands of Washington and Benton Counties.[15]

Many of the area's first settlers moved up from the Arkansas River valley. William McGarrah's story illustrates the circuitous route several of these pioneers followed to northwestern Arkansas. Born in South Carolina in the 1790s, McGarrah made a brief sojourn in Tennessee before settling with his family in the swampy St. Francis River country of eastern Arkansas around 1809. After two years there, the McGarrahs ascended the White River and settled at Poke Bayou, from which the men conducted hunting and trapping expeditions deep into the Ozarks via the White River and its tributaries, eventually settling on the right bank of the White River far upriver from the Laffertys. Still later the family went west, settling at the junction of the Poteau and Arkansas Rivers, the present-day site of Fort Smith. When Washington County opened to white settlement a decade later, William McGarrah and his extended family were among the first settlers of the Fayetteville area.[16]

Not all immigrants to the western Ozark region lived such vagabond lives. In one of the most intriguing settlement stories, a well-established and relatively prosperous central Arkansas community pulled up stakes and moved almost en masse to Washington County. The Crystal Hill settlement on the Arkansas River in Pulaski County was by 1828 the latest in a series of temporary settlements undertaken by a group of families who had left Charleston, South Carolina, shortly after the American Revolution. In 1827, upon hearing of the government's plan to remove the Cherokee, two young men from Crystal Hill journeyed to northwestern Arkansas on a surveying trip for their neighbors. The following year, after the Cherokee had indeed left the area, one of the men, James Buchanan, returned to Washington County and built a log cabin on a fertile rise in the southwestern part of the county. Cane Hill, named for the switch cane that grew so densely among the sycamores and walnuts in the area, soon attracted dozens of Buchanan's old neighbors, so many, in fact, that some claimed with little exaggeration that the village of Crystal Hill had relocated to Cane Hill. The rich soil of the Cane Hill area and the abundance of springs helped it become one of the state's most agriculturally prosperous communities in the antebellum era.[17]

In northwestern Arkansas settlement proceeded at such a rapid pace that by 1833 Washington County, which was home to more than 6,000 people, and Benton County had become two of the most populous and prosperous counties in the territory. By the 1840 census, the first after Arkansas achieved statehood, the eight Ozark counties contained more than 20,000 inhabitants. Washington County, the state's most populous, accounted for one-third of the total Ozark population and more than half of the region's 1,515 slaves.

In his study of migration into Arkansas, Robert B. Walz traces the settlement trails of immigrants before 1880. According to Walz, almost half of all Ozark settlers before 1850 came from Tennessee, and another 20 percent simply migrated across the state line from Missouri. In the decade preceding the Civil War, Tennessee and Missouri continued to supply more than 60 percent of immigrants to the Arkansas Ozarks. The Ozark region's popularity among Tennesseans is logical considering the tendency to migrate westward along similar latitudes. Furthermore, many people raised in eastern or middle Tennessee were drawn to the Ozarks by the familiarity of the terrain. As historian Frank L. Owsley observed of these southern plain folk, most sought "a country as nearly as possible like the one in which [they] formerly lived in matters of soil, rainfall, temperature, and appearance." Of the remaining pioneers, about one in five families originated in Illinois, Alabama, Mississippi, or Kentucky.[18]

A few points regarding immigration and settlement patterns deserve mentioning. The Arkansas Ozarks inherited the ethnicity of the upper southern backcountry. Consequently, the region's pioneer settlers possessed a homogeneity rarely witnessed west of the Mississippi. With the exception of a few descendants of eighteenth-century German immigrants whose Protestantism and generations in the United States had been conducive to assimilation, antebellum Ozarkers were of British origin. It is quite possible, as geographer Russel L. Gerlach suggests, that the offspring of the Scotch-Irish dominated the interior region, and it is even more likely that the aggregate of Celtic descendants constituted a majority of the region's inhabitants. Nevertheless, even a detailed analysis of surnames listed by the Census Bureau is inadequate proof for such a proposition. What one can surmise about the Ozarks is that few non-British settlers found their way to northern Arkansas and that by the time they arrived in the early and middle nineteenth century, their culture and lifestyle reflected the southern backcountry, not Scotland, Ulster, or Wales.[19]

Although the Ozark region has long been considered an offspring of Appalachia, and for good reason, the settlers of the northern Arkansas hills did not always come directly from the mountain region back east. For many Appalachian-born people, their settlement in the Ozarks followed a series of westward relocations. We have already seen the westward odyssey of William McGarrah; his friends at Cane Hill had taken up residence in the Tennessee River valley of northern Alabama and in Logan County, Kentucky, before crossing the Mississippi. Born in Rutherford County, North Carolina, to Virginian parents, Jehoida Jeffery moved with his family to eastern Tennessee, western Kentucky, and then southern Illinois before settling in the White River valley. As a child, Jacob Wolf left his native Rowan County, North Carolina, with his family to settle in Hopkins County, Kentucky, in 1799. Two and a half decades later he too settled in the White River valley. Washington County farmer Brackin Lewis, born in western North Carolina, lived in Kentucky and Illinois before moving to northwestern Arkansas in 1835. David Price, a native of Warren County in middle Tennessee, made sojourns in Alabama and Missouri before reaching Washington County in 1851.[20]

An in-depth look at the origins of settlers by county reveals that Arkansas Ozark counties drew their settlers from eastern locations sharing common physiographical characteristics. Migrants from Tennessee tended to settle in Ozark areas similar in elevation and terrain to those of their previous homes. Remote and rugged Newton County, the most mountainous of Arkansas's Ozark counties, attracted many immigrants from the higher elevations of the Appalachian region. Of twenty-eight families listed in the 1860 Newton County census who could be positively identified in the 1850 Tennessee census, nineteen originated in the mountain counties of eastern Tennessee. Only three had resided in western Tennessee in 1850. A study of Tennessee migrants to the rolling foothills of Fulton and Izard Counties in the decade after 1850 turned up ninety-three families in the 1860 census who could definitely be identified in the 1850 Tennessee census. Of those, only eighteen were living in mountainous eastern Tennessee in 1850. The majority resided in a middle Tennessee corridor stretching from Jackson County southwest to Hardin County. Wayne County alone, just about one hundred miles east of Memphis, was home to eleven of the ninety-three families in 1850. It is likely that many of these middle Tennesseans had been born in Appalachia or at least had roots there. If so, such information underscores the notion that the Ozarks served as a western terminus, temporarily at least, of a great migratory trail. As we shall see, this trail would remain active into the twentieth century, when the Ozarks would become the eastern jumping-off point for another westward migration.[21]

The thirst for movement was not always quenched by the time one reached Arkansas, even in the antebellum era. Marion Crutchfield was born in Orange County, North Carolina, in 1846. Shortly thereafter his parents brought him to Arkansas, first settling in White County in the central part of the state. In 1849 the family relocated to mountainous Newton County, which they eventually left for Izard County in the eastern Ozarks. Born in Massachusetts, E. F. Smith lived in Tennessee before settling in the lower White River town of Jacksonport in 1859. Six years later he moved into the hills, settling in what would become Sharp County. He eventually made his way to Izard County, where he became a successful merchant and erected a cotton gin and sawmill. Squire B. Marrs definitely possessed the spirit of a wanderer. Born in Logan County, Indiana, in 1811, Marrs came with his family to Lawrence County, Arkansas, in 1817. While he was still a teenager, his family settled in newly opened Washington County. Marrs maintained a farm there throughout his life, in addition to traveling to the California gold mines in 1849 and spending the war years in Texas.[22]

Although Squire Marrs and the vast majority of Ozarkers were farmers, the earliest pioneers were generally hunters and trappers, the first wave of settlement described in historian Frederick Jackson Turner's famous frontier litany. We have already witnessed John Lafferty, the Tennessee hunter-trapper-keelboatman who decided to turn his favorite hunting ground into his home. Most of the inhabitants of the region that Schoolcraft came in contact with qualified as hunter-trapper–subsistence farmers. Schoolcraft's first meeting with a pioneer in what is now Arkansas was with an illiterate hunter named Wells, whose new one-room log cabin lay just off Bennett's Bayou, a tributary of the North Fork of the White River. Although the abundance of deer, bear, and other skins strung on poles outside the cabin attested to Wells's primary activity, the family, all clothed in deerskins, also had several acres under cultivation and provided Schoolcraft and his partner a supper of cornbread, butter, honey, and milk. At the home of the McGarrah family on the west bank of the White River, Schoolcraft found a more civilized, though still clearly frontier life. The large family had a field of corn and several horses, cows, and hogs. In addition, the McGarrahs owned a hand mill for grinding corn into meal and a smokehouse filled with bear and buffalo meat. Farther up the river, the young traveler found the Coker family living off corn and bear meat, "much like savages." The Cokers most closely adhered to the traditional hunter-trapper lifestyle. They informed Schoolcraft that they frequently moved to find game. In the fall the Cokers would sell their hides to traders who came up the river in exchange for salt, iron pots, axes, blankets, knives, rifles, and anything else deemed a necessity on the frontier.[23]

On the fertile lands in the vicinity of Poke Bayou, Schoolcraft found neat farms with fences made "in the zig-zag manner practiced in western Virginia and Kentucky." Such farmsteads were rare at this early stage of settlement and would not be duplicated in some areas of the Ozarks for more than a generation. Nevertheless, the existence of fences denotes the presence of livestock in the area. According to Turner, the hunter-trappers were followed by the herders. In his pioneer study of the region, geographer Carl O. Sauer recognized that many Ozark settlers from the hills of Tennessee, Kentucky, and other states of the Upper South combined hunting and livestock raising and sought out hillside clearings where cattle and hogs could graze and forage for mast amid an abundance of wild game. The McGarrah family reflected a combination of the hunter-trapper and the herder; it may have been in the midst of transformation to the latter. Jehoida Jeffery, who brought several head of livestock from Illinois, appears to have been an early Ozark herder.[24] In all likelihood, the distinctions among different occupations were blurred.

The agricultural census of 1840 revealed an Ozark region of subsistence and semisubsistence farms. Farmers in the eight core counties possessed 13,693 horses and mules, 34,040 head of cattle, 17,662 sheep, and 92,229 hogs; they raised 43,583 bushels of wheat, 72,844 bushels of oats, 1,105,652 bushels of corn, 59,618 pounds of tobacco, and 53,159 pounds of cotton, the equivalent of about 133 bales. Washington County led the state not only in population but also in almost every agricultural category: the number of horses and mules, cattle, sheep, and hogs, and the production of wheat, oats, and corn. The rolling prairies of the Springfield Plain had become Arkansas's agricultural oasis in little more than a decade. Almost all the products listed above were consumed at home. Since steamboat service had not yet reached the upper White River in 1840 and no cotton gins existed within the Ozarks, it is likely that what little cotton was produced was used at home or in the community. It appears, however, that at least a few farmers in the Izard County area marketed tobacco. Although the 16,100 pounds harvested in the county was a minuscule figure in comparison with tobacco-producing areas east of the Mississippi, Izard did have one small tobacco manufactory in 1839 that produced $750 worth of plug tobacco. By 1840 each Ozark county had at least four gristmills for grinding corn, and Washington County had four flour mills to service the county's bumper wheat crop.[25]

The 1840 census also revealed growing diversity within the Ozark region. While Washington County dominated the state's agricultural output, the rugged interior maintained characteristics of the Ozarks Schoolcraft had visited two decades before. The six counties other than Washington and Benton produced over $10,000 in skins and furs, and Searcy County, covering a large section of the Boston Mountains, counted 104 trappers and hunters in a total population of fewer than 1,000 people. Although farms and occasionally even small plantations occupied the fertile river bottoms and more level uplands by this time, vast acreages of hill and hollow lands remained to be claimed.[26]

While the Ozarks could be considered a subsistence farming region in 1840 and, in most areas, throughout the antebellum period, this was not due to a lack of fertile lands or the absence of large farms. As we have seen, the region's first generation of settlers were drawn to the best farming lands: the Springfield Plain and the White River bottoms. Just as early arrival resulted in political power for pioneers such as Jeffery and Wolf, early arrival could also result in agricultural prosperity. In his study of slavery in Washington County, historian Ted J. Smith notes that the county's earliest settlers, many of them slaveholders, laid claim to the fertile bottomlands along the White and Illinois Rivers. Consequently, these slaveholding farmers (by 1850 only three slaveholders owned more than twenty slaves and could thus be considered planters) played the "single largest role in the county's economic development." In 1850 slaveholding farmers on the most fertile landholdings, though comprising less than 3 percent of the farming population, owned 42 percent of the county's hogs, horses, and cattle; raised 40 percent of the corn and 50 percent of the oats; and accounted for more than half the total farm value in Washington County.[27]

The influence of slave owners in the White River valley was considerably less than in Washington County. (It should be remembered that more than half the Ozarks' slaves resided in that county in 1840.) Nevertheless, the benefit derived from early settlement on choice land was likewise evident in the White River region. In 1850 Daniel Jeffery, youngest brother of the late Jehoida and a fellow pioneer, was one of the White River valley's most prominent agriculturists. On his 220-acre farm Jeffery owned 5 horses, 67 head of cattle, 41 sheep, and 100 hogs. In addition he raised 1,000 bushels of corn, 125 bushels of oats, and 60 bushels of Irish potatoes. Farther up the river Jacob Wolf had capitalized on his early arrival as well. In addition to operating a trading post, two river ferries, a gristmill, and a blacksmith shop and being appointed as postmaster, in 1850 he owned a 182-acre farm worth $2,500, and his eldest son William owned a 97-acre farm worth $2,000. The elder Wolf, who with 15 slaves was Izard County's largest slaveholder, owned 16 horses, 49 head of cattle, 36 sheep, and 150 hogs. His cultivated land produced 2,500 bushels of corn, 150 bushels of wheat, 250 bushels of sweet and Irish potatoes, and 50 bushels of rye, and his cattle provided milk and 400 pounds of butter.[28]

After the most fertile plains and river bottoms had been claimed, settlers drifted into the interiors of the Salem Plateau and Boston Mountains. This wave of settlement, commencing in about 1840 and reaching astounding proportions in the decade preceding the Civil War, signaled the most intense phase of inmigration in antebellum Ozark history. The settlement boom between 1840 and 1850 almost doubled the population; by 1850 the ten core counties were home to almost 40,000 inhabitants, of whom more than nine in ten were American-born whites. Settlement in the 1840s reflected a dispersion of immigrants into the initially avoided interior areas. Whereas the fertile plains of the northwest, which had been heavily favored by newcomers in the 1830s, experienced an increase of about 33 percent of the 1840 population, the remainder of the region grew by more than 140 percent. Settlement in the Boston Mountains and on the Salem Plateau became significant enough in the decade to merit the creation of a new county in each subregion, Newton and Fulton, respectively. Nevertheless, the four northwestern counties that encompassed the Springfield Plain continued to account for more than three-fifths of the region's population and more than three-fourths of its 2,328 slaves. Washington County alone held one-fourth of the Arkansas Ozarks' people, including more than half of the area's slaves.[29]

Prosperous herders or farmers were not limited to the prairies and river bottoms, though their numbers were always minuscule in areas such as the Boston Mountains or Salem Plateau. The story of one family reveals the existence of prosperous slaveholders even in these relatively infertile, isolated areas. In the spring of 1844, the three Watkins brothers left their father's farm east of Franklin, Tennessee, and settled the following year on a rocky but relatively flat section of the Salem Plateau in Izard County. William F. Watkins, the eldest, soon returned home to resume his profession as a steamboat clerk, regularly sending significant portions of his paycheck to his brothers, James D. and Owen Thomas, to use for purchasing land. Like Jeffery, Wolf, and others who had migrated to a sparsely settled region and who had taken advantage of their early arrival and their wealth to become agriculturally prosperous and politically influential, the Watkins brothers began to establish the foundation of a farming and business enterprise that would dominate the community of Wild Haws (renamed Lacrosse in 1869) for half a century.[30]

In addition to the money sent by William and the farming activities of the other two brothers, Owen, a trained physician, built a large practice serving much of north central Arkansas. James, who had been responsible for the establishment of a post office with himself as postmaster in 1848, was in the same year elected to represent his district in the state senate. The following year, William returned from Tennessee to open the first general store in Wild Haws. By 1852 two sisters with their families had also moved into the area. The 1850 census revealed Owen Watkins to have been the most prominent agriculturist in his township, and perhaps in the county. On 900 acres he raised 2,000 bushels of corn, 500 pounds of tobacco, and 200 bushels each of wheat and oats, as well as 5 bales of cotton. His primary interest, however, lay in raising livestock. Owen

Watkins owned 4 horses, 17 mules, 120 head of cattle, and 50 hogs. His 12 slaves also ranked him among the region's leading slaveholders.[31]

The development of the Watkins farm also provides insight into the difficulties of raising cash crops in the antebellum Ozarks as well as into the state of the region's agriculture on the eve of war. Owen Watkins, who had raised small amounts of both cotton and tobacco in 1849, invested no money or land in either crop in 1859.[32] By 1860 the South's cotton culture had yet to embrace the Ozarks. The white fiber had begun to make its way up the White River, occasionally adorning river and creek bottoms and smooth plateaus; nevertheless, Ozark farmers grew less than 1 percent of Arkansas's chief cash crop in 1859. The primary drawbacks to cotton cultivation were poor transportation to ginning and marketing facilities and the availability of other sustainable if not profitable farming activities.

The only means of transporting goods in the antebellum Ozarks was by steamboat, flatboat, or wagon. Steamboats first began ascending the White River to Batesville in 1831, but another decade would pass before they ventured above Batesville to the upper reaches of the river's navigable waters. The impact of the steamboat's arrival for Batesville-area farmers was immediate. A young Pennsylvanian who arrived in Batesville in early 1831 wrote to his brother, "They raise fine cotton here. There has been 500 bales made here this season." But farmers in the interior who sought to utilize river ports for trade often had to travel dozens of miles over treacherous roads that were actually little more than widened trails. In the eastern Ozarks the best roads followed the rivers, though one early trail connected the upper White River valley with Fayetteville. The region's most adequate road, a portion of the trail between St. Louis and the Arkansas River port of Van Buren that crossed northwestern Arkansas, proved a boon to that section's early agricultural prominence.[33]

Although the Ozark region never became a significant cotton-producing area before the Civil War, the introduction of steamboat service on the upper White River in the 1840s had an immediate impact on agriculture in the eastern Ozark river bottoms, especially in Marion County. In that county, which encompassed the valley's most expansive and fertile bottoms, cotton production ballooned from about 8 bales in 1839 to 1,100 in 1849. The importance of steamboat access is reflected in the observation that the rest of the Ozark counties combined produced only 221 bales of cotton in 1849. Farmers far removed from the river occasionally attempted to raise cotton, but the difficulties of transporting crops to market often rendered their efforts unprofitable or suitable for domestic use only. Owen Watkins harvested five bales of cotton in 1849 and in subsequent years attempted to expand his production of the crop. In 1853 he and his brothers constructed a gin at Wild Haws, from which they hauled the bales by wagon some forty miles to Jacksonport on the White River below Batesville. It appears that the expense of the trips to Jacksonport and the paucity of other local cotton growers to patronize the Watkinses' gin coaxed Owen and William Watkins out of cotton cultivation before 1860. The 1860 census revealed a still-prosperous Watkins family with over 6,000 acres of land and fourteen slaves. The farm produced no cotton or tobacco as it had in 1849, though the production of corn and oats had increased 200 percent and 150 percent, respectively.[34]

The Watkinses' production of a surplus of corn in 1860 presents another aspect of antebellum Ozark agriculture. As Ted J. Smith discovered in his work on Washington County, corn was often used as a cash crop. Washington County farmers, who produced a state record of 663,540 bushels of corn in 1860, as well as other northwestern Arkansas agriculturists, could barter their surplus corn at most stores before the Civil War for up to 18 cents per bushel. Merchants then sold the corn to Fayetteville industrialists or to plantations in the Arkansas River valley. The substantial livestock holdings in the area suggest that corn and fodder may also have been in demand for the fattening of hogs and cattle.[35]

Even more important as a cash crop for much of the region was tobacco. In 1859 the ten Ozark counties produced more than 450,000 pounds of tobacco, and Izard County farmers accounted for 200,000 pounds of the leaf. Although the Watkins brothers grew no tobacco in 1859, most of their neighbors did. Reflecting the prominence of settlers from middle Tennessee and central Kentucky, Izard County surpassed all other counties in the state in tobacco production and produced more than one-fifth of the state's total crop. As early as 1839, when the county ranked second to neighboring Independence County in tobacco production, Izard claimed the only tobacco manufactory in the state, which employed three workers and produced $750 worth of tobacco products. The existence of a local market for tobacco accounted in part for the raising of only 184 bales of cotton in Izard County in 1859.[36]

Although Owen and William Watkins grew no cotton or tobacco in 1859, they continued to raise an abundance of livestock. The brothers owned 21 horses, 40 mules, 49 head of cattle, and 70 hogs. In an 1854 letter, Fanny Watkins Hunt mentioned that her brother Owen had ceased practicing medicine and claimed "cow driving" as his primary occupation. Although typically not the primary occupation of most Ozarkers by the beginning of the Civil War, raising livestock was nevertheless an integral part of Ozark agriculture and not infrequently a source of income for farmers. In sparsely settled areas with difficult access to markets, the raising of cattle and hogs continued to occupy a position of agricultural prominence up to and after the Civil War. It was also a key activity among farmers on the grassy prairies of the Springfield Plain. The 1860 census attributed more than 75,000 head of cattle, 190,000 hogs, 56,000 sheep, and almost 30,000 horses and mules to the ten Ozark counties. The open range, whereby farmers fenced in crops and not animals, facilitated the development of extensive livestock raising throughout most of the region. Ozark cattle herders grazed stock in open meadows and in cane brakes, almost impenetrable jungles of switch cane found growing along the sandy banks of many large streams. Cattle and hogs both scoured the hardwood forests for mast—acorns, hickory nuts, walnuts, and beechnuts. The abundance of hardwood forests rendered the region particularly suited for ranging swine, which could survive quite well in the forests regardless of the season by rooting for food beneath leaves and soil on the forest floor. The treeless prairies of northwestern Arkansas were well suited to the raising of sheep. Consequently, by 1860 Washington and Benton Counties led all others in the production of sheep, while the four counties of the Springfield Plain claimed almost 20 percent of the state's sheep population.[37]

It is impossible to know how many Ozark farmers actually sold livestock. It is reasonable to assume that many, perhaps a majority, of them did so. Practically all Ozarkers owned livestock of some kind, and it was common for farmers in the late antebellum period to possess fifty or more hogs and as many as a dozen cows. Such holdings certainly provided for subsistence needs and left a surplus that could be marketed. Cattle, and often even hogs, were driven to markets as far away as St. Louis and Kansas City or as close as Arkansas Post and Little Rock. Washington County herder Peter Mankins, at one time the upper White River valley's wealthiest man, made cattle drives to Chicago and hog drives to Louisiana. In 1857 he sold $34,000 worth of cattle to the U.S. government; he continued to deal in livestock until the outbreak of war in 1861. Mankins also participated in the first transcontinental cattle drives from the Ozarks to California. Northwestern Arkansas was the starting point for numerous cattle drives to California in the decade following the gold rush of 1849. A few Ozark cattlemen even established ranches in northern California to supply San Francisco and its environs with fresh beef. One of the largest drives took place in 1853, when a crew of drovers left Washington County with 550 head of cattle bound for a ranch in the Trinity River valley of northern California. In 1855 Wythe Walker, son of prominent Washington County farmer and judge David Walker, drove 432 head of cattle to market in Kansas. Most large drives of this kind were handled by experienced cattlemen who covered familiar areas, buying a few head from various small farmers on the trail to market. This allowed small farmers and herders to sell one or two steers, old cows, or hogs without having to spend weeks or months on an arduous drive. By the end of the antebellum era, however, most Arkansas Ozark cattle drives were oriented toward nearby Missouri markets.[38]

The primary use of livestock for most Ozarkers involved subsistence. Horses, mules, and oxen pulled stumps, plows, and wagons. Cattle provided milk and beef, though hogs and wild game provided the majority of smokehouse meat. Sheep's wool provided clothing material, and chickens supplied eggs as well as the main course for special meals. Livestock was an integral part of subsistence agriculture, and the Ozarks on the eve of the Civil War was still a land of subsistence and semisubsistence farms. Despite the introduction of small-scale cotton and tobacco growing and corn bartering, the business of the vast majority of Ozark folk was not prospering, but living.[39]

Although the existence of Jacob Wolf, Owen Watkins, and David Walker belies the notion of an impossibly isolated region hiding behind a wall of mountains, separated or immune from developments elsewhere in the Southwest or in the United States, these prosperous antebellum Ozarkers were exceptional, the beneficiaries of early arrival, business acumen, or previous wealth. More typical was Stephen McElmurray, owner of a 160-acre Fulton County farm. Young McElmurray, who had migrated to Arkansas with his family from Missouri, owned 1 horse, 9 cows, 8 sheep, and 20 hogs. Without the help of slave labor, he and his wife raised 200 bushels of corn, 100 pounds of tobacco, and small amounts of peas and sweet and Irish potatoes. His livestock supplied 150 pounds of butter and 14 pounds of wool. Small landowners such as McElmurray inhabited the hillsides and hollows throughout the region by 1860. Joel Farley of Benton County grew 42 bushels of wheat and 150 bushels of corn and made 25 gallons of sorghum molasses on his 90-acre farm. He owned 1 horse, 3 cows, 12 sheep, and 30 hogs. In mountainous Newton County, J. W. Whitely conducted a diverse array of activities on his 55-acre subsistence farm in the Buffalo River valley. In addition to producing a corn crop of 1,000 bushels, Whitely used 6 horses to grow small patches of wheat, oats, and Irish and sweet potatoes. The family collected 45 pounds of wool from 15 sheep and churned 100 pounds of butter from the production of 8 cows. Whitely, like his neighbors, lived off pork and found the hives of wild bees sources of sweetening in the absence of sugar. In 1860 he owned 20 hogs and gathered 600 pounds of wild honey.[40]

The prevalence of the yeoman farmer in 1860 reflected a two-decade period of migration that followed the initial settlement of the fertile prairies and river and creek bottoms. According to Ted J. Smith, a massive wave of yeoman immigrants in the decade before the Civil War diluted the power and influence of the small class of slaveholders in Washington County. These last antebellum settlers, in Washington County and else-where in the Ozarks, inhabited the less fertile hillsides and hollows and the rocky, wooded uplands passed over by a generation of pioneers. As did the majority of their predecessors, they came with meager posses-sions, but unlike the earliest arrivals on fertile soils, they settled on mar-ginal lands that afforded them few opportunities to move beyond sub-sistence. Consequently, by the end of the antebellum era, the Ozark region was for the most part a relatively isolated semifrontier dominated by first-generation yeomen settlers. The region could boast of areas as prosperous as any the state had to offer; nevertheless, geography dictated that the widest expanses of the Ozarks would be the domain of small landowners whose diligence and labor were rewarded with survival and perhaps comfort and happiness, but almost never with wealth.[41]

Southerners, Midwesterners, and Mountaineers

EARLY ONE CLOUDY spring morning in 1862, Will McGuire set out from Batesville on horseback with three other young men. Although they were not yet soldiers of the Confederacy, their mission was to travel toward the northwest and reconnoiter the federal troops on their way to Batesville. The foursome rode far enough to encounter local residents who possessed ample knowledge of the enemy's numbers and whereabouts; on the return journey they "had some fun [and] saw the country." For the twenty-one-year-old McGuire, it was the first taste of military activity and the last youthful expedition of a man facing a life-changing decision. Three months later, spurred by federal troops' theft of his saddles, bridles, ropes, blankets, oats, and corn, McGuire enrolled as a private in Company D of the Confederate First Arkansas Cavalry.[1]

McGuire, like many men in the Ozarks, faced difficult decisions. The oldest child in a fatherless family, he watched his brother Charley leave to fight the Union in the summer of 1861 but stayed behind to tend the farm and care for his mother and younger siblings. Although Will had been educated at the Literary and Military Institute of St. Louis and although his family held no stake in the South's slave economy, his and his family's preferences seem never to have been in doubt. Many of his neighbors faced the question of loyalty with more trepidation, however; the bluecoats gathered a number of recruits in Independence County and elsewhere in the Ozarks. In the months before he joined the Confederate forces, McGuire's life followed routine patterns, with the occasional military interruption. Between visits by Union foraging parties, McGuire planted crops, cut firewood, repaired equipment, gardened, made candy, fished, and hunted. After weeks of considering the alternatives, such as moving his family to Missouri, McGuire opted to join his friends in Confederate service, a decision that would almost cost him his life and would leave his family to fend for themselves until war's end. By the time he left for war, the visits by occupying forces had become more frequent and hostile. Three more years of war would exact a terrific toll on Batesville and the other communities that lay in the paths of southern and northern forces.[2]

The Civil War interrupted the development of the Ozark region, and the destruction wrought by four years of skirmishing, battling, and marauding altered the subsistence and semisubsistence patterns of Ozark agriculture. Few areas in the region escaped damage inflicted by the Union and Confederate armies or raids by roving bands of bushwhackers and jayhawkers. The region's two most populous settlements, Fayetteville and Batesville, suffered particular hardships at the hands of both sides, and Benton County witnessed the Battle of Pea Ridge, the trans–Mississippi region's largest engagement. Stealing and impressment stripped many farms of livestock, crops, implements, and money. Sharply divided between northern and southern sympathies, the Ozarks became a dangerous, lawless land abandoned not only by the men going to war but also by scores of their families looking for safer homes free from the unofficial bands of Union and Confederate sympathizers who sought out their enemies and their enemies' families in the isolated backcountry.[3]

As Ozarkers returned to their homes after the war and as thousands of new immigrants filtered into the region, the Ozarks remained an area dominated by yeoman farmers. Nevertheless, for most communities the final three decades of the nineteenth century marked a dynamic era of rapid inmigration and agricultural experimentation highlighted by increased participation in the market economy. In addition, this transformation divided the region geographically and agriculturally more sharply than ever before.

By 1880, farmers in the eastern counties had begun to be absorbed into the South's cotton economy, although the continued diversity of semisubsistence practices and the dominance of small landowning family operations distinguished the Ozark cotton-producing areas from the increasingly monocultural bottomlands of eastern and southern Arkansas. The small prairie farmers of the western counties, meanwhile, developed an agricultural system that resembled the practices of the Ozarks' midwestern neighbors. The five counties of the Springfield Plain, especially Washington and Benton Counties, continued to lead the state in the production of small grains and livestock, while virtually ignoring the South's most popular cash crop. This most agriculturally prosperous and diverse section of the Arkansas Ozarks eventually achieved recognition as one of the United States' leading apple-producing areas. Lying between the two extremes was an already shrinking class of subsistence farmers sprinkled throughout the region but found in greatest proportions in isolated mountain coves and on barren hillsides. Only in these enclaves did life resemble the isolated, backward existence that would come to characterize the region in the following century.

Cotton production in the eastern Ozarks had undergone a significant increase after the introduction of steamboat service on the upper White River in the 1840s. Several factors served to continue its expansion after the Civil War. Farmers who had raised cotton prior to the conflict and who lived to return home generally continued to cultivate the crop. New settlers from cotton-producing states frequently brought their knowledge of cotton cultivation with them. Although settlers from the states of Tennessee, Georgia, Alabama, and Mississippi accounted for just 28 percent of the Ozark region's immigrants in the decade before 1870, they made up almost half of the newcomers to Searcy, Izard, Sharp, and Van Buren Counties, the region's four leading cotton-producing counties in 1869. In addition to these two classes of cotton growers, a third group was composed of antebellum Ozark settlers who entered the cotton market after the war for a variety of reasons: to take advantage of better marketing and transportation facilities; out of a desire for a larger, more dependable cash income; or in response to demands placed upon them by credit merchants or landlords in a cash-starved economy. In addition, farmers who before the war had entered the cash-crop market by raising tobacco, after 1865 often found cotton to be more profitable and marketable. Whatever the reason for taking up cotton cultivation in the years after the Civil War, a steadily increasing number of eastern and southern Ozark farmers did so. By 1869, cotton production in the eastern Ozark counties had increased to 6,410 bales; ten years later, over 50,000 acres produced 27,688 bales. Although these numbers paled in comparison with those of the fertile lands of eastern and southern Arkansas and the chief cotton-growing areas elsewhere in the South, they represented a significant change in eastern Ozark agricultural practices and signaled the development of a small-scale cotton economy.[4]

Before the turn of the century, the White River and its steamboats provided the only means for transporting most Ozarkers' cotton to the docks of Memphis, New Orleans, and other port cities. By the late 1860s,

Harvesting wheat in northwestern Arkansas using a mule-drawn harvester, date unknown. Courtesy of Mary Ellen Johnson/Shiloh Museum of Ozark History.

steamboats were already plying the waters above Batesville to collect bales of cotton and other products at landings and towns deep in the Ozark interior. Boats such as the *Argos*, the *Batesville*, the *Alberta*, and the *Green* came steaming down out of the hills with anything from venison and turkey to wool, bacon, and oats. By the 1870s the primary cargo of most boats was cotton, and each boat attempted to haul as many bales as could be stacked up without sinking the vessel. In 1877 the *Hard Cash* arrived in Batesville with 1,324 bales from upriver, although boats generally carried between 100 and 300 bales in addition to a variety of other products. The cargo of the *Alberta* in May 1877 is indicative of the variety of agricultural products marketed in the Ozarks; in addition to 47 bales of cotton, the *Alberta* carried 1,700 bushels of wheat, 5 hogsheads (6,800 pounds) of tobacco, 1 bale of wool, 1 bale of hides, 20,000 pounds of flour, 14,300 pounds of bacon, and 900 pounds of lard. The volume of cotton shipped during the wet season reflects its growing importance in the Ozark interior. Between October 1876 and January 1877, the *Alberta* shipped more than 3,200 bales to Memphis, New Orleans, and St. Louis. Another White River steamer, the *Green*, transported almost 3,000 bales from September 1875 to January 1877.[5]

In 1883, the Kansas City, Fort Scott & Memphis Railroad extended its line through Mammoth Spring and Hardy, giving the eastern Ozark interior its first rail service and connecting eastern Fulton County and

Southerners, Midwesterners, and Mountaineers

northern Sharp County and their environs with Memphis. The same year witnessed the extension of the St. Louis, Iron Mountain & Southern Railroad from Newport up the White River to Batesville. The coming of the railroad proved a boon for farmers near towns such as Hardy, Mammoth Spring, and Batesville; it provided a convenient market for cotton as well as for livestock, grains, fruit, vegetables, and lumber. The steamboats of the White River continued to carry on a brisk business, however, for it would be another two decades before the railroad would render their services obsolete.[6]

The improvement of roads leading to riverboat landings or railroad depots spurred the construction of cotton gins in communities throughout the eastern Ozarks, which provided a more convenient means of marketing crops for small farmers in the interior. An analyst of agricultural census schedules reveals the growing practice of cotton raising among these small farmers. In Izard County, which led the region with 4,800 bales produced in 1879, dozens of small farmers began growing cotton in the late 1860s and 1870s. Near the Franklin community, situated on rolling Salem Plateau lands thirty miles from the White River, Jesse Riggs and his neighbors began planting a few acres in cotton after the Civil War. Riggs raised 2 bales in 1869, although he did not grow cotton a decade earlier. Samuel McElmurray produced 5 bales in 1869, and William Hightower 1 bale; neither grew cotton in 1859. The greatest expansion of cotton cultivation occurred in the decade after 1869. In the same area of Izard County, John Black increased his cotton acreage from none in 1869 to 12 acres in 1879. John Porterfield planted 6 acres of the fiber in 1879, and Robert Powell 20 acres; both began raising cotton only after 1869. Before 1870, even the area's largest cotton farmers grew small amounts of the crop or none. In 1879, William Cooksey harvested 16 bales on 22 acres, and William Floyd cultivated 75 acres, producing 50 bales. In 1869, Cooksey had harvested only 2 bales, and Floyd had not yet begun to raise cotton.[7]

Floyd and Cooksey were atypical of Ozark cotton growers in 1879. Most farmers raised less than 10 acres of the crop. Nevertheless, cotton served as a significant and usually primary source of cash income for these agriculturists; it grew amid various other crops and animals on semisubsistence farms. Of the 91 farmers in New Hope township, Izard County (home to all the farmers mentioned above), 83 grew an average of 9 acres of cotton in 1879. The New Hope farmers grew more than twice as much corn as cotton; one-third of them raised wheat, oats, or sorghum cane. Livestock could be found on almost all farms, with hogs outnumbering cattle about three to one. Fifty-eight farmers sold at least one cow in 1879, which augmented the income from the sale of cotton.[8]

Eastern Ozark farmers carried out a variety of agricultural practices to maintain their livelihoods. In his autobiography, Izard County native De Emmett Bradshaw recalled the plethora of activities with which his father David supported the family and generated cash income. On a small farm in the community of Nubbin Ridge (now Sage), David Bradshaw raised small crops of corn, wheat, hay, and cotton, which he and his neighbors hauled twenty-five miles to Batesville until local gins sprang up in the late 1870s and early 1880s. The elder Bradshaw frequently purchased calves from neighbors, fattened them on corn over the winter, and sold them to cattle buyers on their annual spring treks. He also found a market for the hogs that the family had not butchered during the winter. Bradshaw sold surplus corn to local farmers, who used it to fatten their own stock, and during the winter he chopped firewood to sell in the nearby village of Lacrosse.[9]

Similarly, William Swan of Stone County carried out numerous farm activities designed for both self-sufficiency and cash income. His nephew John Quincy Wolf Sr. recalled that in the 1870s Swan rotated his crops of millet, corn, clover, cow peas, cotton, and wheat. Swan also maintained an orchard of more than 100 apple and pear trees, a strawberry patch, and raspberry bushes. In addition, the Swans "had honey on the table at every meal in the year," thanks to a dozen beehives on the farm, and stored garden produce such as cabbages, lettuce, turnips, potatoes, and beets through the winter in straw-lined holes four feet deep. The family's meat, primarily pork, was provided by 8 to 10 razorback hogs, which were fattened on corn in late autumn and butchered in the winter. Like David Bradshaw, William Swan received his small cash income almost exclusively from the sale of cotton and cattle. Swan had several dozen head of cattle that ranged on the hillsides and in the cane brakes along the river and creek bottoms. Swan butchered a few calves between October and March and in the spring "sold from ten to twenty-five head of cattle to Missouri buyers and in the fall two or three bales of cotton, which brought in more than enough money for the family needs."[10]

Like many Izard County farmers, David Bradshaw and William Swan increasingly came to rely on cotton as their primary means of cash income. Cotton production in the Ozarks peaked around 1890, although the southern and eastern counties would experience severe declines in cotton cultivation only in the 1930s, after New Deal legislation limited acreage. Despite the region's obvious agricultural diversity in the waning decades of the century, by 1889 the practice of dedicating small patches of land on hill farms to cotton was so common that one observer of agriculture in Izard County wrote: "Cotton is king, and some lands are being exhausted by its constant cropping." By the same date there were at least eight cotton gins operating in neighboring Fulton County, where none had existed before the Civil War. The 1890 census indicated that in the Ozark region, small farmers east of Madison and Carroll Counties devoted almost 100,000 acres to cotton cultivation. The region's combined harvest of more than 30,000 bales represents the pinnacle of cotton production in the northern Arkansas hills. Three counties—Izard, Sharp, and Van Buren—contained more than 10,000 acres of cotton land in 1889. The Ozark region's contribution to the state's total cotton crop had increased from less than 1 percent in 1859 to almost 6 percent in 1889. Even the remote Buffalo River valley was not immune to King Cotton. By the 1880s, cotton was the chief cash crop in the valley, and the prosperity of isolated Wilcockson (later Marble Falls), which would gain infamy in the next century as the site of the Dogpatch, U.S.A., theme park, depended upon its cultivation. Located midway between Harrison and Jasper on a tributary of the Buffalo River, Wilcockson claimed two cotton gins, one powered by a steer-operated treadmill and the other by a waterwheel. By the time Willis Moore purchased the gristmill and cotton gin on Marble Falls in 1889, the hamlet boasted, in addition to the general stores, a hotel and a newspaper. Moore ginned more than 800 bales over the next decade.[11]

The Ozark region could not sustain the furious expansion of cotton raising into the final decade of the nineteenth century. The eastern and southern counties, such as Izard, Sharp, Van Buren, and Cleburne, saw their cotton production level off or decline slightly before 1900. Although farmers in these counties would continue to cultivate small cotton patches for another half-century or more, in the central Ozarks most agriculturists moved away from the cotton economy and culture. Between 1889 and 1899, the number of acres devoted to cotton in Newton County decreased from 4,289 to 1,622. Boone County's cotton acreage declined by more than half over the same period, from 7,461 to 2,348. Carroll County farmers, who had uncharacteristically grown more than 1,200 acres of cotton in 1889, almost totally abandoned the crop afterward; by 1899 the county's total cotton crop had been reduced to only 86 acres. A number of factors influenced this decline. By 1890, the best cotton-growing land had already been brought under cultivation in most areas. The decline in cotton acreage after 1890, especially in the eastern and southern counties, probably represents an effort by farmers to take out of cultivation the least productive lands that had been broken during the furious expansion of cotton growing in the 1880s. Furthermore, as the observer in Izard County recognized, cotton exhausted lands that were only marginally productive to begin with. Perhaps most important, declining prices in the late 1880s and early 1890s (from 11 cents per pound in 1880 to 9.4 cents in 1886 and finally to a low of 6 cents per pound in 1898) forced many farmers, especially those in the mountainous areas of Boone, Newton, and Searcy Counties, to abandon cotton growing in favor of a more general subsistence type of agriculture.[12]

Interestingly, tobacco, which had been an integral crop for several eastern Ozark farmers in 1859, lost its popularity in that area after the Civil War. The upland southerners who peopled the Ozarks brought a knowledge of tobacco raising with them; furthermore, tobacco grew well on newly cleared land and demanded a good, steady price. When soil infertility began to affect tobacco crops after two or three plantings, and when Ozarkers developed shipping facilities for other, lower-priced agricultural commodities, according to geographer Carl O. Sauer, most hill farmers converted their lands to corn, cotton, or some other crop. Jesse Beaver, William Woods, and James and John Porterfield had raised a combined 3,725 pounds of tobacco in 1859 but grew none two decades later. Tobacco production in Izard County, the state's leading producer of the leaf on the eve of war, fell to 24,795 pounds in 1879, just over 12 percent of the 1859 harvest. Ozark farmers continued to raise tobacco in the late nineteenth century, though the center of cultivation shifted to the west. The establishment of tobacco factories at Yellville (Marion County) and Melbourne (Izard County) in the 1870s would suggest a resurgence of the crop, but this was not the case. Farmers whose lands supported the cultivation of row crops gradually found cotton to be a less soil-exhausting, less time-consuming, and more profitable crop. By 1889, Izard County farmers planted 600 acres of cotton for each acre of tobacco.[13]

The prevalence of cotton-state settlers in the eastern and southern Ozarks and the role of the White River as a direct link with the plantation South affected the rise of cotton culture among the hill farmers of Izard, Sharp, and other counties east of the Boston Mountains in the decades following the Civil War. The western Ozark counties, those with the most fertile prairie lands, followed a different agricultural path in the postwar years. Although the region's soils were suitable for cotton cultivation— Washington County had produced at least twice as much cotton as any other Ozark county in 1839—an influx of midwestern settlers after 1865

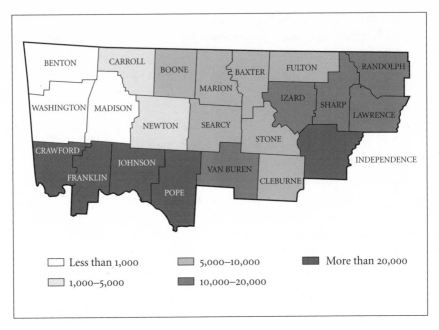

MAP 2.1. Cotton Acreage, 1890

and a long tradition of small grain and livestock agriculture influenced most farmers to eschew raising cotton. Furthermore, the preexistence of a market for small grains and the emergence of new cash crops freed the farmers of northwestern Arkansas from the stifling demands of the cotton lien system, a system of agricultural mortgages that effectively reduced thousands of southern farmers to a status little better than peonage.

We have already witnessed the influence of settlers from cotton-producing states on the agriculture of the eastern Ozarks. Settlers from other areas had an equally important impact on the course of agricultural development in the western Ozarks. Whereas immigrants from a four-state block of the cotton-growing South—Tennessee, Mississippi, Alabama, and Georgia—comprised almost half of all settlers in the eastern Ozarks in the 1860s, the same immigrant group accounted for less than one in five settlers in the western Ozarks. In Benton and Washington Counties, the two westernmost counties and the most popular destinations among all Ozark newcomers, immigrants from these four southern states comprised only 15 percent of the total number of immigrants in the decade after 1860. The percentage of settlers coming from southeastern states declined even further in the 1870s. Conversely, Missourians made up over half the newcomers in Carroll and Boone Counties and accounted for at least 30 percent of immigrants settling in Madison, Benton, and Washington Counties in the 1860s. The prairie counties also received substantial numbers of settlers from Texas, Kansas, and Illinois. Significantly, of the five prairie counties, only Boone County received over a quarter of its immigrants in the 1860s from the Southeast. By 1889 Boone County farmers raised almost 7,500 acres of cotton; the other four western counties raised a combined total of less than 2,000 acres.[14]

The western counties forged a link with their midwestern neighbors to the north; and the subregion's increasing production of tobacco and orchard products diversified its agricultural output beyond grain and livestock. The influence of midwesterners and of the rolling openness of the Springfield Plain was evident in the western counties' production of small grains. Although the per-farm averages for livestock production varied only slightly between the eastern and western sections of the Ozark region, the western counties gained a clear ascendancy in grain production. According to the 1880 census, the average farmer in the five western counties of Boone, Carroll, Madison, Washington, and Benton produced 20 percent more corn than his eastern Ozark counterpart, twice as many bushels of oats, and more than three times as many bushels of wheat.[15]

Perhaps the most distinguishing characteristic of the western counties was the sheer number of farms and people as compared with the eastern Ozark counties. From its earliest settlement, the Springfield Plain had been characterized by an abundance of small yeoman farmers. By 1880, Washington and Benton Counties contained more farms than any other county in Arkansas, and the five western, or prairie, counties held 10,312 farms, 11 percent of the state's total and more than the other nine Ozark counties combined. Washington County had more land under cultivation than the combined improved acreage of Baxter, Fulton, Newton, Searcy, and Stone Counties. The proliferation of relatively small, intensively cultivated, diverse farmsteads resembled the pattern prevalent in the Midwest. The western counties also accounted for 56 percent of the Ozarks' population of almost 200,000 people in 1890; Washington County alone counted more than 32,000 inhabitants within its borders.[16]

Like farms across the Midwest, farms on the prairies of northwestern Arkansas were devoted to a diverse array of agricultural pursuits. In addition to growing small grains, various farmers in the western counties raised livestock, grew tobacco, or maintained orchards of fruit trees. Goodspeed's Benton County biographies contain the names of several stockmen. LeRoy Camden, a Tennessee native raised in Missouri, moved onto a 180-acre Benton County farm in 1876, from which he began buying and selling cattle. M. R. Blevins moved with his family from eastern Tennessee to Arkansas in 1851, eventually settling in Benton County on the eve of the Civil War. After service in the Confederate army, he ran a cattle business on his 340-acre farm. Another native of Tennessee, Catlett Fitch, left Iowa for Benton County in 1852. By 1889, he had amassed 3,000 acres and had built one of the region's largest cattle farms, marketing 300 head per year. In Washington County David Divelbiss, a Union veteran from Indiana, settled on a 320-acre farm in 1876, where he raised a herd of Jersey cattle. In 1887, he earned $700 from the butter he sold. Other Washington County farmers also bred blooded stock, an uncommon practice throughout much of the Ozarks until after World War II. In 1889, Washington County contained more than 10 percent of Arkansas's graded cattle. Union veteran and Indiana immigrant Jonathan Foust was among the region's earliest breeders of Poland-China hogs. B. F. Holway, a New York native who moved to the county from Iowa in 1886, listed himself as a raiser of trotting horses, and Captain Samuel Pittman claimed to be the first breeder of Cotswold sheep and Shorthorn cattle in his native Washington County.[17]

While tobacco raising declined in the eastern counties after the war, cultivation of the leaf spread westward into the prairie counties. As early as 1868, reports out of Searcy County praised the profitability of tobacco: "This county is well adapted to the culture of tobacco and it would certainly pay far better than cotton." Several farmers shared this opinion—at least for a time. The 1869 tobacco crop in Searcy County represented a 500 percent increase over that of the previous decade. If tobacco did pay better than cotton, the decline of tobacco production in the 1870s fails to reflect such a condition. By 1879 Searcy County's tobacco harvest had declined by 16,000 pounds to less than 9,000 pounds.[18]

Farther west, tobacco factories sprang up in Washington and Benton Counties, and to the north, Bellefonte became the manufacturing center of the Boone County tobacco industry. Elias Boudinot, a prominent Arkansas newspaperman and tobacco manufacturer who owned a factory in Benton County near the Cherokee Nation border, assured readers of the *Arkansas Gazette* that Arkansas-raised tobacco was equal to the best Virginia brands. Through such promotion by manufacturers, newspapers, and agricultural societies, raising tobacco quickly caught on in northwestern Arkansas. By 1869, Washington County had become the state's leading tobacco-producing county, with a harvest of 116,176 pounds, and Boone and Benton Counties ranked second and third, respectively. A postharvest report indicated that one Benton County community had produced 100,000 pounds in 1873. Four years later, the *Arkansas Gazette* reported that tobacco culture was still on the rise in the five prairie counties.[19]

Tobacco production in northwestern Arkansas peaked in the late 1870s and early 1880s. Benton County became the state's chief tobacco-growing area during this period. The sandy limestone soils of the rolling Springfield Plain proved ideal for raising small grains and tobacco. Most Ozark tobacco farmers cultivated White Burley; other varieties grown in the region included Virginia Yellow Leaf, Yellow Pryor, and Orinoco. In 1879 Benton County's farmers planted 547 acres in tobacco, more than one-fourth of the state's total; their harvest of almost 400,000 pounds represented more than two-fifths of Arkansas's combined harvest. Tobacco farmers sold their crops to local dealers or manufacturers in the fall and winter; prices ranged from just over 1 cent to 40 cents per pound, although most farmers received between 4 and 8 cents.[20]

Like their eastern neighbors before them, the farmers of northwestern Arkansas eventually gave up on tobacco as a viable cash crop. Tobacco production exacted a severe toll from the soil. Most Ozark farmers found it necessary to plant soil-replenishing grasses after only two years of tobacco cultivation. The necessity of crop rotation and declining tobacco prices influenced many Ozark farmers to abandon tobacco after the Frisco Railroad arrived in 1881. Benton County's tobacco production declined by almost one-third in the decade after 1879.[21]

Tobacco growing was a short-lived activity in northwestern Arkansas, and cotton raising never caught on in the prairie districts. Livestock raising and dairying remained common practices among Ozark farmers, although specializing in livestock was relatively uncommon. The emergence of a new cash crop, apples, in the final two decades of the nineteenth century reduced tobacco to insignificance in northwestern Arkansas by 1900. The area, especially Washington and Benton Counties, had been known for its apple production for many years. The introduction of rail service in 1881 supplied the transportation network necessary for successful fruit farming and marketing. Within the decade the apple industry began to transform Arkansas's northwestern corner into a prairie of vast orchards amid diversified farms that raised livestock, dairy, and grain products. The growing of apples and other orchard and truck crops would come to dominate agriculture in the area for the better part of four decades.

As early as 1852, Washington County farmers had sent shipments of their "striped Ben" apples over the Boston Mountains to be sold at ports on the Arkansas River. The prairie soil of northwestern Arkansas—a stony, silty loam with a subsoil possessing good water-retaining capacity —and a fine combination of altitude, rainfall, and temperature resulted in an ideal orchard farming area. Nevertheless, orchard production was minimal until after the Civil War. One of northwestern Arkansas's first orchard keepers was H. S. Mundell, who bought an abandoned farm with a neglected orchard in western Benton County in 1866. Within two years he had salvaged the valuable trees and had begun selling apples at 50 cents per bushel to freighters who hauled them to Kansas or Texas. When Mundell began earning as much as $40 off a good tree, his neighbors took note. After harvesting only $890 worth of orchard products in 1859, Washington and Benton Counties claimed about half the state's sales of orchard fruits in 1869, with combined sales of more than $68,000. De-spite strides in fruit production, the lack of rail transportation stymied the apple industry throughout the 1870s. A freighter wagon could haul only 40 to 50 bushels at once, and a good orchard could produce several times that many. In 1872 the *Arkansas Gazette* reported the shipment of Washington County apples to Texas but lamented the loss of many to rot. By 1879, largely due to transportation shortcomings, the sales of orchard products in Benton and Washington Counties had fallen to less than $20,000.[22]

The chief obstacle to an orchard boom fell in 1881, when the St. Louis, Arkansas & Texas Railway (later the St. Louis & San Francisco Railroad, or the "Frisco") extended its line from Springfield, Missouri, to Fort Smith, Arkansas, bisecting Benton and Washington Counties. The rail-road had an immediate impact. Within the decade, orchard keepers found a ready market for their products. Healthy apples were sold to cold stor-age houses to await shipment. Cull apples were sold to evaporators, vine-gar plants, and a brandy distillery that opened for business along the tracks. In 1886, sixteen Springdale-area farmers formed the Northwest Arkansas Horticultural Society, and other Washington County agricul-turists established a similar organization the following year. While the primary purpose of the horticultural societies was to share information and compare products, the Western Arkansas Fruit Growers' and Ship-pers' Cooperative Association, organized at Springdale in 1888, provided a valuable boost to growing and marketing activities in the burgeoning orchard industry.[23]

One other important impetus to orchard culture was the 1888 estab-lishment of an experiment station at Fayetteville's Arkansas Industrial

University (now the University of Arkansas). In 1887 Congress passed the Hatch Act, which provided federal funds for state university–operated agricultural experiment stations. The Arkansas Agricultural Experiment Station was established the following year at Fayetteville under the direction of Albert Menke. Because of northwestern Arkansas's isolation, the experiment station became in practice a regional, rather than a state, institution. In the 1890s director Robert Bennett concentrated on livestock and fruit raising at the university's experimental farm. Farmers' institutes, demonstrations performed by traveling experiment station and university personnel, encouraged orchard farming in Benton and Washington Counties, and in 1897 the Arkansas Agricultural Experiment Station issued a handbook for truck farmers that stressed the importance of crop rotation and fertilizer. The presence of the experiment station provided farmers of northwestern Arkansas with valuable scientific information and helped spur the development of a prosperous and diverse agricultural community; conversely, the station's isolation and subsequent narrow subregional focus denied farmers elsewhere in the Ozarks and in much of the state the benefits of research results and information until the establishment of the extension service on the eve of World War I.[24]

By 1889, the western Ozarks' production of apples had increased to almost 570,000 bushels, about one-third of the state's total harvest. Washington County's 375,000 bearing trees produced over 200,000 bushels. Several of the subregion's most prominent agriculturists raised apples, which could generate as much as $500 per acre at 50 cents or more a bushel, and other fruits. Some of these farmers were newcomers to the Ozarks after the Civil War. Goldsmith Davis, an Indiana native who left Minnesota for a section of Benton County land in 1867 at the age of twenty-three, owned the largest orchard and nursery in the county in 1889. Davis's orchard consisted of 20,000 trees, and from his nursery of 1 million trees he shipped seedlings throughout the United States. Thomas Gilbert Brown made his way from New York to Nebraska before settling on a Benton County farm in 1875. Fourteen years later, his orchard consisted of 2,000 trees. Ozark natives also entered the orchard culture after the war. Richard Bean, a Washington County native and livestock raiser, established the Cane Hill Canning and Evaporating Company; another Washington County native, James Russell, owned a 225-acre farm with an orchard of 3,600 trees in 1889.[25]

In subsequent decades, railroad companies extended branch lines into various communities, spurring a widespread movement to establish orchards by the turn of the century. In 1896, Rogers, the seat of Benton

County, shipped 287 carloads of apples and 20 additional cars of dried apples. By 1900, northwestern Arkansas ranked among the leading apple-producing regions in the country. According to the 1900 census, the five prairie counties of northwestern Arkansas produced more than 1.5 million bushels of apples, over half the state's harvest. Horticulturists in those counties received almost $500,000 for their crops. Both Washington County and Benton County contained more than 1.5 million bearing apple trees in 1899. Two years later, shippers and manufacturers in Rogers exported 440 carloads of first-grade and dried apples.[26]

Although orchard products made up the vast majority of northwestern Arkansas's fruit harvests in the late nineteenth century, the arrival of the railroad also opened the way for the marketing of truck crops. The last two decades of the century witnessed the expansion of the cultivation of strawberries, tomatoes, grapes, and other field and vine crops. The self-titled fruit king of Arkansas was perhaps the most prominent farmer of such crops. Ohioan D. D. Ames arrived in the western Ozarks as a traveling nursery agent shortly after rail service began. Smelling great possibilities in the prairie soil of Benton County, he leased 17 acres in 1883 and founded a small fruit and orchard operation. After clearing more than $1,000 on 5 acres of strawberries and 1.5 acres of raspberries, he purchased 130 acres. By 1889 Ames maintained a large orchard and 64 acres planted in small fruits. To the south in Washington County Alexander Caton arrived from Texas the same year railroad crews connected the western Ozarks with the outside world. In 1889 his Richhill Fruit Farm was among the county's most successful small fruit and orchard operations. By the turn of the century, Springdale had become the focal point of a significant Ozark strawberry industry. Farmers in Benton and Washington Counties combined to produce almost 5 million quarts of strawberries in 1899 on more than 4,000 acres. The two counties also combined to produce more than half the state's 348,450 quarts of raspberries and loganberries.[27]

Near the end of the century, Washington County became the location of the Ozark interior's first extensive community of vineyards when Father Pietro Bandini led a group of almost three dozen Italian immigrant families from southeastern Arkansas to Tontitown, a community of small farms west of Springdale. Each family settled on ten acres, one of which was devoted to the cultivation of grapes. In 1899 Washington County, largely due to the Tontitown settlement, produced 2,359 gallons of wine. A decade later, Tontitown had grown to seventy families living on 1,400 acres.[28]

The western Ozarks enjoyed a greater variety of moneymaking crops in the post–Civil War years than did the eastern Ozarks. The railroad cargoes leaving Rogers in 1887 attest to the diversity of marketable crops. Over 400 carloads of agricultural products left the town, including 123 loads of flour, 89 cars of livestock, 51 of apples, and at least 10 carloads each of wheat, potatoes, dried fruits, and eggs. Like farmers in the eastern counties, many western Ozark agriculturists operated by and large at the semisubsistence level, and the diversity of their crops and livestock included one or more cash-producing activities. Although such farmers may have represented a clear majority before the arrival of the railroad in 1881, the relative importance of these small producers to the overall western Ozarks agricultural community was clearly diminished in the face of wealthy orchardists and large livestock raisers.[29]

Between the eastern Ozarks, with its growing dependency on cotton as a cash crop, and the western Ozarks, an area of uncommon agricultural diversity for the Upper South, lay the rugged Boston Mountains. In the late nineteenth century, the impenetrable hollows and ridges of this subregion represented the last bastion of isolated, self-sufficient mountain life in the Arkansas Ozarks. Many Boston Mountaineers would greet the twentieth century farming and living much as their ancestors had generations before. Twentieth-century America would be happy to meet them—so happy, in fact, that writers and travelers would seize upon their anachronistic ways and label them representative of an entire region's populace and continue to do so even after the mountaineer's extinction.

In 1879, the farmers of mountainous Plumlee Township in Newton County practiced a subsistence style of agriculture little different from what they and their fathers had practiced before the Civil War. Most owned about a quarter section (160 acres) of land, of which the majority was woodland where cattle and especially hogs ranged for grasses and mast. Corn was the primary crop, often accounting for more than half a farmer's cultivated acreage; many farmers cultivated varying amounts of oats, wheat, Irish and sweet potatoes, fruit, and sometimes tobacco and sorghum cane. The preponderance of corn on remote Ozark farms also suggests the existence of a quasi-agricultural activity long associated with mountainous areas but certainly not restricted to them. Although perhaps not as universal as Hollywood would have us believe, the making of moonshine, or corn liquor, was not an unusual occupation in the Ozark region, especially in the remote coves and hollows of the Boston Mountains. Farmers who avoided prosecution realized far greater profits from converting surplus corn to whiskey or beer than they did from selling corn in an area where there was at best a limited market for the crop; furthermore, in the most remote reaches of the region, the difficulty of hauling corn out of the mountains made moonshine the easier and preferred product. At least one Boston Mountain community in the late nineteenth century staked its health and survival on the illegal distilling of whiskey. During a one-term tour of duty as Happy Hollow's teacher, Wayman Hogue found that those who did not maintain stills benefited by selling their surplus corn to neighbors who did. An intensive effort by federal revenue officers to destroy the stills and moonshine of Arkansas resulted in numerous raids across the region in the late 1890s and early 1900s, including one—a state record—in the Boston Mountains of northern Pope County that netted eleven stills and twenty-seven prisoners, among them a preacher, a constable, and a justice of the peace. Nevertheless, moonshining continued to offer an underground market for corn and even sorghum, and it was a source of cash income for a number of rural Ozarkers throughout the twentieth century.[30]

Representative of the mountain farmer, although not necessarily of the moonshiner, were William Plumlee and Francis Edgmon. Plumlee owned 3 horses, 8 head of cattle, 10 hogs, and a small flock of sheep that produced 38 pounds of wool. The Plumlees churned 225 pounds of butter, gathered 170 dozen eggs, and picked 170 bushels of apples and peaches. Plumlee's crops consisted of 20 acres of corn, 10 of oats, and 3 of wheat. Edgmon's farm production slightly exceeded that of Plumlee. He tilled more than 50 acres to produce 700 bushels of corn, 16 bushels of oats and 55 of wheat, 40 gallons of sorghum molasses, and 12 bushels of potatoes, in addition to the family's garden produce. Edgmon owned 2 horses and 20 hogs, as well as 15 head of cattle that produced 100 pounds of butter. He also had sheep that produced 20 pounds of wool. The family gathered 400 dozen eggs and 70 pounds of wild honey. It is unlikely that any of Edgmon's crops were sold for cash, although surplus corn and eggs may have been bartered for goods. Neither Plumlee nor Edgmon sold cattle, and they probably maintained their hogs primarily for pork. Isolated by the encircling ridges, these mountaineers and their neighbors were indeed subsistence farmers whose lifestyles had yet to be dominated by the market economy.[31]

Although his final demise lay a half-century in the future, the self-sufficient subsistence farmer was a dying breed by 1900 and already comprised only a minority of the Arkansas Ozarks' farm population. Even in the remote Boston Mountains, farmers who lacked the valley land for

Sorghum mill, Baxter County, ca. 1930s. Animal-powered sorghum cane mills such as this one were common in the Ozarks during the late nineteenth and early twentieth centuries. Courtesy of the Keller-Butcher Photo Collection, University of Central Arkansas Archives, Conway.

cotton cultivation practiced other forms of commercial agriculture, or at least other methods of earning cash income. Isaac Coonrod Wishon, a Union veteran who lived in the Low Gap community of Newton County, subsisted on scratch farming, blacksmithing, and hunting after the Civil War until the bear population was depleted in the 1880s. In 1885 he ordered fruit trees and berry plants from a Nashville, Tennessee, company; within a few years, Wishon's orchard produced such a surplus that he built a fruit cellar and an evaporator. The Hogue family of Gravel Hill typifies the diverse economic efforts of highland families in the late nineteenth century. The Hogues raised sheep and hogs and grew corn, wheat, oats, tobacco, sorghum, potatoes, and cotton for home use—the women of the family carded and spun wool and cotton into thread—and periodically sold cattle to drovers. In addition, Mr. Hogue traveled by wagon to Little Rock every year to sell turkeys and furs. In particularly hard years, the entire family, along with neighbor families, would trek to the bottomlands of the Arkansas River valley and pick cotton for several weeks.[32]

William Plumlee, Isaac Wishon, and other small subsistence and semi-subsistence farmers found themselves no longer alone in a sparsely settled country but increasingly surrounded by other small farms. The frontier was gone. Decades of intensive immigration had transformed the wilderness into a landscape of small farms and crossroads hamlets. A quarter of a million people lived in the Arkansas Ozarks in 1900. Settlers from Appalachia and elsewhere back east would continue to settle the region until the outbreak of World War I. Even more important to the growth of population was the region's penchant for large families. Broods of ten children and more were common, basic medical advances assured that most of them would reach adulthood, and few of them left the Ozarks. As a result, by 1900 the Census Bureau found more than 35,000 farms in the fifteen Ozark counties, an increase of 90 percent in just the previous two decades. Such intensive peopling of the rural countryside and farming of the tired soil took its toll on Ozarkers and their land. Tenancy increased by almost one-fifth between 1880 and 1900. Acres previously deemed unsuitable for cultivation came under the plow, forced to produce cotton for market or corn for livestock. As had happened in Appalachia a half-century before, the population of the Ozarks began to exceed the land's ability to support it.

By 1900, the Ozark region had begun to display its agricultural diversity. The twentieth century would witness further crystallization of intraregional differences. The southern wave of cotton culture that had rushed over the eastern half of the Ozarks in the two decades after the Civil War had begun to recede by the turn of the century, leaving a vast interior devoid of a solid cash crop system or of any consistent means of farm income. The eastern quarter remained a poor satellite of the South's cotton culture, and the western edge of Arkansas's hill country continued to cement its position as an agricultural oasis, a countryside of orchards, livestock, and small grains that shared little in common with other areas of an impoverished southern state. The new century would continue to chip away at the dwindling community of isolated subsistence farmers at the same time that the nation would first discover their existence.

Life beyond the Leatherwoods

IN 1854 a twenty-one-year-old graduate of the University of Alabama, Michael Shelby Kennard, followed his Baptist missionary father to Batesville, Arkansas, where he became editor of the *Independent Balance,* a local Whig paper. A member of the secession convention who had abandoned Unionism after Fort Sumter, Kennard enlisted in the Confederate army as a private, was wounded and captured at Arkansas Post, and rose to the rank of major. He returned to Batesville after the war and taught school until 1868, when he moved to Izard County and established the Lacrosse Collegiate Institute. Professor Kennard and his little college thrived until a cyclone destroyed the school and most of the town in 1883. Over the next few years, Kennard accepted a variety of teaching appointments around the state while trying to rebuild his college. After a year as a high school principal at Newport, Kennard, a devout Baptist, moved to Mountain Home in the fall of 1893 to assume the position of professor of languages at the new Mountain Home Baptist College. Three years later he became president of the struggling institution; unfortunately, financial hardship and poor health forced Kennard back to Lacrosse only a couple of years later. The professor died in 1901, having spent the last two years of his life engaged in farming and a final effort to revive the Lacrosse Collegiate Institute.[1]

The story of Michael Shelby Kennard chronicles the life of one relatively obscure and somewhat unusual man in the Ozarks of the late nineteenth century; at the same time it provides insight into the institutions and activities that defined the lives of Ozarkers outside of their fence rows, corn patches, and barn lots. As a classically educated man in a rural region, Kennard certainly was atypical, but his interests were not. His concerns in life were family and community—his children, the church, the village or hamlet, and education. These institutions and concerns rested at the center of rural life and culture; although nonagricultural by nature, they were intimately linked with the well-being of the region's primary economic and cultural activity, farming.

Kennard's wife Mary and their seven children occupied the most important position in the teacher's life. This was true of almost all Ozarkers. The family played a particularly important role on the farm. Many children meant plenty of farmhands. Large families often allowed small farmers to forgo reliance on seasonal hired laborers for activities such as chopping and picking cotton and harvesting hay or small grains. In the late nineteenth-century Ozarks, Kennard's brood of seven would not have been considered large.

As in most rural families of the era, tasks were apportioned according to sex, age, and skill. The male head of the household, teenage sons, and other adult males—grown sons or an unmarried brother or brother-in-law—labored outside the house. The men planted and cultivated the various crops; cared for work stock, cattle, hogs, and sheep; maintained fences and farm buildings; chopped firewood; supervised harvests; and hunted and fished. Boys were introduced to field work at an early age, often placed behind a small mule as soon as they were able to grab hold of the plow handles. John Quincy Wolf Sr. described his experiences as a teenager on his uncle's farm in the White River Hills: "Life on an upland farm was quite a shocker to me. First of all, there was work to do. We got up at 4:00 A.M., and in the warm months we planted, plowed, hoed, chopped cotton, picked cotton. In the winter we cut wood, made fires, cleaned out fence corners, cleared land, shucked corn, fed the horses, often nubbined some thirty head of cattle, and gave corn to the hogs. We went to bed not long after dark."[2]

Most Ozark farm women had responsibilities both inside and outside the home. Child rearing and housework occupied the majority of a woman's time. A woman who raised ten children spent most of her life caring for children and expecting another. As daughters grew older, they were asked to relieve some of this burden by babysitting, changing diapers, and feeding their younger siblings, thereby freeing the mother to tend to her other chores—cleaning, cooking, sewing, and washing. In addition to household duties, many Ozark women milked cows, chopped kindling and firewood, and tended gardens. In the summer, while the men worked the fields, mothers and daughters busied themselves preserving, making jams and jellies, and drying fruit. An Independence

County man was probably correct when he recalled, "The women would work so much harder than the men and never get no credit."[3]

The difficulties of the farm woman's life were multiplied during harvest time. The harvest's demand for abundant labor and quick work drew women out of the kitchens and into the fields. Most Ozark women and girls picked cotton and gathered corn alongside their husbands and brothers, while continuing to care for and feed their families. During corn gathering or cotton picking, a woman's day started before daybreak, in the kitchen; she may even have had to milk the cow as well. After cooking breakfast and dressing the children, she joined the others in the field. At midday she rushed back to the house to prepare the family's dinner, probably ate little herself, cleaned the kitchen, and returned to the cotton or corn rows to work until she had to cook supper. After supper, she probably worked into the night's darkness washing, mending, or caring for a sick child. A woman's life was demanding and offered little respite beyond an afternoon at church or an occasional trip to town. Despite the demands of rural life on women, however, the Ozarks did not harbor eighteenth-century patriarchal attitudes. According to historian Janet Allured's study of Boone County in the late nineteenth and early twentieth centuries, Ozarkers were not ignorant of "the changes underway in the definition of male and female roles within the family, and women often occupied positions of prominence and respect in family life and in the community."[4]

Perhaps the institution in which women exercised the greatest degree of influence was the church. Women constituted a majority of members in most Ozark churches and often served as the voice of righteousness and morality in their families. Churches offered spiritual and moral guidance, as well as a venue for community socialization; in the backcountry, a church often provided the only means of socialization. Weekly or monthly services, annual church revivals, and brush arbor preachings were popular events that offered neighbors the opportunity to visit and gossip and provided young adults a public place in which to carry out courting rituals.

From the early days of Ozark settlement, religion and churches played an integral role in migration patterns and community development. Faith was a valued tool of the frontier; it served as a commission to "work till Jesus comes" and as a balm in times of hardship and distress. The rural church was as integral to Ozark life as was the smokehouse, the corn row, and the cold-water spring. Ozarkers named their settlements

Goshen and Zion and Sharon and their churches Barren Fork and Caney Creek and Spring Hill. Just as family ties and kinship networks influenced settlement choices, denominational and congregational associations also affected migrational decisions. A congregation's cohesiveness often resulted in the resettlement of an extended family of Appalachian communicants in the Ozarks. In 1842, the congregants of Cedar Grove Baptist Church in Jefferson County, Tennessee, migrated en masse to the Greenbrier Valley of Independence County, Arkansas, where they established the Jamestown Baptist Church.[5]

Perhaps the most extraordinary example of congregation- or denomination-inspired settlement involved a group of Cumberland Presbyterians. In 1809 the Pyeatts, Carnahans, and several other families migrated south from Logan County, Kentucky, the site of the Gasper River and Cane Ridge revivals of 1800 and 1801, to Cherokee lands near Huntsville, Alabama. Forced off the Cherokee lands by the Georgia militia, the Pyeatts and Carnahans floated down the Tennessee, Ohio, and Mississippi Rivers to settle at Arkansas Post above the mouth of the Arkansas River. In the spring of 1812, the two extended families fled the Roman Catholic–dominated post, traveled up the Arkansas River to the mouth of Palarm Creek (fifteen miles above present-day Little Rock), and there established the community of Crystal Hill. In subsequent years Crystal Hill underwent significant growth as the Pyeatts and Carnahans were joined by other Cumberland Presbyterians from Kentucky, Tennessee, and Alabama. A decade and a half later, the majority of Crystal Hillers, led once again by the Pyeatts and Carnahans, moved into the Ozarks and established the community of Cane Hill in Washington County. Here they organized northwestern Arkansas's first Cumberland Presbyterian congregation in 1828 and in 1835 founded Cane Hill School, a private secondary institution designed to train young men for the ministry. The school grew into Cane Hill College in 1852, Arkansas's second institution of higher learning.[6]

The denominational makeup of the Arkansas Ozarks reflected the frontier's influence on American Protestantism. The Great Revival exerted a tremendous effect on the frontier churches of Kentucky, Tennessee, and other western states around the turn of the nineteenth century. The Ozark region was quickly dominated by the "people's churches" that had been successful in the southern frontier states—Baptists, Methodists, Cumberland Presbyterians, and Christians (Disciples of Christ).[7] These evangelical bodies thrived on the frontier because of their flexible, decentralized organization and their use of uneducated clergy—those without a degree from an approved college and a mastery of Latin and Greek—and because of western prejudices against the wealth and urbanity of older, established churches. Their brand of southern Protestantism, according to historian John B. Boles, "remained individualistic, provincial, conversion-oriented, and pietistic."[8] Denominations such as the Episcopalians and Old School Presbyterians, which relied on college- or seminary-trained clergy, failed to establish themselves on the frontier and exercised practically no influence in the Arkansas Ozarks.

Methodism owed its success in the Ozarks to the camp meeting and the labors of circuit-riding preachers and farmer-preachers. During most of the antebellum period, settlement throughout the region was sparse and widely scattered. Rural communities and their small congregations generally could not support a full-time minister. Consequently, Methodists utilized a system developed in the late eighteenth century whereby itinerant preachers traveled circuits, conducting services each Sunday with a different congregation on the circuit. Between pastoral visits, Methodists made use of lay exhorters to oversee Bible studies or regular church services designated as "classes." As settlements grew, Methodists generally adopted the Baptists' use of the farmer-preacher.[9]

The first Arkansas Ozark circuit, the Spring River Circuit, was established in 1815 by the Tennessee Conference of the Methodist Church. The circuit's first full-time minister, Eli Lindsey, mixed well with the frontier Methodists of the backcountry. A native of North Carolina and only nineteen years old when he came to Arkansas, Lindsey did not object to dances before his preachings, and on at least one occasion the young minister gladly interrupted his sermon to accommodate a spontaneous bear hunt. Lindsey's circuit covered a vast area comprising roughly the eastern quarter of the Arkansas Ozarks, from the Little Red River in the south to the Spring River in the north.[10]

Eventually even more successful than the Methodists were the Baptists. The congregational polity—which resulted in various shades of Baptistry and ultimately in denominational splintering—combined with the practice of ordaining uneducated preachers to render the Baptist church a perfect fit for the frontier and the rural South. The farmer-preacher became a staple of the South's most popular denominational body. The farmer whose "calling" led to his ordination as pastor to his local congregation could preserve local autonomy to a degree unknown in most denominations. Baptists' nonhierarchical system extended to their associations composed of equal and independent congregations. The popularity of the association further reflected frontier egalitarianism.

Whereas Methodists used circuit riders to ensure the continued practice of Christianity on the Arkansas frontier, Baptists sent missionaries into the region to form congregations and establish churches. The earliest Baptist missionaries in northern Arkansas were sent by the Bethel Association of southeastern Missouri. Most notable among these was David Orr, a Kentuckian who moved into the eastern Ozarks in 1828. A tireless worker, Orr helped establish churches throughout the upland area east of the White River, from Little North Fork Church on the river to Spring River Church near Imboden. By 1831 the Spring River Association, which he had founded, consisted of ten different congregations.[11]

Like most frontier Baptist preachers, Orr possessed little formal education. After surviving in territorial Arkansas on the meager funds provided by the Bethel Association and, beginning in 1832, by the American Baptist Home Mission Society in New York, in later years Orr settled into the role of farmer-preacher. Perhaps even more representative of the egalitarian nature of frontier Baptists was Orr's friend Henry McElmurray. Another Kentuckian who had moved to Missouri as a young man, McElmurray could neither read nor write when he married in 1814. After his wife taught him to read the Bible and a hymn book, McElmurray became a preacher-farmer and missionary in Missouri and later in Arkansas.[12]

One of northwestern Arkansas's most successful Baptist missionaries was George Washington Baines, a great-grandfather of President Lyndon B. Johnson. Unlike McElmurray, Baines was an educated man. The North Carolina native graduated from the University of Alabama shortly before settling on a 160-acre tract on the upper reaches of Crooked Creek in Carroll County, Arkansas, in 1837. An ordained minister, Baines worked for the American Baptist Home Mission Society and established three churches in northwestern Arkansas, personally baptizing 150 converts. After a term in the state general assembly, Baines carried the gospel and his plow to more fertile lands in Louisiana.[13]

Baptist missionary activity continued until the eve of the Civil War. In 1854 George W. Kennard, father of Michael Shelby Kennard, moved from Alabama to Batesville, Arkansas, after being hired as a missionary by the White River Baptist Convention, a young division of the Southern Baptist Convention that covered the Ozark region of Arkansas.[14] Kennard and his Southern Baptist brethren found a hodgepodge of Baptists in the Ozarks at midcentury—Primitives, Hard-Shells, Landmarkers, Missionaries, and Anti-Missionaries. Religious ferment in the early nineteenth century and Baptist congregational polity resulted in a collection of diverse beliefs and practices under the Baptist umbrella.

Many Arkansas Baptists who opposed such splintering eventually left their churches to join the followers of Alexander Campbell, Barton Stone, and others who denounced denominationalism and urged a return to true Christian principles. The "Campbellites," as adherents of the Disciples of Christ or Christian Church movement were generally referred to by their religious competitors, gained influence in northwestern Arkansas in the 1830s and 1840s. In 1836 Stephen Strickland, a "reformed Baptist," organized a Christian Church at West Fork in Washington County. By 1840, northwestern Arkansas contained several similar congregations. Fayetteville became an early center of Christian Church activity in the Ozarks. In 1848 John T. Johnson, a Kentucky congressman and brother of Vice President Richard M. Johnson, left his home state to spread the teachings of his close friend Alexander Campbell. After preaching in Little Rock and Van Buren, Johnson arrived in Fayetteville, where he converted several of the town's most prominent members, including a Cumberland Presbyterian minister, and organized a church. Robert Graham, a graduate of Campbell's Bethany College, became the Fayetteville church's first preacher in the same year. Four years later, in 1852, Graham was appointed president of Arkansas College, a Christian Church institution and the state's first college.[15]

The "Campbellites" were dissenters from dissenting churches. Campbell had been a Baptist and Stone a Presbyterian, and many of Arkansas's early Disciples of Christ were former Baptists or Presbyterians. Like the frontier culture that spawned it, the Christian Church appeared to be rootless, made up of believers who had consciously denied their religious heritage in the quest for a pure form of New Testament Christianity. Of the religious bodies that settled the Ozarks in significant numbers, the Cumberland Presbyterians were perhaps most unlike the Campbellites. Although the Cumberlands had splintered away from regular Presbyterianism, this did not diminish the power of community and ethnic heritage among the Scotch-Irish adherents. Perhaps more vividly than any other denomination, the Cumberland Presbyterians embodied the egalitarian forces at work in frontier America, the dominance of those forces in the Ozarks, and the importance of church and family to migration and settlement.

The Cumberland Presbyterian Church grew out of the embers of the fire started by the Great Revival. It was founded on the Tennessee frontier by four Presbyterian clergymen, three of them from Logan County, Kentucky. Old Side Presbyterians objected to several developments among their brethren on the western frontier: the use of emotional revivals and

Gathering at the Ash Flat Church of Christ, Sharp County, ca. 1900. Courtesy of Hayden Estes.

Methodist-style circuits to convert and maintain members and the recent appointment of uneducated clergymen in the church's westernmost presbytery. On the other hand, a growing number of Presbyterians, especially on the frontier, began to take umbrage at the strict Calvinistic doctrine of election. The combination of these conflicting views resulted in the severance of a group of New Side revivalists of the Cumberland Presbytery from the Presbyterian Church in 1810.[16]

The prominence of Cumberland Presbyterians reflected the Scotch-Irish heritage of many Ozark settlers and lends credence to the idea of the Ozarks as a continuation and temporary western terminus of the advancing southern frontier. Cumberlands were especially plentiful in and east of the White River valley, an area that became the destination of hundreds of migrating families from middle Tennessee and south central Kentucky, and in the northwestern corner of Arkansas. The Cumberland tradition of community-centered Presbyterianism and its cohesiveness engendered in part by a common ethnic heritage resulted in settlement patterns and church foundations that were more focused on community and extended family—to the point of being clanlike—than those exhibited by other denominations. The odyssey of the congregation that settled at Cane Hill in 1828 is an excellent example of this cohesion. Other

Cumberlands had already founded churches near the Strawberry River and at Mount Olive on the White River.[17]

In the late nineteenth century, the Arkansas Ozark region was still dominated by these four Protestant groups. In 1888 Sharp County contained thirty-two congregations: six of the Christian Church, seventeen Methodist, six Baptist, and two Cumberland Presbyterian. Neighboring Izard County was home to nineteen Baptist congregations, eighteen Methodist, ten Christian Church, and ten Cumberland Presbyterian. In northwestern Arkansas, Benton County—more populous and, because of greater inmigration of nonsoutherners after the Civil War and the arrival of the railroad, more economically and politically diverse—returned similar findings. Of the county's eighty-six congregations in 1888, thirty-five were Methodist, thirty-one Baptist, nineteen Christian Church, and six Cumberland Presbyterian. As a reflection of a slight degree of cultural diversity and the growing class distinctions of Bentonville, the county's seat and largest town, the regular Presbyterians, Congregationalists, and Quakers were also represented in Benton County.[18]

Divisions existed within the two largest denominations in the region, the Methodists and the Baptists. The rift in the Methodist Church from before the Civil War remained unsettled, and the existence of both northern and southern Methodists in the Ozarks mirrored the region's ambiguity over secession and war and displayed the effects of northern inmigration in certain areas. Of the thirty-one Methodist congregations in Fulton County, eight belonged to the Methodist Episcopal Church, or the northern branch. Eleven of Benton County's thirty-five Methodist churches belonged to that denomination. Nevertheless, churches affiliated with the Methodist Episcopal, South, denomination dominated the region, claiming some 90 percent of Methodists in most Ozark areas. Even within the northern and southern branches of Methodism, the Holiness movement and its acceptance by many rural congregations by the 1880s created further tension. The Ozarks proved to be a particularly fertile ground for Holiness devotees; consequently, the late nineteenth century witnessed a significant Methodist decline as members abandoned established denominations for new ones and as adherents of the Holiness movement took control of existing congregations. Likewise, Baptist congregations included Missionary, Free-Will, Primitive, and southern and northern Baptists. Unlike in the old Confederacy and other areas in Arkansas, in the Ozarks Baptists affiliated with the Southern Baptist Convention remained in the minority, especially outside the towns and villages, reflecting the frontier tradition of congregational independence as well as the region's often ambiguous and ambivalent connection to the plantation South.[19]

Despite denominational tags, most Ozark churches were very similar, although not homogeneous. Baptists, Methodists, Disciples of Christ, and Cumberland Presbyterians shared a reliance on evangelical, revivalistic methods and a faith in a righteous, caring, and omnipotent God, whose hand was witnessed more often in the miracles of the weather and in the healing of the sick than in the tragedies and failures of Ozark life. These common threads, of course, did not prevent religious debate and conflict. The differences among congregations and denominations in the Ozarks appeared slight and inconsequential to outsiders but were exceedingly important to most church members. In such an egalitarian region, denominational practices and doctrines became distinctions proudly worn or bitterly attacked by Ozarkers. Methodists and Baptists resented the Disciples of Christ's claim of "true Christianity." Many Baptists, partly in response to this tenet, turned to the teachings of Landmarkism, which attempted to prove that the Baptists were the modern representatives of a succession of churches, independent of Catholicism, from the time of Christ until the present. Non-Baptists rejected this teaching as well as other Landmark doctrines, including the rejection of "alien," or non-Baptist, baptism; an adherence to closed communion; and the prohibition against non-Baptist preachers exhorting in Baptist pulpits. Baptists and Disciples of Christ also found plenty of room for debate over the issue of salvation. Baptists ridiculed Disciples for their Arminian reliance on good deeds, or for "working their way to heaven." To the Disciples, meanwhile, the Baptist doctrine of the security of the believer represented the prospect of lethargy and contentment. Another popular point of contention was baptism. Baptists, whose reliance on total immersion gradually became for many a demand for immersion by only a Baptist minister, castigated Cumberland Presbyterians and Methodists for "sprinkling" converts, while the latter two groups replied that Jesus himself had not been immersed.[20]

Despite doctrinal disputes, groups such as the Cumberland Presbyterians had much in common with Baptists and Disciples in the region. All believed unflinchingly in the Bible, and all officially stood for the foundations of evangelical Christian moral order, especially in their opposition to drinking and dancing. The absence of Catholicism in the Ozarks influenced many congregations to exaggerate the seemingly superficial differences among the practitioners of evangelical Christianity, whose hegemony in the region was complete in the late nineteenth century. As settlements grew into towns, congregations of High Church Protestant-ism often appeared; nevertheless, Episcopal and Old School Presbyterian churches remained rare institutions in the Ozarks, limited to larger towns such as Fayetteville, Eureka Springs, and Batesville.

Because Arkansas lacked a public education system before the Civil War, churches often led the way in establishing institutions for secondary and higher education. As settlement progressed, education took its place beside religion as a cornerstone of community life in the Ozarks. Churches and denominations established high schools and colleges, most with an emphasis on Bible study or theology, and community church houses frequently served during the week as one-room schoolhouses.

In the antebellum era, schools of any kind were rare in the region, although by the 1850s most larger villages had at least one academy. In rural areas a group of families occasionally pooled their resources to hire an itinerant teacher to conduct a subscription, or "pay," school. In general, the absence of a state public school system and the meager financial resources of Ozark farm families demanded that children be taught to read and write at home, if a parent's own skills were adequate to instruct a child.

For the vast majority of Ozarkers after the Civil War, schools were extensions of the agricultural community. After Arkansas's Democratic Redeemers severely curtailed Republican-era state and local spending on public schools, the underfunded institutions rarely operated for more than a quarter of a year—when they were open at all—and then during the winter and possibly during the summer after crops had been laid by and before the harvest. Students learned traditional subjects—reading, writing, and arithmetic, of course, were universal—and often undertook Bible study. The basic function of rural schools was to provide local boys and girls with the tools necessary to one day take their places in the community of farmers, and schools almost never extended beyond the elementary level. In larger towns such as Fayetteville or Batesville, private academies and public high schools sometimes prepared students for college or professional life with a broader range of subjects. J. P. Womack, who had been taught in a one-room Benton County school until the age of nineteen, was amazed at the variety of courses offered at the Pea Ridge Academy: mathematics, sciences, English, Latin, Greek, history, psychology, and ethics. After the Civil War, academies similar to the one at Pea Ridge sprang up in smaller towns and villages such as Lacrosse and Mountain Home, whose academy reported four teachers and more than one hundred students in 1870.[21]

By the late nineteenth century, basic public education remained inaccessible to thousands of Ozark children. A report from the state superintendent's office for the year 1888 found that barely half the school-aged children in Izard County had attended school during the year. A similar report two years earlier discovered that only 3,219 of the 6,019 school-aged children in Madison County were attending school. Those who did attend were often crammed into small church houses or community buildings with several dozen other children ranging in age from five to twenty, often instructed by one underpaid teacher. Total education funding for Izard County in 1888 amounted to $9,433.45, less than $4 per student. Most of these limited funds came from local sources. In Madison County, the annual state apportionment for education equaled slightly more than $1 per child. Teacher salaries also suffered from a lack of funds. By the late nineteenth century, most rural Ozark teachers received less than $40 per month, and young women, who made up an increasingly significant percentage of teachers, often brought home less than $30 for a month's work. In addition, most teachers were expected to procure firewood and clean the schoolhouse without extra pay. In Stone County in the early 1880s, John Quincy Wolf, only seventeen years old at the time, was hired to teach at the local "free" school, as public schools were often called in the early days of the public education system. Young Wolf's salary was only $25 per month; like all his students, he came to the one-room school barefooted. Wolf had obtained a teaching certificate from the county examiner, but, according to one account, many rural school boards cared less about a prospective instructor's educational background and pedagogical abilities than about his or her reputation as a disciplinarian. The preference for stern masters did not always result in superior education. The one-room school dominated the educational landscape of the Ozarks. In 1888 Madison County had one hundred separate school districts, only thirty of which had arranged to partially fund their school with local tax money. Sharp County and Fulton County, both with fewer than 4,000 school-aged children, contained sixty-six and sixty-nine districts, respectively. Madison County claimed only one secondary academy, and Fulton County had two.[22]

In the establishment of institutions of higher learning, Arkansas lagged behind even its southern neighbors. Just as northwestern Arkansas had been an early leader in state agriculture, in the 1850s the area took the lead in the founding of colleges, and the Ozarks, or at least the edges of the region, was the site of several nineteenth-century colleges. On 14 December 1852, the Arkansas General Assembly issued a charter to a group of Fayetteville Disciples of Christ for the incorporation of Arkansas College, the state's first institution of higher education. The following day, a similar charter granted Cumberland Presbyterians the right to establish Cane Hill College. Less than two years later, Arkansas College, whose enrollment never exceeded 200, conferred the state's first bachelor's degrees. The Civil War ended Arkansas College's brief existence, but Cane Hill College limped on for more than two decades before falling victim to a new institution in nearby Fayetteville.[23]

In 1871, the Reconstruction Republican legislature voted to locate the new state university, partially funded by federal money through the wartime Morrill Land Grant Act, at Fayetteville, where Confederates, scalawags, and carpetbaggers had put aside their differences to support an effort to lure the university to the most isolated corner of the state. The university, originally called Arkansas Industrial University, opened for business the following January with a couple of frame buildings on the former hilltop farm of William McIlroy, one mile northwest of the center of town. The regional nature of the institution—Fayetteville and the surrounding plains were isolated from the rest of the state by mountains until the railroad came in the 1880s—limited enrollment and forced the university to operate a preparatory academy to attract local students. By 1883, the college half of the campus counted only eighty-three students; at the turn of the century, after the construction of dormitories, only 234 students enrolled for college courses at the newly renamed University of Arkansas. Despite a rocky start, the university would become the centerpiece of northwestern Arkansas's success, helping perpetuate the tradition of the Springfield Plain as an agricultural, economic, and perhaps cultural oasis in the Ozark desert.[24]

In the fall of 1872, on the other side of the Ozarks, a second Arkansas College was established at Batesville by southern Presbyterians. On the southeastern fringe of the region, Arkansas College, like the University of Arkansas, remained a local institution throughout the nineteenth century. The student body, which did not surpass 200 until after World War I, was drawn almost exclusively from the Batesville area and from Presbyterian congregations in southern and eastern Arkansas. Few rural Ozark young men and women found their way to Batesville or Fayetteville.[25]

Higher education was a luxury enjoyed by few interior Ozarkers. In most areas outside the northwest and border towns such as Batesville, the scarcity of high schools and the absence of wealthy concentrations of population precluded the establishment of colleges. A few determined educators and religious leaders fought the odds, nevertheless. One of the most notable was Michael Shelby Kennard. The Alabamian established the Lacrosse Collegiate Institute in Izard County in 1868. Lacrosse was a hamlet only two decades old, with a few small stores in an area that would soon become one of the Ozarks' chief centers of cotton production. The small institution, a two-year college by nineteenth-century Arkansas standards and perhaps an academy by modern ones, educated more than 3,000 young men and women in its sporadic existence before closing its doors for good in 1900. Due to the absence of dormitories, most students, those from the region and other areas in Arkansas or from out of state, boarded and worked with families in Lacrosse.[26]

Kennard's college was not state- or denomination-funded; consequently, like most small private institutions, Lacrosse Collegiate's existence and health relied completely on tuition payments. Because most Ozarkers in the vicinity of Lacrosse were farmers and because almost all farmers who possessed the means to send a child to college relied on cotton for their cash income, Kennard's and the college's well-being became intertwined with the success of the cotton crop. Lacrosse Collegiate's enrollment rose or fell on an annual basis in accordance with cotton prices and harvests. In the waning years of the institute's life, Kennard wrote his son, George, to inform him, "Lacrosse Collegiate Institute will become a thing of the past. . . . Many who intended to come here for a year were unable to come for want of means,—the result of the low price of cotton—, and many who came had to leave before the year was out for the same reason." Nevertheless, the elder Kennard sounded optimistic as he noted in closing: "The prospect for a [cotton] crop is good. Wheat is very fine, oats are unusually good, and the corn crop is in excellent condition."[27]

Kennard later faced the same problem at another interior Ozark college. Established and funded by the White River Baptist Association, Mountain Home Baptist College began conducting classes in the fall of 1893 in a two-story brick building on a 10.5-acre campus. One of several small Baptist colleges established in Arkansas during the late nineteenth century, Mountain Home College, advertising "Healthful and Christian" coeducation in music, art, elocution, stenography, typewriting, and traditional studies, attracted 166 students in its initial year. Kennard, whose Lacrosse Collegiate Institute had closed after the 1891–92 academic year, joined the new college's eleven-member faculty as instructor of Latin, Greek, and French.[28]

Despite its denominational ties, Mountain Home College's enrollment was also at the mercy of the cotton harvest. Even more isolated and remote from the centers of financial power in Arkansas than Lacrosse had been, the college struggled from the start, beset by low cotton prices, poor crops, and a lack of transportation facilities in hilly north central Arkansas. The good crop of 1893 presented the college and its faculty with false hope. As Kennard prepared to assume the presidency of Mountain Home College in the summer of 1896, he found the future all too familiar. "Much will depend, of course, on the crop now growing. If it is good, throughout North Arkansas, the attendance will probably be large." By Thanksgiving George Kennard heard his father's dire news: "If we can barely pay expenses this year, it will be doing well, considering the short crop throughout this section of country and the general financial stringency."[29]

Kennard's dependence on crop prices and harvests mirrored the region's reliance on agriculture. By the late nineteenth century, the Ozarks was still the most rural region of a rural state. Although the region was inhabited primarily by farmers who ranged from valley cotton raisers to self-sufficient mountaineers to wealthy apple orchardists, northern Arkansas had also developed a network of villages, hamlets, and crossroads stores to cater to and profit from these agriculturists. The existence of hamlets and villages, and even a few larger towns such as Fayetteville and Batesville, lent diversity to the Ozarks and provided valuable services to rural residents in their trading areas.[30]

At the turn of the century, the Ozark region was completely settled. More than a quarter of a million people inhabited the northern Arkansas plateau, and all but the most rocky and hilly lands had been purchased or homesteaded. Scattered settlers would filter into the region until World War I, but the land, in terms of its ability to support life, had reached its capacity. The population of the region would remain almost unchanged until World War II. The peopling of the countryside effected the growth of a network of trade centers. By the 1890s almost all Ozarkers lived within a "team haul"—the distance a team and wagon could travel round-trip in a day—of at least a crossroads store. Consequently, on any given road a traveler would probably have encountered a village, hamlet, or crossroads center every five miles.[31]

The ubiquitous center of trade throughout the Ozarks was the hamlet of fewer than 250 inhabitants. The majority of Ozark families headed for one of these settlements when they "went to town," except for the yearly trip to the county seat to pay taxes or for the rare occasion—especially before 1900—that banking necessitated a visit to a larger village. Even hamlets of fewer than 100 people generally contained a blacksmith, general store, physician, post office, gristmill, and cotton gin (in cotton-growing areas). Kennard's adopted home of Lacrosse provides a good example. In 1898, the hamlet of 100 people offered local farmers the services of three physicians, a general store, a druggist, a carpenter, and one hotel. Mail was delivered daily to the post office, but banking required a five-mile ride to Melbourne, and a person wishing to catch a train faced a bumpy eighteen-mile trip to Cushman. Even in the isolated Boston Mountains, the Searcy County hamlet of Witts Springs, fifty miles from the nearest bank and railroad, contained three general stores, a druggist, two physicians, a blacksmith, a wagon maker, and a carpenter.[32]

Throughout most of the region, only the county seats were large enough to qualify as villages. In 1898, Marshall, the seat of Searcy County, offered services not provided by Witts Springs. In addition to doctors, gristmills, churches, a cotton gin, and six general stores, the village of 350 also contained two lawyers, two grocers, a newspaper, a hotel, and county offices. In Madison County, Huntsville offered even more services and stores to its area farmers. Located on War Eagle Creek some thirty miles from the nearest railhead, the village of 550 people advertised both steam- and water-powered gristmills, four churches, a high school, a bank, and two weekly newspapers—one Republican and one Democratic. In addition to the usual general stores, a shopper also found specialty businesses: jewelers, barbers, a gunsmith, grocers, undertakers, and milliners.[33]

Jewelers, milliners, and other skilled artisans were rare in the Ozarks. In most hamlets and crossroads centers, patrons depended on the general store for anything they could not grow or make at home. The late nineteenth century was the heyday of the little general store in the Ozarks. The railroads had not yet penetrated the interior, and mail-order companies such as Sears, Roebuck, and Company and Montgomery Ward were still in their infancy. Rural folks relied on the country store for ready-made clothing, dry goods, tools, and food not raised on the farm. John Quincy Wolf Sr. recalled that his uncle William Swan purchased only a few such items—coffee, salt, spices, sugar, rice, shoes, hats, nails, and horseshoes.[34] Most stores accepted hides and agricultural products as credit toward accounts, and in cotton-producing areas, country store-keepers often became supply merchants.[35]

The ledger of E. N. "Nick" Rand provides a glimpse into the activities of the country merchant and the needs and desires of his rural customers. A native of Tennessee and a Union veteran, Rand farmed and operated a small mercantile establishment in the Fulton County hamlet of Wild Cherry in the late nineteenth century. In his ledger for the years 1885–86, most of the items sold reflect the popular demands of the time.

The *Ozark Queen* on the upper White River, with a ferryboat in the foreground. Courtesy of the Lyon College Archives.

Farmers purchased hames, axes, curry combs, backbands, shovels, hoes, horseshoes, horse collars, and barlows. Clothing items were also popular; Rand sold suspenders, brogans and other shoes, sole leather, calico and domestic cloth, bed ticking, pant goods, and even one man's suit. Judging from food purchases, Rand's Ozark clientele were highly self-sufficient. Coffee was the only commonly sought item, although plug tobacco and snuff were popular luxury items. In addition, the Wild Cherry store peddled gunpowder, lead, and caps for hunters, and washboards, thimbles, and lamps for home use. Rand also offered the popular curatives of the era: Godfrey's Cordial, Bile Beans, Worm Candy, castor oil, and iron tonic.[36]

Rand's and other general stores also served as markets for local farm families. In 1885–86 Rand paid 40 cents each for a fox hide and a gallon of sorghum molasses, a nickel for handmade ax handles, and 13 cents per pound for honey. Other products accepted for cash or credit included squirrel hides, lard, vinegar, feathers, homemade socks and baskets, onions, potatoes, butter, chickens, and eggs. Rand probably sold or traded these goods at West Plains, Missouri, or Mammoth Spring on the Kansas City, Fort Scott & Memphis Railroad, or closer by at Calico Rock on the White River. Rand hired wagoners to transport goods to and from these larger villages, although crossroads and hamlet merchants often made such trips themselves.[37]

Life beyond the Leatherwoods 65

The general store brought Ozark farm families to the hamlets and villages on occasion, but the scattered settlements offered more than businesses and churches. Social organizations became increasingly popular in the final quarter of the nineteenth century. By 1900, it was difficult to find a professional or a prosperous farmer who was not a Freemason. Other popular organizations included the International Order of Odd Fellows, Knights of the Horse, the Patrons of Husbandry (Grange), and the Agricultural Wheel (later the Farmers' Alliance). Although women's social life commonly centered on the church, many Masonic wives joined that fraternity's auxiliary, the Order of the Eastern Star. The Ozark region was also rich in political debate, with the ruling Democrats finding strident challenges from Wheelers within their ranks and, in certain areas, from Republicans. In counties such as Benton and Carroll, the prominence of Union veterans and northern immigrants delivered Republican votes and swelled local chapters of the Grand Army of the Republic. In mountain counties such as Newton and Searcy, the residual effects of antisecessionism and feuding between bushwhackers and jayhawkers created a strong local two-party system.

As the twentieth century dawned, the Arkansas Ozarks shared many similarities with other rural regions across the nation. Although more isolated and self-sufficient than Americans in most other rural areas, Ozarkers lived their lives on the farm but transacted business and found social and political diversions in the hamlets and villages. Like those of other rural Americans, the lives of Ozarkers were not confined to the land; the monotony of seasonal labor was broken by school sessions, church services, social club meetings, and political events. With road improvements and increasing population density, these activities came to be centered in settlements that ranged in size from a few families to 500 or more people. These hamlets and villages offered the services of doctors, blacksmiths, and merchants; the larger villages contained newspapers, secondary academies, and even specialty businesses. The Census Bureau's declaration of Ozark rurality obscured the nuances and diversity of settlements in the region and undermined the significant contrasts between the isolated farmstead and the crossroads hamlet.

Shortly after the turn of the century, Nick Rand left Wild Cherry to open a business in Calico Rock after the White River Division of the Iron Mountain & Southern Railroad transformed the river port into a railroad town. Here he would eventually grow prosperous in the wholesale business, his days as a country merchant a memory. By the late nineteenth century, the majority of Ozarkers had been little affected, if at all, by the railroad. The vast interior, its rich timber resources, and its small farmers stood untouched by the century's great transportation development. The Ozarks' isolation, or immunity, from the rest of America would soon come to an end as two rail lines penetrated the heart of the region in the first decade of the twentieth century. Some Ozarkers, like Nick Rand, would profit from the business and commerce generated by railroads. Some nineteenth-century citizens such as Shelby Kennard, who had recognized the potential for college growth that railroad service offered, would not live to see its coming and the fulfillment or failure of the railroads' promises. Still others, whose communities and farms lay isolated far from the nearest track, would carry on their lives as usual. The railroad, to them, would remain a distant, imagined dream.

PART TWO

Transitions and Discoveries

THE LATE NINETEENTH and early twentieth centuries marked an era of starts and stops, false hopes, important transformations, and stubborn continuities. Railroad lines first entered the Ozark periphery in the late nineteenth century but penetrated the rural interior only in the first decade of the twentieth. The railroads did not fulfill their promise to bring prosperity to farming folk in the interior. They did bring loggers and miners, but even these newcomers found long-term development in the region a precarious endeavor. The railroad and mining companies' expansion into the Ozarks in the late 1800s coincided with the discovery of mineral springs in the region, which spawned a nascent tourism industry. The sixty years preceding World War II also saw increased diversity among Ozark subregions; at the same time, the era said goodbye to the last of the semisubsistence farming families of the Boston Mountains and other isolated areas. The Great Depression and New Deal programs not only hastened the disappearance of the semisubsistence lifestyle but also set in motion the forces that would depopulate the Ozark countryside and bring about an unprecedented degree of agricultural homogeneity.

Despite their obvious forthcoming demise, and just as likely because of it, these hill folks were "discovered" in the depression decade by writers and travelers. Although few in number, these highland families came to dominate popular perceptions of the Ozark region before World War II and would continue to play a key role in those perceptions for much of the latter half of the twentieth century.

The following three chapters focus on the above themes primarily within the first four decades of the twentieth century, although tentacles of Chapters 4 and 6 stretch well back into the nineteenth century. Chapter 4 explores the timber and mining booms that brought environmental change and heightened activity to the Arkansas Ozarks for a brief period but had little long-term effect on the region. Chapter 5 picks back up the story of agricultural change and development, from the pinnacle of intraregional diversity at the beginning of the depression to the New Deal policies that would plant the seeds of agricultural homogeneity and massive abandonment of the Ozark countryside—seeds that would be watered by the forces of World War II. Finally, Chapter 6 offers our first look at tourism and the development of Ozark stereotypes, and with it our first opportunity to chronicle the chroniclers.

Big Dreams, Brief Diversions

PETER VAN WINKLE was an anomaly in the Ozarks for a number of reasons. He was born and raised in New York City. He made his living in a nonagricultural pursuit. And he was a lumber baron in the days before the coming of the railroad. As a twenty-five-year-old mechanic, Van Winkle settled in Washington County in 1839. After a decade of farming and mechanical labor, he moved to the Benton County community of War Eagle and built a gristmill and steam-powered sawmill on the White River. Van Winkle amassed a considerable fortune, at least by Ozark standards, and a stock of slaves, both of which he lost in the Civil War. Helping rebuild his region's towns and prospects, he recouped his fortune in the 1870s by supplying most of the lumber used in the construction of businesses and houses in Fayetteville and Eureka Springs. Van Winkle fought vigorously to ensure the railroad's arrival in 1881, an event that, as fate would have it, proved of little personal benefit. Peter Van Winkle died the following year as the northwestern Arkansas lumber boom was just getting under way. He would be forever remembered by locals as the first lumber baron in the region and the last whose activities and profits depended solely on local markets.[1]

The railroad rendered obsolete many of Van Winkle's methods. He had hauled the timber for University Hall (now Old Main), the original building of Arkansas's land grant university, by ox-drawn wagon from his War Eagle sawmill to Fayetteville.[2] By the mid-1880s railroad cars carried the majority of the region's lumber, in the form of railroad ties, staves, and posts, to destinations outside the Ozarks. Although railroads only skirted the Arkansas Ozarks in the late nineteenth century, they sparked an increase in nonagricultural economic development, specifically the growth of extractive industries. The Ozarks remained an overwhelmingly agricultural region, but the mining and lumbering made possible by the railroad offered Ozark farmers opportunities for off-farm income and presaged a regionwide extraction of natural resources in the early twentieth century.

The entrepreneurs responsible for bringing railroad service to northwestern Arkansas came to the region not for its apples, grains, or livestock, but for the thousands of acres of virgin hardwood timber on the Boston Mountain slopes of southern Washington and Madison Counties. Particularly appealing were the ancient white oaks, whose wood made fine railroad ties and barrel staves. Such hardwood stands covered much of the Ozarks, from the Boston Mountains to the White River Hills, but most forests were inaccessible and isolated. Ozarkers had harvested small numbers of trees since the beginning of settlement, but the lack of adequate transportation limited lumbering activities. On the eve of the Civil War, the Ozark region contained about twenty sawmills. The largest, in Carroll County, employed ten men and produced $15,000 worth of lumber annually. Most of the others were small one- or two-man operations that served limited community demands.[3]

In the decades following the Civil War, lumbermen penetrated the Ozark interior well ahead of the railroad. After 1875, lumber companies established operations along the Buffalo River. Boston Mountain cedar, walnut, and oak logs were dumped into the rapid waters in the winter or spring and floated down the Buffalo and the White Rivers to lumber mills at Batesville and other points farther down the river. Handford Cedar Yard, established at Batesville in 1884, was among the state's largest lumber companies in the late nineteenth century. Lumbermen from as far away as Newton and Searcy Counties created cedar rafts of 150 to 200 feet and floated downriver with the rafts for a week or more before being stopped midstream by the cable that Handford had stretched across the White River. Elsewhere in the Ozarks, the Spring, Little Red, and Strawberry Rivers carried logs out of the backcountry. For loggers in the extreme southern reaches of the Boston Mountains, the completion of the Valley Division of the Iron Mountain & Southern Railroad in 1879 provided transportation. Nevertheless, because water provided the only means of transporting large numbers of logs, lumbering in the interior Ozark areas remained a small-scale endeavor throughout the nineteenth century.[4]

The Arkansas Ozarks' first real lumber boom occurred in the 1880s after the completion of the St. Louis & San Francisco Railroad (the Frisco). If Peter Van Winkle reigned as the lumber king of northwestern

Arkansas before the arrival of the Frisco, Hugh McDaniel qualified as the region's first railroad-era lumber baron. An Ohio native and Union veteran, McDaniel followed the Frisco to Fayetteville in 1881 and established a railroad-tie shipping business. McDaniel's business grew as quickly as the ancient white oaks of Washington County fell. In 1886 he began construction on a branch line from Fayetteville to St. Paul, deep in the Boston Mountains of Madison County; the branch eventually extended forty-five miles from the main line to the hamlet of Pettigrew. In 1887, a year before his death, McDaniel shipped from Fayetteville 15,000 cars of railroad ties—almost the year's supply for the Santa Fe Railroad—worth $2 million.[5]

In the following decade, the Northwest Arkansas Lumber Company became the region's premier establishment. Founded in 1885 by C. W. Phillips, the Northwest Arkansas Lumber Company harvested and purchased timber from all of northwestern Arkansas and the northeastern Indian Territory; by 1900, it shipped a total of 200 cars of lumber daily from its yards in Springdale and Fayetteville. Woolsey, Winslow, and other railroad villages grew into timber shipping points as well. Northwestern Arkansas also became home to several lumber manufacturing plants, including Fayetteville Wagon-Wood and Lumber Company, Ozark Wagon Works, Red Star Spoke Company, Ayer and Lord Tie Company, and J. H. Phipps Lumber Company, which employed as many as 200 workers at its Fayetteville plant.[6]

Even after the construction of railroad lines through the northwestern corner of the state, a large interior region of the Ozarks remained beyond the reach of entrepreneurs and lumbermen for the remainder of the nineteenth century. Other rail lines in the Ozarks only skirted the region or sent dead-end branches slithering into some previously isolated valley or hollow. In 1883 the Eureka Springs Railway began service between the Carroll County resort town and Seligman, Missouri. In the same decade, the St. Louis, Iron Mountain & Southern Railroad sent a branch from its trunk line at Newport to Batesville and eventually to Cushman, and the Kansas City, Fort Scott & Memphis Railroad dissected Arkansas's northeastern Ozark foothills. None of the lines penetrated the rugged but settled interior White River drainage basin.[7]

This oversight by the powerful American railroad interests was remedied after 1900 with the simultaneous construction of two parallel roads through the heart of the Arkansas Ozarks. Boone County farmers and citizens had long clamored for the extension of a line from Eureka Springs to the most isolated corner of the fertile Springfield Plain at Harrison. Rail service in the area became a reality, however, only when depletion of the timber supply in northwestern Arkansas and the discovery of zinc deposits south and east of Harrison led entrepreneurial railroaders to brave the rugged, steep country of the Buffalo and the White Rivers. In 1899 Richard Kerens, a St. Louis businessman and president of the Eureka Springs Railway, and his partner, former Arkansas Republican governor and senator Powell Clayton, organized the St. Louis & North Arkansas Railroad, which absorbed the Eureka Springs Railway as its first stretch of line. Two years later, after citizens of Boone County had contributed $40,000 and the rights of way for the road, the St. Louis & North Arkansas Railroad reached Harrison. By late 1903, the line had been constructed southeastward to Marshall and Leslie. Despite construction delays and treacherous terrain, the newly reorganized and rechristened Missouri & North Arkansas Railroad (M&NA) reached Shirley and Heber Springs in 1908, and by the end of that year the Ozark section of the line was completely operational.[8]

The country traversed by the M&NA quickly became one of America's hardwood lumber bonanza sites. The central Ozarks grew stands of virgin timber—white oak, red oak, walnut, cedar, and even shortleaf pine—similar to the ones that had attracted railroaders and lumbermen to Appalachia and northwestern Arkansas. Prescient Ozarkers had recognized this potential long before 1900. In 1886 the editor of the Yellville *Mountain Echo* observed: "One of the greatest and most valuable products of the county [Marion], and one which will greatly augment its wealth and general prosperity, whenever our present transportation facilities are improved, is our immense timber resources."[9] Without rail service, harvesting timber could be carried out economically only near rushing streams such as the Buffalo or the White Rivers. Ozark farmers who owned acres of forest lacked the tools and incentives to fell the ancient canopies. Trees that avoided girdling and burning were generally left standing, and inaccessible hillside and ridge-top woods were reserved as a place for hogs and cattle to graze and forage for mast.

Sawmills were not uncommon in the interior Ozarks in the late nineteenth century. Hamlets and villages such as Big Flat, Evening Shade, Newburg, Omaha, Sage, St. James, and Salem boasted sawmills by the late 1880s, and small furniture shops could be found at Elizabeth, Leslie, and other places. Nevertheless, such establishments were invariably small, locally oriented businesses, most of whose customers were wagon makers or village carpenters. Furthermore, due to their reliance on inadequate tools and roads, many prerailroad sawyers harvested cedar and pine, which were easier to fell and haul than hardwoods but were also less prevalent in the region.[10]

Lumber and wood manufacturing companies followed the railroads into the central Ozarks. In 1903, at the same time the M&NA reached Marshall and Leslie, the Houston, Ligett & Canada Cedar Company started harvesting operations along the Buffalo River, seeking to profit from the large Newton County red cedars that in the previous two decades had been floated down the river. Lumbermen continued to utilize the natural transportation supplied by the river, but the rafts' destination switched from Batesville to the Searcy County hamlet of Gilbert, where a spur line extended to the bank of the Buffalo River and allowed the Eagle Pencil Company to load logs directly from the water to waiting railroad cars.[11]

Villages up and down the M&NA profited from the region's abundance of timber. Although Harrison, Marshall, and Heber Springs would ultimately become the primary points of trade along the line, the Searcy County village of Leslie grew into the M&NA's first lumber boomtown. In 1901, two years before the arrival of rail service in Leslie and in anticipation of the line's construction, the Great Western Mill Company of Kansas established the first of many lumber-related companies in the tiny hamlet of fewer than 100 people. A few months after construction crews extended the line from Marshall southward to Leslie in late 1903, Geyhauser and Galhausen erected the village's first stave mill. Three years later, Leslie received its biggest economic stimulus when the H. D. Williams Cooperage Company relocated its entire factory there from Poplar Bluff, Missouri. By 1910 Williams Cooperage claimed to be the largest manufactory of its kind in the world, producing between 3,000 and 5,000 barrels a day at its 68-acre plant in Leslie. In addition to the barrel factory itself, which at peak production employed as many as 500 workers, Williams operated 13 portable sawmills in the hills surrounding the town and constructed and maintained a 17.5-mile branch rail line that penetrated the white-oak forested ridges west of Leslie. At the peak of barrel construction on the eve of World War I, Williams Cooperage held leases on 85,000 acres, housed many of its 1,200 employees, ran company-owned hotels, and kept stables for some 300 teams of company horses.[12]

Williams Cooperage Company was only the largest of many lumber manufactories that established works in Leslie between 1903 and 1920. In the years after Williams's arrival, the boomtown welcomed the Pekin Stave Manufacturing Company, Mays Manufacturing Company, Export Cooperage Company, Leslie Handle Works, and Curtis Mills. Within

Williams Cooperage Company, Leslie, Arkansas. Peg Leg Decker Photographs (MC 1025), photo 19. Courtesy of the Special Collections Division, University of Arkansas Libraries, Fayetteville.

seven years after the M&NA's arrival, Leslie's population grew to almost 2,000 and perhaps doubled by the end of World War I, when it began to decline. At the height of its prosperity, the town boasted four newspapers, four banks, four hotels, and a hospital, as well as a number of nontimber manufacturing plants such as canneries, flour mills, and a creamery.[13]

Elsewhere along the line of the M&NA, the changes were less drastic but important nonetheless. Two stave mills and several sawmills sprang up in Marshall, which also added a canning factory and stockyard to its list of businesses after 1903. Southeast of Leslie, Heber Springs and Edgemont grew into lumber centers. Although the railroad reached Heber Springs only in 1908, within two years the village's population doubled to more than 1,000 inhabitants, and the former resort's fortunes switched from healing waters to the timber and lumber industry. When the M&NA reached Edgemont in 1908, the Globe Cooperage and Lumber Company moved its operation from Indiana to the Cleburne County rail town. At full production, the company employed 150 workers, and, as Williams Cooperage had done in Leslie, Globe boosted its own and the village's profits by establishing a bank and other business ventures in Edgemont.[14]

The influence of Williams, Globe, and other lumber factories extended beyond the railroad towns and villages and far into the surrounding hinterland. Railroad construction and the timber bonanza altered the demographic composition of the region. Railroad construction crews were often composed of immigrants and African Americans, and lumber companies frequently brought with them their previous employees. In the case of the Williams Cooperage Company, a significant number of black workers and their families settled in a previously all-white area. For the most part, the infusion of racial, ethnic, and religious diversity into the interior Ozarks was only temporary. The newcomers to the region rarely stayed once their employers pulled up and followed the trail of virgin timber farther west. The few who did remain after the timber boom had subsided tended to gather in small enclaves such as Green Thomas Hill north of Leslie or the Mountain View community north of Clinton.[15]

While companies often brought many employees with them to the interior Ozarks, they also relied heavily on the labor of local farmers and their sons. Many young men and struggling farmers found full-time employment in stave factories, cooperages, or sawmills; many more felled white oaks in isolated coves and on ridge tops. One Searcy County man whose father was a farmer-timberman estimates that at the peak of the hardwood lumber harvest, 70 percent of the county's residents were engaged in some timber-related occupation. When the boom times faded after World War I, Benson Fox and his family continued to cut white oaks on their farm near Leslie to supply railroad ties and rough lumber to a local wagon-hub mill. They also supplied walnut lumber for furniture stock. Even a farmer whose primary focus remained his crops and livestock could "in the summer, after he laid his crop by . . . take a load of timber and make a hundred dollars." The financial incentives were evident. A wagon load of white oak stave bolts, logs or parts of logs from which barrel staves were cut, could bring a hundred dollars in times of high demand, and a strong and industrious worker could render twenty to twenty-five rough-cut railroad ties—worth 25 cents apiece—in a day's time. Daniel Boone Lackey recalls the financial benefits his family received from timber work. Lackey's father, a Newton County farmer who cut and sold cedar logs during the winter, earned enough cash from one season's labor to buy himself a new set of harness, a metal washboard and clothes wringer for his wife, and a mail-order diamond ring for his daughter. The work was back-breaking and tedious, but this was nothing new to the Ozark farmer; besides, the immediate dividend of cash pay for a day's labor proved exciting and helped allay the uncertainty of the harvest and of agricultural prices.[16]

Employees of the Doniphan Lumber Company pose with a massive white oak log, Cleburne County, ca. 1915. Courtesy of the Ray Rains Photo Collection, University of Central Arkansas Archives, Conway.

Even in the most remote communities, timber and lumber companies brought brief periods of excitement and off-farm employment. In 1915 two Hot Springs entrepreneurs leased land in Dare Mine Hollow on Moccasin Creek in the remote Boston Mountains of northern Pope County. There they erected a stave mill and several company houses using lumber supplied by the Pages, the family on whose land the mill sat. The stave company owners bought and leased tracts of virgin timber, hauled their mill machinery into the hollow on wagons, and brought into the mountains a band of timber and mill workers whose drunken weekend revelries proved exciting to children and unsettling to their parents. In addition to the initial timber-cutting employment, the stave mill community also provided the Pages and some neighbors with a captive market for milk, butter, vegetables, meat, and moonshine. The demands of mill workers and timbermen in the isolated hollow grew substantial enough to convince farmer Scott Page, the family patriarch and landowner, to set up a small general store in a corner of his smokehouse, from which he sold tobacco, candy, coal oil, lard, and canned goods.[17]

The timber bonanza had sinister effects as well. Lumber companies sometimes took advantage of the locals' lack of business acumen. Most companies grossly underpaid for the timber rights to forest property, leaving the owner with cut-over land and little to show for the destruction. Other companies gobbled up unclaimed parcels, evicting unsuspecting families from the land that they had farmed for many years but had failed to officially claim as homesteaders.[18]

Environmental damage clearly represented the farthest-reaching ill effect of the timber harvest. As had happened in the western Boston Mountains in the 1880s and 1890s, timbermen and farmers quickly stripped the interior Ozarks of its most valuable trees, leaving in their wake scarred hillsides subject to erosion. Timbermen looking for bolt and tie logs often sawed off a felled tree at the first limb or knot, leaving the top and the bulk of the lumber to rot on the forest floor. As a result of such wasteful practices and the failure to plant replacement trees, by the depression much of the Ozark region was a cut-over wasteland. Amid the huge white oak and cedar stumps and decaying tree tops emerged a new woodland of saplings and scrub timber, surrounded by an impenetrable undergrowth of briars, vines, and brush. Ozark stockmen who had for decades ranged hogs and cattle on the mast of the forests found their supply of acorns, walnuts, and beechnuts dwindling in the early twentieth century as they and their neighbors leased forest lands to lumber companies for valuable income. In this way the timber bonanza effected a transition in agricultural practices as well.

One other agricultural tradition affected by intensive timber harvesting was the annual woodland burnings. A practice with both European and Native American precedents, springtime burning of woodlands continued after the depletion of the hardwood forests, and in infrequent cases continues to this day. When the rain and sunshine of spring brought green grass to the meadows and buds to the trees, cattle and swine emerged from their wooded winter habitats. Agriculturists set fire to the woods to burn quilts of leaves and needles and to destroy any blossoming bushes, briars, and small trees, thereby cleansing the forest floor in anticipation of the new season's mast and providing fertilization for nascent grasses. In the twentieth century, another justification for wood burnings was the killing of ticks, which plagued the livestock of hill farmers across the South. The gutting of woodlands by timber workers created an unforeseen problem for Ozark burners. Whereas the undergrowth of virgin forests had been sparse and the thick weathered bark of old trees helped them survive the flames, the dry, decaying tops—especially the parched, torchlike remains of cedars—and thick undergrowth of the cut-over woodland stoked the spring fires into raging infernos; the young trees that avoided the saw stood little chance of surviving the lapping flames and searing heat. By the late 1920s, remembers one Van Buren County man, "the forest fires would burn for weeks. They'd burn until the next rain."[19]

In anticipation of such ecological damage, the administration of Theodore Roosevelt set aside almost 2 million acres of sparsely settled Ozark forest lands, mostly in the Boston Mountains, as public domain in 1907. With this he established the Ozark National Forest in the following year. After the domain was reduced during Woodrow Wilson's presidency, more than 1.1 million acres of this land would comprise the national forest. But even these woodlands were subject to extensive logging as a result of the conservationist, not preservationist, policies of Gifford Pinchot and his Forestry Department successors.[20]

The majestic virgin forests of white oaks had almost disappeared by 1930. In little more than a century, white settlers and entrepreneurs had almost succeeded in taming the ancient Ozark wilderness, in the process eliminating from the region bison and elk and driving the bear and deer to the most inaccessible reaches of the interior. The Osage would scarcely recognize their former domain, and the white farmers who had supplanted them faced a future in which their parents' and grandparents' reliance on the woodlands for food, shelter, and livestock range would become increasingly obsolete.

Nevertheless, after almost four decades of cutting, the forests along the route of the M&NA continued to supply enough second-growth trees and scattered virgin oaks to sustain a steady lumber industry on the eve of World War II. Information gathered by Works Progress Administration writers in 1939 revealed that Boone and Newton Counties together contained 28 lumber manufacturing firms employing a total of 222 workers. While most of the firms produced rough lumber for barns, houses, and other buildings, the area also contained a few specialty firms; the largest of these, Harrison's Motor Wheel Corporation, employed 40 workers in its stave factory. Down the line in Cleburne County, Heber Springs ranked among the state's leading lumber centers in the late 1930s. Almost 300 people in the county made a living working in lumber mills and plants; the Lincoln Creosoting Company maintained 150 to 200 employees at its Heber Springs plant, and the Bruner-Ivory Handle Company claimed to be one of the largest hickory handle factories in the South.[21]

The isolated country of coves and ridges along the line of the M&NA became the undisputed center of Arkansas's hardwood timber and lumber industry in the World War I era. To the east a similar scenario, albeit

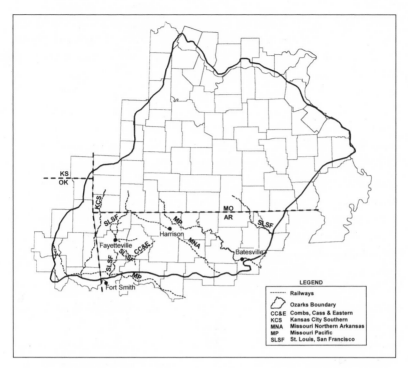

MAP 4.1. Railroads in the Ozarks, 1920

on a smaller scale, played out along the Ozark interior's other twentieth-century railroad. In 1903, the White River Division of the St. Louis, Iron Mountain & Southern Railroad, which became the Missouri Pacific in 1917, connected Carthage, Missouri, to Newport, Arkansas. It followed a southeasterly path through Boone County into Marion County, along the smallmouth bass–filled waters of Crooked Creek to the White River, and down the river's narrow, bluff-hidden bottoms through Baxter, Izard, and Independence Counties.

Because the Missouri Pacific generally followed the river valley, the line could not claim the drastic exposure of isolated people and hidden forests effected by the M&NA. Significant portions of the valley's best timber, especially the yellow pine of the Salem Plateau in Fulton and Izard Counties, had been harvested in the late nineteenth century and rafted or barged to Batesville. Nevertheless, the White River Hills contained enough white oaks, cedars, and pines to keep timbermen and lumber companies busy for a couple of decades. Stone County farmer Tom Ross, having grown up in the World War I era, recalled stave mills in the area harvesting "good timber. . . . Big old steel-backed white oaks." Across the

White River in Izard County, the most popular shipments leaving Sylamore were carloads of stave bolts, many of which were hauled in from small mills operating deep within the White River Hills. Up the river and railroad line from Sylamore, Mt. Olive was home to a thriving stave bolt manufactory before World War I; down the line at Guion, a hickory golf stick factory employed several workers until it closed in 1924. Mountain Home, although not on the line of the White River Division, still benefited from the lumber boom. In the 1920s, the Baxter County seat contained sawmills and a baseball bat factory. By the end of the depression, the village was still home to two lumberyards and the Sick and Treat Cooperage.[22]

To the entrepreneurs behind the Missouri Pacific, and perhaps even to those responsible for the M&NA, even more enticing than timber was the potential mineral wealth in the region. By 1900, the southeastern Ozarks possessed a flourishing manganese mining district; for years, geologists and Ozark natives had known of rich zinc and lead deposits in the hills along the Buffalo and the upper White Rivers. Due to the conspicuous absence of coal, the Arkansas Ozarks' level of mineral extraction would never be more than a fraction of Appalachia's—but the mining of various ores continued sporadically for three-quarters of a century, and the potential of mineral wealth played no small part in the railroad's exposure of the Ozark backcountry.

Mining activity in the Arkansas Ozarks centered on two general areas, each possessing different resources. In the southeast lay the Batesville District and its manganese ore, limestone, and marble. In north central Arkansas, the Yellville Formation contained rocks bearing zinc and lead. Both areas experienced a boom-and-bust cycle between the late nineteenth century and the 1950s, yet neither area bears much record of this past today.

Manganese ore was the first mineral to be mined and exported from the Arkansas Ozarks in significant amounts. The ore occurred in an east-west belt only twenty-four miles long and four to eight miles wide, centered in northern Independence County and spilling over into Sharp, Izard, and Stone Counties. About a decade before the Civil War, Colonel Matthew Martin of Batesville was prospecting for gold in the sparsely settled White River Hills northwest of the village when he discovered a heavy blue ore in the area's stone. Despite the district's isolation and ruggedness, Martin began efforts to extract the manganese ore, which was hauled by wagon to Batesville or Penter's Bluff Landing and there sent downriver by barge in loads of one to two tons. Low demand and

Manganese miners, Independence County, ca. 1914. Courtesy of Becky Wood and the Cushman History Project, Cushman High School, Cushman, Arkansas.

cumbersome transportation methods precluded any chance for profit, and the outbreak of the Civil War temporarily halted mining in the Batesville District.[23]

Manganese is used in steelmaking to impart toughness, malleability, and elasticity. After the Civil War, it became a highly prized mineral as American industries switched from iron to steel for the construction of railroad ties, skyscrapers, ships, and machine tools. Although the Ozarks' ore was coveted for its high percentage of manganese and low silica content, efforts to mine it were slow to get off the ground. In 1868 William Rinstein shipped 10 tons of Arkansas ore to a Pittsburgh steelmaker, but the Batesville District remained practically abandoned for another decade. In 1881 E. H. Woodward of the Ferro-Manganese Company opened several mines in the center of the district, which produced 1,475 tons in the first four years. For two years Woodward's operation was little more advanced than Martin's had been, for the ore was hauled by wagon to Batesville and then traveled by river to Newport, where it was loaded onto railroad cars. In 1883 the St. Louis, Iron Mountain & Southern Railroad built a branch line from Newport to Batesville; three years later, after mining companies from the Northeast began buying mineral rights in the district, it extended the line to a spot near the center of mining activity that became the manganese boomtown of Cushman. Railroad service provided an immediate jolt to ore shipping in the district. In 1886,

Big Dreams, Brief Diversions

the year the branch line reached Cushman, the amount of ore produced by the Batesville District more than doubled to 3,316 tons and the total value of the ore tripled to almost $20,000. The earliest beneficiary of railroad service was the Keystone Iron and Manganese Company of Pennsylvania. By 1889 the company's property and equipment were valued at more than $1.2 million, and in the first five years of operation Keystone shipped 18,000 tons of ore.[24]

By the late 1880s, other shippers, such as the St. Louis Manganese Company, the Missouri Furnace Company, and local buyers, joined Woodward and Keystone to make the Batesville District the most heavily capitalized and third most productive manganese field in the United States. Mining activity peaked in 1892, with 6,708 tons earning more than $60,000, but by 1900 the first boom was over. After the buyout of Keystone by W. H. Denison, a local man who had started as a laborer for the Pennsylvania company and whose personal interest in the community and its people spurred his efforts to revive mining, the manganese industry in the Ozarks underwent transformation and rejuvenation. Concentrating on reddish, ferruginous manganese ore, less pure and less valuable than the black oxide type, Denison oversaw a mining resurgence in the decade before World War I. Demand for high-grade manganese ore returned with the outbreak of war. In the years 1916 to 1918, the Batesville District enjoyed its greatest prosperity to that time, producing almost 40,000 tons of high-grade and ferruginous ore worth more than $1 million. Prices for high-grade ore ran as high as $40 to $50 per ton during the war years, and even low- and mid-grade brought $8 to $15. Cushman became the mining-town version of Leslie, and Denison, with a diverse array of businesses that included mines, a cotton gin, a canning factory, and a large general store, became the town's most wealthy and revered citizen.[25]

After World War I, manganese mining remained a steady but unspectacular activity, generating between $100,000 and $150,000 per year in the 1920s and 1930s. Despite a drop in prices and increasing competition from cheap Brazilian ore, miners continued to scour and scar the White River Hills during the depression. Many saw their persistence pay off in World War II as demand by the military pumped another million dollars into the coffers of Cushman companies. But this time around, the end of war did not spell doom for manganese miners and mining companies. While market forces dictated a severe reduction in demand after 1945, resulting in limited mining in the immediate postwar years, the threat of nuclear war and the looming presence of the Soviet Union granted the

Batesville District one last great period of prosperity and activity. In the frenzy of the Cold War and McCarthyism, Congress and the Pentagon in 1952 established a program for stockpiling various essential minerals and resources, among them manganese. Before the program was abandoned seven years later, the U.S. government purchased—at extremely generous prices; high-grade ore often brought $75 to $100 a ton—28 million tons of manganese, approximately 140,000 tons of which came from Arkansas. Between 1952 and 1959 shippers in Arkansas, primarily from Cushman, sold more than $10 million worth of manganese ore.[26]

The end of the government stockpiling program brought the manganese mining industry to an abrupt close after almost eighty years of commercial activity in the Batesville District. Unlike the timber industry, manganese mining exercised a localized but long-term influence on the area. The existence of ore in northern Independence County was responsible for the construction of a branch railroad line, which in turn made Cushman an important railhead for agricultural communities as far away as Lacrosse and Melbourne. Ultimately, however, these developments had little impact on the Ozark hinterland beyond the ore-bearing hills, even in times of high prices and prosperity.

The social effects of manganese mining within the Batesville District did, however, resemble those of the timber bonanza areas along the Ozarks' interior railroads. Even more than the timber industry did, mining attracted a diverse collection of laborers and businessmen into the once-homogeneous hills. Keystone and other companies recruited miners from other regions but also relied heavily on seasonal labor by local farmers. Mining companies generally employed contractors who in turn hired miners to obtain the ore from company-leased or -owned veins. In the early twentieth century a typical mine worker, whether a professional miner or a moonlighting farmer, earned $1.25 per day or $4 per ton. In the winter months, many farmers who lived in the vicinity of mines worked diligently for such wages, and those who owned a strong team and good wagon could earn money hauling ore to Cushman or Pfeiffer. Pay-per-work arrangements also allowed the independent-minded to set their own schedules and work without supervision. During the boom days of World War I, when ore prices frequently exceeded $50 per ton, the Batesville District hosted an influx of newcomers from outside the region—zinc miners from southwestern Missouri; coal miners from Alabama, Tennessee, and Illinois; and immigrant laborers. Companies imported some 900 Italian workers into the area, many of whom lived in caves and tent cities in booming Cushman. Most of the immigrants left the district after the war, but many of the other miners settled there permanently. Bulldozers and other power equipment gradually replaced traditional miners after the 1920s; before that time, the presence of both mine operators and laborers in Cushman and its environs offered a picture of industrial-age class distinctions rarely witnessed in the egalitarian, rural Arkansas Ozarks until recently.[27]

Although mining manganese ore would prove to be a stable industry in the Batesville District, entrepreneurs and railroad men in the first decade of the twentieth century were most excited about the plentiful deposits of zinc and lead ore spread across north central Arkansas. The potential of this mineral wealth was a key factor in the construction of the White River Division of the St. Louis, Iron Mountain & Southern Railroad. Nevertheless, zinc and lead never generated the quick, easy profits of the timber industry or developed the steady demand of manganese. The mining boom in north central Arkansas, coinciding in part with the timber bonanza, would prove short-lived.

Lead and zinc were prevalent in much of the Ozark region, especially in Missouri. Schoolcraft observed lead ore deposits on his journey, and on the eve of Arkansas's statehood in 1836, a lead mine was established on the Strawberry River in the eastern Ozarks. Lead smelting was a common activity for early Ozark settlers, who made bullets and shot with the plentiful ore. By the 1850s, lead ore was being commercially smelted near a Marion County (now Boone County) settlement aptly named Lead Hill. In 1876, the Illinois-based Boston Mountain Mining and Smelting Company started mining operations along a tributary of the Buffalo River in Newton County. For two years, the company shipped lead ore by wagon to Russellville over terrible mountain roads. But the real attraction for investors and entrepreneurs was zinc, which was used in the production of various items such as electric batteries, medicines, tombstones, and galvanized iron. Zinc ore could be found in at least eight counties, from Lawrence in the east to Boone and Newton in the west. The Arkansas Ozarks' first zinc smelter was erected at Calamine in Sharp County (then Lawrence County) in 1857. After the Civil War halted smelting in 1861, activity revived for a short time during Reconstruction.[28]

In the early 1880s, prospectors discovered zinc deposits on Rush Creek, a Marion County tributary of the Buffalo River, which set off a frenzy of prospecting between Harrison and Mountain Home. The richest sections of the northern Arkansas zinc field, named the Yellville Formation after the village that would become the center of zinc mining, covered Marion and Baxter Counties and included the Rush Creek mines. Miners loaded the first barge shipment of zinc ore on the Buffalo River in early 1888. The potential of the zinc fields drew the Buffalo Zinc and Copper Company and the Arkansas Mining and Investment Company to the Rush Creek area, which by this time was the site of a mining settlement appropriately named Rush. As the Batesville manganese district had been in 1881, the Yellville Formation and Rush Creek area were without railroad service in the late 1880s. Unlike the manganese industry, however, the northern Arkansas zinc field would have a long wait before rails penetrated the deep hollows of the Buffalo, an area even more naturally isolated and rugged than northwestern Independence County. Before 1901, miners and prospectors on their way to the zinc fields south of Yellville faced a daunting journey by wagon or horseback. Most traveled by rail as far as Eureka Springs, by coach or wagon fifty miles to Harrison, and then another treacherous thirty miles to Yellville. The primary means of shipping ore, by water down the Buffalo and White Rivers, was abandoned even before the coming of the railroad. Nevertheless, determined miners and companies continued to drift into the region throughout the last decade of the nineteenth century.[29]

Despite regular mining activity in northern Arkansas, by 1900 the region had produced only 1,500 tons of zinc and 500 tons of lead. The first full-scale run on the zinc mines occurred only in 1899 when, in anticipation of coming railroad service, miners invaded the hills around Yellville. Farther east, the Hawkeye Mining Company led a bevy of zinc and lead mining companies into Baxter County. By 1901 that county contained dozens of ore sites and twenty companies. The arrival of railroad transportation bolstered zinc mining. Along the M&NA, Pindall sprouted as a shipping point for zinc from the Big Hurricane Mine, and Gilbert shipped zinc as well as timber. The White River Division of the St. Louis, Iron Mountain & Southern Railroad traveled through the heart of zinc country, navigating through and near mining areas from Zinc in Boone County to Buffalo City in Baxter County. In contrast to manganese mining, zinc mining experienced only one great period of demand and prosperity—World War I. Between 1914 and 1915 the number of active zinc mines in northern Arkansas increased from 30 to 100, production tripled, and earnings jumped from $62,000 to almost $800,000. Zinc mining peaked in 1916 and 1917, when the region produced a total of 13,506 tons of ore. Rush, the epicenter of the zinc boom, grew to perhaps 5,000 inhabitants at the height of demand. The zinc craze then subsided as quickly as it had arisen. By 1924, the region's ore production had dropped to a paltry 4 tons. While zinc and, to a smaller extent, lead min-

Limestone mining operation, Independence County, ca. 1950s. Courtesy of the Arkansas Lime Company Records, Lyon College Archives.

ing continued sporadically in the Rush Creek area until the early 1960s, it would never experience the ongoing resurgence of the manganese mining industry. Only hundreds of abandoned mines and the shell of Rush, now a ghost town, remain to commemorate Arkansas's Ozark lead and zinc industry.[30]

Most other industrial or extractive endeavors in the Arkansas Ozarks had lives as brief or more so than the lead and zinc mining phase. In the late nineteenth and early twentieth centuries, the White River valley contained two marble mines, one near Batesville and another on the upper reaches at Beaver. World War I marked the beginning of decades of silica mining along the White River in Izard County, in the southeastern corner of Boone County, and in northwestern Arkansas near Rogers; the only active silica sand mines in the region today are nestled in Izard's White River Hills in and around the hamlet of Guion. Before the depression stymied industrial expansion, Williford, a Sharp County village on the Frisco rail line, grew prosperous from the quarries of the Greenville Stone and Gravel Company, makers of gravel for railroad beds. In the 1880s, Mammoth Spring became home to the Calumet Cotton Factory, a two-story brick textile mill with 120 looms, 5,000 spindles, and 150 employees. While textile mills had sprouted like cotton plants along the Piedmont of the Southeast, Calumet, constructed on a hydroelectric dam across the Spring River, was a rare representative of this southern industry in the Ozarks and, ultimately, not a successful one.[31]

One Arkansas Ozark industry that has enjoyed a much longer life than zinc mining or textile manufacturing is lime production. Concentrated in the White River valley in Independence and Izard Counties, the Ozarks' first lime company began operation in 1887 at Denieville on the Cushman branch of the St. Louis, Iron Mountain & Southern Railroad. Two decades later, after the Denieville operation closed, Edgar Young, a former kiln superintendent there, opened his own lime company up the White River near Sylamore in Izard County. In 1910 this business was incorporated as the Arkansas Lime Company with limestone mining interests, two lime kilns, and a barrel-making facility. By 1919, Arkansas Lime's kilns at Ruddells produced 35 tons of lime per day, or 10,000 barrels per month. In the 1920s, with oak fuel-wood becoming scarce and limestone beds depleted, the newly renamed Batesville White Lime Company established a new Independence County plant near the Cushman branch, two and a half miles from the river, and constructed a small-gauge railroad line to the plant and quarry. By 1928 the new Limedale plant alone produced 25,000 barrels of lime per month. Demand dropped during the depression, but the development of myriad uses for lime after World War II has resulted in steady production over the past forty years.[32]

In his study of modernization in Appalachia, Ronald D. Eller chronicles the rise of industry and the building of towns and cities in the once-agricultural hills and mountains. The historian finds the socioeconomic conditions of mid-twentieth-century Appalachia—industrial violence, social strife, dislocation, and the loss of local political control—direct results of the modernization of the United States.[33] Using this model, it is safe to say that the timber and mining booms of the early twentieth century did little to modernize the Ozarks. A few mining towns emerged to prosper for a season or more and to bring a taste of class division, immigration, and boomtown violence and entertainment to the backcountry, but they never imparted a permanent industrial influence to the agricultural Ozark hinterlands. Mineral resources found in the region were at best on the periphery of industrial America, which proved to be a mixed blessing for the Ozarks. The absence of coal and lack of waterpower denied the region the infusion of capital and modernization experienced in the Piedmont South and Appalachia; this same absence delivered the Arkansas Ozark region from the domestic colonialism of the eastern mountains, saved its hills from scarring, and spared its inhabitants the pain of black lung and landlessness. The Arkansas Ozark region would ultimately pass through the depression and World War II as one of the most agriculture-dependent regions in America, as well as one of the poorest.

The Making of the Migrant

THE TWO MOST famous sons of the Arkansas Ozarks were born five years apart and grew up only twenty-five miles from each other. Beyond their uncommon ambition and political skill, however, the lives of J. William Fulbright and Orval E. Faubus diverged sharply. Born in a red ginger-bread house on main street in Sumner, Missouri, in 1905, Fulbright moved with his family to Fayetteville, Arkansas, in 1906. His father, Jay, a banker and businessman, followed his own father, a well-to-do farmer, to northwestern Arkansas.[1] As Jay amassed a small fortune and a combina-tion of businesses as great as any in the region, young Bill grew up in comfort, his youth "an idyll of small-town happiness and success." It is a gross understatement to pronounce Bill Fulbright's life atypical of the re-gion as a whole. According to one biographer, the youngster who had the run of a thousand-acre farm just outside town acquired a distaste for manual labor. "He never knew hardship; he never lived in a log cabin or studied by candlelight or even worked his way through school."[2]

His young adulthood was a tale of success and adventure worthy of an F. Scott Fitzgerald novel, without the anxiety and imminent fall. After graduating from the University of Arkansas in Fayetteville, where the athletic teenager became a football hero, Fulbright departed for Oxford on a Rhodes Scholarship. He completed his studies in the spring of 1928 and spent the better part of the following year touring Europe, living for several months in Vienna on the $200 his mother sent each month. Upon his return to the States, Fulbright earned a law degree from George Wash-ington University, married Philadelphia socialite Betty Williams, and re-turned to Fayetteville to teach at the University of Arkansas's new law school. Three years later, at the age of thirty-four, Fulbright became the country's youngest university president when Governor Carl Bailey—at

least in part as a show of gratitude to Bill's mother, Roberta, for the unflagging support of her influential Fayetteville newspaper, the *Daily
Democrat*—placed him in charge of his alma mater. After one term in
the U.S. House of Representatives, in 1944 Bill Fulbright defeated Governor Bailey's old nemesis, Homer Adkins, for a seat in the Senate, where,
as chair of the Foreign Relations Committee from 1959 to 1974, he would
exercise a level of influence on foreign policy unrivaled in the twentieth
century.[3]

To the southeast, just a day's wagon ride from the Fulbright home, a
vastly different story played out, a story whose early scenes were far more
typical of the average Ozarker's experience. In the winter of 1910, Orval
Eugene Faubus was born in a rented log house on a hillside farm two
miles north of Combs, a railroad hamlet deep in the Boston Mountains
of southern Madison County. Orval's parents, John Samuel and Addie
Joslen Faubus, were both natives of the area, hard workers, and barely educated. Sam was a semisubsistence farmer whose livelihood increasingly
came to depend on cutting and selling timber. His passion, however, was
politics and, more specifically, socialist politics—the socialism of Arkansas and Oklahoma farmers that represented only the most recent incar-
nation of three decades of agrarian protest.[4]

The oldest of seven children, Orval grew up in what might be referred to
as comfortable poverty. Shortly after Orval's birth, Sam and Addie homesteaded a quarter section of hillside land across the valley on the other
side of Greasy Creek, a farm that Sam eventually expanded to 320 acres.
The Faubuses grew practically everything they and their cattle, hogs,
horses, mules, sheep, and chickens ate. In addition to staples such as
wheat, sorghum cane, and corn, their gardens, fields, and orchards produced radishes, lettuce, onions, parsnips, turnips, carrots, peas, beans,
okra, cabbages, sweet and Irish potatoes, pumpkins, squash, cantaloupes,
muskmelons, watermelons, strawberries, rhubarb, peaches, apples, cherries, peas, and plums. The Faubuses also took from the forests and wild
meadows poke greens, muscadines, grapes, blackberries, and huckleber-
ries; they hunted squirrels, rabbits, raccoons, and possums. Orval and his
brothers helped Sam cut rough lumber, fence posts, and cross ties, which
they sold at Combs. Addie and her daughters made all the family's gar-
ments from store-bought cloth. Young Orval Faubus's Ozarks still witnessed an occasional log rolling and house or barn raising, as well as annual social events such as spelling bees and pie suppers. In an area where
postmasters and county employees were looked upon as socially and
financially elite, Sam and Addie Faubus and their seven children could

live on a gross annual cash income of $360, less than two months' allowance for Bill Fulbright in Austria.[5]

Like Fulbright, Faubus first supported himself in the Ozarks by teaching, although his own formal education was limited and his classrooms somewhat more rustic than those of the university. Orval attended the local Greenwood school and occasionally the larger two-room Combs school through eighth grade; at the age of eighteen, he passed the state teacher's exam. In 1928 he took his first teaching job at Pinnacle, a one-room school midway between his home and Fayetteville. On a salary of $40 to $70 per month, Faubus saved enough money to attend the vocational high school at Huntsville during a hiatus from teaching and earned his diploma in 1934. In the meantime he married former student Alta Haskins of Ball Creek. During the depression, bare existence became a precarious effort throughout the region. When not teaching or attending school, Orval worked on local farms and at sawmills, traveled through the Midwest as an itinerant fruit worker, and spent a year picking apples and piling brush in Washington. After a brief stint in local politics and a couple of years as a farmer near Japton, Faubus served in World War II. His letters from the front, published in a Huntsville newspaper, kept his name before the public and allowed him to launch a political career that would take him to the Arkansas governor's mansion in 1955. He served as governor for an unprecedented six two-year terms, during the second of which Orval Faubus became a household name across America for his resistance to the integration of Little Rock Central High School. His actions made him a champion of massive resistance for millions of white southerners.[6]

The patrician and plebeian backgrounds of Fulbright and Faubus present an extreme contrast. Nevertheless, comparing the lives of the two reveals the diversity of this misunderstood region. The Arkansas Ozark region was not the monolith of poverty and backwardness reported by travel writers and novelists, nor was it a bustling area teaming with modern businesses and progressive people, as the town boosters and chambers of commerce declared. The region contained examples of both, as well as a large middle group that existed somewhere between backwardness and progress.[7] The economic and agricultural diversity of the Ozarks was both subregional—the residents of the Springfield Plain bore little resemblance to those of the Boston Mountains—and local—as settlements and villages matured in the early twentieth century, town and country dichotomies became more prevalent even among farm families. Technological and governmental influences operated within the confines of subregional and economic differences to exacerbate the polarization between haves and have-nots, semisubsistence tillers and progressive farmers, as the country approached the depression. In the meantime, with the introduction of mechanical machinery, automobiles, and government programs, the semisubsistence lifestyles of isolated families became obsolete.

Before World War II, outside of mining and timber towns such as Cushman and Leslie and beyond the limits of Fayetteville, Harrison, and other regional business centers, the vast majority of Ozarkers, like the Faubuses, made their living from the land. As the region entered the twentieth century, farming practices diversified rapidly, hastened by the introduction of rail service and the existence of natural differences in soils and terrain. Fruit production and livestock raising were on the rise in northwestern Arkansas. Cotton continued to supply eastern Ozarkers with their primary cash income. Farmers of the interior, limited by poor rocky soils and transportation shortcomings before 1900, remained trapped in the difficult world of general semisubsistence agriculture. Before 1900, these areas had been agriculturally dynamic as farmers slowly entered the market economy and constantly searched for new products and crops. Conversely, in the early twentieth century, agriculture in much of the Ozarks beyond the Springfield Plain would grow stagnant and farm families less self-supporting. Government intervention in the region and the technology and rhetoric of progressive agriculture would come to challenge tradition; however, only the destitution and desperation of the depression could permanently alter Ozark agriculture and, in the process, shape the region's destiny.

The construction of the two railroads through the Ozark interior after 1900 failed to affect agriculture in the way the Frisco had done in Washington and Benton Counties two decades earlier. Nothing comparable to northwestern Arkansas's apple bonanza occurred along the M&NA or the White River Division of the St. Louis, Iron Mountain & Southern Railroad (after 1917 the Missouri Pacific). Nevertheless, the interior railroads did provide a market and transportation for traditional Ozark farm products such as livestock, dairy, and poultry, as well as for fruit and other new crops. Only when the cooperative extension service and other government agencies arrived in rural northern Arkansas and began collaborating with railroad representatives, local businessmen, and farmers did agriculture in the region undergo noticeable changes. A look at pre–World War II agricultural change reveals how the ongoing interplay of government, business, and technological influences brought about the

Ozarks' greatest era of subregional polarization and foretold the demise of the shrinking remnant of isolated, semisubsistence agriculturists.

The arrival of rail service in the interior had almost no immediate impact on agricultural production in the surrounding area. Lumber and mining interests dominated the railroads' business for two decades. In the eastern Ozarks, cotton had developed into the one dependable cash crop, and farmers had already discovered overland or water outlets for their crops before the turn of the century. Throughout the central Ozarks, the absence of a cooperative tradition among farmers and isolation from the centers of agricultural progressivism in Fayetteville prevented the development of large-scale, profitable fruit or truck production. Furthermore, poor grades of cattle and a paucity of urban centers inhibited the growth of a dairy industry and resulted in low prices for beef cattle.

Ultimately, the potential of improved transportation to market was realized through the intervention of state and federal agencies. The increasing influence and power of such agencies would become the defining characteristic of pre–World War II agriculture in the Arkansas Ozarks. Unlike farmers in the northwestern corner of the state, whose proximity to the university exposed them to the tenets of progressive agriculture as early as the 1880s, most early twentieth-century Ozark farmers outside Benton and Washington Counties continued to toil in stubborn independence and methodological ignorance. Since the late 1880s, the agricultural experiment station had churned out studies and reports on crops, livestock, and farming techniques, but few Ozark farmers read them and fewer still possessed the money and ability to follow their progressive guidelines. Most Ozarkers followed the practices of their fathers, even though depleted soils and population pressure took their tolls on crop yields and family security. Ozark farmers' isolation from the representatives of progressive agriculture came to an abrupt end in the second decade of the twentieth century.

Arkansas's cooperative extension service, which came under federal supervision with passage of the Smith-Lever Act in 1914, grew out of attempts to alleviate two serious problems affecting livestock—hog cholera and cattle ticks. In 1911, during the heart of the Progressive Era, the Arkansas General Assembly enacted a law enabling the Arkansas Agricultural Experiment Station to produce an anti–hog cholera serum and providing for the selling of the serum to the state's farmers. High costs and the lack of a distribution network delayed use of the serum, especially in remote, hilly areas; however, the efforts of state agents in various counties represented the first direct extension effort in the rural Ozarks.[8]

More controversial and crucial was the effort to alleviate the cattle tick, or Texas fever tick, a parasite that left its host sickened and almost unmarketable. Due to the effects of cattle ticks Arkansas, like most other southern states, had been placed under federal quarantine, meaning that cattlemen and farmers in the state were prohibited from shipping their livestock to tick-free states. In 1907 the veterinarian of the Arkansas Agricultural Experiment Station, in cooperation with the federal Bureau of Animal Industry, undertook the daunting task of tick eradication. Beginning in northwestern Arkansas, agricultural agents organized cattle growers' associations and oversaw the building of dipping vats, concrete and wood structures filled with an arsenic formula or some other solution. The voluntary nature of these early attempts was soon replaced by direct intervention when the general assembly passed the "Tick Law," a bill that divided the state into two sections for the purpose of efficient tick eradication. East of the White River a state-funded agency, the Northeast Tick Eradication Commission, cooperated with the federal Bureau of Animal Industry to construct dipping vats and carry out the systematic dipping of cattle. Eradication efforts in the remainder of the state were managed by the veterinarian of the university's agricultural experiment station in Fayetteville. Because all farmers were expected to drive their cattle to be dipped periodically, in most counties agents built numerous vats. After cows were dipped, they would usually be painted or marked to signify compliance.[9]

This first taste of government intervention met local displeasure in many Ozark areas. In the spring and summer of 1912, anxious farmers in the White River Hills of Izard County expressed their resentment by dynamiting dipping vats at Guion and Lunenburg. In connection with the destruction of the latter, a posse of twenty-five night riders chased a "tick inspector" into the remote hollows of Hidden Creek. Although the destruction of government-constructed dipping vats became a common symbol of resistance throughout the region, the work of the tick inspectors continued with success. By 1914, fifteen Arkansas counties had been released from federal quarantine, eight of them—Benton, Washington, Carroll, Madison, Boone, Newton, Fulton, and Sharp—in the Ozarks. In the region, only Stone, Van Buren, and Cleburne Counties awaited the arrival of their first tick inspectors. Antidipping demonstrations erupted once again after World War I, culminating in the murder of a federal inspector on Hutchinson Mountain in Independence County in 1922. Nevertheless, within a few years the entire region would be declared tick free.[10]

The reception for government programs such as hog vaccination and tick eradication was more favorable among the prosperous farmers of the Springfield Plain, which was the birthplace of such progressive intervention. The farms of the fertile, rolling prairies of Fulbright's boyhood stood in stark contrast to the semisubsistence farms of the hollows and hills to the east, and the differences became more pronounced as the early decades of the twentieth century rolled by. At the dawn of the new century, four main factors accounted for the divergent paths of the "two Ozarks"—the prosperous Ozarks of the Springfield Plain, comprising Benton and Washington Counties and stretching into western Carroll and Madison Counties, and the mostly poor remainder of the region. First, the fertile soils, subtle climatological differences, and relatively smooth terrain of the Plain had decades earlier engendered a distinctive, somewhat midwestern brand of farming based on livestock and small grains. Second, a peculiar post–Civil War immigration pipeline had brought in hundreds of farmers from midwestern states such as Iowa and Illinois whose previous farming experience and recent Union army service fostered an environment of experimentation and cooperation. Third, the construction of the Frisco in 1883 had provided a valuable outlet at a key moment in the area's development, resulting in the birth of a large-scale orchard culture. Fourth, and perhaps most integral to the prosperity of northwestern Arkansas, the scientific and agricultural experts at the university shared their knowledge and experimental data with local farmers, a practice that, until the development of the cooperative extension service, was limited to Washington and Benton Counties.

The best example of the interworking of these factors was the fruit industry of the Springfield Plain. By 1900, Benton and Washington Counties ranked among the nation's elite fruit producers. The arrival of the Frisco had spurred the expansion of an indigenous apple industry into a full-fledged fruit culture. The agricultural experiment station provided farmers with valuable advice and research. In 1899 the station began a two-year program of "farmers institutes" in which traveling representatives presented orchard demonstrations and helped establish trial orchards on the farms of northwestern Arkansas. Fruit raisers also benefited from an atmosphere of cooperation. One of the region's most influential organizations, the Benton County Horticultural Society, was founded in 1893; its members, most of whom were postwar immigrants from non-Confederate states, read eastern agricultural journals and followed scientific practices.[11]

During the first two decades of the twentieth century, fruit growing developed into the dominant agricultural enterprise in Benton and Washington Counties. The 1901 Benton County apple crop was reported to be the largest in the United States; Rogers, the rail center for the industry, shipped more than 400 carloads of first-grade and dried apples. At the St. Louis World's Fair three years later, apples from northwestern Arkansas captured all the major prizes in the horticultural division. John Henry Keith, a Benton County farmer with a 400-acre orchard, won a gold medallion and a large check for his Ben Davis Number Ones. By 1919, at the height of the Ozark apple bonanza, apple pickers in Keith's orchard harvested 250 barrels a day, which brought a price of $8.50 per barrel. In that year, fruit crops in Benton and Washington Counties were valued at more than $9 million, more than the value of all other crops combined.[12]

The increasing popularity of apple production in the late nineteenth and early twentieth centuries influenced the growth of apple manufacturing facilities as well. By the early 1900s, evaporators for drying apples could be found in almost every community in northwestern Arkansas; during the fall harvest each one employed between ten and forty local workers, most of them girls and young women. Vinegar plants and canneries cropped up in a few larger towns, and Bentonville claimed one of the nation's largest apple brandy distilleries. Apple production peaked around World War I. The 1919 crops of Benton and Washington Counties, the largest on record, exceeded 5 million bushels and earned more than $5 million. The following decade witnessed a precipitous decline; disease and late frosts frequently decimated harvests, expensive insect sprays drove up production costs, and competition from the Pacific Northwest reduced prices.[13]

At its peak, the beauty of the Springfield Plain apple country was legendary. In 1907, a newcomer to the region had written to a friend in Massachusetts: "With a friend I drove out the other day to see the orchards adjacent to Rogers and this country is nearly all orchard; a perfect forest of apple trees. . . . The trees are simply loaded; bending to the ground with their weight of big red apples." During the period of decline, in April 1924, the citizens of Rogers, whether out of anxiety over the impending demise of their chief industry or out of hope for its recovery,

Packing apples on the Grabill Farm, Washington County, ca. 1910. Courtesy of
W. B. Grabill/Shiloh Museum of Ozark History.

held their first annual Apple Blossom Festival. The rains came year after
year to dampen the festivities, the apple industry refused to rebound, and
Rogers ended its celebration after 1927. On the eve of the depression,
northwestern Arkansas's apple crop had fallen 75 percent from World
War I production levels. In 1934 a Fort Smith newspaper sponsored an
Apple Blossom Pilgrimage through Washington and Benton Counties.
But by then the apple boom was over, and visitors drove through the countryside to take a last look at the blossoms of pink, white, and green whose
brilliance had illuminated the Springfield Plain for half a century.[14]

While apples commanded most attention from the area's farmers, the
Springfield Plain gradually developed a diverse array of fruit and vegetable crops. Shippers in Springdale began exporting peaches as early
as 1908. The peach harvest in Washington County peaked around 1915,
when local growers shipped 225 carloads. Like apple trees, peach orchards
suffered from drought and frost, and production declined severely after
World War I. In 1919 Benton County produced more blackberries and
cherries than any other Arkansas county, and Washington County led the
state in the production of grapes and strawberries.[15]

As apple production declined in the 1920s, strawberry, grape, and tomato growing experienced significant increases in northwestern Arkansas.

First grown commercially in the 1890s, grapes and strawberries generated considerable cash income by 1899. In that year Washington and Benton Counties ranked second and third, respectively, in strawberry production—almost 4 million quarts from more than 4,100 acres. A year earlier a bumper strawberry crop had led the Shippers' Union of Springdale to advertise for 3,000 pickers, many of whom camped out for weeks at a time or lived in migrant shacks on large farms. In 1919, Washington County farmers raised 255,034 pounds of grapes and almost 3.6 million quarts of strawberries. Over the following decade, strawberry production increased by almost 400 percent, and Washington County's grape crop, buoyed by the Welch Company's construction of a plant in Springdale in the early 1920s, exploded to more than 9 million pounds. In the same period, tomato farming also emerged as a viable alternative to apple raising.[16]

This boom in small fruit and vegetable production resulted in the construction of canneries across northwestern Arkansas. By the 1930s canneries in Benton and Washington Counties sealed more than thirty kinds of food. Among Washington County's largest canners were the Appleby brothers, George and Charles, who began packing blackberries as early as 1907, organized the area's first strawberry growers' association, and eventually operated eight canneries. T. U. Jackson's cannery in Summers, opened in 1925, packed spinach, beans, and tomatoes, turning out one carload a day during peak production. On the eve of World War II, canning operations were still plentiful in Benton and Washington Counties and had expanded into neighboring counties as well. In early 1941 Benton County contained eleven tomato canneries and nine other businesses that packed beans, spinach, poke greens, peaches, apples, blackberries, and grapes. These canneries shipped some 500 carloads of food in 1940. Down the road in Springdale, strawberry packers continued to export between 400 and 500 carloads annually. Thirty-two canneries, including eleven in Green Forest alone, operated in neighboring Carroll County; the largest, Alpena Canning Company, employed forty workers during the harvest season. Even mountainous Madison County was affected by cannery development. In the mid-1920s, fifteen canning companies were erected in the county; each plant contracted with area farmers to pay a given price for each ton of tomatoes. By the late 1930s, twenty-four canneries packed the produce of the county's farmers' 4,856 acres of tomatoes and 555 acres of beans. As early as 1925, tomatoes were the biggest cash crop of Carroll County, furnishing thirty-four local canneries.[17]

The development of canneries and a market for small fruits and vegetables after World War I provides another example of the dynamic interworking of commercial interests, government agents, and farmers in northwestern Arkansas. Declining profits from lumber and apple shipments persuaded railroads' agricultural representatives to look elsewhere for much-needed business. In the 1920s, county extension agents in northern Arkansas began collaborating with agents from the agricultural department of the M&NA in a campaign to encourage fruit growing among farmers along the line. In their annual reports for 1925, the extension agents for Carroll and Newton Counties both mentioned the assistance of W. L. Flanery of the M&NA. The two counties had recently acquired tomato canneries, and farmers in both were strongly urged by railroad and government agents to undertake the cultivation of grapes. G. C. Watkins, Newton County extension agent, claimed grape promotion as the "most outstanding piece of work we have accomplished this year" and noted "some valuable assistance in this particular project from W. L. Flanery." In adjacent Madison County, a movement was under way among farmers along the St. Paul Branch of the Frisco to plant strawberries for shipment in 1926.[18]

In addition to its cooperation with railroad agricultural agents, the extension service also offered demonstrations of grape and other fruit production and, in conjunction with the University of Arkansas College of Agriculture, sponsored an annual grape tour of the vineyards of northwestern Arkansas. A group of twelve Newton County farmers from Western Grove accompanied their extension agent on the 1925 tour. Upon their return, they organized a grape growers' association and made plans to plant 500 acres or more in grapevines. Such associations were common in fruit-raising areas and were often organized with the assistance of extension or railroad agents. In 1925, Washington County was home to six grape growers' associations and two sweet potato growers' associations. In Carroll County, fruit growers had organized near Eureka Springs, Berryville, Green Forest, and Alpena. Farmers in the last community also formed a strawberry growers' association after World War I.[19]

Cooperative extension agents used associations and other methods to entice mountain farmers of Madison and Newton Counties to enter the cash-crop market system in the 1920s. Their models for progressive agriculture lay on the prairies of the Springfield Plain, where the majority of agriculturists had long raised crops for market. Young agents like G. C. Watkins sought to re-create the grain-dairy-livestock-fruit system of agriculture prevalent in Benton and Washington Counties in the rocky, mountainous country to the east. But Watkins and other progressive-minded agricultural experts encountered a situation in the isolated parts of the Ozarks for which they could have been little prepared. Communities in the Boston Mountains and other areas not conducive to market agriculture were in the midst of a social and agricultural revolution, a gradual transformation from a lifestyle based primarily on semisubsistence agriculture to one dependent on off-farm labor or more intensive, market-oriented agriculture.

The reasons behind the transformation and its timing are numerous. One obvious cause was population pressure. In his study of the development of economic dependency in Appalachia, Paul Salstrom argues that the postfrontier stage of preindustrial life in the plateau subregion, which took place in the decades following the Civil War, witnessed a decline in the spirit of enterprise and a reversion to subsistence agriculture in response to overcrowding. A similar process appears to have occurred in the most isolated reaches of the Arkansas Ozark interior in the first quarter of the twentieth century. Rural population levels reached their peak in the Ozark region around the turn of the century and leveled off or declined in most localities in the following decades. Large families and continual immigration sorely taxed the infertile, rocky soils. Farmers in the mountainous areas gradually abandoned the grain and livestock economy that had developed after the Civil War. Between 1899 and 1929, Madison County's corn crop fell by more than half, its wheat crop dwindled to insignificance, and its farmers decreased their holdings of swine —a diet staple and once a valuable, marketable commodity—by 70 percent. In Newton County, corn production decreased more than 40 percent, and the average number of hogs per farm fell from 16 in 1900 to 4.5 in 1930, a drop from surplus production to subsistence levels.[20]

One reason for the decline in hog production was the timber industry. Lumbermen harvested the best mast-producing trees—white oaks, walnuts, and beeches—depriving hogs of much of their traditional winter and fall range. But the timber industry also provided cash work for many mountain farmers; this new income could be used to replace money previously earned through the sale of hogs or other livestock, and the off-farm labor might have proved profitable enough to convince farmers to reduce or retire their annual grain crops of corn, wheat, and oats. After World War I timber jobs grew scarce, forcing many old farmers back into a lifestyle now altered by time and the knowledge of the power of money. For these families the options were obvious but never easy: enter the cash-crop market by raising tomatoes, grapes, or whatever else the railroad and extension agents were peddling; by some miracle perhaps find an off-farm job; or hit the trail with other migrants, either the seasonal laborers who followed the ripening fruit up and down the Midwest, like Orval Faubus, or the permanent movers searching for greener pastures out west.

The machine that made the last option possible in the 1920s, the automobile, represented a third factor driving the transformation—the introduction of technological advances. After World War I, telephones, radios, and automobiles began trickling into the rural Ozarks, each one chipping away at the region's isolation by introducing the world beyond the hills and hollows or by offering the freedom to leave in search of that world. In the early twentieth century, the new technologies exercised practically no direct influence on Ozark farming in the interior areas. For a generation after the introduction of small, relatively inexpensive tractors by International Harvester, Ford, and other companies in the 1920s, farm tractors remained oddities in most Ozark communities. Small hillside plots were better suited to mules and horses, and the money received from meager cash crops rarely inspired farmers to invest in labor-saving machinery. More often, technological developments operated in the agriculturally marginal lands as pull factors. As we shall see repeatedly, machines lured Ozarkers out of their native hollows and into the factories of distant cities or the fields and orchards of other states with greater frequency than they improved their agricultural efficiency and thereby kept them on the farm. Unlike the people of Appalachia, many of whom crowded into mine and mill towns, most marginal Ozarkers adjusted to the demands of post–World War I rural transformation by leaving their native region in the initial wave of a half-century tide of outmigration.

Extension agents often found themselves overwhelmed in the face of such change, especially in counties such as Newton whose mountainous terrain and lack of transportation facilities prohibited cultivation of the university's current experimental crops. One alternative was to urge farm families to meet their subsistence needs first and market the surplus. In this spirit, Governor Thomas McRae and the University of Arkansas College of Agriculture launched a "Live at Home" movement in 1924. Typical of many programs of the time, the movement used a variety of means to encourage small farmers to increase self-sufficiency. Distressed that "in many counties in Arkansas the folks of the farm [were] living out of tin cans and bakeries and store bought food," proponents of "Live at Home" advised farm families to achieve a number of goals, including raise enough corn, hay, and meat for the year; keep at least thirty hens; start small orchards; terrace and drain land where needed; and maintain a twelve-month gardening and canning budget. Although this call for diversification targeted the one-crop systems of the fertile flatlands, it addressed the declining emphasis on subsistence in the twentieth-century Ozarks as well.[21]

One important component of the "Live at Home" philosophy was dairy production. An agent who began work in Madison County in 1925 found "many homes . . . without sufficient milk and butter." Except for thoroughbred cattle in Benton and Washington Counties and near larger towns such as Harrison or Batesville, Ozark dairy cows were of common stock and produced small amounts of milk. Extension agents attempted to import purebred Jerseys, Guernseys, or Holsteins to improve bloodlines and encouraged farmers to market surplus dairy products. In Madison County, the extension agent assisted a few farmers in developing small dairy operations. One farmer purchased five purebred cows and a milk separator, which helped earn him $10 to $15 per week in cream sales to a Fayetteville creamery. In Stone County, Nat Rushing converted eight head of range cattle to milk cows and earned $250 in cream sales over the first eight months. Newton County agent G. C. Watkins helped four farmers purchase Jersey bulls and oversaw six new small dairy farms. The six farmers milked between three and ten cows and received monthly checks for cream sales of up to $75.[22]

Poultry raising and egg production were also areas of "Live at Home" farming stressed by extension and railroad agents. Although egg sales had long provided Ozark families with extra cash or bartering value, by the 1920s it was not uncommon for poor farmers to ignore this sideline. In 1925 the extension agent of Carroll County cooperated with produce dealers, county merchants, and George McKinney of the agricultural department of the M&NA to sponsor a better-egg campaign. But because poultry demonstrations were generally carried out by female home demonstration workers and because there were few such workers in the region, poultry raising made few strides before World War II in most Ozark counties.[23]

Poultry, dairy, and livestock producers in the interior Ozarks were hampered by a lack of electricity and transportation services. No such barriers stood in the way of most agriculturists in Benton and Washington Counties. As we have seen, livestock raising had been an integral component of agriculture in the prairie counties since before the Civil War. By 1900 Washington and Benton Counties still ranked first and second in the state, respectively, in the value of livestock. Gradual depletion of virgin forests and closing of the open range substantially reduced the number of hogs in the two counties over the next three decades, a com-

Cattle auction on the square in Mountain Home, ca. 1930s. Courtesy of the Keller-Butcher Photo Collection, University of Central Arkansas Archives, Conway.

mon trend that was repeated elsewhere in the Ozarks. Between 1900 and 1930, the swine population of Benton and Washington Counties declined by two-thirds, while cattle herds experienced a 50 percent increase, reflecting a movement away from traditional, frontierlike livestock raising and toward a midwestern model based on purebred British cattle breeds, enclosures, scientific breeding, and a greater emphasis on pasture maintenance and forage crops. Again, the agricultural experiment station at Fayetteville and extension agents played a key role in the importation of thoroughbred beef and dairy cattle. In 1930, all but one of the Ozark members of the American Aberdeen-Angus Breeders' Association resided in northwestern Arkansas. Irma Giffels, who grew up on a cattle farm near Hindsville in northwestern Madison County—an area whose gently rolling terrain and proximity to Fayetteville and Springdale set it apart from most of the mountainous county—recalled that her grandfather's most prized possession was his Hereford bull. Beef and dairy farming grew in popularity across northwestern Arkansas in the 1920s and 1930s as the apple industry slumped.[24]

Several factors influenced the expansion of dairy farming in northwestern Arkansas. Railroad agricultural departments transported dairy products and recruited farmers to supply cream, milk, and butter. Rural electricity allowed farmers to use milk coolers and occasionally even automatic milking machines. Growing towns such as Fayetteville, Springdale, and Rogers provided whole-milk markets for surrounding suppliers. This last factor delayed the development of dairy farming in other Ozark areas where towns were small and scarce. By the late 1930s, northwestern Arkansas contained numerous milk processing companies, including Armour's Cheese in Bentonville, Pet Milk in Siloam Springs, a Carnation plant in Rogers, United Dairy Products in Huntsville, and Berryville Cheese Company. In 1939 Benton County farmers marketed almost half a million dollars' worth of whole milk, cream, and butter. Washington County farmers received more than $300,000 from the sale of dairy products, an increase of over 40 percent from 1919. Nevertheless, as World War II approached, successful dairy farming continued to depend on one's proximity to urban areas and the availability of electricity and transportation to market. Interior counties such as Newton, Searcy, and Stone lacked the above prerequisites, and, consequently, their farmers realized few profits from dairy sales. In Newton County only about 10 percent of farm families sold dairy products; their $18,138 in sales in 1939 was the lowest county total in the state.[25]

Poultry raising, which would eventually become the most profitable agricultural enterprise of northwestern Arkansas, also found a receptive audience in the farmers on the Springfield Plain. Farmers in Benton and Washington Counties had made money from poultry sales as early as the 1890s, but the dominance of fruit growing relegated poultry to a peripheral activity on most farms. In 1914 a representative of Kansas's Aaron Poultry and Egg Company, a subsidiary of the Armour Company, erected a small processing and shipping shop on the Frisco in Fayetteville, promising to pay up to 50 cents for a healthy chicken. At the same time, the Arkansas Agricultural Experiment Station inaugurated its poultry division. When the Aaron plant closed in 1916, Jay Fulbright and other local business leaders built a new plant, which began shipping its products out of the region in refrigerated cars stocked with crushed ice and rock salt.[26]

The genesis of the modern poultry industry awaited the aftermath of World War I and the demise of apple raising. A decade and a half before John Tyson made his first poultry haul to Chicago, young Jeff D. Brown, the "Father of the Broiler Industry" in Arkansas, raised and marketed his first broilers. In the early 1920s Brown, who had grown up on a small farm near Springdale, used kerosene incubators and coal-burning stoves to grow broilers over the winter. He began mixing and making his own poultry feed, took correspondence courses on poultry production, and read journal articles and experiment station bulletins to improve his infant operation. In 1929, just two years after a severe freeze had devastated the beleaguered northwestern Arkansas apple industry, Brown convinced an official at Springdale's First National Bank to loan him $700 for a down payment on a 10,000-egg electric incubator. The young entrepreneur set up his hatchery in Springdale and began supplying chicks on credit to local farmers, who raised them in small wooden houses 14 by 16 feet or smaller. By 1936, Brown produced 94,000 chicks annually, and the growing demand for birds influenced him to build hatcheries in Fayetteville and Centerton. The Arkansas Agricultural Experiment Station observed Brown's success and constructed a poultry research facility on its Fayetteville farm in 1931. The following year Brown constructed his first poultry feed mill. By World War II, 6,750 poultry loans had been extended to Benton County farmers by feed companies, hatcheries, banks, and private citizens. The census of 1940 reported a combined total of more than $2.2 million in poultry and egg sales for Benton and Washington Counties, an increase of two-thirds in just two decades. Carroll and Madison Counties also ranked among the state's top five poultry-producing counties, making the northwestern Ozarks the undisputed center of the industry in Arkansas.[27]

The successful marketing of dairy and poultry products reflected an increasingly diverse agricultural economy in northwestern Arkansas and an extended community of farmers, especially in Benton and Washington Counties, firmly devoted to market agriculture. As we have seen, other Ozark subregions were less diverse and often less market-oriented. While farmers in interior counties such as Newton and Searcy tended to entrench in the interwar years and rely on semisubsistence farming combined with limited market production or income from timber labor, most farmers in the eastern and southeastern Ozarks found themselves on the eve of the Great Depression mired in the stifling cycle of cotton production, their capacity for self-sufficiency undermined by eroding fields, depleted soil, large families, and expanding cotton patches.

The wave of cotton planting that swept up from the bottomlands and over the hillsides and hollows after the Civil War had receded in the early twentieth century; in the central Ozarks, the fiber was grown only in the fertile valleys and on the relatively level plateaus, but it spread over broader areas around the region's periphery. In Searcy, Newton, Marion, and other marginal, interior counties with limited creek and river bottomlands and an abundance of steep, rocky terrain, cotton acreage leveled off or, more commonly, declined after 1900. Even in the rugged Boston Mountains and White River Hills, however, cotton frequently served as the primary source of cash for small farmers. Aaron Stevens, who was raised on Roasting Ear Creek in northern Stone County, recalled that his family depended heavily on the three to five bales of cotton they harvested each fall. "That was all we had to getting a little money, was out of the cotton."[28]

Farther east and south, however, on the Salem Plateau and beneath the rim of the Boston Mountains, farmers grew more and more dependent on cotton. By 1929 thousands of Ozark farmers relied on cotton for their primary cash income, and for some their only income; eight Ozark counties were classified as cotton counties. One Izard County farmer recalls: "Cotton was the only money income we had at all. And we'd make from four to six bales of cotton a year. And what we got out of that had to do til the next year."[29] Another remembers only one other source of cash. "Nobody had any money hardly. About as far back as I can remember they'd sell their cream. It was about all the income they had from the time they picked their cotton in the fall til the next fall."[30] Farmers in each of the region's four leading cotton-producing counties—Izard, Cleburne, Van Buren, and Sharp—planted more than 20,000 acres in cotton. Between 1899 and 1929, the combined acreage in cotton of the four counties increased 134 percent to 97,231. On the eve of depression, more than four in five farmers in these counties grew at least some cotton.[31]

The signs of cotton culture were not as visible in the hills as they were in the bottoms, but they existed nonetheless. In 1929 farmers in the previously mentioned four counties as well as Fulton County devoted more than one-third of their harvested lands to cotton. This emphasis on cotton resulted in a decline in small grain and livestock production, two areas associated with diversified or subsistence farming. In the thirty years after 1899, oat production in the four primary cotton-producing counties fell 84 percent, to 3,211 acres. By 1929 wheat cultivation was practically a lost art in those counties; farmers raised only 19 acres where more than 29,000 had grown three decades earlier. In the meantime, the number of hogs declined by two-thirds, cattle herds fell off 20 percent, and the sheep population decreased to insignificance in many areas. Tenancy was also more common in cotton-growing counties. Of the five Ozark counties with tenancy rates above 50 percent in 1929, only Searcy contained fewer than 5,000 acres of cotton land. The noncotton counties all possessed ownership rates of more than 56 percent, almost double the state average.[32]

Although extension agents had carried the gospel of diversification and progressive agriculture into the Ozark cotton counties for many years, their efforts brought about few "Live at Home" results before the New Deal. Agents who worked in the Ozark counties, especially during World War I, usually "did the work that seemed most urgent, and had no year-round plans."[33] Furthermore, according to historian Pete Daniel, many agents catered to the needs of local farm-supply businessmen and larger farmers who could afford the costs of converting row-cropped fields to pasture, a class of agriculturists in short supply in the eastern Ozarks. Despite the fact that declining cotton prices after World War I rendered agriculture in Izard, Cleburne, and similar counties less profitable, few farmers possessed the resources and scientific knowledge necessary for wholesale farm restructuring along the lines of expert programs. Even when farmers were willing to experiment and change, advice was not always available. Only two counties benefited from the service of agents every year during the 1920s, and several others lacked extension service aid over half the years between World War I and the depression.[34]

Most Ozark farmers in the 1920s probably received more encouragement from local newspapers than from extension agents. Humble celebrations of agricultural diversity could be found in almost any local publication. More often, however, the local farmer—who feared changing practices would jeopardize his family's well-being—received encouragement to continue planting familiar crops and raising livestock in hopes that people elsewhere would reduce operations in cotton and cattle farming. The following passage from a Marion County newspaper is typical: "There seems to be but one hope for farmers and stock-growers and that is, since the dawn of civilization, it has been impossible to very long keep anything below the cost of production. It is an economic law that sooner or later adjusts itself. . . . So while cattle and cotton are now below the cost of production they can't be held there always. . . . So let no one lose courage."[35]

The Ozark cotton counties never descended to the depths of monoculture witnessed on the alluvial plain of eastern Arkansas, but it was not due to lack of effort. The post–World War I decade brought an unprecedented intensification of cotton cultivation. Ozark farmers expanded their cotton patches to reap the benefits of generous wartime prices, and when prices plummeted, many found themselves trapped in the crop lien system so familiar to southern farmers from Texas to South Carolina. Writing during the depression, a historian of Sharp County lamented: "So many farmers during the fifteen years preceding 1930 turned their attention to cotton that it . . . almost spelled economic disaster to the county, due to a one crop system."[36] His statement was no exaggeration.

Between 1919 and 1929 cotton acreage in Sharp County increased 55 percent. Neighboring Izard County, the region's leading cotton producer in 1929, experienced an even greater increase. Particularly dramatic was the expansion of cotton planting in marginal, mountainous counties. Farmers in Searcy County raised their total crop from 2,581 acres to 4,327, and Stone County's cotton crop almost doubled.[37]

These predepression years of intense cotton cultivation in the eastern Ozarks represent an important period in northern Arkansas's agricultural history. Perhaps at no other time in Ozark history have the farming practices and economies of the subregions been so divergent from one another. The South's cotton culture had laid claim to almost the eastern half of the region. In geographer Charles Johnson's *Statistical Analysis of Southern Counties*, eight of the fifteen counties in this study were classified as cotton counties in 1930. While semisubsistence activities—primarily the practice of a family raising its vegetables, meat, and milk at home—were still common here, market-oriented diversity was on the wane. On the Springfield Plain, however, that diversity was still found in abundance. Since the earliest days of white settlement, the fertile prairies had boasted a superior and diversified agriculture. In 1930 Benton County, with its grain-dairy-livestock label, more closely resembled a midwestern county; Washington, Arkansas's only fruit and vegetable county, was from an agricultural standpoint equally heterogeneous and prosperous.[38] The Ozark interior, meanwhile, provided a final, temporary haven for subsistence and general farming, although the farming profiles of the five counties so labeled ran the gamut from grape-growing dairymen to sharecropping cotton growers.

In 1930, all Ozark farmers—from Imboden to Decatur and from Omaha to Scotland—stood on a precipice of change. The worst depression in American history would soon prompt a monumental program of federal intervention. This intervention would lay the foundation for rural agricultural and economic change so intense and rapid as to be almost unimaginable. For several years, however, the programs comprised just that, a foundation. The Ozarks, and the country, would ultimately rely on the unleashed forces of war to galvanize and realize the visions of governments and bureaucrats.

The Great Depression failed to catch most rural Ozarkers off guard. In fact, low crop and livestock prices had created a recessionlike atmosphere in American farm communities long before the stock market crash of 1929 foretold a fundamental sickness in the marketplace. Following the 1920s Republican free-market method of encouragement rather than enforcement, the Hoover administration created the Federal Farm Board with the passage of the Agricultural Marketing Act of 1929. The board sought to minimize speculation, prevent inefficient and wasteful methods of distribution, prevent and control surpluses, and encourage the organization of farmers into marketing cooperatives. The board's goals depended on voluntary participation, however, and the average farmer continued to ignore cutback requests. When crop demands declined, the only way the farmer knew to cope with the situation was to increase planting. Consequently, crop acreage rose in 1930 and did not decline in 1931, while farm prices plummeted.[39]

As if the market crash did not do enough damage, Ozark farmers suffered the Great Drought of 1930 and another almost as damaging the next year. The combination of economic and climatic woes made survival the greatest challenge for many families. For the thousands of marginal farm families in the Ozarks, the 1930s saw the hardships suffered throughout the 1920s intensify. For the few prosperous farmers, the depression often brought poverty and blurred the local lines of economic status that once had existed. For all Ozarkers, this trying time revealed the inefficiency of self-reliance and general farming in a countryside inextricably linked to the economic forces of the nation and the world. One newspaper encouraged the Ozark farmer to "make every effort possible to take care of himself before assistance from any source is given. The individual who sits down for this relief will doubtless have a long, hungry wait." Such brazen calls for rugged individualism tended to perpetuate the problems of overproduction and low prices, while requests for cooperation—"Those who can, from a financial standpoint, hold their cotton, should not rush the product to the market"—went unheeded.[40]

When Franklin D. Roosevelt took office in 1933, it was obvious that the agricultural sector was not recovering under the leadership of the Farm Board. After four years of depression, the board had lost $50 million on cotton alone and, together with the new cooperatives, held 3.5 million bales of the unmarketable product.[41] Roosevelt and the Congress decided to pursue a different plan of action, government intervention, with a series of acts and laws the president called the New Deal. The independent Ozark farmers who two years earlier had read with approval the question: "What right has Congress or the legislature got to tell the farmer what crops he shall not plant or how much he may plant?" now seemed quiet, forlorn, and resolved to accept the little that Roosevelt offered in these strange programs.

While the memories of depression-era Ozarkers cannot measure the

Farmstead and cornfield, Baxter County, ca. 1930s. Throughout the row-crop era in the Ozarks, corn was the most commonly raised crop. The fence around this cornfield suggests that, like many Ozarkers before World War II, this farmer lived in an open range district. Courtesy of the Keller-Butcher Photo Collection, University of Central Arkansas Archives, Conway.

revolutionary effects of the New Deal or government involvement in farming, they reflect the day-to-day challenges that occupied their minds. Most Ozarkers remember the physical hardships. "We didn't miss airy a meal, but we come blamed short. . . . And the dust was knee deep."[42] "I've went to the breakfast table when all there was was sawgrum molasses and cornbread. That's not a very good combination, but you'd eat it. That's all there was."[43] Others recall their experiences with the Civilian Conservation Corps (CCC) or the Works Progress Administration (WPA). New Deal programs made their way into every community in the Ozarks, bringing both positive and negative results and establishing a pattern for federal intervention in rural life.

Many Ozarkers, just as other Americans, found their basic ability to survive linked to federal programs. Direct relief, rehabilitation loans, and crop benefits often accounted for substantial portions of hill family incomes. In September 1934, over three-quarters of Van Buren County farmers received Federal Emergency Relief Administration (FERA) money through direct aid or drought relief. Other Ozark counties had similar numbers on relief. The FERA also operated canning centers for rural families in federal relief or rehabilitation programs.[44] Some state and federal agencies loaned money to farm families that experienced difficulties obtaining private loans. The Arkansas Rural Rehabilitation Corporation (ARRC) loaned money to needy Ozark farmers and stressed reduction of cotton acreage. Rexford Tugwell's Resettlement Administration (RA), later renamed the Farm Security Administration (FSA), lent thousands of dollars to Ozark farmers in the mid-1930s. Nevertheless, the modernizing forces of agriculture trapped the average hill farmer in an unrewarding situation, with or without federal aid; of the 155 Izard County families who received RA loans in 1936, only 7 greeted 1937 with sufficient supplies and food for the new year.[45]

Perhaps even more important to the alteration of the Ozark countryside during the depression were New Deal work programs. Employees of the WPA repaired poor mountain roads and constructed new ones. The National Youth Administration's (NYA) young work crews left the most recognizable legacies of the Roosevelt era in the Ozarks. The NYA built dozens of public buildings with their trademark flat sandstone in various shades of brown. NYA building projects produced community centers, courthouses, and school buildings, many of which remain in use. Many rural Ozark schools had no gymnasiums or vocational education buildings before the arrival of NYA crews.

Of all the New Deal work programs, the CCC effected the most long-term changes for Ozark farmers. Established in 1933, the CCC employed young men to work in military-style rural camps on projects under the direction of the Departments of Agriculture and the Interior. CCC programs generally concentrated on either soil conservation or forestry projects. Workers at Sage (Izard County), Eros (Marion), Harrison, and other camps encouraged soil conservation by terracing hillsides and helping farmers plant cover crops and trees. The Soil Conservation Service also built stock ponds using CCC labor. Typical of Ozark CCC projects were the activities at Camp Sage. Between December 1938 and September 1941, young men housed at a fifteen-acre site leased by the federal government carried out projects all over the area. They erected 48 bridges; built 47 miles of roads, a lookout tower, and a house; and raised 125 miles of telephone lines. In addition, CCC companies at Sage built 80 rods of fence and a sewage and water system for a local town. CCC camps working on Department of the Interior projects, such as the ones at Jasper (Newton), Fifty-Six (Stone), and Calico Rock (Izard), built mountain roads and parks and carried out various forestry activities.[46]

Because the Ozark region of Arkansas was still overwhelmingly rural, the New Deal's agricultural programs exercised the most immediate and long-term effects. The foundation of all New Deal farm programs was the Agricultural Adjustment Administration (AAA), established in 1933. The AAA, funded by taxes on agricultural processing companies, attempted to increase farm incomes and purchasing power through price supports and production adjustments that would raise commodity prices. The AAA program, carried out by extension workers in each county, resulted in the plowing up of 10 million acres of cotton across the South and the slaughtering of millions of head of livestock in the summer of 1933. Slightly improved prices and subsidy checks kept the most fortunate off relief roles for another year.[47]

Ozarkers began to witness the revolutionary nature of New Deal programs and the sweeping changes in store the following year when two separate agencies reacted to overproduction and drought. In an effort to further reduce corn yields and swine population, the AAA instituted a corn-hog program, which provided subsidies for farmers who reduced corn acreage and slaughtered hogs. The program proved attractive to more successful farmers with large corn crops and surplus hogs, especially in the severe drought conditions that overtook the region in 1934. In Benton County, 966 farmers received a total of $76,300; 548 farmers in Fulton County and 382 in Newton County received an average of more than $1,000 each for their participation. In the cotton counties, where corn acreage and hog ranges had given way to cotton fields in the 1920s, the program had less impact. Only 6 percent of Izard County farmers received corn-hog subsidies.[48]

The drought that helped extension agents convince farmers to slaughter hogs also threatened the lives of Ozark cattle. In late summer of 1934, FERA conducted an emergency cattle purchasing program in the Midwest and Southwest to relieve farmers and ranchers of their starving livestock. FERA bought thousands of head of Ozark cattle for $12 to $15 each. Benton County farmers received more than $87,000 in drought cattle payments for 6,634 head; other Ozark counties shipped anywhere from fewer than 1,000 to more than 6,000 cattle, earning farmers valuable income for cattle that might have died had they stayed in the parched Arkansas hollows. In addition to drought cattle purchases, FERA also contributed to the foundation of an Ozark cattle industry when, also in 1934, the agency provided financial assistance to the town of Harrison for the purpose of establishing a municipal stockyard. The Harrison stockyard, site of the first regular livestock auction in Arkansas, contained twenty-seven different pens to be used for cooperative marketing and cattle shipping.[49]

Important as these programs were to the farmers of the eastern Ozarks, even more significant was the Bankhead Cotton Control Act of 1934, which established the long-term mechanisms for market controls. Under the act, which would again be carried out by the AAA and the extension service, if two-thirds of the cotton growers in a referendum consented, a 50 percent tax would be levied on all cotton ginned in excess of a farmer's allotment. The program had a drastic effect on the eastern Ozarks' cash crop. Acreage allotments reduced the 1934 Ozark crop by almost 50 percent from pre–New Deal levels. Farmers continued to receive subsidy payments for cotton lands taken out of cultivation; in Cleburne County, farmers received more than $77,000 for the 11,187 acres lost in their 1934 allotments. In Izard County, where the extension agent and twenty-four farmer-committeemen conducted educational meetings in each community, 93 percent of the cotton crop was brought under the Bankhead contract system in 1934, resulting in a decrease of 9,275 acres. Participating farmers, who expected to receive about $65,000 in subsidy payments for imaginary crops, earned even less after their real harvests. The drought of 1934 reduced the county's production to 2,050 bales, well below the number of tax-free bales allotted.[50]

Crop and livestock prices did not dramatically improve during the 1930s; only the economic boom surrounding World War II could accomplish the goals of the New Deal. But the AAA and other New Deal programs permanently altered agriculture in the eastern Ozarks and laid the groundwork for transformation elsewhere in the region. In 1934, Baxter County's extension agent reported: "The trend of interest of the average citizen is drifting away from cotton to diversification and live stock."[51] For a generation, agricultural progressives had dreamed of making such an observation. The trend was almost wholly the result of the Bankhead allotment system, and the interest of the average citizen was born out of necessity. Throughout the remainder of the depression decade, most Ozark farmers who had planted cotton before 1933 continued to do so on smaller plots and received subsidies for the rest. Some also received assistance from the Soil Conservation Service or the CCC in converting their fallow cotton fields into pastures and hay fields. The rolling hills of the eastern Ozarks had never been fit for cotton raising, but neither had most of the South's cotton lands. It was time to halt the destruction of a tired and rocky soil that rewarded its worker's labor with only a few pennies for a pound of white fluff. This land, like the rest of the Ozarks, was overextended and exhausted, never meant to support so many families. The AAA, a political, impersonal bureaucracy, recognized this fact only

This picturesque view of a Washington County farm taken during the late depression era defies the stereotype of the Ozark "subsistence" farm and reflects the progressive and modern style of agriculture prominent on the Springfield Plain. Photograph by J. Laurence Charlton, ca. 1938–41. Courtesy of the J. Laurence Charlton Collection, group 9, number 1, Special Collections Division, University of Arkansas Libraries, Fayetteville.

because of Ozark farmers' low yields. Fortunately for the bureaucracies, and even more so for the people on the land, such explanations became superfluous when the onset of war absorbed the largest group of displaced farmers and rural laborers in American history.

On the eve of World War II, Bill Fulbright and Orval Faubus still lived in two very different Ozarks. To the north of Fulbright's Washington County lay Benton County, the region's most prosperous agricultural county. To the east of Faubus's Madison County stood Newton County, the region's most inaccessible and rugged. Even farther still, beyond the White River, cotton-growing Izard County offered yet another picture. When employees of the WPA Writers' Project observed the Ozarks in the late 1930s, they recorded the divergent economic situations of the various areas. Benton County farmers enjoyed markets for their diverse array of crops and products—five flour mills, twenty fruit and vegetable canneries, two evaporators, a large vinegar factory, five bakeries, a broom factory, six wineries, two meatpacking plants, and four dairy manufactories. Although fruit raising had declined somewhat, Rogers held on to the appellation "Center of the Arkansas Fruit Belt"; poultry and dairy farming were rapidly gaining popularity. Benton County's farm communities were among the most technologically progressive in Arkansas. By 1940 more than 20 percent of farmers had electricity, and telephone lines reached over 15 percent, both well above the state average. While tractors were rare on the county's farms—fewer than 5 percent of farmers owned one—an automobile could be found on almost half the farms. Benton County's lumber industry, although far removed from its boom days of the early twentieth century, continued to thrive, employing almost 250 workers, while another 117 residents found employment with a silica-sand mining company and two large gravel mining companies. Rogers, Bentonville, and Siloam Springs, all in Benton County, were three large towns by Ozark standards with the usual businesses and modern conveniences of southern or midwestern towns: electrical power plants, soda bottling plants, banks, stores, filling stations, theaters, and restaurants.[52]

Newton County, a favorite destination for travel writers and colorists, presented a stark contrast to progressive Benton County. The county had never possessed a thriving market agricultural system, and the absence of rail transportation only exacerbated the problem of marketing crops and produce. Consequently, farmers had few of the choices found in Benton County. Some farmers with river and creek bottomlands received small cotton allotments; in 1940 Johnson's gin at Mt. Judea served as the county's last local cotton market. In the eastern part of the county a few farmers grew tomatoes for small seasonal canneries at Bass and Western Grove. Despite poor mountain roads, many farmers found markets in Harrison for small amounts of dairy and poultry products. Only 14 of the county's 1,926 farmers owned a tractor in 1940, and fewer than 10 percent of farm families possessed an automobile. With the bulk of Newton County's forests contained within the Ozark National Forest, only about 100 people found employment in the lumber industry; most of them worked at rough lumber mills scattered throughout the backcountry or at Sutton's handle mill at Lurton. Small-scale zinc mining and an infant tourist industry, concentrated upon Diamond Cave near Jasper, provided perhaps another three dozen off-farm, seasonal jobs. The poverty of Newton County supported few small businesses and left the infrastructure weak and underfunded. A visitor in 1940 would have found only one bank, one drugstore, one hotel, one printing press, five general stores, three cafés, and two garages. Only three villages had the benefit of electricity. One-room schools continued to dominate education, and the county contained no high school.[53]

Izard County on the eve of World War II was a rural county oriented toward market agriculture but with an economic status much closer to Newton County's than to that of Benton. Enough farmers maintained their cotton allotments to keep seventeen gins in business. A roller mill in Melbourne, the county seat, ground corn and occasionally wheat, and a new cheese factory in that village promised to spark a rise in dairy farming in the area. In 1940 only 7 percent of Izard County farms used electricity, and only one-fourth as many owned telephones. Only fifteen farmers owned tractors, but almost 15 percent owned an automobile. Off the farm, the lumber industry employed almost 100 workers, and mining—silica sand at Guion and manganese near Lafferty and Croker—provided jobs for about 75 others. Mount Pleasant was the site of one of the few hospitals in the region. The Presbyterian Church USA built the small structure in 1928 and constructed a new gymnasium for the high school three years later. Although most of the county's children no longer attended one-room schools by the late 1930s, only 77 percent of school-age children were enrolled, and only 286 attended high school.[54]

The report on Izard County revealed a trend in the Ozarks toward a more regionwide homogenization of agricultural practices. Several factors accounted for this new development on the eve of World War II. Most important, the AAA's allotment program forced many farmers to find a supplement for lost cotton income or to develop an altogether new agricultural strategy. Extension agents urged expansion into dairy and poultry production and assisted farmers with the purchase of purebred dairy cattle, and the new cheese factory in Melbourne offered area farmers a market for their products. One major obstacle to commercial dairying—the lack of rural electricity—was gradually overcome after the mid-1930s. Another New Deal agency, the Rural Electrification Administration (REA), was largely responsible for this. Through its local cooperatives, including one at Salem that served many Izard County farmers, the REA brought electricity to thousands of remote Ozark families in the decades after 1933 and spurred the Arkansas Power and Light Company to extend its lines into the countryside as well. By 1940, through the efforts of the Farm Bureau Federation of Arkansas and the extension service, thousands of Ozarkers were served by electric cooperatives headquartered at Berryville, Fayetteville, Clinton, and Salem. A 1950 extension service report for Fulton County, which received its first REA line in 1940, hailed the effects of low-cost electricity as a "peaceful revolution" on the farm. Electricity proved invaluable to dairy farmers for powering milk coolers, automatic milking machines, and other appliances. In fact, in order to qualify for grade A dairy status—selling milk for the whole-milk market instead of to manufacturing plants such as the Melbourne cheese factory—a farmer had to have access to electricity. A fourth factor spurring the development of dairy and other livestock-related activities in the eastern Ozarks was the Arkansas Agricultural Experiment Station's establishment of a livestock and forestry branch near Bethesda (Independence County) in 1937. This branch station, founded in anticipation of the imminent collapse of cotton raising in north central Arkansas, provided area farmers with demonstrations and information for livestock farming on the soils of the eastern Ozarks.[55]

The growth of dairy farming was one part of a larger trend in the eastern Ozarks toward the development of an agriculture resembling that of northwestern Arkansas. A survey of ninety-three farms in the subregion, conducted by the Arkansas Agricultural Experiment Station in January 1940, reflected the changes under way after less than seven years of government controls. The farmers surveyed had decreased cotton and corn crops, increased pastures and hay crops, and expanded poultry flocks and dairy and beef cattle operations. Much of the land taken out of row-crop cultivation, one-third of which was classified by the Soil Conservation Service as severely eroded, had been sown in lespedeza and other soil-restoring grasses. On average, the ninety-three farmers realized only one-third of their income from cotton sales, considerably less than a few years earlier. More than one-fourth of the average income was generated by sales of livestock and livestock products, and another 13 percent came from AAA subsidy payments.[56]

The Ozark region of Arkansas was in the initial stage of a process that would create a greater degree of agricultural homogeneity and usher even the most remote sections of the region into the modern world of twentieth-century America. Nevertheless, the economic and cultural differences between the Ozarks of Fulbright at Fayetteville and Faubus on Greasy Creek belied two trends in characterizing the region: travel writers' increasingly popular portraits of a monolithic region of moonshiners and ridge runners, and the chambers of commerce's dogged boosterism and progressive materialism. At the very moment the nation was discovering the Ozarks, the image that would come to represent the region no longer applied in reality. Not that this mattered; the image crafted by writers and tourist hawkers was never meant to be based on fact, but on the nostalgic yet condescending desires of urban America.

In the Land of a Million Smiles

HEMMED-IN HOLLER has long been a popular attraction for Ozark travelers. Today its rugged beauty and isolation attract hikers and awe canoeists floating through on the swift upper reaches of the Buffalo River. Hemmed-in Holler was especially appealing to writers who "discovered" the Ozarks after World War I and whose preconceptions of Ozark people seemed to be satisfied by Holler dwellers. Perhaps no other community in the Arkansas Ozarks—a region that appeared staggeringly remote to most Americans—was as isolated and removed from the forces of modernization as Hemmed-in Holler. One observer described the exotic terrain in 1935: "There [were] no roads into the holler. One usually enter[ed] it, afoot, fording the river from one to a dozen times, following a mountainside trail steep enough to become discouraging to a mountain goat."[1]

Up until a couple of generations ago this Newton County hollow was home to a community of people as isolated and anachronistic as any the United States had to offer in the middle of the twentieth century. When Charles Morrow Wilson, a Fayetteville native and freelance journalist, visited the Holler in the midst of the Great Depression, he found twenty-two families living lives similar to those of their ancestors a hundred years earlier. There were no automobiles, radios, or telephones; no electricity or indoor plumbing; no doctors, teachers, or even preachers. Although the Buffalo River bottoms were fertile, the difficulty of transportation rendered the inhabitants subsistence farmers. Most raised their own tobacco, and the women continued to spin and weave wool cloth and make the families' clothes. Cash incomes—estimated at only $60 a year per family—depended upon "by-products and incidental crops" such as wool, honey, sorghum molasses, cow hides, chickens, eggs, furs, and herbs. The residents of Hemmed-in Holler, their "names outstand-ingly English," could, according to Wilson, "swap talk and break bread with farmers of Chaucer's England, and suffer few misunderstandings."[2]

Hemmed-in Holler was an anomaly on the eve of World War II, an anachronistic, quaint model of a region as it had existed half a century earlier. Yet for all its unrepresentativeness—in the Holler were no cotton tenants, apple orchards, or broiler houses—Hemmed-in Holler matched the Ozark image that developed after 1930. The Holler and other remote communities scattered across the region satisfied the demands of that image so well, in fact, that one must presume they served as the model for the popular Ozark portrait. Not surprisingly, writers and tourism pro-moters found the region and its Hemmed-in Hollers only as the quaint relics of frontier existence—the "diverting and picturesque" qualities so appealing to nostalgic urban Americans—were fading from the scene, rendered obsolete by the modernizing forces of government intervention and technology. As historian Janet Allured comments in her study of women and family life in the Ozarks: "Though many outsiders were loathe to admit it, not everyone was poor, few families kept a still at the spring house, even fewer women smoked a corn-cob pipe, and not every person was superstitious."[3] Thus, the image of the Ozarks first formed during the depression—of log cabin homesteads inhabited by broad-brimmed hat-wearing, barefooted moonshiners and wrinkled women weaving homespun—was based on nostalgia and whimsy and sup-ported briefly by a select cadre of remote twentieth-century families liv-ing almost wholly lives of the nineteenth century.

By most standards, life in the Arkansas Ozarks before World War II would have been isolated and difficult, but the isolation and harshness of existence were relative and in most areas decreased in the first four decades of the twentieth century. Isolation and accessibility, like agricul-tural practices, differed from subregion to subregion and community to community in the Ozarks. Two recent archaeological studies reveal these contrasts. Artifacts at the Moser site northwest of Lowell in Benton County dispute the backward image and "indicate that by the late nine-teenth century the people were integrated through a flow of information and goods that connected the site to the community, the region, and be-yond." On the Moser farm "what was not sold was consumed at the stead and not the reverse." The farm family owned Ball jars from Indiana and other items manufactured in nine different states as well as in England, Germany, and the Far East, all of which suggests that the Mosers "be-long[ed] to a wider information network than just their neighbors."[4]

Conversely, sites excavated in the Sullivan Creek area near Sandtown in northern Independence and southwestern Sharp Counties reveal a more isolated existence. Researchers found stoneware and pottery manufactured in the Northeast but little else—none of the decorated whiteware, stemmed glass goblets, and porcelain doll fragments of the Moser homestead—to indicate that the Sullivan Creek residents were anything but economically restricted and isolated in the early twentieth century.[5]

Contemporary accounts of predepression conditions in the most remote counties of the region reveal a high degree of isolation and inaccessibility. The extension agent who arrived in Madison County in 1925 reported that his rustic new home county possessed no telephone connection, only fifty-six miles of gravel-improved state highway, and "not more than fifty miles of county roads that could be negotiated by auto." Bridges were so rare and streams so plentiful that often in winter and spring travelers could exit and enter the county in only one direction. The agent, who maintained both a car and a horse for local travel, could visit the southern part of the county during the wet months only by driving to Fayetteville and riding the train to Pettigrew, St. Paul, and other depot villages. This lack of transportation and communication facilities hampered market agriculture and often resulted in impoverished conditions. In neighboring Newton County, the agent observed: "Home conditions are frightfully bad. Hogs fare better in the progressive agricultural sections of the country than do many of the children of Newton County."[6]

Over the following decade and a half, large-scale highway construction and the introduction of electricity, radios, and automobiles improved traveling and living conditions in most areas. School consolidation made available high school educations to a greater number of Ozarkers. Mail-order catalogs, rural free delivery, and automobile travel gradually supplanted drummers and peddlers. On the surface, however, by 1940 the rural Ozarks in many localities appeared to be little changed from a generation or more earlier. Most rural families continued to rely on the local crossroads or hamlet merchant for necessities and for petty cash from sales of eggs, chickens, and cream. Thousands of children continued to walk three or four miles to one-room schools. Horse- and mule-drawn wagons and buggies outnumbered automobiles, and telephones and electricity remained luxuries enjoyed only by town folk and farmers on the outskirts of those towns.

Nevertheless, a transformation was under way. The signs could be as blatant as a noisy Model T or as subtle as a little white AAA cotton card. The influence of modern outside forces is evident in one study of musical styles that challenges the idea of Ozark cultural stability. In his study of musical life in Stone County, H. Page Stephens found that by the late 1920s and 1930s the traditional musical style was dying out in the face of the onslaught of radio, the phonograph, and travel outside the Ozarks. Among Stephens's subjects—all pseudonymous—were Bill Jackson and Herbert Keller. Jackson, born in 1881 to a prosperous farm family in the fertile West Richwoods community south of Mountain View, became a banjo player for traditional local dances and singings. Nevertheless, Jackson's family owned a pump organ and ordered popular sheet music from Sears, Roebuck and Company. Before the arrival of radio and the phonograph in Stone County, Jackson had become familiar with national styles from visits to Mountain View stores, from contact with African American riverboat workers, and from mail-order music. Herbert Keller, seventeen years younger than Jackson, had also abandoned any unadulterated traditional mountain musical style by the late 1920s. Like many other young Ozarkers, he began listening to phonograph recordings of popular national songs in the 1920s, and in the 1930s Keller looked for inspiration to the musical styles emanating from radio broadcasts in Nashville and Chicago.[7]

By World War II, the foundation had been laid for massive transformation and depopulation in the Ozark region. War would provide the impetus for swift and momentous change. In the meantime, as the world marched toward war in the latter part of the depression, the Ozarks stood on the threshold of modernity, a threshold that a few Ozarkers had already crossed and across which thousands more would wander in the coming decades. Even Hemmed-in Holler would not avoid the influence of the modern world outside the region. Even at the time of Wilson's visit, the signs were evident; this was no untouched Arcadia. Several of the Holler's young men had left to fight in World War I—none returned—and to join the hordes of migrant Ozark workers. These folks were mostly literate, and Wilson found among them books "ranging from paper-bound dime-thrillers to collections of great poetry"; in most homes he spotted the second most treasured publication, a Sears, Roebuck catalog.[8]

Many writers would have conveniently overlooked such un-Ozarkian appurtenances as mail-order catalogs, although scarcely a family would have been without one by the 1930s. Their search was at best for the quaint and picturesque, the living anachronism, and at worst for a mythical, fantastical land of slovenly dullards divorced from the march of time or independent rustics defying modernity and materialism. This search for rejuvenation, both physical and spiritual, has a long history in the Ozarks. The most conspicuous examples were the health resorts and tourist camps that sprang up in the half-century after the Civil War. Like the romantic articles of depression-era writers, the resorts usually bore little resemblance to the region in which they were set.

While Ozark farmers scratched meager livings from the thin soil, a phenomenon completely unrelated to their agricultural existence took place in their midst. The healing mineral water craze of the late nineteenth century enriched speculators and entrepreneurs across the nation. Blessed with an abundance of such springs, the Arkansas Ozarks became home to some of the trans-Mississippi's busiest health resorts. The mineral spring boom brought thousands of outsiders into the remote hills— albeit into overnight resort towns that bore little resemblance to surrounding towns and villages—and first introduced the region to the tourist industry, a relationship that would intensify after World War II. The pioneer of the resort towns, and the most prominent, was Eureka Springs. In 1854 Alvah Jackson, a quack medicine man, hunter, and trader, discovered the head of a healing spring in Carroll County and began marketing the water in Missouri and Arkansas as "Dr. Jackson's Eye Water." A quarter-century later, when a prominent judge claimed to have had a leg sore cured by the water, the area began attracting visitors. By 4 July 1879, twenty families had settled around the spring. Incorporated in February 1880, by midyear the population of Eureka Springs had grown to almost 4,000. Three years later, the Eureka Springs Railway connected the booming town with the St. Louis, Arkansas & Texas (later incorporated into the Frisco) at Seligman, Missouri. The railroad's leadership reflected the clientele of Eureka Springs. President and chief stockholder was Richard Kerens, a St. Louis businessman and prominent Republican supporter. The man spearheading the railroad's construction was former Reconstruction Republican governor Powell Clayton, a one-armed Union veteran from Pennsylvania who had settled on a large cotton plantation in southeastern Arkansas after the war.[9]

During the heyday of the resort, thousands of visitors came from St. Louis and other midwestern cities and towns to bathe in the healing spring water. In 1886 former Republican presidential candidate James G. Blaine attended the dedication of the magnificent Crescent Hotel, the center of the town's bathing and tourist activity. (Its closing on the hotel's fiftieth anniversary in 1936 marked a low point in Eureka Springs' fortunes.) For twenty-five years beginning in 1898, the town also boasted an electric streetcar system, an unusual sight to local farmers who ventured into town. Although the mineral water craze wilted around the turn of the century, Eureka Springs—dubbed "Top of the Ozarks" and "America's Little Switzerland" for its steep, rugged terrain and peculiar Alpine architectural style—continued to attract dwindling numbers of wealthy midwesterners throughout the early twentieth century before becoming a small haven for writers and artists in the 1930s.[10]

In 1881, only two years after the public's discovery of Eureka Springs, Max Frauenthal, a Bavarian Jewish merchant with businesses in Conway, Arkansas, and in Memphis, sought to profit from a group of white sulfur springs in Cleburne County. Frauenthal bought the land containing the springs and promptly organized the Sugar Loaf Springs Company with ten other investors, mostly from Conway. Sugar Loaf Springs, as the town was known until changed to Heber Springs in 1910, became a prosperous health resort for wealthy patrons from Conway, Little Rock, and other Arkansas cities in the 1880s. Nevertheless, poor accessibility limited growth. By the time the M&NA arrived in 1908, the healing water fad had long passed.[11]

Not all Ozark resort towns relied on spring water. One of northwestern Arkansas's most popular resorts was Winslow. When the St. Louis & San Francisco Railroad reached Summit Home in 1882, entrepreneurs renamed the Boston Mountain hamlet Winslow, after the president of the railroad, and developed a thriving resort town with fine hotels and dining facilities. Like Eureka Springs, Winslow was almost completely divorced from its rugged subsistence-farming surroundings. By the mid-1880s, the Washington County town's largest investor was a Chicago businessman whose plush resort attracted wealthy visitors via railroad from as far away as Texas and Louisiana.[12]

On the other side of the region, the Kansas City, Fort Scott & Memphis Railroad spawned a similar town in Sharp County. Although the railroad connected Hardy, also named for a railroad executive, to Memphis and other cities in the 1880s, only after the turn of the century did the town become a resort destination. The primary reasons for the growth of vacationing in Hardy were the lure of the Spring River and the booster activities of a Memphis physician. Unlike Winslow, Hardy was not a mountain town, but the cool Spring River, whose headwaters flow from the Mammoth Spring some fifteen miles away, attracted sightseers and swimmers. When Dr. George Buford visited in the early twentieth century, Hardy was a modestly progressive farming community of livestock and fruit raisers. In 1908 Buford purchased land south of the river on

Wahpeton Hill, built the Wahpeton Inn and several guest cottages, and began selling riverfront lots. Buford used his Memphis connections to promote Hardy as the "Playground of the Ozarks." By 1920 Hardy was a popular vacation destination for Memphians and the site of summer camps for Boy and Girl Scouts, the YWCA, and orphans, all sponsored by Memphis groups. So many residents of Memphis had relocated to Hardy or vacationed there annually that in 1920 a group of them established St. Mary's Episcopal Church, a sign of wealth and affluence amid the humble Baptists, Methodists, Christians, and Pentecostals of the surrounding countryside.[13]

Hardy, unlike many other Arkansas resort towns, experienced a minor resurgence during the depression. When the Wahpeton Inn burned in 1932, a new owner rebuilt the inn and added a bowling alley, shuffleboard court, and dance floor. The new Guthrie Wahpeton Inn conducted a steady business before it too was destroyed by fire in 1939. The year the original Wahpeton Inn burned, a second summer resort was established in Hardy by Blytheville businessman Loyd Ward Sr. Rio Vista, a community of rental cottages, served vacationers from Memphis, Little Rock, and eastern Arkansas until the 1950s.[14]

Undoubtedly, the two most ambitious resort schemes of the early twentieth century took shape in Benton County. The two communities, Monte Ne and Bella Vista, shared common beginnings but little else. Monte Ne was established in 1900 by William Hope "Coin" Harvey, a West Virginia native and sometime Rocky Mountain land speculator who had earned a fair degree of fame as author of *Coin's Financial School* in 1894 and as an adviser to Democratic presidential nominee William Jennings Bryan in 1896. In the latter capacity, Harvey accompanied Bryan to Rogers, Arkansas, to which he returned four years later because the area reminded him of his boyhood home in West Virginia. Harvey, whose wealth was derived primarily from sales of his book, bought 320 acres in the community of Silver Springs five miles southeast of Rogers; with the financial assistance of Chicago investors and several local businessmen, he established the Monte Ne Investment Company. In short order, the 320-acre spread was divided into lots worth between $24 and $300 and streets and parks were constructed; the Hotel Monte Ne opened for business in April 1901. The following year Harvey completed a five-mile railroad spur to transport visitors from Lowell. By the end of the decade, Monte Ne included a small lake (on which a Venetian gondola transported tourists from the depot to the hotel), a golf course, a swimming pool, an auditorium, and a dance pavilion. The origination of most of Monte Ne's visitors was revealed by the names of the two most popular sections of summer cottages—Missouri Row and Oklahoma Row.[15]

Faced with declining numbers of visitors, Harvey headed up highway-building efforts and in 1913 helped establish the Ozark Trails Association (OTA), whose purpose was to signpost and promote 1,500 miles of hill country highways in Arkansas, Missouri, Oklahoma, and Kansas. Harvey's dream was that all Ozark roads would lead to Monte Ne, but the automobile dealers and chamber of commerce people who made up the OTA had other ideas. The Monte Ne Railroad ceased operation in 1914, and by 1917 Monte Ne was practically a ghost town. The aging Harvey, unfazed by the failure of his resort town, began work on a grand concrete pyramid time capsule in 1926, a project that attracted film companies from Hollywood and newspaper reporters from London, Paris, and across the United States. Never completed, the concrete remains today lie partially submerged under Beaver Lake. In the meantime, Harvey tried to recoup his fortune and his prestige by publishing a financial newspaper, *Liberty Bell*. He engineered Monte Ne's last hurrah when he gathered a convention to establish the short-lived and insignificant Liberty Party, under whose banner he received over 50,000 presidential votes in 1932.[16]

More successful than Harvey's Monte Ne was Bella Vista. The story of this north central Benton County community dates back to 1909, when a Bentonville minister, William S. Baker, and his wife Mary bought 159 acres along Sugar Creek four miles north of their town for $4,500. For six years the land sat idle amid the surrounding family farms. In 1915, with the decline of Monte Ne, the Bakers decided to turn their land into a summer resort. The following year they built a small lake by damming Sugar Creek and began selling lots of 40 by 100 feet or larger. The Bakers also made plans for the construction of tennis courts, a golf course, and a hydroelectric plant.[17]

After selling twenty-six lots, the Bakers sold all but nine acres of their planned resort to Forrest W. Linebarger, a Texas realtor and entrepreneur. Forrest Linebarger and his brother Clayton began building the Arkansas Ozarks' most successful summer resort of the 1920s. The Linebargers were not strangers to the area. In 1900 the brothers had moved with their father and mother from their native Indiana onto a farm south of Bentonville in the hope of relieving Mrs. Linebarger's tuberculosis. When she died six years later, the elder Linebarger took his three sons to Dallas, where in 1908 Clayton and Forrest formed a real estate business. Forrest found his way back to northwestern Arkansas in 1917 after successfully promoting a new town site, Tomball, north of Houston. In addition to purchasing the Bakers' land, Forrest Linebarger bought fifty-six adjoining acres from farmer Thomas McNeil. The entire plot cost him $6,100.[18]

Forrest Linebarger had to scramble to prepare Bella Vista for the 1917 summer season. He ordered construction of roads, a lodge, a dining hall, a dance pavilion, and bathrooms; arranged for the acquisition of a water system and electricity; and printed maps that he distributed to 250 members of the Arkansas Press Association at a May meeting in Bella Vista. Linebarger dispatched brochure-toting salesmen to Tulsa, Oklahoma City, Dallas, Texarkana, Little Rock, and other southwestern cities to peddle lots ranging in price from $300 to $750. Bella Vista opened in June 1917 with a thirty-room lodge; rooms rented for $2 per day or $12 per week. By the end of World War I, Bella Vista was a prosperous resort of 375 acres with a fifty-six-room lodge, a grocery store, a golf course, and dozens of personally owned cottages. Activities available included hiking, tennis, horseback riding, fishing, swimming, and automobile touring.[19]

Several factors accounted for the success of Bella Vista in the 1920s. As historian Gilbert C. Fite observes, the increasing financial mobility of a growing middle class allowed greater numbers of business and professional people to enjoy activities once reserved for the wealthy. The proliferation of automobiles permitted travelers to reach out-of-the-way places, and the postwar improvement of county roads connected Bella Vista with Bentonville. Perhaps most important, savvy marketing by the Linebargers targeted wealthy oil families in Dallas, Fort Worth, Bartlesville, Tulsa, and later El Dorado. The resort was so dominated by oil interests that residents from cities such as Dallas and Tulsa had their own cottage colonies in the "Summer Capital and Playground of the Oil Men of the Southwest."[20]

By the mid-1920s, Clayton Linebarger was practically the manager of a small town. In the summer of 1926 alone, 4,700 guests, including Sam Rayburn, Will Rogers, and Harry Truman, stayed in the resort's 600 cottages. In 1930 Clayton Linebarger opened Wonderland Cave, a nightclub in a natural cave that attracted national attention from newspapers and magazines. No amount of publicity could save declining lot sales during the depression, however, and Bella Vista's fortunes bottomed out in 1933. The resort limped through the remainder of the decade on the limited income from recreation facilities, house rentals, and food sales. By 1940, after an aborted attempt at establishing a winery on company lands, Wonderland Cave remained the only tourist draw at the resort.[21]

The Linebargers' venture was also quite unique in its relationship with local farmers. Because Bella Vista was located inside a farming community that lay several miles from the nearest substantial town, Bentonville, the Linebargers were careful to cultivate a sense of partnership with their agricultural neighbors. About thirty local farmers were allowed to sell milk, cream, butter, eggs, chickens, honey, fruit, vegetables, and meats to resort guests, and their teenage and young adult children often found employment at Bella Vista. One of these farm families was Roy Ritter's. As a young man on his father's Elm Springs farm, Ritter would take truckloads of early grapes into the resort town to peddle to Bella Vista residents.[22] Such positive interaction between tourism entrepreneurs, tourists, and native Ozarkers, according to Vance Randolph, was the exception rather than the rule. In his 1931 book, *The Ozarks: An American Survival of Primitive Society*, Randolph complained that "the realtors who are booming the Ozarks as a summer playground talk a great deal about how the tourists help the poor hillfolk by bringing money into the country, but the truth is that the hill farmer sees very little of this money." He claimed that tourists fished and hunted without permission, trampled and stole crops, and to top that off ridiculed the hill man almost to his face. "The tourist brings nothing but trouble to the real hill-billy."[23]

If Randolph's estimation of the negative effects of tourism was correct, then fortunately for the natives of the Ozarks, resort visitors and tourists were typically temporary guests. But another group of early twentieth-century arrivals envisioned the region as a permanent abode, or at least they did so when they first arrived. Spurred by the frenzy around the closing of the frontier and the turn of the century and stimulated by Theodore Roosevelt's Country Life movement and the Arts and Crafts movement, thousands of middle-class urbanites left the city to find moral rejuvenation through rural life and work in the nostalgic countryside.[24] Many of these original back-to-the-landers found their way to remote Ozark sections where unoccupied mountain lands could still be homesteaded. A popular destination was the region's most remote county, Newton, especially the rocky mountain sides that even mountaineers avoided, "keeping . . . at arm's length, always handy, there to see, there to climb, but not there to plant, any more."[25]

In the century's first decade, lawyers, ministers, bankers, artists, and other energetic homesteaders invaded the hills and hollows around Jasper. Upon arriving in the county seat, most homesteaders hired a local citizen to direct them to their mountain Shangri-la. Isaac Coonrod Wishon, an old Union army veteran, blacksmith, and farmer from Low Gap, was the busiest of these pioneer tour guides. Along with his son Milas, the colorful Wishon, for a small fee, escorted the wide-eyed immigrants to their forested and rugged farms deep in the Boston Mountains and helped them contact local carpenters who would erect one-room log cabins in a matter of days, usually at a price of $50.[26] In Donald Harington's fictional Newton County hamlet Stay More, the homesteaders first requested that their houses resemble a picturesque local barn, but when "assured that the barn was a barn," they settled for an anachronistic log cabin.[27]

While we cannot be certain that a barn satisfied the urbanites' preconceptions of Ozark shelters, it is quite likely that their rustic log homes were anachronisms in the early twentieth century. The back-to-the-landers were not in search of authenticity, were not interested in joining their new physical community, and were not concerned with taking their new neighbors at face value. Instead, for the most part, theirs was an exercise in fantasy, an interlude of nostalgia in an otherwise normal existence, with "the city dudes putting on one act and the hill people the other, each group enjoying the show." Isaac Wishon, though perhaps unaware of the urban currents directing these outsiders into his hills, came to realize how he was perceived by his guests and probably enjoyed acting the part, exaggerating his drawl or dress to coax a wink of satisfaction between two Chicagoans. The nostalgic and poorly conceived nature of this homesteading movement was evident in the attrition rate among back-to-the-landers. By World War I, almost all the original homesteaders had vanished from their Ozark domiciles, most having sold their free land to timber speculators.[28] As historian T. J. Jackson Lears has observed, "Many reduced the simple life to a vacation cottage or a rustic exurban home."[29]

Homesteaders continued to brave the Ozarks and filter into the region after World War I, though far less frequently. In one of his many articles on life in the Ozarks, Charles Morrow Wilson told the story of Tom Puddister, a former New Jersey railroad conductor who homesteaded 160 acres in Hemmed-in Holler in the early 1920s. Erstwhile Ozark chronicler Otto Ernest Rayburn purchased a small farm near the Madison County hamlet of Kingston in 1925; using this farm, which he named Kingston-in-the-Ozarks, as a base, Rayburn tried in vain to establish a communal enterprise for aspiring writers, artists, and craftspeople.[30]

The depression era brought another wave of back-to-the-landers to the Ozarks, many of them urbanites influenced by the example and books of New Yorker Ralph Borsodi.[31] Perhaps the best firsthand account of an Ozark back-to-the-land experiment was written by Charlie May Simon, who moved with her first husband Howard, a New York artist, to

Arkansas in 1931. Charlie May, who would later marry John Gould Fletcher and earn fame for her children's books, was the daughter of one of the Arkansas Ozarks' first memoirists, Wayman Hogue, but had been raised in Memphis and trained as an artist in Chicago. Her account of their sojourn on a 60-acre homestead was mostly respectful of native Ozarkers but revealed fundamental misconceptions and ironies inherent in most back-to-the-land efforts. Although they reportedly lived ten miles from the nearest post office—an amazing distance, if accurate, even in the most remote reaches of the region—Charlie May and Howard owned a comfortable home, again built by locals, that included a studio, library, kitchen, washroom, indoor plumbing, and a stone-paved courtyard. The couple purchased a cow, calf, and chickens, baked bread, made cheese, and plowed and hoed the garden; however, they also hired a local teenage girl to cook and clean in exchange for clothes and an education. Simon's neighbors were burgeoning Ozark archetypes, such as Uncle John, "who lives alone with two half-starved hound dogs in a tumbledown shack," and Oval, a young, blonde moonshiner, with his "tall, gawky" wife and infant. Ultimately, life in the country—albeit an existence more akin to a squire than an Ozark farmer—was not for Charlie May and Howard. Although she boasted, "We have never before had so much leisure," Simon warned her urban readers that the back-to-the-land movement was not the answer to depression woes, that life on the farm was too hard, and that the city offered conveniences no modern person would intentionally forfeit. Charlie May and Howard were making preparations to leave their homestead as she wrote.[32]

Charlie May Simon's back-to-the-land account was one of many Ozark stories to appear in national magazines in the 1930s. The Great Depression marks the "discovery" of the region by journalists and artists. Ozark scholar Milton D. Rafferty argues that the timing of this discovery, when Ozarkers were at their poorest state and perhaps most unlike mainstream America, explains the development of the backwoods image that persists to this day. Such an explanation fails to consider both the development of an earlier "Arkansas image" based largely on the Ozarks and the long tradition of Appalachian stereotyping that greatly influenced depression-era writers and travelers. The hillbilly image of backwoods Arkansans dates to antebellum times, especially in the "Arkansas Traveler" legend and the writings of C. F. M. Noland and Thomas Bangs Thorpe. In the late nineteenth century, former *Arkansas Gazette* editor Opie Read contributed to the legend in the pages of his humorous,

Chicago-based *Arkansas Traveller* magazine, through which he became the "voice of Arkansas" to the nation.[33]

But it was primarily the Appalachian tradition that the post–World War I writers perpetuated. As Henry Shapiro has shown, the Ozarks' motherland, Appalachia, had been discovered by writers and missionaries a full half-century before the New Deal.[34] The Ozark region toiled on, almost isolated from the eye of the novelist or reporter. The reasons are numerous. Most Americans, when they considered the region at all, thought of the Ozarks as an arrested frontier throughout much of the late nineteenth and early twentieth centuries. In fact, the Arkansas Ozarks, with the Indian Territory obstructing its view of the Rockies and the Pacific, was in many regards a frontier in the late 1800s, and in the most remote sections—Hemmed-in Holler, for instance—frontier characteristics clung to the mountaineers after 1900. Many writers, even among later Ozark chroniclers, believed the other southern mountains merely a smaller replica of Appalachia, and hence reasoned that any study or stereotype pertaining to the latter could be applied to the former. The geographical location of the Ozarks also cloaked the region in obscurity. Appalachia was much closer to New York, Washington, D.C., and other eastern cities that served as headquarters for magazines and their writers. Most of the reporters and travel writers who would eventually infiltrate the Ozarks had midwestern backgrounds or ties to some area west of Pittsburgh. Furthermore, a major focus for writers in Appalachia, especially after 1890, was the havoc wrought on rural communities by industrialization and mining, developments that, as we have seen, exercised little long-term influence on the Arkansas Ozarks.

Nevertheless, the timing of the Ozark discovery is significant. In *Appalachia on Our Mind,* Shapiro traces the evolution of the American idea of Appalachia through the half-century ending in 1920. Although the popular conceptions of the region's inhabitants varied from quaint mountain folk to criminals and social deviants, the one constant was Appalachia's status as a psychic need for Americans, a reassuring model against which to gauge American well-being and self-worth. The various literary efforts of Appalachia watchers generated movements by outsiders, from missionary activity in remote hollows to preservation of indigenous crafts and musical traditions. The discovery of Appalachia coincided with the Progressive Era to create an atmosphere of observation and action.

The Arkansas Ozark region's experience with observers, which became intense well after the end of the Progressive Era, assumed a different form. If the formation of the idea of Appalachia had been accompanied by the missionary's zeal, both religious and otherwise, the genesis of the idea of the Ozarks occurred in an atmosphere of sociological and anthropological detachment. The story of the discovery of Ozark "otherness" is one of observation without concomitant action. This phenomenon can be traced back to the Appalachian experience, but such an explanation goes only so far. As Shapiro observes, by 1915 the tide of missionary activity in Appalachia had shifted from a focus on benevolent salvation and modernization to the maintenance of mountain distinctiveness. The establishment of a conscious community within Appalachia, a kind of "folk society manqué," became the new goal.[35] By the 1920s, according to Appalachian scholar David E. Whisnant, "the solutions to problems in the mountains were judged to lie in integrating the region's politics and economy into the mainstream while preserving, if possible, its picturesque and nostalgic folkways and religion."[36]

The Arkansas Ozarks was not completely devoid of missionary efforts. Randolph proclaimed that "another thing which has prejudiced the hill people against outsiders is the fact that so many of them feel called upon to save the hillman's soul, or show him how to build a new-fangled privy, or advise his wife about the proper feeding of her children." Despite Randolph's blustery condemnation, such efforts were quite rare in the Ozarks when compared to developments in Appalachia. Between 1903 and 1932 the Episcopal Diocese of Arkansas operated the Helen Dunlap School for Mountain Girls in the Washington County resort town of Winslow, and for about half a dozen years beginning during World War I the Arkansas Synod of the Presbyterian Church in the United States (the Southern Presbyterians) maintained Mountain Crest School near Combs in the southern Boston Mountains. Southern Methodists in Arkansas also dabbled in mountain mission education between the two world wars, most notably at Valley Springs, south of Harrison. The Board of Missions of the Presbyterian Church, USA, however, sponsored the most notable missionary endeavors. The board established small hospitals in Mount Pleasant and Kingston and funded the construction of a gymnasium for the former's high school. The Kingston project of the board was perhaps the most ambitious example of missionary outreach in the region. In 1924 the Brick Presbyterian Church of Rochester, New York, sent the Reverend Elmer J. Bouher to the Madison County hamlet to survey religious and educational opportunities. When he found such opportunities lacking, he received board funding for the construction of a church house, a ten-bed hospital, and for the establishment of the community's first high school. The departure of Bouher in 1929 and the onset of the depression doomed the short-lived mission, and the board eventually withdrew financial aid.[37] The Presbyterian efforts in Kingston and Mount Pleasant are significant not as representatives of a larger movement in the region, but rather as unusual occurrences. The scarcity of such missionary activities in the Ozarks underscores a significant point of divergence between the experiences of highlanders in Appalachia and the Ozarks. The Ozark region was, and would remain, relatively free of one of the scourges of Appalachia, what Whisnant calls "systematic cultural intervention."[38]

The urge to intervene had largely passed by the 1930s. Simultaneously, observers and reporters of life in the Ozarks borrowed from earlier Appalachian models and from current political and social trends. The loss of the ability to support oneself financially during the depression brought about a reappraisal and celebration of subsistence cultures. Communities such as Hemmed-in Holler, while by American standards backward and unprogressive, seemed to defy the depression and reinvigorate one's faith in mankind and in American vitality. An acceptance of certain socialist, antimaterialistic tenets common among the young and educated of the era influenced some writers to search out and praise remnants of traditional folk societies relatively unadulterated by twentieth-century technological and economic trends. And, of course, a good deal of the "contemporary ancestors" theme from earlier Appalachian studies carried over as writers applied tested interpretations to a virgin region.

The genesis of the twentieth-century idea of the Ozarks dates back to 1907 and the publication of Harold Bell Wright's *Shepherd of the Hills*.[39] Set in southwestern Missouri, the story concerns "a careworn and spiritually burdened city pastor . . . who retreats to the wilderness . . . in an attempt to recover inner peace and heal his tormented soul." It is typical of the arcadian genre and is reminiscent of romantic Appalachian works by John Fox Jr. and other nineteenth-century writers. Wright's novel, which by 1918 had sold 2 million copies, spawned a local tourism boom in the neighborhood of its setting and "transform[ed] the region into a commercialized imitation of the novel itself."[40]

Nevertheless, it was only in the late 1920s and early 1930s that American readers began to catch regular, "non-fictional" glimpses of the region in magazines and periodicals.[41] These depression-era portraits of the Ozarks grew out of previous Appalachian studies but also tended to diverge sharply with the style of observation in vogue in the older mountains at the time. In his monumental study of Appalachia, Cratis D.

Williams found that "by the mid-thirties, as new writers turned toward the mountaineer, they tended to see less of the folk quality in him and, possibly because so many of them were mountaineers themselves, became less concerned with romantic and sentimental aspects of his history."[42] Such realistic, unromantic interpretations of the Ozarks were rarely found, however, stemming in part from the belated discovery of the region. Historian Ronald D. Eller notes the irony in the emergence of the static image of Appalachia as the dominant literary theme in the late nineteenth and early twentieth centuries, the same time that an industrial and social revolution shook the foundations of mountain social order.[43] In much the same fashion, the image that would come to represent the Ozarks was first articulated in the two decades between the world wars when revolutionary forces—though not industrial ones—undertook a fundamental restructuring of Ozark agricultural and social life.

Several different elements or themes were found in these pre–World War II books and articles. Often more than one is evident in a given work, reflecting the ferment of ideas emanating from the fresh evaluation of the Ozarks. Most of these ideas were also found at one time or another in Appalachian literature. On the extremes were the interpretations of the region as either a romantic Arcadia of contemporary ancestors or a backwater of lazy, inbred deviants. Not infrequently, both sentiments poured forth from a single writer's pen. Other writers concentrated on the extraction of folk tales, songs, and traditions; to these the contemporary status and lifestyle of their subject was often superfluous or at least of secondary importance. A few writers even followed the lead of the chambers of commerce and rotary clubs and highlighted the progressive element of the region. The most thorough of the observers recognized the era for what it was: a watershed in Ozark history, a last glimpse of an increasingly obsolete lifestyle practiced by a shrinking number of people at the dawn of the triumph of modernization and progress.

The Arkansas Ozarks' first prolific chronicler, and one who fits into the first category as a romantic, was Charles Morrow Wilson. A native of Fayetteville and a graduate of the university, Wilson spent his early career during the interwar years as a reporter and correspondent for such papers as the *Arkansas Gazette, St. Louis Post-Dispatch,* and *New York Times.*[44] Wilson first gained notoriety in 1927 when he edited and introduced Charles Finger's *Ozark Fantasia,* a collection of previously published essays by the Englishman whose Fayetteville-based magazine, *All's Well,* young Wilson served as coeditor. Both Wilson's introduction and Finger's Ozark essays (many of the book's essays had little or nothing to do with the Ozarks) staked out their romantic visions of the region. Wilson's Ozarks was "a world foreign to advertising, and sales luring, and trade slogans, and patched pavements."[45] Finger described rugged Newton County in romantic terms and found there "folk who spent winter evenings, not in sitting each one with nose buried in book, but talking and singing ballads as they made quilts, or burred wood, or sewed harness, or churned."[46]

In a series of depression-era articles on life in the Ozarks, Wilson never wavered from his romantic contemporary ancestors theme. In a 1929 *Atlantic Monthly* article—according to folklorist and Ozark scholar W. K. McNeil, the first work to establish a direct cultural link between the Ozarks and Appalachia—Wilson described the southern highlands as "a land of Elizabethan ways—a country of Spenserian speech, Shakespearean people, and of cavaliers and curtsies."[47] Among his subjects were the staples of romantic treatments of the Ozarks: foxhunting, square dancing, hand-loom weaving, superstition, folk remedies, and Elizabethan persistence in the Ozark dialect. To Wilson, the Ozark region was a land of indomitable neighborliness, of barter and simplicity, a refuge of tradition. His focus on the "frontier temperament" and the "all-American and invincible frontier" was another common romantic theme. In the end, Wilson's Ozarks was an arrested frontier, a region and people that, he thought, had not changed perceptibly in half a century and would likely maintain traditional practices and avoid modernity, the fate of all civilized peoples.[48]

The same romantic contemporary ancestors theme was evident in the work of folklorists as well. Chief among these observers was Vance Randolph. Extraordinary in his passion for the region and his prolific writing, Randolph was nonetheless typical of many Ozark chroniclers who settled among their subjects. Years after his arrival in the region an acquaintance offered her estimation of Randolph's—and most other Ozark writers'—intentions. "I think Mr. Randolph went to the Ozarks, as many writers do, to spend a few weeks then write ridiculous stories about the natives. But after living with and amongst them I believe he developed a deep and sincere love for them, their gullied farms, and for their pitiful but unfailing determination to wrest a living from the rocky soil."[49] This description may have accurately captured the preconceptions of most Ozark writers, but, as we shall see, it is probably too simplistic to encompass the man who would become the region's most famous chronicler.

Raised in a prosperous Republican, Episcopalian family in Pittsburg, an ethnically diverse and politically radical small town on the outskirts of

Hillbilly postcard, Crawford County, ca. 1930s. This early example of a hillbilly postcard was designed to capitalize on the popularity of radio and vaudeville performer Bob Burns, a native of Van Buren. Courtesy of the University of Central Arkansas Archives, Conway.

the Ozarks in the mining country of southeastern Kansas, Randolph at an early age became enamored with marginalized people. After moving in socialist and radical academic circles as a young man at Clark University in Worcester, Massachusetts (where he studied psychology under G. Stanley Hall), and in New York (where he unsuccessfully proposed to Columbia's Franz Boas an anthropology dissertation on "white mountain people"), he found his way to southwestern Missouri in 1919. His first Ozark publication, "A Word-List for the Ozarks," appeared in *Dialect Notes* in 1926, signaling the arrival of a scholar-romantic and reflecting his primary attraction to the region: the survival of obsolete traits among these contemporary ancestors. Much of Randolph's early work derives from previous Appalachian studies and stories. The works of Horace Kephart and John C. Campbell influenced his direction and work in the Ozarks.[50] In fact, in his first book on Ozark life and culture, *The Ozarks: An American Survival of Primitive Society*, he stated, "The Ozark country is, in a sense, only a small edition of the Appalachian highlands."[51]

The Ozarks was the first book-length study of the region, and its publication in New York gave it a national audience, even though the depression killed book sales for the unfortunate and often impoverished Randolph. One cannot classify Randolph as a simple romantic in the mold of Charles Morrow Wilson; he was too savvy, even too ornery, for such pigeonholing. Instead Randolph consciously chose his subjects—the "diverting and picturesque"—and candidly informed his readers that he was "not concerned with the progressive element in the Ozark towns, nor with the prosperous valley farmers, who have been more or less modernized by recent contacts with civilization."[52] Reading Wilson's accounts, one would never suspect that progressive townspeople or prosperous farmers existed in the region. Furthermore, the tone of Randolph's romanticism was more political than Wilson's, harboring in it the sentiments of a former radical put off by the materialism and hypocrisy of modern America. Where Wilson's contemporary ancestors had formed their "Ozarkadia" as much from necessity as from choice, Randolph's "hill-billies" and "ridge-runners" had scoffed in derision at progress, consciously rejecting mainstream America. "With the possible exception of some remote districts in the southern Appalachians, the 'hill-billy' section of the Ozark country is the most backward and deliberately unprogressive region in the United States."[53] Coming from the mouth of a chamber president or Ozark booster, such words would have been meant to demean or degrade. But from Randolph they represented a sly compliment, a jab in the ribs of every small-town banker and insurance salesman, at every semblance of his middle-class background. From the outset, he fearlessly defended the folkways of the most backward people in his adopted region against all detractors, whether they be chamber of commerce progressives or unrealistically romantic outsiders.

Like Wilson and countless Appalachian observers before him, Randolph covered the gamut of stereotypical mountain traits and activities: dialect, superstitions, play parties, folk songs, foxhunting, and moonshining. Unlike many other romantic treatments, however, Randolph's book also included discussions of woman's place in Ozark life, social networks, and the deleterious effects of tourism in a chapter entitled "The Coming of the 'Furriners.'" Such serious fare, inspired by Randolph's academic training, was rarely evident in later romantic, pre–World War II books on Ozark life such as Catherine S. Barker's *Yesterday Today: Life in the Ozarks*.[54]

Randolph was not the only writer to find the Ozarkers stubbornly unprogressive people. In a 1930 *Outlook* article, William R. Draper focused on this obstinance from a different viewpoint. Unlike Randolph, Draper found the Ozarker—or at least Randolph's hillbilly and ridge runner—an easy target for ridicule. "The Ozarkians, if such the tribe could be called, have lived lazy, kin marrying, morally clean, but none too God-loving lives. Feuds of love and passion have flared and died, moonshine has been made and bartered, tie timber has been stolen, some murders have been unnecessary. . . . The crop tenders are none too active in the growing season, and to them winter is a delight because they can group around the fireplace—and loaf." Like Randolph, Draper recorded the dissonance between town and country, noting that industrialization and the damming of rivers for hydroelectricity "is the cheerful vision of the townspeople who live in the hills, but not the native farmer."[55]

Other writers concentrated on this theme of transformation in the Ozarks, but without the derision evidenced by Draper. In July 1934, just one year after it featured a romantic piece by Charles Morrow Wilson, *Travel* magazine carried a much more balanced portrait of the region by distinguished Missouri artist Thomas Hart Benton. Benton's debt to the contemporary ancestors theme was reflected in the title "America's Yesterday," and he freely admitted that the region lent "itself readily to romantic interpretation." Nevertheless, once finished with his tale of a night's sojourn with a rustic Arkansas family and after covering the familiar ground of frontierism, superstition, and fundamentalism, Benton offered a valuable analysis of life in the region. He observed the differences between townspeople and rural dwellers; movies and radio, he stressed, had only moderately affected the fundamental psychology of the hill man at the time. "But the automobile has come, and with it passable roads and an influx from the modern world bringing its load of new ways, beliefs and habits." While Benton did detect a certain degree of resistance to modernity, for the most part he found modern ways, beliefs, and habits being adapted or absorbed into traditional practices. "Tradition and the old ways fight still the entrance of the modern world in this country but in a little while they will break down and the very last of our fathers' America will be gone."[56]

Benton's statement, and others like it, apparently sounded a wake-up call among the collectors of folk songs and tales, a call that many had already heeded. The literary and folk discoveries of the Ozarks during the depression fed off each other and in turn sparked another phenomenon, the folk festival. The original draw for collectors was the wealth of traditional mountain songs, tales, and superstitions, both indigenous and archaic. Ballad, or "ballet" as they were known in the Ozarks, collectors had ventured into the region around the turn of the century. Sallie Walker Stockard's 1904 book of ballads included a number collected in northern Arkansas. Simultaneously, H. M. Beldon, Carl Sandburg, and others visited the Ozarks to collect songs. As an Arkansas College student, John Quincy Wolf Jr. began collecting ballads in the vicinity of Batesville shortly after World War I. By the late 1920s, Randolph had collected enough songs and tales in the region to supply several folklore articles. Nevertheless, before 1930 the bulk of ballad collecting took place in Appalachia. The depression years brought to northern Arkansas a wave of prominent collectors including John Gould Fletcher, Laurence Powell, and John A. Lomax, as well as dozens of lesser-known collectors such as University of Arkansas professor Clement Benson and graduate student Theodore Garrison.[57]

Ballad collectors found in the region a wealth of folk songs, but they also discovered what Benton discovered: that the region was in a state of flux and that even the traditional music was beginning to be eschewed by a younger generation to whom radios and phonographs had delivered the commercial sounds of Nashville, Chicago, or New Orleans. For this reason, the best sources of Ozark ballads were the elderly. Perhaps the very best source was Emma Dusenbury, who actually lived outside the Ozarks by the time ballad hunters found her. A native of northeastern Georgia, Dusenbury was raised and lived for thirty-five years in the foothills of Baxter and Marion Counties. In these hills Dusenbury learned more than one hundred songs. An illness left her blind as a young woman, but she continued to pick cotton and take on other laborious tasks to help support her family in their rambling, hardscrabble existence. By the time Randolph found her in 1928, with the help of a teacher at local Commonwealth College near Mena, she was living in poverty with her daughter and crippled husband in the Ouachita Mountain community of Rocky in western Arkansas. When John A. Lomax visited in 1936, the blind, elderly woman sang continuously for two consecutive days, leaving the venerable Library of Congress collector with eighty-two recorded songs, among them the greatest collection of Child ballads ever recorded from one singer. Later that year, Dusenbury was the featured singer at Arkansas's centennial celebration in Little Rock. Despite her brief renown, the woman Randolph called the "greatest ballad singer I ever knew" was penniless and forgotten when she died a few years later.[58]

By the time Randolph and Lomax sat down to record Dusenbury's ballads, outside influences were beginning to push traditional songs to the side or were combining with traditional music to produce marketable hybrids. As H. Page Stephens illustrates with his study of Stone County, Ozark musical styles were in transition by the late 1920s. Commercial country music had made its debut in 1922 when Alexander Campbell

Robertson, an Ozark native raised in Texas, and Oklahoman Henry Gilliland made their first recordings for the Victor Talking Machine Company. The next year, country music's first star arose in the form of Fiddlin' John Carson. The first Ozarker to achieve success in the world of commercial country music was Sam Long of Kansas and Oklahoma, who won a fiddling contest and recording contract in Joplin, Missouri, in 1926. That same year in Arkansas, Dr. H. Harlin Smith, a surgeon for the Missouri Pacific Railroad, promoted a fiddler's contest in Calico Rock and, with the five local winners, formed the Champion Hoss-Hair Pullers. The Hoss-Hair Pullers accompanied an Izard County quartet, the Hill-Billy Quartet, on a series of Hot Springs radio broadcasts and recorded at least six songs for Victor. Four years later, Victor recorded versions of "Dry and Dusty" and "Ozark Waltz" by Searcy County's Absie and Abbie Morrison, two of the era's best-known Ozark musicians, after a company representative heard them in Little Rock. By the onset of the depression, thanks in large part to the proliferation of barn dance programs on radio stations from Fort Worth to Chicago, hillbilly music was popular in cities and the countryside around the nation. By World War II, the Arkansas Ozarks had produced its first commercial country-music recording star, Eldon Britt, who was born James Elton Baker in Zack, Searcy County.[59]

Not only did the Hoss-Hair Pullers and Hill-Billy Quartet represent the melding of mountain music and popular, contemporary American sounds, but the group's performances reflected another common practice often affiliated with the discovery of folk tradition—boosterism. Before each Hoss-Hair Pullers performance, Dr. Smith delivered a rousing oration imploring listeners to "come to the Arkansas Ozarks, where you can eat the best fruit in the world, where home-cured meat is found in the smokehouse and corn and hay in the barn; where you can juice your own cow, feed your own chickens, [and] fish in the wonderful White River."[60]

The official denizens of boosterism in the region, the Ozark Playgrounds Association (OPA), initially distanced themselves from the mountain music sound. Formed in Eureka Springs in 1919 at the behest of the Joplin, Missouri, Rotary Club, the OPA adopted the slogan "Land of a Million Smiles" and commissioned Green Forest carpenter, musician, and violin- and mandolin-maker James T. Braswell to write a song with this slogan as title. Recorded in 1925, his song was based on a contemporary, popular style, and both song and slogan appeared in innumerable booster efforts before World War II.[61]

By the mid-1930s, most Ozark boosters and promoters had changed their tune, literally. The increased national attention for the region, which was based largely on interest in folk songs and traditions, came at a time when resort profits had dried up. Consequently, Ozark businessmen and boosters were more than willing to support folk peddlers and enthusiasts in their efforts to organize folk festivals in various Ozark communities. The first Ozark festivals were inspired by Appalachian models. Bascom Lamar Lunsford initiated the festival movement in 1928 with the Mountain Dance and Folk Festival in Asheville, North Carolina. After attending the 1933 Mountain Dance and Folk Festival, Sarah Gertrude Knott, director of the St. Louis Dramatic League, decided to organize a similar event for the Ozarks. The first folk festival in the Ozarks took place in the spring of 1934 at the Basin Park Hotel in Eureka Springs, the declining resort and tourist haven that was about as representative of the Ozarks as Beale Street was of Tennessee. Directing the program were May Kennedy McCord, a Springfield, Missouri, newspaper personality known as the Queen of the Hillbillies, and Sam Leath, a Eureka Springs tour guide, Indian enthusiast, and chamber of commerce president. Subsequent weeks witnessed similar but smaller festivals in the Missouri towns of Rolla, West Plains, and Aurora. These four festivals were followed by an All-Ozark Festival in Springfield and, in the fall of 1934, by the first National Folk Festival, sponsored by Knott in St. Louis. These early festivals were light on folk material and heavy on profiteering and promotion. In Springfield, the Ozarks' largest city, many business and social leaders denounced the All-Ozark Festival for promoting an unprogressive image of the region. In other areas, chambers of commerce formed uneasy alliances with festival promoters. Vance Randolph quit the festival scene after 1934, angered by the rampant hucksterism of the folk peddlers.[62]

The festival business experienced a lull in the Ozarks after 1934 but began to gain momentum as the depression waned. In April 1941, Searcy County home demonstration clubs sponsored a folk festival on a bluff overlooking the Buffalo River some seven miles from St. Joe, a village on the M&NA. This first rural Ozark folk festival revealed the misconceptions many folk enthusiasts had concerning the southern highlands and reflected a people and region very much in the process of social and cultural transformation. Home demonstration club members had discovered three mandolins, the instrument of choice for collectors of mountain ballads, but could find no local residents who knew how to play them. The festival's activities, dictated primarily by contemporary local recreation practices and largely free of the cultural intervention of similar festivals in Eureka Springs and in Appalachia, included contests in skills both "traditional" and not so traditional: fiddling, jigging, hog calling, horseshoe pitching, archery, roping, and shooting. Four months later, the Stone County home demonstration agent organized a similar weekend musical, dance, and craft fair at an abandoned CCC camp near Blanchard Springs.[63] Had it not been for the outbreak of war, festivals and the folk movement would probably have soon achieved a high level of popularity.

But the war did touch the isolationist shores of the United States only four months after the old and young of Stone County had gathered to sing, dance, and remember. Similarly, the modernity of the country had already begun to transform the isolated sectors of this American region. No longer a quandary or an eyesore as Appalachia had been two generations earlier, the Ozarks was a quaint, nostalgic comfort, assuring people in Chicago and St. Louis that the frontier was still out there, that the past was not really past for those determined enough to reclaim it; it reminded them that their urban way of life was a superior product of American greatness, even more spectacular for having sprung forth from the Newton and Stone Counties of previous generations and centuries.

Unfortunately, for the purveyors of the arcadian image of the Ozarks and for the observers of contemporary ancestors, the war and its aftermath would not be kind to their "unspoiled" region. The war years would bring about an intensification of the processes of transformation first sparked by technological intrusion and governmental intervention in the Ozarks. By the time the smoke cleared in the Cold War era, the Ozark hawkers and observers would return to a region quickly being absorbed into regional and national patterns of life and rapidly becoming unrecognizable. But images die slowly, even in the face of damning evidence.

On the eve of World War II, one more portrayal of the Ozark region appeared. In December 1941, the last prewar Ozark book hit stores around the country in the form of Otto Ernest Rayburn's *Ozark Country*, the latest in a long line of regional works in Duell, Sloan and Pearce's American Folkways Series. Rayburn provided a good bridge figure—he was active in Ozark writing circles before and after World War II—and his book, like the Ozark region, struggled to come to grips with modernization. Like Randolph, Rayburn, who was born in Iowa in 1891, grew up in eastern Kansas. After reading Wright's *Shepherd of the Hills* as a student at Baker University in Baldwin, Kansas, Rayburn moved to the backcountry of southwestern Missouri in 1917; his stay was short, however, since service in World War I and three subsequent years of teaching in

Kansas pulled him out of the Ozarks. The young teacher and writer returned to his adopted region in late 1923 to accept a short winter-term teaching assignment at a one-room school in southern Baxter County. He remained in northern Arkansas and southern Missouri for the next decade, teaching school, penning Ozark-themed columns for the *Arkansas Gazette* and the *Tulsa Tribune*, and editing his first two magazines, *Ozark Life* and the *Arcadian*. Rayburn left the region in 1933 and did not return until after World War II. Nevertheless, while teaching at high schools in Texas and southwestern Arkansas, he continued to write about his beloved Ozarks.[64]

Ozark Country, published shortly after Rayburn accepted a position as superintendent of a small rural school district in Garland County, Arkansas, resembled Randolph's *The Ozarks* in its unfortunate timing. Six days after the book's release, the Japanese bombed Pearl Harbor, banishing more than a year of Rayburn's work to inconsequentiality, at least temporarily, and dampening book sales; despite the popularity of the well-established American Folkways Series, *Ozark Country* sold only 1,200 copies in its first thirteen months.[65] Rayburn's work also resembled Randolph's in its mixture of realism and romanticism. Although Rayburn admitted in later years that *Ozark Country* had been written in the "spirit of romanticism," Randolph praised it as one of the "very few 'hillbilly' books which do not seem ridiculous to those of us who live in the Ozarks."[66] The romanticism of Rayburn's Ozark magazines—he had already started his third, *Arcadian Life*, by 1941—was balanced considerably by editorial demands. Editor Erskine Caldwell, no stranger himself to the perils of realism and stereotype in treating southern regional groups, informed Rayburn that he had "always been dissatisfied with the manner in which the Ozarks [were] almost always treated" and warned him "to stay away from the 'cute' conception of folkways." "I would suggest that you plan your book with the idea of presenting the Ozarks, not as a tourist area, but as though you were seeing it as a historian of contemporary America."[67]

The product of Rayburn's "spirit of romanticism" and Caldwell's entreaties for a more sociological approach was a mostly balanced but sometimes contradictory evaluation of the region at the end of the depression. *Ozark Country* is a mix of history, folklore, sociology, and anthropology. The book recalled Randolph's of a decade earlier in its selection of topics as well as in its tone of regret for the passing of traditions and the fate of these contemporary ancestors. Rayburn's phrases sometimes come across as schizophrenic, but they reflect the divergence within the region, the rapid but uneven modernization and transformation of the homes of J. William Fulbright and Orval Faubus, of Fayetteville and Greasy Creek. In a chapter entitled "Anglo-Saxon Seed Bed"—the title a reflection of the contemporary ancestors theme and a long tradition of Anglocentricism among collectors of mountain folk materials—Rayburn waxed romantic: "Regardless of the contrasts and inequalities of the Ozark Country, I have found it to be a modern Arcadia where one may enjoy simple happiness, innocent pleasures, and untroubled quiet. . . . It is still possible in some sections of this romantic land to turn back the clock and listen to the hum of the spinning wheel, the creak of the loom, the groan of the water-wheel at the mill, the rhythmic poetry of the cradle in its golden sea of grain, and to enjoy the generosity that springs from every true hillman's heart."[68]

Most of Rayburn's evaluations were more balanced. He realized that the previous quarter-century had significantly altered his arcadian region. Whereas "social life of the Ozarks a quarter of a century ago had many of the primitive trappings of pioneer days," by 1941 "the tempo of fun and frolic [had] been greatly accelerated . . . by the use of the automobile, and by the invasion of modern entertainment in the form of movies and road houses." Furthermore, Rayburn concluded his book by tracing recent trends in the Ozarks, including government intervention in farming. A litany of government programs affected farmers by the late 1930s: the CCC, FSA, NYA, the Soil Conservation Service, vocational agriculture, the Farm Bureau, the Protective Credit Association, the U.S. Forest Service, and the WPA. "The Ozarkian desire for freedom still lives in the hearts of thousands of the people and I believe this feeling will continue as long as the blood stays pure Ozarkian. But the Machine Age has brought a New Order of life to the backhills and the Elizabethan remnants are in the Melting Pot. No one knows what the outcome will be."[69]

PART THREE

Endings and Traditions

WORLD WAR II was a watershed era in the Ozarks and in the United States in general. The massive gears of industry and government that had been activated by war fulfilled the economic promises of the New Deal and set in motion a quarter-century of Ozark agricultural change and outmigration, as well as an unprecedented era of national prosperity. Ozarkers left the countryside in droves, only to be replaced by retiring midwesterners in the 1960s and 1970s. In the process, the region underwent fundamental economic and social alterations.

As we have seen, the forces of modernization and transformation had been at work almost since the beginning of white settlement in the Arkansas Ozarks. Only after Pearl Harbor would rapid modernization become the dominant theme of the region. And only after World War II would the majority of Ozark families find life on the farm too precarious an endeavor to bother with any longer. The postwar decades would produce the sharpest paradoxes in the region: stereotype and reality, Ozark migrant and midwestern retiree, business tycoon and contemporary ancestor. The postwar era would produce stereotypes based on fading realities and would witness a region whose economic salvation, so it often seemed, depended in large measure on the perpetuation of images that bordered on myth.

The three chapters that follow explore the themes of modernization, adaptation, migration, tourism, and imagination in the Arkansas Ozarks after 1941. Chapter 7 traces agricultural development in the region, focusing on the demise of the family farmer and the homogenization of Ozark farming practices. Chapter 8 deals with a broad range of subjects that, taken as a whole, round out the process of rural modernization: outmigration, retirement communities, religion, education, politics, and business and industry. We find at the end of this exploration, at the end of the twentieth century, an Ozarks of significant intraregional economic and social disparity, a region that is materially much like other rural American regions. Finally, Chapter 9 relates the postwar era's most important developments in the Ozarks and the ones that perhaps best reflect the forces of late twentieth-century American modernization at work: the growth of the tourism industry and the stubborn persistence of a depression-era Ozark image.

7

Fallow Are the Hills

DOYLE AND LEOLA WEBB, like so many Ozarkers of their generation, endured a precarious existence for decades. Born in 1924 to sharecropper parents near Union, Doyle grew up in southeastern Izard County near Mount Pleasant, where his father had purchased a small hillside farm shortly after Doyle's birth. The Webbs raised cotton, corn, sorghum, hogs, chickens, and a few milk cows; their meager income came from the sale of two or three bales of cotton, three or four gallons of cream delivered to the Mount Pleasant cream station each week, and chickens and eggs sold in town or to roving peddlers. As a teenager in the late 1930s and early 1940s, Doyle took on a succession of barely remunerative jobs: sawing cordwood for lime kilns for 50 cents per day, building chairs on a National Youth Administration project for $13 a month, and working at a lime plant for 60 cents per hour. In the summer of 1944, after Doyle laid by his three rented acres of cotton, he and seventeen-year-old Leola "borrowed fifty dollars to get married on." The three acres produced just over two bales of cotton, which brought enough to pay the rent and reimburse the $50, but did not leave much for the rest of the year.[1]

Doyle would not have to bother with making a crop the following spring. He was drafted into the army, but the war ended while he was in basic training. When he returned to Mount Pleasant in late 1945, Doyle and Leola purchased their first small farm, which they soon sold to his father. During the next dozen years the couple had three sons and "moved from here to yonder," sharecropping cotton lands and trekking annually to Washington State with friends and neighbors headed for the orchards. In 1958 they bought a 200-acre farm from Doyle's uncle for $1,800 and began milking cows for the grade C markets at Salem and Batesville, in addition to raising 10 or 12 acres of cotton and corn. In the early 1960s, after the Webbs stopped their seasonal trips to Washington and gave up dairying, Doyle found work at a poultry processing plant twenty miles away in Batesville. His sons were old enough to raise a cotton crop using a secondhand, two-row, Allis-Chalmers tractor that Doyle had just purchased, the family's first tractor and a machine that "we didn't know one thing about." The Webbs planted and harvested their last cotton crop in 1968 (the same year that they built their first broiler house), converted all their row-cropped fields to pasture, and bought eighteen Black Angus heifers from a local stock raiser. When he discovered the broilers and beef cattle required full-time attention, Doyle quit work at the processing plant and built a second broiler house.[2]

Something resembling the odyssey of the Webb family was repeated by thousands of Ozark farm families after World War II. Theirs was the story of a quarter-century of change and adaptation, of migration and struggle. The technological and governmental forces that had comprised the foundation of long-term agricultural transformation before 1941 were intensified by the war and its aftermath. The Webbs' experience involved most of the major postwar agricultural trends in the region: the movement away from row cropping and toward dairy and beef cattle farming or poultry raising. Changes on the Webb farm also reflected the homogenization of Ozark farming. Increasingly after World War II, farming in the eastern Ozarks, the former domain of King Cotton, came to resemble agriculture in northwestern Arkansas. Finally, most Ozark farmers, as Doyle Webb did for a time, were forced to seek off-farm employment or simply chose to do so for a more secure living, although part-time farming frequently provided a financial supplement and a conscious link with an agrarian past.

Another postwar trend—one that the Webbs ultimately avoided—was the massive abandonment of farms. World War II opened the gates on an impoverished region, and thousands of Ozarkers fled to military service or to industrial jobs created by the need for matériel. Outside of Arkansas, booming war industries created jobs for thousands of men and women. As a result, many Ozark residents headed for defense plants in Kansas, Missouri, Michigan, Illinois, Indiana, and on the West Coast. Because older couples were generally more financially established, often found it difficult and costly to move, and were less likely to participate in the war, they tended to stay in the Ozarks while young adults fled the hill country in droves. As a consequence, the Ozark region lost a large percentage of its World War II–generation residents. Perhaps most Ozarkers of Doyle and Leola Webb's generation never returned or returned only for a time before permanently leaving the hill country for more comfortable lives up north or out west. And as more and more families left the region, holdings became larger and efficiently consolidated. Land values escalated. In the quarter-century after 1940, the number of Ozark farms declined by more than 50 percent. This era marked the largest out-migration in Ozark history. Especially affected were the old cotton counties of the east, where strict allotments and mechanical developments left Ozark cotton raisers on the periphery of a shrinking zone of cotton cultivation.[3]

Row crops were the chief casualties of postwar agricultural change in the Ozarks. Corn, which had long dominated hillsides and creek bottoms across the region, became increasingly superfluous as tractors and other machines gradually replaced animal muscle. Between 1939 and 1963, the number of Ozark acres devoted to corn decreased by 90 percent. By the latter year, fewer than one in five of the region's farmers harvested a corn crop. Likewise, sorghum and small-grain crops such as wheat and oats had become insignificant long before the 1960s.[4]

Whereas the declining popularity of corn and grain crops generally reflected the disappearance of work stock, the demise of cotton raising involved other factors, both technological and governmental. Since the late nineteenth century, cotton had been the only row crop grown in the Ozarks solely for market. New Deal allotment programs had severely curtailed cotton raising in the eastern Ozarks; nevertheless, in 1939, 7,761 Ozark farmers—or more than one-third of agriculturists outside the four-county northwestern section—produced an average of 3.25 bales of cotton each. Constricting allotments, outmigration, and the "Food for Victory" campaign took a serious toll on the Ozarks' cotton region during the war years. In the five years after 1939, cotton acreage in the fifteen-county region fell from 58,365 to 37,006. Fewer than 4,500 Ozark farmers grew cotton in 1944, although average production grew to 4 bales per farm. The movement away from cotton cultivation was so pronounced that by the early war years cotton had fallen to third place among Baxter County's agricultural products, and in 1942 Stone County farmers used only 65 percent of their allotted cotton acreage.[5]

In the postwar years, a combination of technological and governmental forces doomed Ozark cotton raisers. Technological forces in the form of mechanical cotton pickers, tractors, implements, and improved strains of cotton seed directly and indirectly affected the region's farmers. Hill farms of 5 and 10 acres could not compete with the completely mechanized rich cotton lands of eastern Arkansas; the money gained from 3 to

5 bales was not nearly enough to afford expensive cotton pickers. A tractor-mounted picker made by International Harvester cost almost $6,000 in 1948, and a small Farmall tractor cost another $1,600, a far cry from affordability for the average Ozark farmer.[6] As historian Jack Temple Kirby writes, "Southern farmers in particular had but one question before them: would they accept expensive but labor-saving agricultural science, governmental regulation, and subsidies, or would they perish?"[7] For the majority of Ozark farmers, this was a question that had only one answer; perishing was not a choice, but a sentence.

The machine age was slow in coming to the Ozarks. Even the most basic of agricultural machines and "the key to mechanized farming," the tractor, remained a scarce commodity in the region for many years after World War II.[8] Despite a threefold increase in tractors on Ozark farms during the war years, in 1945, 95 percent of Ozark farmers continued to rely exclusively on animal power, compared to less than 75 percent nationally. It was not until the mid-1960s, when cotton planting had almost stopped, that at least half of all Ozark farmers owned a tractor.[9] An observation by historian Gilbert C. Fite adequately explains the delayed adoption of mechanical power: "Tractors and related machinery cannot perform efficiently on a few acres and are thus not practical for the production of small quantities."[10] Consequently, the results of postwar mechanization were generally negative ones for the bulk of the Ozarks' agricultural population. As late as 1957, the extension agent for Izard County observed that cotton "growers are still making a profit but are being left behind during this time due to inability to mechanize to compete with other areas."[11] Thus, according to Fite, "the ultimate effect was to eliminate most of the small growers who could not, for a number of reasons, become large and efficient enough to produce a decent living."[12]

Even if mechanization had not occurred after World War II, government influence and intervention probably would have brought an end to Ozark cotton raising. The two decades after World War II proved a hectic era for farmers in the old cotton-growing communities. Faced with shrinking allotments, new alternatives to cotton raising (especially dairy and poultry farming), and pleas from extension agents to replace row crops with pastures, most Ozark farmers dropped out of the cotton market before 1960. Just two years after encouraging his constituents to plant their best lands in cotton in 1950, an Ozark extension agent declared in his annual report: "Cotton is no longer king in Izard County." In neighboring Sharp County, cotton acreage decreased by 65 percent in the three years after 1949. Another agent noted: "The yield of cotton per acre in

TABLE 7.1 Row Crop Acreage in the Ozarks, 1929, 1949, 1969

County	1929		1949		1969	
	Corn	Cotton	Corn	Cotton	Corn	Cotton
Baxter	12,961	6,900	3,544	441	102	0
Benton	41,954	0	15,387	0	1,128	0
Boone	18,274	1,521	5,073	144	240	0
Carroll	23,028	0	5,989	0	265	0
Cleburne	18,132	25,411	14,673	13,827	792	219
Fulton	17,869	12,719	6,153	3,767	164	110
Izard	24,357	25,637	11,781	10,434	367	28
Madison	24,025	0	9,617	0	318	0
Marion	15,820	6,686	4,060	200	191	0
Newton	16,871	1,928	7,010	295	109	0
Searcy	19,474	4,327	7,764	1,154	342	20
Sharp	18,801	21,382	9,593	10,192	205	243
Stone	13,547	7,139	7,193	1,287	359	0
Van Buren	25,383	24,801	12,197	7,602	837	16
Washington	40,658	43	14,615	11	373	6

Source: U.S. Department of Commerce, *Census of Agriculture, 1935,* 685–91; *Census of Agriculture, 1954,* 140–45; *Census of Agriculture, 1974,* 19–437.

Cleburne County together with insect control and the smallness of the fields makes cotton an economic liability rather than an asset on the majority of farms in the county." In 1957 the Soil Bank cut Izard County's already diminished allotment by 54 percent, and other counties received similar cutbacks. One Izard County farmer recalled that by the time he raised his last cotton crop in 1961, his allotment had been reduced to three acres. "They cut it down so many acres by the time you paid expenses you didn't have anything left." The following year Cleburne County's agent urged unwilling planters to release their cotton allotments to the Soil Conservation Service for use by other farmers, "in order that the cotton history of the county may be preserved."[13]

Sentimental calls for the maintenance of tradition in the face of imminent crop collapse could not stop the ultimate death of cotton growing. Most alternatives to cotton raising and other kinds of row cropping involved livestock or poultry. For several years during and after World War II, however, some Ozark farmers kept their plows and work stock busy producing for the truck-crop market. Farmers in northwestern

Arkansas had long produced a variety of fruits and vegetables for market, but before the World War II era, such crops failed to catch on elsewhere in the region. The "Food for Victory" campaign conducted by the extension service and the cotton allotment system helped spread truck farming into the western sections of Ozark cotton country in the 1940s. During the first year of war, commercial tomato acreage in Newton County increased from 60 acres to 800; in 1942 seven Newton County canneries produced 35,000 cases of canned tomatoes. In Marion County, where tomato canning had existed on a small scale since the arrival of railroad service, a Flippin cotton gin owner whose livelihood was threatened by severe allotment cutbacks built a tomato cannery in the late 1930s. During the war years, Marion County became a leading tomato producer. In 1942, farmers there devoted almost 1,200 acres to tomatoes, and the county's four canneries shipped 78 carloads of canned tomatoes.[14]

Similarly, strawberry production increased in the central Ozarks during the war. In 1937 the Searcy County extension agent and 26 local farmers organized the Flintrock Strawberry Growers Association based on similar organizations in Benton and Washington Counties. The farmers, who planted their strawberry vines on mountaintops and steep slopes, paid a $1 annual fee to the association and turned over 3 percent of gross sales. The following spring the association marketed 5,000 24-quart crates for $9,500 in its first sale held inside a Marshall cannery. By 1942, the association had branched into neighboring counties and claimed 128 member farmers who produced $50,000 worth of strawberries. Even after tomatoes and other truck crops disappeared from the region after World War II, strawberry growing continued for more than a decade. In 1956, 456 members of the Flintrock association auctioned off almost $1 million worth of strawberries to buyers who shipped the crates around the country and into Canada. In the 1960s, the focus of Arkansas strawberry production shifted back to its original center in White County, and commercial strawberry growing followed tomato farming into memory.[15]

In the midst of the movement away from cotton raising in the postwar era, most Ozark farmers and extension agents gave up on the possibility of finding a savior crop, as many had thought tomatoes to be during the war, and instead looked for small, contracted acreages of fruits and vegetables. After World War II, the Atkins Pickle Company provided a valuable market for cucumber farmers in the southern Ozarks, and in the mid-1950s, various other pickle companies began contracting with eastern Ozark farmers through extension agents and local produce buyers. In 1955, for example, farmers in Izard County marketed 130 acres of cucumbers to the Brown-Miller Pickle Company of Texarkana and the Brine-stock Pickling Company of Birch Tree, Missouri. By the early 1960s, most counties had developed a small yet diverse array of supplemental contract and noncontract crops. In 1962 the Searcy County extension agent, in conjunction with the Stillwell Processing Plant, oversaw the planting, harvesting, and marketing of small but profitable acreages of strawberries, tomatoes, cucumbers, Irish potatoes, green beans, and turnips. The following year almost 100 farmers in Izard County contracted with a local buyer to produce 150 acres of cucumbers for the Atkins Pickle Company, several dozen acres of peas for the Monarch Company, and 15 acres of grapes. In the meantime, independent growers near Cave City and Evening Shade in Sharp County developed a substantial watermelon industry. By the early 1960s, that county's annual melon crop exceeded 1,000 acres.[16]

With the exception of watermelons in Sharp County, fruits and vegetables proved to be only temporary, supplemental crops that relieved some farmers' financial uncertainties in an era of agricultural transformation. A more popular alternative was dairy farming. Ozark farmers had always maintained milk cows for family use, but before World War I, isolation, poor transportation, and the paucity of urban markets prevented the development of a substantial dairy industry. Farmers near Fayetteville, Springdale, Harrison, and other large towns could often take advantage of a small, local market for whole milk, and after the construction of rail lines, farmers who lived near the M&NA or the Missouri Pacific frequently shipped 5-gallon cans of cream to creameries in southern Missouri. Highway construction in the 1920s allowed dairy manufacturing plants to establish cream stations in rural areas far from railroad tracks, presenting small farmers with a valuable opportunity for cash income. Nevertheless, the fluid milk market remained confined to the environs of large towns.

This market, more lucrative than cream sales, began to grow in the latter years of the depression and blossomed during the war. By the end of World War II, dairy farming was the chief source of income for hundreds of Ozark farmers. Several factors accounted for the timing. New Deal agricultural programs stressed the conversion of row crops to pastures and hay fields, and extension agents helped secure thoroughbred dairy cattle for interested farmers. The Rural Electrification Administration (REA) began supplying electricity to greater numbers of farmers and in turn spurred the Arkansas Power and Light Company (AP&L) to extend its services into the countryside. By 1940 there were REA cooperatives or

REA-financed AP&L lines in several Ozark counties, providing electricity for coolers, lights, and automatic milking machines. The war not only brought about an increased emphasis on food production, but it also generated price increases. The average price paid to farmers for fluid milk increased each year between 1939 and 1948 from $1.65 per hundredweight to $5.22.[17] When these factors led to the establishment of milk plants across the region, thousands of farmers rushed to enter the market.

Between 1940 and 1945, whole-milk sales in the fifteen-county region experienced a 210 percent increase to more than $5 million, and in most counties the number of farmers selling whole milk increased at least twofold. In 1949, there were eight fluid grade, or grade A, dairy plants—those that sold milk directly to the public—and ten manufacturing, or grade C, plants—mostly cheese manufacturers—in the Arkansas Ozarks, as well as several other plants in southern Missouri and in peripheral towns such as Pocahontas, Conway, and Clarksville. Five years later 8,867 farmers, or one-third of the region's agriculturists, marketed almost $8.75 million worth of whole milk. As with most other agricultural trends in the Ozarks, the growth of dairying was not uniform. In 1945, farmers in Benton and Washington Counties, the prairie counties that had long dominated Ozark production, marketed over half the region's whole milk. Of the twenty dairy plants operating in the region in 1949, one-half were located in the four-county northwestern quadrant of Arkansas. In Benton County, the state's leading dairy county, more than 1,000 farmers derived their principal income from dairy sales, and almost all farmers marketed some form of dairy product. The county's dairy industry was so advanced by the postwar era that the extension agent there was assisted by a full-time dairy specialist. Conversely, the dairy explosion had less impact on farmers in areas only partially served by milk routes such as Stone and Cleburne Counties, the only two in the region whose 1954 whole-milk sales failed to generate at least $100,000.[18]

In most areas, dairy farming evolved gradually as farmers abandoned row cropping and adopted new technology; rarely did dairy production account for a farmer's sole income. The story of Floyd Burleson is indicative of the development of Ozark dairy farming after the depression. In the 1940s, Burleson and his wife Irene began milking cows on his father's Marion County farm. Like most Ozark dairy farmers, they owned a hand-operated cream separator. Dairy farming in these pre-electricity days was difficult, especially since it was accomplished alongside row cropping and other facets of livestock raising. Burleson recalls: "We started about 5:00 in the morning with our milking, then we went to the field and worked all day and at the end of the day we milked again. By the time we turned the separator and fed the stock we seldom ever got to bed before 9:00 at night." The Burlesons mixed the skimmed milk with shorts (a by-product of milling wheat) and corn to make pig feed and sold the cream to the Carthage Cream Company in Carthage, Missouri. By World War II, nearby Harrison already possessed two milk plants, a grade A whole-milk company, and a cheese plant. After World War II, a cheese plant was established at Yellville, the Marion County seat just a few miles from the Burlesons' farm. But because the Burlesons lived on a rather inaccessible road, they continued to market only cream until 1950, when they were placed on a route of the Farmers' Cooperative cheese plant in Yellville. When the cooperative plant went bankrupt two years later, the Burlesons began selling their grade C milk to the Carnation Milk plant in Harrison, manufacturers of powdered and evaporated milk.[19]

The Burlesons milked their cows by hand—Floyd and Irene each milked eight—until they purchased a Surcingle milking machine in 1956. This automatic milking system funneled the milk into a tank strapped to the cow; when full the tank was strained into a 5-gallon can or a cooling tank. The Burlesons were able to use the Surcingle machine while continuing to milk in the shed on the side of their all-purpose barn. In 1959 they constructed a new walk-in parlor barn and purchased an electric cooler. Seven years later Floyd and Irene Burleson completely modernized their operation, installing a pipeline milker. The new system featured stainless steel lines and cooler; the milk, ultimately pumped from a holding tank into a milk truck, never touched human hands. As a result of this upgrade, the Burlesons cut their milking time in half and improved their receipts. The quicker machines allowed Floyd Burleson to increase his herd from twenty-three to forty head. And, like most dairy farmers of the era, he replaced his Jerseys, whose rich milk produced more cream, with Holsteins, the now-dominant dairy breed whose higher milk production was also lower in butter-fat content. The Burlesons sold their herd and dairy equipment in 1976, just two years after their neighbors, the Wades, had closed their grade A dairy. By the 1980s, a declining northern Arkansas dairy market and the retirement of aging farmers left the Burlesons' Cedar Grove community bereft of dairy farms.[20]

Not all farmers kept up with the changing dairy technology. On his small farm north of Leslie, Benson Fox milked a half-dozen or so cattle by hand until he sold out in 1962. His small herd made it impractical to adopt labor-saving machinery. But most farmers who grew to depend on dairy income adopted some sort of automatic milking system. Some of the earliest simply pumped milk into a pail, which the farmer then poured into a larger can or tank. More advanced portable systems included the Surcingle and the Chore Boy or De Laval "cow-to-can" milker. By the early 1960s, the latter, which pumped milk through a strainer and directly into a 40-quart can, was especially popular.[21]

In general, the dairy farming boom spread gradually eastward from northwestern Arkansas after 1940. By the time it reached the eastern Ozarks, dairy farming was a welcome supplement, and for many an alternative, to cotton raising. In the cotton sections, dairy farming became a key element in a dynamic period of transformation and adjustment. The development of this agricultural industry, which for a time dominated the attention of farmers and extension agents in Fulton, Izard, and other cotton counties, involved the actions of individual farmers, business leaders, and government representatives. An examination of the experiences of farmers and markets in Izard and Fulton Counties reveals the inner workings and nuances of the post–World War II dairy industry in the Ozarks.

On the eve of World War II, both counties were completely rural according to census bureau standards, and their seats of government, Melbourne and Salem, were among the smallest county seats in the state. Only 6 percent of the counties' farms had access to electricity. In 1939, the North Arkansas Electric Cooperative was established at Salem and began constructing rural electric distribution lines in Fulton and neighboring counties. The number of farms with electricity in Fulton and Izard Counties increased by 150 percent during the war years, and by 1950 more than three in five of the counties' farmsteads enjoyed electricity. In his 1942 annual report, the Izard County extension agent noted that 255 of his constituents were already using electrical refrigeration instead of the traditional method of submerging buckets and jars in spring water for cooling milk, cream, and butter; by 1950, 25 farmers had also purchased electric-powered milking machines. In the mid-1920s, the construction of the Mammoth Spring–Batesville Highway (modern-day Arkansas Routes 9 and 69) connected Salem and Melbourne to Mammoth Spring and the Frisco Railroad on the north, and Batesville on the south. This highway and other improved state and county roads led to the development of a wide network of cream stations over the following decade and a half. By 1942, Izard County contained thirty-three cream stations operated by dairy companies in Batesville and other regional market centers. The 1940s also marked the beginning of a whole-milk market in the area. In 1940, Rex McCuistian built a cheese plant in Batesville. By the late

1940s, others had sprung up at Yellville and at Thayer and Gainesville in Missouri. In 1950, Fulton County farmers had access to four cheese plants and one grade A milk plant.[22]

In 1941 Vernon Wells became one of the first farmers in Izard County to market whole milk. After getting married in 1937, Wells had left his parents' farm near Franklin and moved onto a tenant farm. Although the Wellses were still tenants in 1941, they owned six dairy cows; this new market opened up for them when a local man started driving a milk route for a manufacturing plant in southern Missouri. Two years later, the Wellses bought a 240-acre farm between Franklin and Violet Hill, where they continued to milk cows while growing cotton, corn, oats, and hay, a typical selection of crops for the area. The absence of electricity in their community required the Wellses to milk their cows by hand until 1957 and relegated them to grade C status.[23]

In the decade after the war, most of the Wellses' neighbors joined them in the whole-milk market. Extension agents and even local high school vocational agriculture teachers helped arrange purchases of thorough-bred Jersey, Guernsey, and Holstein cattle, and extension agents conducted field days at successful dairies. County agents also devoted a good part of their time to the procurement of grade A routes for their con-stituents. One of the area's first grade A producers was Kennard Billings-ley of Myron. Billingsley's father had been among the region's first farm-ers to purchase Jersey cattle in the 1920s and had for years sold cream to supplement the family's cotton-based income. Kennard Billingsley, like Wells, first entered the grade C market in the early 1940s while operating his elderly parents' farm. He eventually obtained a job driving a milk truck for a cheese plant run by Cudahay Packing Company in Kosh-konong, Missouri, that maintained a route in his area. A few years after the war, with growing urban centers creating a rising demand for bottled milk, a representative of the Patton Milk Company, a grade A dairy at Paragould in northeastern Arkansas, ventured as far west as Izard County looking for suppliers. Billingsley had recently constructed a small dairy barn with a concrete floor, a requirement for a grade A dairy. Further-more, his farm had received electricity in 1948, another prerequisite, which allowed him to utilize an electric milking machine. Billingsley pur-chased an electric cooler, made slight repairs and adjustments to his barn, and kept his barn "cleaner than a pen" to earn a substantially larger check from his new grade A dairy.[24]

Discouraged by droughts and declining prices, Billingsley left the farm in 1954 and moved to Tulsa, Oklahoma, where he would spend the next dozen years as the assistant manager of a grocery store. He left the Ozarks just as dairy farming was becoming the leading activity among his neighbors. In 1954, 245 Izard County farms, or almost 1 in 5, were classified as dairy operations. The following year, the American Cheese Company established a receiving station for grade C milk in Salem, which increased the number of grade C routes in the two-county area to four.[25] The year 1955 also signaled the entry of the North Arkansas Electric Cooperative (NAEC) into the arena of local dairy promotion. The actions and programs of the NAEC would prove invaluable to the dairy industry of north central Arkansas and to the survival of hundreds of farm families.

The NAEC introduced two programs to promote dairy farming in 1955. First, it inaugurated a loan program of up to $3,000 for farmers converting from grade C to grade A dairy production. Farmers could use the money for the purchase of equipment or the construction of a barn and repay the loans by turning over to the cooperative the amount of the increased payments as a result of their upgrade. The second program involved the cooperation of the NAEC and local county extension agents. In November, the NAEC and extension service started an artificial insemination program for farmers in the electric cooperative's region. The NAEC originally purchased semen from the University of Arkansas and funded the actual insemination of clients' dairy cows. In 1957, the NAEC gave up full direction of the program but continued to purchase semen; farmers paid for the service calls, most of which were supplied by an NAEC employee during his off-hours. The withdrawal of the NAEC from direct contact with the insemination program led to the establishment of artificial breeders' associations in Baxter and Fulton Counties.[26]

The late 1950s and early 1960s were the most dynamic years of dairy growth in Izard and Fulton Counties. In 1957, the extension service arranged purchases of over 500 head of dairy cattle by Fulton County farmers. In Izard County, extension agent Jack Justus arranged a cooperative purchase of 238 Holstein and Guernsey heifers from dairymen in Waukesha County, Wisconsin. The heifers, which were sold for $40 a head, were delivered to the farms of thirty-six different farmers in early 1956. Some farmers even purchased cattle directly from or through their manufacturing plants. In June 1956, the Salem chamber of commerce and extension agents for Fulton, Izard, Baxter, and Sharp Counties sponsored the first North Arkansas Dairy Festival in Salem. The life and popularity of this annual event mirrored the health of dairy farming in the area. Subsequent Dairy Days in the late 1950s were used to drum up financial and moral support for the construction of a cooperative dairy manufacturing plant in Salem, 20th Century Foods, which provided a new local market for small grade C dairymen.[27]

An increasing number of farmers were also entering the grade A market by that time. Between 1955 and 1957, the number of grade A dairies in the two counties grew from seven to thirty-six. The area's grade A dairymen formed the North Arkansas Milk Producers Association; shortly afterward, many of these producers signed with the Central Arkansas Milk Producers Association in Conway. The association, which supplied whole milk to the Little Rock market and other central Arkansas towns, paid better prices for milk than smaller grade A dairy companies in southern Missouri and northern Arkansas, according to one extension agent. By 1959, annual sales of dairy products had exceeded $1 million in the Fulton-Izard area.[28]

Many farmers who entered the grade A market in the late 1950s and 1960s did so with the financial assistance of the NAEC. Almost all of them constructed their new barns according to a standard blueprint. The three-stanchion, electric-powered parlor barn, made of concrete blocks or tiles and generally painted white or blue, became a common site throughout Izard and Fulton Counties and the entire region. Guy and Zela Rhoads of Fulton County built such a barn in 1959. The Rhoadses had progressed from hand-milking a few Jersey cows for the local cream market in the immediate post–World War II years to operating a grade C dairy with a portable electric-powered milking machine in the mid-1950s. When a central Arkansas dairy organized a grade A route in their area, the potential price increase enticed the Rhoadses to construct a certified, concrete barn in 1959. Shortly thereafter, at the behest of their contracting dairy, they installed a bulk tank system. By the time the Rhoadses abandoned their dairy in 1977 for beef cattle, Zela had established a substantial list of local customers (most of them elderly neighbors who no longer kept a milk cow but preferred fresh, unpasteurized milk) who helped themselves to fresh milk from the bulk tank for a small price.[29]

Nevertheless, as recently as the mid-1960s, the majority of dairy farmers, usually due to the financial inability to expand, continued to market less lucrative grade C milk. Most did so without the benefit of specially designed dairy barns. They generally milked their cows, often by hand, in multipurpose loft barns that became popular after World War II. These barns were usually designed for general diversified farming purposes, with a large loft for storing loose hay; one or more cribs for storing corn, fodder, or small grains; stalls for work stock; perhaps a side shed for handling beef cattle or hogs; and an enclosed, ground-level section with stanchions for milking cows by hand or with portable electric milkers. Even grade C barns benefited from improvements. By the early 1960s, a farmer milking on a concrete surface and storing his milk in an electric cooler could receive as much as 10 percent more money than one without these modern conveniences.[30]

Such small grade C operations resembled the dairy farming techniques of most farmers in the region, including the Webbs and Hugh Tanner. Doyle and Leola Webb first entered the fluid milk market after purchasing their farm in 1958. For five years they sold grade C milk to cheese plants in Batesville and Salem until the latter plant closed temporarily and the local market for manufacturing grade milk began to tighten in the early 1960s. Similarly Hugh Tanner, another Izard County farmer, began milking Jerseys and Holsteins on his Wiseman farm in the 1950s to supplement a declining cotton income. Unlike Webb, who found work at a Batesville poultry processing plant, Tanner lived too far away from Batesville, Mountain Home, or any other regional center to find off-farm work; like many agriculturists in the NAEC region, he held on to his twenty-cow grade C dairy long after his county agent declared that the lower grade of milk was not profitable. Tanner supported his family through the 1960s with his small dairy and by running a custom hay baling service in the summertime with a neighbor. By the time he replaced his dairy cows with beef cattle in the early 1970s (after finding work as a carpenter-painter at a local retirement community), Hugh Tanner was among the last of the grade C dairymen.[31]

Despite the pessimism of Izard County's extension agent in 1962, his office and other organizations and institutions continued to promote dairying in the area during the 1960s. A market for manufacturing grade milk still existed, and most of the farmers who remained on the land but lived far away from growing centers of employment found this avenue their best hope for survival. Besides, many wives and mothers had grown accustomed to transforming the decorative dairy feed sacks into girls' dresses. In 1964 the Livestock and Forestry Branch Experiment Station at Bethesda transferred most of its beef cattle to an eastern Arkansas site and began concentrating on improved dairy production for Jerseys and Holsteins on the region's hill farms. Even before 1964 the Bethesda station had sponsored an annual Dairy Day, to which extension service personnel and Farm Bureau representatives had transported interested farmers. In the late 1960s, although the number of dairy farmers was steadily declining and the North Arkansas Dairy Festival in Salem had been absorbed by a local homecoming celebration, another government program attempted to improve dairy farming in north central Arkansas. In 1967 and 1968, yearlong training projects were conducted at Melbourne, Salem, and other county seats under mandate of the Manpower Development and Training Act of 1962. Each class provided advanced information on feeding, testing, and other dairy issues for trainees—most of them, including Tanner, veteran farmers who had operated grade C or grade A dairies for years—selected by the Employment Security Division. Ultimately, the most beneficial service of the dairy training project was the cooperative purchasing of additional heifers from Wisconsin.[32]

The dairy training courses were designed to help a depressed area, but trends in the dairy industry and in local employment opportunities effectively gilded any long-term benefits they might have brought to the region. The dairy industry was rapidly centralizing, leaving in its wake casualties such as local cheese plants and their grade C suppliers. New U.S. Department of Agriculture sanitary regulations required significant outlays of money and time by dairy farmers; specialization rendered the diversified dairyman a thing of the past. Scientific breeding and feeding techniques also improved milk production, which translated into fewer and larger farms. Perhaps as important as changes in the dairy industry were changes related to new employment opportunities and local agricultural trends. Regional centers such as Batesville, Mountain Home, and Harrison began to offer plentiful opportunities for off-farm labor in the 1960s and 1970s.

In the case of many dairymen, the off-farm jobs came about as a result of a different phenomenon in the region—the development of retirement communities. Vernon Wells, Hugh Tanner, and Kennard Billingsley all found work in the late 1960s or early 1970s in Horseshoe Bend, a retirement village established in the early 1960s. Wells had already sold his farm by the time he went to work in the community near Franklin. Tanner continued to milk cows for a while after taking a job in Horseshoe Bend, where his wife was already employed. The effort of rising early to milk before going to work and facing the chore again at the end of the day, coupled with a declining market, soon influenced Tanner to take up beef cattle raising. Billingsley, who returned to Izard County in 1967, found work in Horseshoe Bend after three years of working with his father-in-law, who had built a typical three-stanchion, grade A parlor barn in the late 1950s, and sharing the profits. While Kennard and his wife Juanda Lee continued to help run the dairy for a few years after he started to work in 1970, they too eventually converted to beef cattle.[33]

By the mid-1970s, dairy farming in Izard County had declined to insignificance, ranking sixth among agricultural activities in terms of revenue. Only 12 of the county's farmers sold at least $2,500 worth of dairy products for a total of $89,000, the third-lowest figure in the fifteen-county region. In neighboring Fulton County, dairy farming remained a significant profession, although it was practiced by a severely reduced number of farmers. In 1974, 49 Fulton County dairy farmers sold more than $1.2 million worth of milk. As had been the case during the World War II era, northwestern Arkansas continued to pace the region in dairy production. Farmers in the counties of Benton, Carroll, Washington, and Madison produced a combined total of more than $12 million worth of dairy products in 1974. Even there, however, specialization and centralization had reduced the number of dairy farms to fewer than 500. In the two decades after 1954, milk sales in Benton County, the region's most prosperous dairy county, grew by 70 percent, but the number of producers declined by a staggering 92 percent to only 182 in 1974. By the latter date, six Ozark counties contained fewer than 20 dairy farms, and 3 generated less than $100,000 in dairy sales.[34]

Another Ozark farming alternative has enjoyed better staying power than dairy farming. Poultry raising generated more money in Arkansas than any other agricultural activity by the 1990s and (thanks partly to Ross Perot in the 1992 presidential election) came to represent the state in the national consciousness. Like dairy farming, poultry raising had its Ozark origins in northwestern Arkansas and from there spread unevenly across the region. Poultry raising also offered struggling farmers an alternative to declining, traditional practices; it replaced apple and grain production in the western Ozarks and cotton planting in the east. Furthermore, the poultry industry directly and indirectly spawned some of Arkansas's most profitable corporations. In the process, the industry altered the face of Ozark farming, challenging the traditional independence of the small farmer and injecting a dose of agribusiness mentality rarely witnessed before the rise of John Tyson.

Throughout the Ozarks, poultry and eggs had long provided a small source of cash income for farm families, although tending to laying hens, like gardening, was generally considered women's work and thus little more than a supplementary activity. In areas with railroad transportation, local merchants often purchased eggs, chickens, turkeys, and ducks to ship to cities such as Springfield, Missouri, or Memphis. Small urban centers in the region also provided a limited poultry market for farmers in their hinterlands. In areas with no access to a railroad, merchants and roving peddlers, or drummers, generally limited their purchases to eggs, which were taken by wagon and later by truck to urban markets. In the 1930s, after the expansion of broiler raising in northwestern Arkansas drew interest from the agricultural experiment station and extension service, farmers in communities across the region began building small chicken houses for laying hens and for growing birds. Simultaneously, small commercial hatcheries sprang up in most counties, and processing plants were established in a few locations. By the late 1930s, hatcheries in Batesville and Harrison were producing tens of thousands of chicks and tons of poultry feed for sale to area farmers. In Mammoth Spring, a vacant soda bottling plant was transformed into a poultry processing facility and egg station. By 1942 this plant, the Chester B. Franz Company, had begun buying broilers from Fulton County farmers.[35]

By the onset of the Great Depression, northwestern Arkansas had already begun to develop a small broiler industry, although transportation and refrigeration shortcomings limited it to a local market. That situation began to change in the 1930s. While most agricultural prices plummeted early in the decade, poultry prices remained somewhat consistent. Poultry raising was primarily a supplemental occupation; most producers maintained two or three small broiler houses in the wintertime. But when new transportation networks brought about increased demand for birds, many growers decided to expand their poultry operations. The man behind this transportation breakthrough was a pioneer of the poultry industry, John Tyson. A Missouri produce buyer and trucker, Tyson arrived in Springdale in 1931 and for the next few years made a living trucking hay for local farmers and hauling chickens to sell in Kansas City and St. Louis. Tyson's most memorable trip, and the one that launched him on his journey to the top of the poultry world, took place in the spring of 1936, almost a decade after the first northwestern Arkansas chickens had been trucked to midwestern cities. Having read a newspaper report that chickens were bringing much better prices in markets far away from Arkansas, he loaded 500 cooped birds on his flatbed truck and made the 700-mile journey to Chicago. The newspaper report had not been erroneous. Tyson made $235 profit, all but $15 of which he wired back to Arkansas with instructions to buy another load of chickens and have them waiting upon his return.[36]

Within a year, John Tyson was hauling chickens to cities from Detroit to Houston. Tyson soon found himself more deeply involved in the poultry business when a shortage of birds prompted him to buy a couple of used incubators from a local hatchery. From selling chicks to growers it was a short step to the feed supply business, so Tyson began distributing poultry feed for Ralston Purina. By the late 1930s, thanks to Tyson, northwestern Arkansas was quickly becoming a national center of poultry production, with some 5,000 brooder houses on Ozark farms. By the time the United States entered World War II, poultry farming had become a million-dollar business in both Benton and Washington Counties. Over half of the broilers bought and shipped by Tyson and other businesses were destined for Chicago, with St. Louis and Milwaukee the next most popular markets.[37]

The war catapulted poultry farming into elite status in northwestern Arkansas. Rationing of red meat helped increase America's annual consumption of chicken from 16.8 pounds in 1938 to 30.5 pounds in 1943. Because the federal government placed the entire production of the Delmarva poultry industry under army contract, the domestic market was opened to upstarts such as Tyson and his Arkansas competitors. During the war Tyson expanded once again, building his own feed mill, establishing company-owned broiler houses on his Springdale farm, and importing a new meat-type chicken, the New Hampshire Red Cristy, for distribution to growers. By the end of World War II, almost four in five Arkansas broilers were produced in the northwestern corner of the state, and the entire Ozark region accounted for nearly 90 percent of poultry produced. Between 1940 and 1945, poultry sales in Benton and Washington Counties increased more than twofold to over $7.1 million, and poultry raising became the most profitable agricultural enterprise in the area.[38]

In the immediate postwar years, national corporations rushed to claim a piece of the northwestern Arkansas poultry processing industry. Swift, Swanson, Armour, Campbell Soup, and a host of other national and regional companies built processing plants in the region. These new plants utilized refrigerated railroad cars and tractor trailers, or "chicken pullmans," to ship birds around the country. By the early 1950s, Springdale alone contained nineteen different poultry companies, and the tentacles of the industry had spread eastward to towns such as Huntsville and Harrison. Northwestern Arkansas's position as the national center of poultry raising and processing was solidified in 1951 when the National Broiler Council sponsored the "Chicken of Tomorrow" contest at the University of Arkansas, an event substantial enough to attract Vice President Alben Barkley as keynote speaker. Within the state, the poultry industry became a potent political force. When Governor Francis Cherry reneged on a promise to sign a bill abolishing the processing tax on poultry industries, Roy Ritter, poultryman and founder of the nationally renowned AQ Chicken House restaurant in Springdale, and fellow Springdale poultryman Luther George paid Orval Faubus's $1,500 filing fee. Ritter then served as manager of Faubus's gubernatorial campaign in 1954. The Madison County politician consciously cultivated the favor of his fellow northwestern Arkansans in the poultry industry during his dozen years in office.[39]

Tyson entered the processing business in 1957 when he built his first plant in Springdale. With this move, Tyson's Foods became the first fully integrated broiler company in northwestern Arkansas. It supplied breeder stock, hatched eggs, grew broilers, provided feed for other growers, processed chickens, and delivered them to market. In 1963 Tyson's Foods (the name was changed to Tyson Foods in 1971) purchased a local poultry pioneer, Garrett Poultry Company of Rogers; it was the first in a long line of acquisitions. The 1960s marked one of the most dynamic periods in Tyson's development and in the northwestern Arkansas poultry industry as new, larger broiler houses sprang up on hillsides across the subregion. In 1986, after the acquisition of Lane Processing, Inc., Tyson Foods became the nation's number-one poultry processing company. Arkansas had already achieved a similar national status in the farm production of poultry.[40]

In another corner of the Arkansas Ozarks a similar scene played out, albeit on a smaller stage, in the Batesville area. The pioneer of the eastern Ozarks' poultry industry, J. K. Southerland, claimed even more humble beginnings than did Tyson. Southerland grew up the son of a lumberman-farmer in the early twentieth century in Independence County. After teaching at country schools and working for a short time in St. Louis, in 1935 he and his wife Cleo bought a 60-acre farm near Floral in southwestern Independence County. Here in the midst of the depression, Cleo Ferguson Southerland recalled years later, the young couple made their first foray into poultry farming quite by accident. Upon examining their new farmstead, the Southerlands found a nesting hen with a dozen eggs under a corn crib. J. K. raised the chicks and sold them for a dollar each. Recognizing the possibilities of poultry raising, Southerland soon constructed a small, 500-bird brooder house. By the late 1930s he was selling chicks to neighbors and hauling truckloads of chickens to Memphis.[41]

In 1944, with the financial assistance of his rural merchant father-in-law, Southerland established a warehouse in Batesville from which to conduct his growing hatchery and feed business. Nine years later, he built his first processing plant at Concord, a Cleburne County village about twenty-five miles west of Batesville and only ten miles from his home in

Floral. In 1957, Southerland built a larger plant in Batesville and established a feed mill and growout operation in Melbourne. By the early 1960s, Southerland had established another feed mill–growout center in Mountain View and had purchased the Clinton Poultry and Egg Company in Van Buren County. In 1969, Southerland merged his business with a Missouri company and began marketing products under the Banquet Foods brand. Ten years later ConAgra, at the time the nation's largest poultry processor, bought out the old Southerland operation.[42]

The expansion of broiler raising quickly placed poultry production at the top of Ozark agricultural activities in terms of sales. In 1954, 2,644 farmers in the fifteen-county area marketed broilers; thousands more continued to sell eggs and chickens to local merchants and peddlers. Nevertheless, broiler production remained localized around the large northwestern Arkansas market and smaller markets in the eastern Ozarks. While poultry production generated more than $11 million in sales in both Benton and Washington Counties, in seven other Ozark counties poultry sales amounted to less than $250,000 in 1954. The following two decades dispersed broiler raising over a larger Ozark area, but the focus continued to be northwestern Arkansas and the Batesville region. By 1974, Ozark poultry sales had almost reached one-quarter of a billion dollars; six Ozark counties—seven, counting Independence—surpassed $10 million in sales, with Washington County accounting for more than $100 million. Poultry raising was not the most valuable agricultural pursuit in six Ozark counties, however, and in four—Fulton, Marion, Newton, and Searcy—the broiler industry was nonexistent.[43]

By the late 1960s, poultry raising produced more farm dollars than any other agricultural activity in Arkansas. With this success came a restructuring of farmer-market relationships. The most distinctive characteristic of the modern poultry industry is its vertical integration. After World War II, most broiler growers conducted their farms much like other independent Ozark farmers. When declining prices compounded the existing problems of high fixed costs, diseases, and a reluctance by banks to loan money to high-risk broiler growers, feed dealers offered broiler growers a safety net in the form of one of various contracts that limited the farmer's financial liability. Gradually the conditional-sales contract, whereby the feed company retained ownership of the birds and the grower-caretaker received a flat fee per bird or a predetermined sale price, emerged as the dominant relationship between farmers and marketers. Under this safe arrangement, broiler production climbed rapidly in the early 1950s, so rapidly, in fact, that in late 1954 supply outran de-

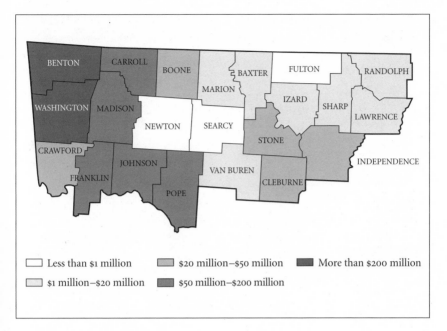

MAP 7.1. Poultry Sales, 1992

mand. Left reeling by the low prices offered by poultry manufacturers, the feed companies responded by canceling many of their grower contracts. This proved only a temporary salve, since prices tumbled again in the spring of 1955.[44]

This intense period of boom-and-bust quickened the nascent integration movement among poultry firms. Processors, who needed a steadily growing supply of birds to maintain their market positions, began buying feed mills and contracting with growers. In some instances, Tyson's for example, feed and hatchery companies expanded vertically by purchasing or building processing plants. By the mid-1950s, vertical integration had already taken root in most poultry companies. Under the seven-part system, each farmer fitted into only one phase of the production of poultry. Foundation breeder flocks produced breeder hens and roosters. Laying houses provided broiler eggs, which were then hatched in company-owned commercial nurseries. The most recognizable phase of the farm side of poultry production was the broiler farm, where long, narrow, metallic houses sheltered growing birds. Broiler growers received company-made feed in company-owned trucks. From the broiler farms, company trucks delivered birds to automated processing plants. Finally, Tyson and other poultry companies controlled distribution channels that

Scattering new chicks in a modern poultry barn, Independence County, ca. 1980s.
Courtesy of the Lyon College Archives.

included warehouses and trucking fleets. By the mid-1960s, this efficient,
agribusiness system described the nation's poultry companies.[45]

This system developed as much through the initiative of poultry processing companies as it did out of necessity. The nature of poultry raising
after World War II, with growers, feed companies, truckers, processing
plants, and hatcheries all competing for limited profits, helped differen-
tiate this industry from other agricultural enterprises and presented a
problem that executives set about solving. Vertical integration had deprived the poultry farmer of the independence traditionally associated
with Ozark agriculturists. Broiler growers especially were little more than
temporary caretakers of the company's valuable property. Company-
owned trucks delivered chicks and feed and picked up mature birds.
Growers' associations, which dated back to World War II, attempted to
maintain a more independent status and better bargaining position in
the early 1960s but lost their battle in *Wintz v. Tyson*. Ironically, in that attempt to force the processors to abide by the Fair Labor Standards Law,
the growers were thwarted by a ruling that denied such a claim because
growers were not employees. The 1966 ruling left broiler farmers in
agribusiness limbo somewhere between independence and peonage.[46]

While the semi-independent Ozark poultry farmer easily exceeded other agriculturists in terms of product sales, the beef cattle farmer was by far the most ubiquitous member of the region's modern farming community. In 1992, more than seven times as many Ozark farmers marketed cattle as they did poultry, and more than 90 percent of all farmers raised cattle. Cattle raising had also become synonymous with part-time farming; the two combined to make up the most important Ozark agricultural trend of the last third of the twentieth century. In contrast to the integrated agribusiness state of poultry raising, cattle farming represented a last bastion of traditional free-market agriculture and for many part-time farmers reflected a conscious link with an agrarian past.

Cattle raising is among the oldest commercial agricultural practices in the Arkansas Ozarks. Before Arkansas's statehood, pioneers in the region were selling cow hides to river traders, and by the late antebellum period cattle drives to Kansas City and Little Rock were quite common. Despite the obvious preference for swine raising and for pork in the hill country, cattle remained plentiful in some areas well into the twentieth century. Even on the eve of World War II, large expanses of the region maintained an open range policy in which farmers enclosed their crops instead of their livestock. Although the open range, where even landless tenants and croppers could turn loose their hogs and cattle, symbolized the egalitarian nature of the region of small farmers, it also served as a barrier to breed improvement. The poor quality of cattle, combined with the dire effects of the fever tick and other parasites and diseases, translated into low prices. In the thirty years after the Agricultural Marketing Service began gathering price statistics in 1910, average annual beef cattle prices exceeded $6 per hundredweight only five times and peaked at $7 during World War I. Poor marketing facilities meant that most Ozark farmers actually received even lower prices for their cattle. One Van Buren County man recalled his father selling fifteen head of cattle to a butcher-trader in 1906 for $92. Another remembered his father receiving $8 for a red cow and trading an old .22-caliber rifle for a heifer. During the depression, cattle became almost unmarketable; by the end of 1933 cattle prices were barely above $2 per hundredweight. During this era, an Izard County farmer "walked down off the side of the hill and sold a Jersey cow and a two-year-old past steer to a cow buyer for fifteen dollars."[47]

Three key accomplishments paved the way for the development of a post–World War II commercial cattle industry in the Ozarks: the establishment of markets, the conversion of row crops to pasture and hay fields, and the replacement of scrub stock with thoroughbred cattle. Of these, the first was a prerequisite for the accomplishment of the latter two. Until the 1930s, Arkansas had no terminal market and nothing resembling a livestock auction. Most Ozark farmers sold their cattle to country buyers, like the one who purchased the Izard County farmer's Jersey cow and steer, who in pre-automobile days made periodic drives to the nearest railroad depot for shipment to St. Louis, Springfield, Memphis, or elsewhere. Country buyers almost never used scales, generally paid for cattle by the head, and most frequently offered less than market prices. After the introduction of trucks in the 1920s, Ozark country buyers often hauled cattle to southern Missouri auctions or to the terminal markets in Kansas City and St. Louis. In small urban centers, local butcher shops and packinghouses created a limited demand for quality beef cattle and, by cutting out the middleman, probably offered better prices than country buyers.

Marketing opportunities began to improve markedly during the depression and World War II. Most significant was the proliferation of livestock auctions. In early 1935 the town of Harrison, with financial assistance from the Federal Emergency Relief Administration, opened Arkansas's first livestock auction in the heart of the Ozarks. Nine other auctions, most of them in the Ozark region, opened for business later that same year. By 1940 the region claimed twelve of the state's fifty-one auctions. Most early auctions were small affairs with makeshift facilities. The first auction company at Flippin held its Wednesday afternoon sales at the old railroad livestock pens on the Missouri Pacific before it constructed a sale barn. In Mountain Home, local businessmen and cattlemen converted the abandoned gymnasium of the defunct Mountain Home Baptist College into a sale barn. And in at least one case, the construction of an auction barn symbolized the Ozarks' agricultural transformation. Erected during World War II, Yellville's first sale barn was fashioned from the lumber of the town's recently dismantled cotton gin. At the beginning of World War II, only two Ozark areas were noticeably deficient in livestock marketing facilities: the mountainous counties of Madison, Newton, and Searcy, and the northeastern cotton triangle of Fulton, Izard, and Sharp Counties.[48]

The auction market provided advantages over previous marketing methods. The bidding process, whereby cattlemen, packinghouse representatives, other local farmers, and feed lot buyers made bids for individual animals or groups of animals while observing them in a central arena, usually resulted in more competitive prices. The year-round, weekly functioning of the auction allowed farmers to decide for them-

Farmers Livestock Auction Company, Springdale, 1958. By the 1950s, cattle auctions such as this one were ubiquitous in the Ozark region. Courtesy of Howard Clark/ Shiloh Museum of Ozark History.

selves when and how many head to sell. Furthermore, although it would be another generation before most farmers could provide their own transportation to market, the convenience of the local auction could save money on hauling expenses and allowed farmers to avoid the railroad and its steep freight charges. Perhaps most important, by simply being there the auction spurred interest in cattle raising as a serious pursuit in an era of agricultural transformation.

The auction market did not immediately become the universal marketing tool in the Ozarks. Country buyers continued to be an option into the 1950s. Individual cattlemen sometimes bought and sold cattle. Between 1936 and 1946, Harrison stock raiser Bob Shaddox maintained scales and holding pens at his barn for buying cattle from local farmers and selling them to Swift and Company. In 1960 another Boone County farmer set up a similar operation from which he trucked cattle to feed lots in Kansas and Iowa. Other farmers bypassed country buyers and local auctions altogether. Stone County cattleman Tom Ross hauled his own cattle to markets as distant as Kansas City even after the establishment of auctions at Mountain View and Marshall. In some areas, the Farm Bureau attempted to circumvent country buyers by providing truck delivery service to railroad depots, from which cattle were shipped directly to terminal markets.[49]

Whereas the growth of markets provided Ozark farmers with financial incentive for cattle raising, the conversion of row-cropped fields to pasture and hay fields provided the physical foundation. The same extension agents who oversaw the removal of thousands of acres from cotton cultivation also encouraged the sowing of pasture and hay grasses such as lespedeza, alfalfa, white and crimson clover, bluegrass, rye, orchard grass, hop clover, fescue, and Bermuda grass. County agents and CCC work crews also terraced eroded hillsides on hundreds of farms. In the hill country of Randolph County, lespedeza, a fertility-restoring legume, practically unknown before the New Deal, was planted on approximately 20,000 acres during the latter half of the 1930s. Between 1933 and 1939, hay production often grew in inverse proportion to the decline of cotton. In Fulton County, this span of a half-dozen years witnessed a two-thirds decrease in cotton acreage and an increase in harvested hay acreage from 14,000 to 63,000. Fertilization provided a boost to young pastures and hay fields. Before World War II, many Ozark farmers received low-cost phosphate fertilizer from the AAA and other New Deal agricultural programs designed to curtail row cropping.[50]

Another New Deal agricultural agency, the Soil Conservation Service (SCS), also provided assistance in the transformation from row cropping to livestock raising. Soil conservation districts were established across the region and the nation. Local farmers who signed up for SCS aid—and most did so in the two decades following the agency's establishment—hosted soil surveys of their farms by government experts. The advice offered Ozark farmers was usually of the commonsense variety: continue to raise cotton, corn, or other row crops on fertile bottomlands; convert steep slopes to hay and pasture; and rotate mildly sloping fields between row crops and grasses. The SCS, in conjunction with local extension agents, also carried out programs in pond building, terracing, and fertilizing.[51]

The Arkansas Agricultural Experiment Station provided the scientific information on hay and pastures that the extension service used and helped extension agents lead the push for the conversion of row crops to grasses. The main station at Fayetteville and the beef cattle unit west of Fayetteville served farmers in northwestern Arkansas. Experimentation with livestock raising in the eastern Ozarks took place at the Livestock and Forestry Branch Station near Bethesda in northwestern Independence County. Founded on 3,000 acres in 1937 with funds provided by the Bankhead-Jones Act of 1935, the lands of the Livestock and Forestry

Branch Station had been restored by the scs and ccc crews by 1939. Soon thereafter, researchers began studying pasture development on a 155-acre plot of overcultivated and eroded hillside and conducted grass and hay experiments with clovers, orchard grass, fescue, and Bermuda grass on the rolling hills of the Salem Plateau and on the steep slopes of the White River Hills.[52]

But the conversion to pastures and hay fields was a gradual one in the three decades after the New Deal. Many Ozark farmers continued to rely on row crops for cattle feed for several years. By the late 1950s, some Ozark farmers, especially dairy farmers, still grew corn and sorghum for silage production. It was not until the mid-1960s that such traditional practices declined to insignificance. The number of Ozark farms harvesting crops fell from 85 percent in 1956 to 66 percent in 1970; by the latter date almost all the fields harvested in the region were hay fields. The same fifteen-year period witnessed an average increase of seventeen acres of pasture land per farm and a 700 percent increase in the number of farmers fertilizing their pastures.[53]

Perhaps the most obvious phase of the growth of commercial cattle raising was the replacement of native scrub cattle with purebred stock. For many years, the raising of thoroughbred cattle was a hobby or at best a diversionary interest among prosperous farmers and businessmen. The high prices for purebred livestock, and even higher prices for animals registered with national breed associations, restricted such beef cattle raising to an elite community. Indicative of this group was the Sloan family of Lawrence County. M. F. Sloan, a Vanderbilt University law graduate whose merchant-banker father was Smithville's wealthiest resident in the late nineteenth century, purchased his first purebred Shorthorn cattle in 1887; in the first decade of the twentieth century, he switched to the more popular Aberdeen-Angus, or Black Angus, breed. His sons Lucien and Fred later divided their father's 1,557-acre farm but continued to lead their region in the production of prized Black Angus cattle. By 1940 Lucien Sloan's Alfaland farm in the Spring River bottoms near Imboden supported 400 head of purebred cattle; he sold his best bulls and heifers to other farmers for breeding purposes and marketed lower-quality animals at local auctions or at terminal markets out of state.[54]

Successful thoroughbred cattle raising required plots of land three or four times the size of most Ozark farms. In the World War II era, few of the region's cattle farms were larger or more modern than the one owned by Ed Mays of Searcy County. In the late 1930s, Mays began consolidating worn-out small farms in the Elberta Mountain area near the old lumber town of Leslie. While most Searcy County farmers continued to scratch out meager livings from their rocky lands or abandoned them altogether, Mays amassed 3,500 acres and developed the state's largest Hereford farm. He raised all his hay and feed on 700 acres and maintained the remainder of his ranch in pasture and forest land. By World War II, Mays owned 450 head of Hereford cattle and had begun to cooperate with local SCS and extension personnel in the construction of stock ponds and tanks.[55] Large-scale cattle raising such as this was beyond the reach of the vast majority of Ozark farmers, who lacked both the extensive amounts of land and the capital required for herd improvement and crop conversion.

One of Izard County's leading cattle raisers was J. H. Landers, a Melbourne merchant and bank president who owned two farms, one south of Melbourne and another near Oxford. On the eve of World War II, Landers owned the largest beef cattle herd in the county and maintained his own dipping vat. A breeder of Hereford cattle, he helped popularize that breed among neighbor farmers who began to import Hereford bulls late in the depression. Many cattlemen such as Landers exercised a significant impact on the growth of cattle raising in their communities. Landers's business peers also influenced the growing industry. The Ozark Commercial Club, originally formed by young men in Boone, Newton, Carroll, and Marion Counties for the purpose of picking up garbage and rubbish in their communities, in 1940 initiated a program to supply beef calves to 4-H club members, Future Farmers of America boys, and other interested youth. The club worked in conjunction with extension agents and vocational agriculture teachers and received financing from a revolving livestock fund at a Harrison bank. In other areas, neighborhood cooperatives purchased purebred Herefords and other breeds of cattle during and after World War II.[56]

The influence of extension agents and the Livestock and Forestry Branch Station at Bethesda was a key factor in the dispersal of purebred cattle. In its first year of operation, the Bethesda station helped distribute at least eleven carloads of Texas Herefords to area farmers. In 1941 the station purchased forty Black Angus heifers and initiated a federally approved study on beef cattle performance. In succeeding years, county extension agents arranged individual and cooperative purchases of purebred beef cattle from outside the region until local cattlemen raised sufficient numbers to supply breeder stock to Ozark farmers. By the end of World War II the open range had been abolished in most Ozark communities, further aiding the cause of thoroughbred livestock raising.[57]

Commercial cattle raising on Ozark farms experienced its most in-

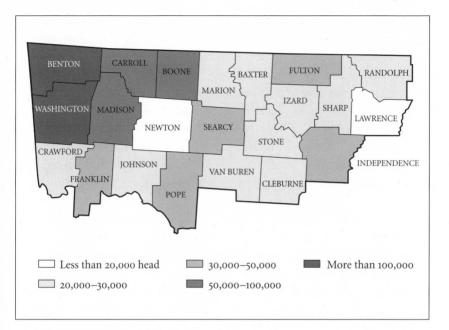

MAP 7.2. Cattle, 1992

tense expansion during the 1960s and early 1970s after the complete demise of row cropping. Dairy farmers such as Hugh Tanner, Guy Rhoads,
and Kennard Billingsley converted their herds to beef cattle, and poultry
farmers such as Doyle Webb often took up cattle raising as a second means
of agricultural income. Unusually high cattle prices resulted in a glut of
beef cattle on American farms in the mid-1970s, and Ozark farmers
played a key role in this development within Arkansas. In the three and
a half decades after 1940, the number of cattle in the fifteen-county region increased from less than 220,000 to more than 640,000 head. Simultaneously, the number per farm grew by more than 700 percent to
47.6 head in 1974. By the 1970s, almost all Ozark farmers raised at least a
few cows, the overwhelming majority of which were beef cattle.[58]

The raising of beef cattle became an integral part of the expansion of
part-time farming after World War II and especially in the last quarter of
the twentieth century. Between 1940 and 1974 the number of farms in the
fifteen-county Arkansas Ozark region declined by more than two-thirds.
Of the remaining farms in 1974, barely more than half produced at least
$2,500 worth of agricultural products. Almost half of all Ozark farmers
earned more money through off-farm employment than they did from
farm production; fully 65 percent of Ozark farms by 1974 were operated

by people who considered their occupation to be something other than farming or by farmers sixty-five years of age or older.[59] By the 1970s, most full-time agriculturists in the region maintained diversified poultry or dairy farms or were retirement-age farmers who raised beef cattle to supplement pensions and Social Security payments or to carry on a familiar way of life on the farm. The family farmer was not yet a memory, but he had certainly become a minority in the hill counties and especially in the old cotton counties of the eastern Ozarks.

Part-time farming was not a new phenomenon of the 1970s; it was a step in the evolving system of rural families struggling for survival and relying on traditional lifestyles and practices. From the first decade of the twentieth century, many Ozark farmers in the Boston Mountains and other areas affected by the timber boom made as much money from seasonal timber and mill work as they did from farming. As early as 1935, a study conducted in Hindsville, a Madison County community located within the market and employment radius of the Springdale-Fayetteville area, found part-time farmers to be the most prosperous people in the area.[60] By 1949, more than one-quarter of the farm operators in most Ozark counties worked at least 100 days off the farm each year. And many more joined the growing numbers of Ozark migrant families. The tired, beaten hills had been overworked for generations; they could take no more. Put matter-of-factly by one observer during the depression, the Ozark region required "labor-extensive use of the land," a small amount of labor in relation to the amount of land.[61] The beef cattle culture fit this description perfectly, but it also dictated larger farms and many fewer families. The bloated attrition rate among Ozark farms in the quarter-century after World War II achieved the necessary decrease in farms, which was generally accompanied by consolidation efforts on the part of farmers who remained. Furthermore, the development of job opportunities in the 1960s and 1970s allowed hundreds of farmers to make the transition to part-time farming in a relatively simple and successful manner.

Unlike raising cotton with human and animal labor (which occupied substantial amounts of time during planting, cultivating, and harvesting) and dairy farming (which required year-round, daily attention), raising beef cattle, especially small herds of less than fifty mature cows, demanded little close supervision throughout the year. Beef cattle needed hay and nutrition supplements during the winter months, occasional vaccination and veterinary attention, a sufficient range of pasture to graze in the warm months, and closer supervision during calving season. With the consolidation of farms into bigger units and the availability of tractors and tractor-drawn implements for the conversion of cropland to pasture and hay field, the stage was set for the dominance of the part-time beef rancher.

Several other factors ensured that beef cattle raising would be dominated by part-time farmers. The land requirements for an extensive agricultural pursuit like beef cattle raising were substantial. Even small herds of fifty or fewer brood cows generally required several hundred acres of pasture and hay, and a herd this size would not support a family by the 1990s. Furthermore, the capricious and unbridled nature of the cattle market prevented price regularity and promoted drastic highs and lows. A farm family with at least one off-farm source of income could survive periods of low prices better than cattlemen who relied solely on cattle sales. Finally, the nature of the Ozark cattle industry favored the small, part-time raiser. Arkansas, like most southern states, was primarily a cow-calf state by the 1990s, meaning the almost universal practice was for the farmer to maintain brood cows who raised their calves until they were ready for the local auction market at 400 to 600 pounds, where they were then purchased by feed lots or by cattlemen who "fed them out" until they reached a weight desired by packinghouses. The few Ozark cattlemen who depended upon cattle dealing for the bulk of their income often maintained such feed-out operations in addition to or instead of cow-calf farms.

The small, part-time cattle farm was a good representative of modern Ozark agriculture. Although poultry farms accounted for almost three-quarters of the region's agricultural sales by the 1990s, fewer than 1 in 5 Ozark farmers produced broilers or eggs, and more than half the region's poultry production took place in just two counties, Benton and Washington. Conversely, cattle raising was almost a universal activity among Ozark farmers. In 1992, only 400 of the fifteen-county region's 11,858 farmers marketed no cattle. But the average of only $13,170 in cattle sales per farm led to another conclusion: the Ozark region of Arkansas was no longer an agricultural region by the late twentieth century. It was certainly a rural region, but agriculture ranked a distant third behind tourism and manufacturing in terms of revenue produced in the region. In 1992 the net cash income of Ozark farmers in only one county exceeded the state average of $17,720, and in all but the four northwestern counties, farmers reported net cash returns of less than $10,000. The Ozark region continued to lead all other Arkansas regions in the production of practically all poultry- and livestock-related farm products, but it did so with a dual concentration of poultry farmers and a diverse array of part-time cattle raisers.[62] The diffusion of small cattle farms throughout the hill country maintained the agricultural appearance of this rural region, but the farmhouse and barnyard were rarely the centers of economic activity, even on Ozark farms.

By the 1990s the fundamental structure of Ozark agriculture had changed little since the demise of row cropping and the wholesale abandonment of small-scale, inefficient dairy farming three decades earlier. Even the rate of farm attrition had slowed. By the early 1970s, the agricultural transformation was for the most part complete. The programs of the New Deal and the economic stimulus of war permanently and monumentally altered the farms and the countrysides of the Ozarks and of the United States. Ozarkers who were able to stay on the land in the post–World War II era had to adapt and evolve. But they were a minority. Most farm families eventually left their fields and barns behind; many left their communities and even their region and state as well. Their sagas provide an equally important piece to the story of modernization and adaptation in the Arkansas Ozarks.

Modernization and Migration

IN 1938, Arvin Watkins and Lillie Mae Darty were married in the small Izard County community of Lacrosse. The young couple moved onto a plot of land on the Walter Fudge farm, where they sharecropped for the next sixteen years. Fudge supplied the work stock, equipment, and supplies, and the Watkinses kept half the crop. The Watkinses attended the Sweet Home Baptist Church, sent their children to school there, and bought necessities at general stores in Lacrosse and Zion. The couple, though both from landowning families, never owned an automobile, never got ahead, never owned their own farm. Since their teenage years, the Watkinses had watched as their neighbors left the land and moved to nearby towns or to distant states and cities. Lillie Mae Watkins, beset by declining agricultural prospects and her husband's poor health, finally moved the family to Batesville, thirty miles to the south. There she supported her husband and children by doing housework and by working as a maid for the First Presbyterian Church. The community they left behind soon disappeared. Every family moved away, and both church houses closed their doors, leaving buildings to the animals and the elements. Within a decade of the Watkinses' departure, only abandoned houses and barns hinted at the life of the past.[1]

The technological and governmental forces of rural modernization affected more than farming practices in the Ozarks. The decline of cotton raising and semisubsistence farming, the rise of cattle ranching, depopulation, and the other facets of rural modernization deeply altered the fabric of Ozark society and culture. As families vacated the land, rural communities dwindled, crossroads stores closed their doors and boarded their windows, church rolls shrank, and consolidation closed small country schools. The life of the full-time worker in town and weekend farmer replaced the seasonal life of the row-cropper and general farmer.

The backdrop to so much of this rural transformation was provided by a quarter-century or more of outmigration by native Ozarkers and an even longer period of inmigration by retirees, especially from the states of the Midwest. Between 1940 and 1960, the population of the fifteen-county Ozark region fell by 14 percent, and even this figure is deceiving. By 1960 Washington and Benton Counties, the only Ozark counties with significant urban populations, contained almost one-half of all Arkansas Ozark residents. In the primarily rural counties beyond the northwestern corner of the state, the population declined by almost one-third during the twenty-year span to fewer than 13 people per square mile, less than half the state average. Particularly deserted were the former cotton counties —Izard, Sharp, and Van Buren all lost more than 40 percent of their inhabitants—and the mountainous counties such as Newton and Searcy. By the late 1960s and early 1970s, the agricultural transformation was basically complete; the introduction of small-scale, low-wage industry and the development of tourist enterprises provided enough jobs to stem the flow of young people out of the region. Even more integral to the Ozarks' population growth since the mid-1960s has been the rise of retirement communities across the region, a phenomenon that ultimately brought about the replacement of thousands of World War II–era Ozark outmigrants with their midwestern peers.

Like most rural areas, the Ozarks suffered from outmigration after World War I. Of the fifteen Arkansas Ozark counties, only Washington gained residents during the 1920s, and the populations of some counties fell by more than 10 percent. As we have seen, the Ozark region reached agricultural capacity around the turn of the century. The discovery of oil and the opening of lands in the new state of Oklahoma offered a relief valve for many desperate Ozark farmers after World War I. The scarcity of opportunities during the Great Depression and the ravages of the Dust Bowl, however, erased most of the previous decade's population deficit as many families returned to their original homes in the 1930s. Finally, the prosperity and jobs created by World War II, combined with New Deal restrictions placed on farmers, initiated a quarter-century of outmigration that would reduce the region's population to Reconstruction levels and scatter Ozark natives across the country.

The movement of families and individuals out of the Ozarks consisted of two kinds: temporary migratory labor and permanent settlement. The former often led eventually to the latter. The decades of migratory labor

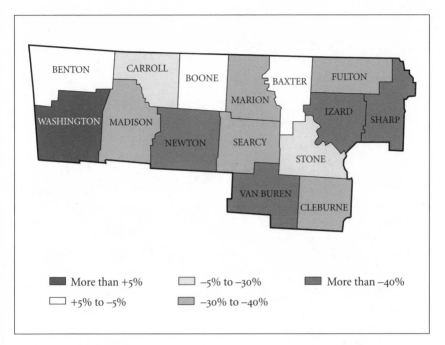

MAP 8.1. Population Change, 1940–1960

activity among Ozarkers are now largely forgotten or overlooked by historians. These Arkies and their Okie cousins were among the last of the great hordes of white migrant laborers who would be replaced in the late 1950s and 1960s by Mexicans and other immigrant groups. This episode of Ozark history is important not simply because of its novelty and color but also for the window it provides into the Ozark psyche and the painful transition from an agricultural, seasonal existence to a modern life based on industrial time and company regulations.

Migratory labor had occurred for decades throughout rural America. Migratory patterns and destinations were generally community phenomena. According to one Ozark native, migration was a "word of mouth thing. Somebody goes and likes it, and their family goes. . . . Then it just mushroomed."[2] Information about faraway harvests traveled quickly from family to family and neighbor to neighbor until entire communities abandoned their farms for a season. Due to the informal style of communication, migratory destinations differed from county to county and sometimes from community to community.

Audrey Thompson, a Fulton County native who operated a traveling picture show business in the eastern Ozarks after World War II, witnessed

Photograph by J. Laurence Charlton of a migrant worker family, Washington County, ca. 1938–41. Courtesy of the J. Laurence Charlton Collection, group 3, number 12, Special Collections Division, University of Arkansas Libraries, Fayetteville.

a variety of migratory trails. In Izard County, where Washington State was the most popular destination, Thompson remembers that his "picture shows didn't do very good during the apple harvest. . . . And around the Black Rock area [Lawrence County] they went to southern Illinois . . . and they worked in the corn patch and things." Other communities dispatched migrants to more diverse destinations. In the Hardy area, "it kindly divided out to Kansas City, St. Louis, and Memphis and, of course, Little Rock."[3]

One of the most common trails, and one that first introduced hundreds of hill families to the life of migratory labor, took Ozarkers to cotton-growing regions as seasonal pickers. Eula Ferrel recalls that her one-room, Madison County school often closed in the fall because so many families traveled southward to the Arkansas River valley to hire out as cotton pickers. In the eastern Ozarks, many poor farmers and tenants supplemented their incomes by picking cotton on the larger farms of the area. Many also traveled to the rich cotton lands of eastern Arkansas before the local harvest commenced. After World War I, the forests were cleared and the swamps were drained in northeastern Arkansas, opening up a virgin land of dark, fertile soil that quickly became a nationally leading cotton-producing region. The experience of one Fulton County family relates the reliance of a significant number of Ozarkers on the income from seasonal labor in the bottoms. Zela Rhoads was raised on her grandmother's 80-acre Agnos farm by her mother, Myrtle Stuart, and her grandmother, Janie Ellis. As a small girl during the early days of the depression, Zela accompanied her mother and grandmother to eastern Craighead County, where the women picked cotton on the small farm of a relative. After the relative, Zela's great-uncle, died in the mid-1930s, Ellis and the Stuarts found cotton-picking jobs as far from home as the Missouri bootheel before striking an annual deal with a farmer in Craighead County. Beginning in the late 1930s and continuing until her marriage in 1943, Zela and her family caught the train each August and traveled to Monett, where their employer, Ben Ball, provided them a one-room house and all the cotton they could ever want to pick. The three generations of Ozark women would stay on at Ball's farm until late October, cooking their meals over an open fire in the small yard and carefully saving their earnings, which grew to a dollar per hundred pounds during the war years. A good day's work could earn the family $7 or $8.[4]

Many farmers such as Ben Ball in Mississippi, Craighead, and Poinsett Counties looked to the Ozarks and other areas for seasonal labor. Cotton planters drove or sent trucks into the region to recruit pickers and transport them back to the bottoms. One Mississippi County planter, L. V. Waddell, journeyed as far west as Fort Smith and Sallisaw, Oklahoma, where poor hill farmers gathered to catch a ride to the cotton fields. Like Ball and the Stuarts, many planters and pickers established long-standing relationships whereby the cotton farmers housed the same workers year after year. When this intrastate migratory labor began in the 1920s, pickers generally earned 50 cents per hundred pounds; a typical picker could earn a dollar or more per day. By the time mechanical pickers began supplanting Ozarkers in the bottomlands in the 1950s, an energetic picker could earn $9 or more for a day's work.[5]

Seasonal agricultural labor demands drew migrant workers to areas around the nation. Jesse Austin and other young men from Madison County made several trips to the hay fields of Wyoming, where they would work for a month or so before returning to Arkansas. Others followed the wheat harvests that began in late spring in Oklahoma. That trail moved north through Kansas and Nebraska and into the Dakotas. So many Ozarkers participated in the wheat harvests after World War II that local newspapers regularly carried help-wanted notices from wheat-

Picking cotton in the Greenbrier bottoms, Independence County, date unknown.
Courtesy of the Lyon College Archives.

farming areas on the Great Plains. A similar migratory trail took eastern
Ozarkers to the cornfields of Illinois and other midwestern states. For
some young Ozarkers, migratory work became a way of life. Baxter
County native Percy Copeland received his initiation in migratory labor
in the vast cotton fields of northeastern Arkansas. Migratory trails eventually carried Copeland to orchards in Michigan, orange groves in
Florida, strawberry patches in central Arkansas, and tomato fields in Indiana. Another Baxter County native, Stonewall Treat, made thirteen different trips to harvest spinach and lettuce in Colorado; Treat followed the
Okie trail to California three times and on another occasion joined hundreds of fellow Ozarkers in the Washington apple orchards.[6]

Thousands of Ozark residents followed the route made famous by
Steinbeck's Joad family in *The Grapes of Wrath*. Benson Fox, a Searcy
County native, found himself among the migrants headed for California
in the 1930s. Fox, who made the first of several trips in 1939, worked in an
orange-packing warehouse and in the redwood forests; he eventually
earned enough money to buy an 80-acre farm near his boyhood home in
Leslie. Irene Jackson followed a brother and several friends to California
during World War II. She found work as an electrician and riveter at an
airplane plant in Fullerton but returned to Madison County upon her
fiancé's military discharge after the war. Another group of Ozarkers in
California illustrates the snowball effect often found in migratory labor
channels. In the summer of 1934, three young men from Carroll County

ventured to California and returned the following autumn bragging about their earnings in the distant fields. A mass exodus from their community followed. The next summer found a migrant settlement in Greenfield, California, made up of about 200 former Carroll County residents.[7]

The farms and factories of Michigan also attracted Ozark labor. As a teenager during the depression, Louie Clark followed siblings and neighbors to the Michigan countryside, where wages doubled those paid by Cleburne County lumber mills. Again, Clark and many others became migrant laborers only as a last resort. Recalling the situation in his community, Clark observed, "Anytime that you needed a little money, take off up to Michigan for two or three months. . . . And when times got rough . . . I'd take the family to Michigan."[8]

Perhaps most popular of all the Ozark migratory destinations was the Pacific Northwest. Thousands of Ozark families traveled to the vast apple orchards and hop vineyards of Washington either to supplement their meager farming incomes with a few months' work or to settle down and begin life anew. The Ozark link with central Washington extends back almost a century. In 1904 a young Izard County family, David and Arrie Billingsley, migrated to Ephrata and soon homesteaded land nearby in Moses Coulee. They were among the earliest of a trickle of settlers from northern Arkansas. Ozarkers in Washington kept in touch with relatives back in Arkansas, and when the depression threatened livelihoods, the migratory treks began. When the pioneer migrants initiated the trail in the 1920s and 1930s, the trip to the Northwest often took as long as ten days, with nights spent not in roadside motels but simply on the side of the road. Sam Faubus and his brother-in-law logged in the forests near Wenatchee in the 1920s and returned during the depression. Sam's son Orval piled brush for logging crews near Omak in the Okanogan River valley and labored in the apple orchards of the Columbia River valley. By 1938 the Wenatchee area contained so many Arkies that the first annual "Arkansas Picnic" attracted almost 200 visitors.[9]

Migrant movement to Washington, especially from the eastern Ozarks, peaked in the 1950s. Constricting cotton allotments meant not only fewer acres for farmers but also fewer opportunities for young Ozarkers to find local cotton-picking jobs. Road improvements and the proliferation of automobiles after World War II eventually reduced the one-way journey to the Northwest to three days or less. Furthermore, the wages for orchard work far exceeded any available in the Ozarks and often provided a migrant family with a better income than could be gained from a year of farming. In 1952 one citizen of Lacrosse, a small Izard County community almost totally abandoned by outmigration, observed: "With so many people talking of going to Washington there is not going to be many people left here."[10] A Marion County chronicler reported an "almost mass exodus of some communities to the Yakima Valley."[11]

The 1952 annual report of Izard County's extension agent described the phenomenon of migratory labor to Washington. Migrating families began leaving their homes in early spring, most headed for the Northwest. Because most did not return until autumn, "from four to six months of the year almost one-third of the county's families [were] away." Furthermore, "one of the characteristics of this migration [was] that different communities [were] affected in different years." The agent noted that a few years earlier the community of Gid "was practically a ghost," whereas in 1952 most Giddites had returned and the most abandoned community was Finley's Creek, from which "so many people moved West that the store-keeper had to close."[12] Almost a decade later, a similar report observed that most farm families in neighboring Stone County resided on their Ozark farms only during the winter months.[13]

Landowning families rarely migrated to Washington year after year, but usually did so only in times of particular financial hardship or during drought years. Many Ozark families—generally young, landless families—made the trek to Washington an annual event, thus providing the backbone of Ozark migrant labor in the northwestern orchards. One such family was Doyle and Leola Webb and their three sons. Between 1952 and 1960, the Webbs spent an entire year in Arkansas only one time. "We'd go out there and work, and we'd make enough money to get back home on and live on til time to go back, and we'd borrow money to go back on. Done that for years," recalls Doyle Webb. The Webbs would leave Mount Pleasant in late winter or early spring and typically return in early November. In the beginning they enrolled their boys in Washington schools, but in later years their children stayed with grandparents in Arkansas except during the summer months. Like Ozark cotton pickers in eastern Arkansas, the Webbs established friendly relationships with employers. They spent their last six seasons in Washington in the orchards of the Davey brothers at Orondo, a small town up the Columbia River from Wenatchee. "We got to know them and worked for them and lived in their house for the rest of the time. They was people about our age and had kids the same age as our kids. We just had a lot in common." Orchard owners such as the Davey brothers would generally pay resident migrants, those living on their farms, a dollar an hour during the pre-harvest season in spring and summer for pruning, watering, and odd

186   ENDINGS AND TRADITIONS

jobs. Ozark workers looked forward to the fall harvest, when employers paid apple pickers 16 to 18 cents per box. Doyle Webb remembers his family trying to earn "a hundred dollars a day during harvest time," which lasted about six weeks. After expenses, the Webbs typically returned home with less than a thousand dollars to carry them over until the cycle was repeated the next spring.[14]

While the precipitous decline in Ozark population after World War II suggests that most migrant laborers eventually stayed in Washington, California, and other destinations, many refused to sever their physical ties with the Arkansas hill country. For many Ozarkers, a sense of place and the devotion to home outweighed the possible financial security offered by permanent residence elsewhere. Perhaps most of the migrants who stayed in the Ozarks echoed the sentiments of Doyle Webb: "That [Washington] would have been alright if I hadn't knowed this place was back here. I liked out there alright. But home is home."[15] In his study of depression-era white migrants in California, historian Walter J. Stein argues that the Okies and Arkies were simply reenacting a drama of geographical mobility that had been a popular practice among southern farm families for over a century. According to Stein, the journey from Oklahoma to California in 1935 paralleled the movement of an Alabama family to Oklahoma a quarter-century earlier. The migrants were not "static, rural peasantry, anchored to the same lands that their fathers and grandfathers had tilled for generations; they were representative farmers, croppers, tenants, and farm workers whose collective pasts included movement every ten or twenty years."[16]

It is hard to argue with that estimation of farmers on the Oklahoma plains, but the Arkies present a more complex picture. By the depression, many Ozarkers enjoyed a century-old heritage of life in northern Arkansas. Many refused to leave their homes; others jumped at the first chance to escape and never looked back. The powerful sense of place kept many on rocky hillsides in the Ozarks, but others found the indescribable contentment of the hills and home a poor salve for lost opportunities and broader horizons outside the region. In retrospect outmigration assumes the fluidity and ease of inevitability, but within the decades of meandering was the tumult of uncertainty, even taciturnity. Ultimately, historical timing, economic status, and individual personality dictated the roll calls for leavers and stickers. Older, established farm families had more to lose—years of toil and sweat and fields of crops and animals—and, as a result, perhaps less to gain from picking up and moving or even migrating by the season. Their children owned no land and little of anything else; they often saw nothing but potential and possibility in faraway regions and cities. The region lost the better part of an entire generation to such a situation. Others whose worlds had been widened by service in war or by labor in distant plants and in fields and orchards returned to find the hills no longer comforting and protecting, but constricting and suffocating. For them the necessity of leaving was superseded by the desire to flee and find something easier, something better somewhere else.

Branches of all Ozark families eventually extended permanently to places outside the region. Kennard Billingsley watched four siblings move to Armona, California, before World War II. In 1954 he moved to another popular Ozark destination, Tulsa, Oklahoma, where he stayed for a dozen years before returning home. His brothers and sisters never returned and have since been buried in a California place where "half the town was from Ash Flat and around." By the 1950s, cities such as Kansas City, Wichita, Tulsa, Bakersfield, and Wenatchee contained large colonies of Ozarkers who kept in touch with their Arkansas relatives and friends through letters and in the columns of small, Ozark newspapers: "News of Arkies in and around Ponca City," "Home Folks in Wichita," and "Home Folks in Kansas City."[17] While one could make a strong case that most of these Ozark enclaves were the results of "forced" migrations, it is also quite probable that most of these outmigrants enjoyed more comfortable and secure, perhaps even more fulfilling, lives than would have been their inheritance in northern Arkansas.[18] For those whose sense of place and attachment to the land was not strong enough to keep them on an Ozark hillside in the most dire circumstances, even if for only months a year, the taxing and mundane chores of farm life, laced with nostalgic memories though they might have been, held little allure when faced with an alternative life of bimonthly paychecks, new automobiles, television, and paid vacations.

The process of permanent outmigration frequently mirrored that of migratory labor movement. As one Ozarker recalled: "They'd go out there for, say, several months and try to make enough to live on the next year. Then eventually a lot of them just stayed."[19] The same family and community networks were also evident. The story of the family of Adam and Grace Moser is indicative of the economic and social forces behind outmigration. Adam and Grace married in 1922, settled in their Izard County community of Possum Trot, and produced five daughters. While Grace was stricken with tuberculosis during the depression, three of her brothers made their way to southern California in the mid- and late 1930s. Adam Moser spent two decades as a sharecropper-handyman and frequently made and sold moonshine to earn cash; he never lifted his family above the poorest in the community. He was overwhelmed and thankful to find $5 in the mail from Grace's brother, Tom Hall, one Christmas during the darkest days of the depression. The following year Tom Hall, a young, single man who had found employment at a Pasadena factory, mailed his sister enough material to sew five dresses for her girls. Tom and his two brothers were by no means prosperous, but the move to California had certainly eased their plight.[20]

When Grace Moser died in 1942, Adam sold the meat from his smokehouse to a generous local merchant for $15, gathered up his five daughters, and headed for Pasadena with two brothers-in-law—eight people crammed in a 1939 Buick Club-Coupe on the road for four days. Once in California, Adam and his three youngest children settled in Pasadena, where the old sharecropper found work at Caltech. His two oldest daughters moved in with an uncle in South Los Angeles before finding work and moving out on their own. The Mosers made several visits back to Arkansas over the following decade until most traces of the community they had known disappeared in the 1950s. Eventually their relatives and friends also left Possum Trot, settling in Washington, California, and Oklahoma.[21]

Outmigration has connected Ozark families to innumerable cities and communities across the nation, mostly west of the Mississippi River. In many northern Arkansas families today place names such as Wenatchee, Yakima, and Independence are as common as Springdale, Harrison, and Mountain Home. Although the migratory trails leading out of the Ozarks closed more than three decades ago, the disparate Ozarkers scattered throughout the West have maintained a remarkable degree of contact with native communities and extended families and have reflected an attachment and loyalty to home that often defies assumptions about the atomistic nature of modern American society and community. In many cases this was probably a defensive reaction to the ridicule leveled on the Arkies for their accents and tattered clothes. The conscious maintenance of heritage manifests itself in various ways. Many Ozarkers, after spending their working years in Washington, California, or Kansas, return to their native region to spend their final years in a place familiar and comforting despite monumental change. Ozark newspapers print obituaries of the deceased who left the region half a century ago, people remembered by only a handful of locals. Ozark outmigrants often subscribe to these same hometown papers and request to be returned to their native communities for burial among ancestors and former neighbors. How long these ties will bind the Ozark region with its exiled and prodigal children remains to be seen. The bonds of family and friendship between the Ozarks and Wayne County, Tennessee, or Watauga County, North Carolina, or Jackson County, Alabama, were severed generations ago, and so shall the bonds of twentieth-century migration be forgotten in years to come. The child of an Ozarker in Oroville, California, is no more an Arkansan than his great-great-grandfather born to pioneers in Arkansas was a North Carolinian.

Twentieth-century outmigration from the Ozarks reached its peak exactly one century after the zenith of migration to the Arkansas region. The settlers of the 1850s searched for better opportunities and a new life, but one based on the traditional practices of farming and livestock raising. Theirs was the transplantation of inherited lifestyles in a strange land rendered less foreign by its physical similarities to Appalachia. The post–World War II exodus from the Ozarks represented a sharp break with the past; it was one element of a watershed in the region's history. Although some of the same push-and-pull factors influenced both migrations—pressures from overpopulation, agricultural change, and brighter prospects farther west—the migrants of the mid-twentieth century were refugees fleeing the final wave of destruction of a rural American region of small farms. They would not re-create their pasts in a distant location, not even in the appealing valleys of central Washington State. They did not even desire to re-create the land of abandoned farms, gullied hillsides, and scant prosperity from which they had escaped. Their futures, even if not their salvation, lay with the lot of other Americans in factories, department stores, filling stations, and steel and glass office buildings.

Perhaps the supreme irony of post–World War II Ozark history lies in the fact that the same economic and social forces that transformed agriculture and depleted the population of the northern Arkansas countryside, the same process that coaxed thousands into migratory labor and threatened farm families and farms alike, lay behind the development of a recent American phenomenon that has repopulated once-deserted Ozark valleys and hillsides and in so doing has begun to fundamentally alter Ozark society and culture. The widespread affluence created by World War II and its economic aftermath—the primary pull factor urging Ozarkers to leave their homes for city factories—and the growth of the culture of leisure had produced a new group of citizens by the late 1950s, middle-class and lower-middle-class Americans whose savings and automobile-induced mobility allowed them to retire. Teachers, military personnel, insurance salesmen, even farmers and factory workers looked to do something their parents and grandparents had not—retire in relative comfort away from the noise and crime of the city but within reach of modern conveniences. And like the wealthy had done in Florida since World War I, many of these new retirees began to search for spots that offered warmth, tranquillity, safety, and scenic beauty. The Ozarks offered midwestern retirees such a place, and, with the exodus of thousands of rural families and the transformation of agriculture, the region also presented the buyer plenty of land at cheap prices.

Midwestern retirees began to move to the Arkansas Ozarks after World War II. An advertisement explained why: "Arkansas offered a quieter, calmer life, free of urban pollution both socially and environmentally. A good standard of living in the state was affordable, another major reason for its early appeal."[22] In the 1940s and 1950s, the most popular destinations were the lake district created by the construction of dams in the upper White River valley and the old resort towns such as Eureka Springs, to which Illinoisians were attracted by Otto Ernest Rayburn's *Rayburn's Ozark Guide* and by Marge Lyon's bucolic descriptions in her *Chicago Tribune* column, "Marge of Sunrise Mountain Farm." By 1950, according to Rayburn, Lyon's "lucid lines [had] lured thousands of visitors to the hills, many of whom came to stay," and Eureka Springs had assumed the nickname "Little Chicago."[23]

The Arkansas Ozarks' first man-made reservoir, Norfork Lake, helped transform Mountain Home from a little farming town to a leading retirement destination. Beginning early in the century, Tom Shiras, a Kansas City native and editor of a successful weekly newspaper in Mountain Home, had clamored and campaigned for hydroelectric dams in the upper White River basin. In 1938 Shiras and fellow dam boosters saw their diligence pay off when northwestern Arkansas congressman Claude Fuller engineered the inclusion of three White River dam projects in a flood control bill passed by Congress. His successor, Clyde T. Ellis of Bentonville, who had defeated Fuller in 1938 by promising his constituents cheap hydroelectricity, envisioned a smaller Ozark version of the Tennessee Valley Authority; his dams would give rise to industry and commerce that would lift his region from the depths of depression.[24] Ellis carried through with his promise by securing hydroelectric facilities for Norfork Dam, but his industrial dream never materialized. The dams would bring prosperity to the region, though not always to its people.

The construction of Bull Shoals and Table Rock Dams would be delayed by war, but Ellis's pet project, Norfork Dam on the North Fork a few miles above its mouth at the White River, went up as scheduled. Work crews from the Northwest, fresh off their labors on Boulder and Grand Coulee Dams, commenced work in the spring of 1941. Constructed for the avowed purpose of flood control—despite the facts that the North Fork had little bearing on White River flooding farther downstream and that the areas most frequently affected by seasonal rises in the tributary were eventually inundated beneath the reservoir—Norfork Dam spurred the creation of three separate boomtowns and attracted desperate job seekers from around the Ozarks and from outside the state. By the time the structure was completed, the focus had clearly shifted from Ellis's promise of flood control and cheap electricity for every home to an emphasis on recreation potential and real estate profits. The 2,624-foot-long-by-242-foot-high dam created a lake covering 22,000 acres. From this basin, the Army Corps of Engineers removed some 400 landowning families from "what was once the most prosperous and thickly settled section in Baxter County." The buildings in the village of Henderson, the center of the county's cotton-producing river bottom section, were auctioned off, and twenty-six cemeteries were relocated to higher ground before the flood gates closed in June 1943.

Completed in 1944, the White River valley's first dam, in accordance with the demands of Ellis and influential Ozark businessmen, was also equipped with hydroelectric generators. The release of the cold water that powered the generators from the base of the dam also altered downstream ecology. Bass, crappie, bluegill, and other warm-water native fish could not survive the cold bursts. Consequently, the Army Corps of Engineers established a trout hatchery in the shadow of the dam in order to stock the lower North Fork with trout, a nonindigenous species unable to reproduce in an alien environment.[25]

The long-term effects on the human community in the Norfork Dam area in many ways paralleled the effects on the fish community. Retired and entrepreneurial midwesterners poured into the Mountain Home area, replacing those uprooted by the dam and the hundreds more whose agricultural pursuits failed to support them after World War II. The newcomers, like the brown and rainbow trout, were and are most often nonreproductive; they lived out their lives in an environment quite different from the one heritage had provided until they were replaced by another midwestern retiree at death. But they came to northern Arkansas in large numbers. By the 1950s, Mountain Home was the third most popular destination for retirees in Arkansas, and Baxter County boasted over 150 resorts, lodges, hotels, and restaurants. Clyde T. Ellis's successor, James W.

Trimble of Carroll County, saw the second of Ellis's dams completed in 1951. The mammoth, 256-foot-high Bull Shoals Dam blocked the White River not far above the mouth of the North Fork and created a lake about twice the size of Norfork extending into southern Missouri. Even more significant for the local population was the 1952 dedication of the dam that attracted President Harry S. Truman to the Arkansas Ozarks, the first active president to have visited the region. The new reservoir proved a further boon to the prospects of Mountain Home, located between the two lakes, and spawned two new resort-retirement communities of its own, Bull Shoals in Marion County and Lakeview in Baxter.[26]

The success of the twin lakes area probably influenced another postwar Ozark development, the planned retirement community. In the past four decades, thousands of retirees have settled in northern Arkansas, and most have done so in communities specifically designed to satisfy their needs and desires. The development of retirement communities in many ways mirrored that of the early twentieth-century resorts. They were generally located in previously rural farming areas of the Ozarks using outside capital and influence. The residents attracted to them by low taxes, low crime rates, and generally mild seasonal weather came overwhelmingly from outside the region and most often from midwestern states north of Arkansas. The profits from land sales were usually funneled to people and places outside the Ozarks. Nevertheless, the new retirement communities would provide some benefits to Ozarkers in neighboring communities and towns. Unlike the early resorts, whose summer visitors stayed in lodges or cheap bungalows, the retirement communities demanded well-constructed permanent homes for their residents. This provided years of great demand and boomlike conditions for local carpenters and construction crews. Merchants in outlying towns benefited from newcomers' patronage, at least until the new communities reached sufficient size to support their own businesses. And the revenues of local schools and county governments increased as a result of growing property tax coffers.

The father of the planned retirement community was John A. Cooper Sr., scion of a wealthy family in the rich Mississippi alluvial plain cotton lands of eastern Arkansas. After earning a law degree from Cumberland University in Lebanon, Tennessee, Cooper practiced law in West Memphis for a decade while developing a diversified range of business interests in eastern Arkansas, including banking, sawmills, machinery, heavy construction, and farming. By his thirtieth birthday in 1936, Cooper had become one of the largest cotton producers and ginners in the delta region of Arkansas. Soon afterward he made his first foray into the real estate and housing market with his development of Avondale Gardens, a West Memphis housing project, but the Ozarks would be the site of his most innovative and significant developments.[27]

Having visited Hardy and the Spring River area with his family as a teenager—the Coopers were just one of many eastern Arkansas families to visit the resort town in the era—John A. Cooper Sr. purchased a summer home and 440 acres on the South Fork of the Spring River near Hardy in 1946 from fellow West Memphian Frank Graham. When his acquisition sparked an interest among friends in the Memphis–West Memphis business community, the opportunistic Cooper began buying abandoned farms and steep, forested lands in the vicinity of his summer home. By 1950 he owned 2,400 acres in a remote section of Sharp County that was rapidly being abandoned by outmigration. In 1954, with the urging of promoter Ralph Johnson, a native of northeastern Arkansas who had moved to Hardy from California in the early 1950s, and bolstered by research data that indicated a retirement rate of more than 7,000 each day within a 500-mile radius of north central Arkansas, Cooper organized the Cherokee Village Development Company (CVDC). Although it was "regarded as the nation's first modern day master planned retirement community," the CVDC was formed in a spirit of confident irresolution.[28] Johnson probably had more faith in the potential of basing the development's future on retirement than did Cooper in the early years, and Cherokee Village's proximity to Hardy tended to shroud the infant community in a resort atmosphere. Johnson's confidence was not shared by residents of the area. Recalls Audrey Thompson, who lived in Hardy in the mid-1950s: "We all thought they [Cooper and Johnson] were crazy. There was absolutely no doubt about all the native people that there was two crazy people out there." Local farmers and townspeople, beset with agricultural transformation and struggling to survive in one of the poorest sections of an impoverished state, could be forgiven for disbelieving that prosperous folks with good homes in Memphis or up north would give it all up to settle hundreds of miles away on a rocky glade teaming with ticks, chiggers, and copperheads.[29]

Cooper's vision began to take shape in the late 1950s and early 1960s, a time when "millions of middle class Americans had sufficient income to purchase additional property and retire in comfort." He developed the concept of "gradual retirement" to appeal to a base of retirees becoming increasingly younger and one whose pensions, savings, and Social Security payments allowed them to enjoy active lives. Under this concept, the

CVDC provided hotel and rental house lodging for weekend visitors who took advantage of Cherokee Village's golf course, tennis courts, lakes, riding stables, and restaurants. Many of these middle-aged visitors purchased lots before retirement and used Cherokee Village as more of a resort until permanently relocating to their new home. By 1962 the CVDC had sold almost 6,000 homesites, and Cherokee Village already contained some 400 homes, paved roads, a water system, and a hobby and craft center in addition to the recreational facilities. In the early 1960s Cherokee Village was an oasis of prosperity plunked down in a depressed area. Perhaps the most surreal example of this strange collision of cultures was recorded without a hint of any recognition of irony in the 1963 annual report of the Sharp County extension agent. Amid his frenzied efforts to bring agricultural salvation to local farmers through cattle, cucumbers, grapes, okra, watermelons, dairy, or anything else that could stave off failure and outmigration for one more year, the agent found himself one morning discussing lawn maintenance with sixty retirees at the Cherokee Village Country Club.[30]

The success of Cherokee Village inspired a rash of similar developments in the northeastern Arkansas Ozarks. In 1957 Cooper's former partner, Ralph Johnson, founded two retirement communities near Cherokee Village. Ozark Acres, established on 5,000 acres five miles east of Hardy, enjoyed the financial and moral support of many local residents, and Hidden Valley, located on a 1,000-acre tract three miles south of Hardy, continued the Cherokee Village practice of luring retirees from outside the region. Three years later, Johnson organized yet another new community, Woodland Hills, north of Hardy. This effort proved less successful than previous community projects.[31]

In Izard County a similar development took shape in the 1960s. In the early 1960s Bill Pratt, a Little Rock businessman, and his brother Dick, a Newport farmer and businessman, began buying abandoned land in a sparsely settled and wooded section of Izard County north of Franklin. In 1963 they established the Horseshoe Bend Development Company (HBDC) about one mile north of a sharp bend in the Strawberry River and began selling lots.[32] A close look at the early boom days of Horseshoe Bend provides valuable insights into several aspects of retirement communities: marketing methods, retiree characteristics, and relations with local communities and native residents.

The successful development of Horseshoe Bend, like all other planned retirement communities, was fueled by intensive marketing. By 1967 the HBDC employed forty-six full-time salesmen and recruiters, about evenly split between locals and outsiders, and additional workers in the summer months. The HBDC mailed brochures and advertised in newspapers across the Midwest. Recruiters brought groups of visitors to the community on chartered buses or in the company-owned small jet by providing free transportation and lodging for a weekend, a free vacation in the Ozarks. Once in Horseshoe Bend, visitors were chaperoned by a salesman whose duty was to prevent his guests from leaving town before purchasing a lot. In 1967 Horseshoe Bend attracted 60,000 visitors in this manner. Lot buyers had several options. If not yet retired, they could build a house and rent it out or simply make periodic visits until retirement. Depending on their financial security, retiring couples could choose to build a house or move into a mobile home park.[33]

Gradual retirement frequently assumed a different form in Horseshoe Bend. Instead of vacationing in the Ozarks for several years before retirement, a significant number of people settled permanently while in their fifties and sixties and continued to work for several years once in northern Arkansas. Wilma and Guy Eubanks, retired Iowa farmers who relocated to Horseshoe Bend in 1965, opened a sandwich and ice cream shop and later a craft and hobby shop in their new hometown. Carl Carlson moved with his wife Edith from Illinois to Horseshoe Bend in 1964; a retired accountant and businessman, Carlson joined the sales staff of the HBDC and worked part-time at the local branch of the Bank of Franklin. Dozens of residents assumed semiretirement status by going to work for the HBDC. Their connections and their knowledge of the targeted clientele were instrumental in the early growth of Horseshoe Bend and communities like it.[34]

An analysis of residents' originations and previous occupations reinforces Cooper's and the Pratts' vision of the Ozarks as a haven for middleclass midwesterners. Perusal of the short biographies found in a year's worth of issues of the *Horseshoe Progress* finds among the village's residents a former decorator, a bus driver, accountants, teachers, postal workers, secretaries, farmers, a barber, railroad workers, construction workers, and factory hands. In most cases wives had worked outside the home for a decade or more. Most of these working couples, almost 90 percent, hailed from somewhere outside of Arkansas. A list of ninety-three home builders in the late 1960s and early 1970s reveals Horseshoe Bend as a definite haven for midwesterners. Of these newcomers, 25 percent were natives of Illinois, and the five midwestern states of Illinois, Missouri, Iowa, Indiana, and Wisconsin accounted for half of all new home builders.[35]

Cherokee Village and Horseshoe Bend came along at a time when the surrounding farms were in the thralls of an agricultural revolution, and many farmers found employment in the new towns. Vera Tanner found work as a restaurant cook in Horseshoe Bend in the 1960s, and her husband Hugh followed her a few years later when he began painting houses in the booming town. Farmers Kennard Billingsley and Vernon Wells also went to work in the retirement community. A few native Ozarkers even grew prosperous from their associations with the retirement villages. Ruth Thompson became one of Horseshoe Bend's first and most successful salespersons in the early 1960s. When Audrey Thompson, at the time the superintendent of a local school district, realized his wife "was making three times as much money as I was," he joined her, and the two stayed there until 1975. "Horseshoe Bend was good to us. It allowed us to put a boy through medical school."[36]

The southern Ozarks' largest retirement community, Fairfield Bay, combined the recreational opportunities of a large reservoir with the town-building methods developed by John A. Cooper Sr. The construction on Greers Ferry Dam across the Little Red River in Cleburne County began in 1959 and was completed three years later. Outmigration had so depleted the rural population of the upper valley's two communities, Choctaw and Eglantine, that only thirty families were removed from the Van Buren County portion of the inundated basin. In October 1963, a month and a half before his ill-fated journey to Dallas, President John F. Kennedy visited the site of this concrete behemoth in an abandoned hollow to dedicate the dam and officially launch the economic revitalization of a depressed area. Greers Ferry Lake, at 31,500 acres the second largest of the Arkansas Ozark reservoirs, rejuvenated Heber Springs as Norfork Lake had Mountain Home two decades earlier and produced immediate profits for realtors and contractors. Louie Clark, a Cleburne County native who had moved to Dallas in the early 1950s, brought his experience as a carpenter back home on the eve of the dam's completion and found work on numerous house-building crews. The demand for resort and retirement housing escalated so quickly in the following decade that Clark was able to establish his own contracting business, which he ran until his retirement in the 1980s.[37]

The new lake also attracted community developers. In 1963 Herbert L. Thomas Sr., president of the First Pyramid Life Insurance Company in Little Rock, began development of Eden Isle, a resort and retirement community near Heber Springs on the southern shore of the lake. That same year George Jacobus, a Fort Smith builder of housing additions, dispatched Clinton Owen to find a suitable location for a retirement community in the southern Ozarks. A native of western Arkansas, Owen was nonetheless familiar with the Greers Ferry area and soon purchased 4,300 acres for Jacobus on the north side of the lake in Van Buren County. In 1966 the newly formed Fairfield Communities, Inc., began construction on a marina and roads, and lots were surveyed and placed on the market. Like Cherokee Village and Horseshoe Bend, Fairfield Bay and its Fairfield Communities Land Company built golf courses, tennis courts, and other recreational facilities targeting midwestern retirees. By the mid-1970s Iowans made up the single largest contingent of settlers in the infant community. By the early 1990s more than 16,000 lots had been sold in Fairfield Bay, and, with over 2,000 residents, the community was the second largest in rural Van Buren County.[38]

By far the most successful of the retirement communities, however, was Bella Vista Village. In 1962, during the heyday of the Cherokee Village Development Company, John A. Cooper Sr. ventured into northwestern Arkansas looking for a new community site. In the final months of the year, he began purchasing land through trustees (in order to prevent a sudden escalation in property values) on the northern border of the old resort town of Bella Vista. By the end of 1963, Cooper's CVDC had spent more than $1 million on about 7,000 acres, and in January 1964, Cooper purchased Bella Vista, including 1,100 acres and physical assets, for $363,000. By the time the now media-savvy Cooper announced his plans for building a new retirement community, Bella Vista Village, at a 1965 press conference, the CVDC held title to almost 14,000 acres in northern Benton County. Cooper used a decade of experience and the booming economy of rapidly growing northwestern Arkansas to launch his largest Ozark effort. He hired a landscape architect, a golf-course designer, and an urban environmental planner; he also commissioned respected Arkansas architect and former student of Frank Lloyd Wright E. Fay Jones to develop an architectural style that blended with the area's rugged natural environment. Cooper hired popular *Arkansas Gazette* columnist Ernie Deane as director of information for the new village. In the first year and a half, more than 2,500 people bought property in Bella Vista Village, and the first permanent residents moved into the community in January 1966.[39]

Its location near the northwestern Arkansas corridor of prosperity has catapulted Bella Vista Village to greater success than the other Ozark retirement villages. By 1990, some 37,000 homesites had been sold in the community, and Bella Vista Village boasted seven different golf courses and more than 4,500 homes. The population surpassed 10,000 in the early 1990s, more than twice the number of inhabitants of any other Ozark retirement community. As historian Gilbert C. Fite explains, much of this success has to be based on location. Northwestern Arkansas offers better and closer medical facilities than do the more isolated areas of other communities. Furthermore, an abundance of jobs attracts younger families and retirement-age persons wanting to find part-time work. Bella Vista has also brought more prosperity to a generally prosperous area. A 1983 study of the community revealed that Bella Vista Village residents generated $43 million annually in retail sales in northwestern Arkansas and supplied banks with $73 million in deposits. Four years later, a second study found that Bella Vista Village contributed almost half of all tax money used in the Bentonville school district, even though the school-age population of the community was less than 500.[40]

Today thousands of retirees live in the Arkansas Ozarks. They have come in such large numbers over the past three decades that retirees now dominate the populations of some counties. In others, midwestern retirees are rarely found. Their effects on the surrounding native communities are in many ways unmeasurable but nevertheless evident. In recent years, a growing trend among retirees has been to settle on old farmsteads or in isolated backroad houses away from towns and villages. Any traveler admiring the quaint houses and simple living of rural Ozarkers would probably stand amazed at the number of these picturesque abodes that are actually inhabited by retired factory workers from Indiana or teachers from Wisconsin. Certainly the retirement communities have never built walls around their towns. The very nature of these communities and the solidarity and homogeneity of their residents prevent assimilation into local cultures and promote isolation and separatism, but retirees do have contact with people in surrounding communities. Some seek county and local office, and others serve on school boards or as substitute teachers. As might be expected, many midwestern retirees confront their native Arkansas neighbors with a condescending attitude based on stereotypical images. Most often the rural Ozarker returns the favor with grumbles and moans about "damn Yankees" and "furriners." Such animosity has become increasingly subdued in recent years because a generation and more has erased the novelty of interaction for natives and newcomers. Furthermore, a recent trend has brought more and more children and grandchildren of retirees to the Ozarks as permanent settlers, which has partially eroded the generation gap inherent in retiree-native relationships.[41] Nevertheless, working relationships between Ozarkers and inmigrants on school boards and in courthouses frequently require periods of adaptation and understanding. Midwestern retirees now occupy a permanent position in the Arkansas Ozarks, and as more and more filter into the backcountry away from the planned retirement communities, their influence will be felt even in the most remote rural communities, the communities that have suffered the most from outmigration and agricultural transformation in the years since World War II.

A less welcomed group of postwar inmigrants was the most recent wave of back-to-the-landers in the late 1960s and 1970s. This group could be divided into three rough classifications: young counterculture proponents (hippies), urban escapists, and disenchanted young people drawn to the region by its image as a haven of traditional, rural life and craftsmanship. Eureka Springs became the most popular Arkansas destination for back-to-the-landers in the early 1970s; the folk culture movement in Mountain View also attracted many to Stone County. Like their urban predecessors in the century's first decade and in the depression, many bought isolated mountain land with no access to roads, water, or electricity. The vast majority stayed only a short time before being driven back to civilization by snakes, chiggers, heat, cold, and starvation. Those who survived often did so by becoming craftspeople or by assimilating into local life with more mundane occupations. But all back-to-the-landers soon discovered what Ozarkers had known all along: "It's nice to live in a pretty place, but there's no time to enjoy it when you're scrabbling for an existence."[42]

We have witnessed the outmigration and migratory labor activities of thousands of Ozarkers and the inmigration of thousands of midwesterners in the last half-century. Postwar economic and social trends have produced prosperous enclaves such as Bella Vista Village and Cherokee Village in the Arkansas Ozarks; those same forces have practically obliterated the traditional rural community. Since the white settling of the region, individuals and their families, despite the agricultural and cultural similarities throughout the Ozarks, have identified themselves as members of a specific community and not, as some scholars argue, as Ozarkers. Poor transportation and communication facilities and the traditional bonds of family and neighbors influenced rural families to rarely look beyond the confines of familiar surroundings.

Rural communities have traditionally taken different forms. Most communities revolved around a village or crossroads hamlet. In all but the most mountainous areas, a village or crossroads hamlet existed every five miles or so. Geographical forces sometimes dictated the formation of communities. For instance, families living in an isolated cove or in a river bottom accessible only by water formed communities set off by nature. Other communities revolved around a church or a mine. Although community populations ranged from less than 50 to more than 500, their boundaries were known by their inhabitants, and families knew the community to which they belonged. The first communities to suffer the negative effects of modernization were river towns bypassed by the railroad at the turn of the century; however, since World War II, the communities experiencing decline or extinction have been those bypassed by state and national highways. Highway construction from one trading center or county seat to another, which began on a substantial scale in the Ozarks in the 1920s, often dictated the prospects of small communities in between. Dozens of obscure communities such as Prim, Denver, Center, and Landis suffered from isolation while popular thoroughfares sustained life and limited business in other equally obscure places: Brockwell, Hindsville, Drasco, and Bee Branch. The state's construction of a highway connecting Melbourne and Batesville in the 1920s bypassed the busy little village of Lacrosse. Once a thriving trade and education center, Lacrosse soon contained only one general store–post office, which closed its doors in 1987.

Widespread use of the automobile after World War II, the proliferation of chain stores, and outmigration spelled doom for the most recognized victim of rural modernization, the country store. Until recent decades, the crossroads general store and village shop were as integral a part of the American rural community as the land itself. Jeff Matthews, in the general mercantile business in Imboden for almost seventy years, remembers carrying "just about everything you can think of. From a sewing needle to a bush hog and a road wagon." In addition to supplying farmers with seed, fertilizer, and other necessities, general stores also could provide their customers with cash for chickens, eggs, nuts, berries, and furs. Matthews attributes the decline of stores such as his to good roads and Wal-Mart. After local highways were paved in the 1950s and 1960s, many customers chose to drive twenty or thirty minutes to Pocahontas or Walnut Ridge. The expansion of Wal-Mart stores into small towns across the region in the 1970s provided a final blow for most general stores.[43]

Matthews's business waned despite the federal highway running through town. General stores located in communities on unimproved roads or on less-traveled highways suffered even more from rural modernization. Outmigration reduced the number of regular customers, and the transition of agricultural practices altered seasonal demands for seed and supplies. And, like rural families around Imboden, Ozarkers in more

Photograph by J. Laurence Charlton of a country store with men sitting on the porch, Boone County, 1942. Courtesy of the J. Laurence Charlton Collection, group 7a, number 17, Special Collections Division, University of Arkansas Libraries, Fayetteville.

remote areas began to travel improved county roads and highways to take advantage of cheaper prices and larger selections at department stores and later at Wal-Marts and grocery stores. Goldie Benedict, who ran country stores near the Madison County community of Forum for more than a quarter-century, recalls that by the mid-1970s, "people were going to town [Huntsville] to buy their groceries, and come back and buy their gas on credit from me." She closed the Forum store in 1976.[44] In the 1980s alone, a half-dozen rural general stores closed their doors in Izard County, all of them for generations centers of farming communities.

A modern phenomenon has been the survival of small villages and rural communities near larger trading centers. Communities within a thirty-mile radius of towns such as Harrison, Conway, Fayetteville, and Batesville have maintained populations but not always businesses. Families in these communities often choose to live in the peace of the countryside and commute to work each day. Businesses have generally suffered in such communities, however, because commuters shop in their towns of employment.

Another twentieth-century casualty of rural modernization has been the country church. Entirely dependent on a healthy population of rural families in the surrounding area, the rural Ozark church suffered from outmigration and the introduction of automobiles. By World War II, many families with automobiles had left their local churches and had begun driving to nearby towns in order to join larger congregations. Most absent members, however, had simply left their farms and homes. Whatever the cause of their departure, rural families left rural churches in great numbers. When too many farms in a community became covered by weeds and bushes, the church house was almost certain to soon be left to the elements as well. In the ten years before 1936, the number of rural churches in Arkansas declined by more than 30 percent.[45] Outmigration after World War II further darkened the prospects of rural churches. Isolated churches that consisted only of generations of the same families held little hope of survival in the quarter-century of mass exodus after 1940.

Retiree inmigration after 1950 did not revive shrinking rural congregations. Instead, the waves of newcomers entering the hills brought with them the denominations of the Great Lakes states and of the Great Plains—Roman Catholicism, Lutheranism, Episcopalianism, and others foreign to the rural Ozarks. Before the growth of retirement villages in northern Arkansas, the Ozark region consisted almost entirely of evangelical Protestant churches. In 1936, Baptists, Methodists, Cumberland Presbyterians, and members of the Disciples of Christ or Churches of Christ constituted over 95 percent of all Ozark religious adherents recorded by the Census Bureau.[46] Members of Holiness and Pentecostal congregations had become a significant minority by this time, but among these varied and disorganized groups, only the Assemblies of God reported membership statistics. The region contained only 723 Roman Catholics in 1936, and Washington County accounted for almost 75 percent of these. Ten counties reported no Catholics among their churchgoers. The near absence of Catholics, Episcopalians, Lutherans, and regular Presbyterians in the Arkansas Ozarks in the early twentieth century reflected several important characteristics of the region. Both the Presbyterian and Episcopal churches clung to traditions of trained clergy. Consequently, both typically found their way into backward regions only after sufficiently large communities had been established, and the interior Ozark region contained no town with 2,000 inhabitants in 1910. Furthermore, most Ozark settlers who had migrated from Appalachia or middle Tennessee brought their religions with them, and those denominations did not include Episcopalianism, Lutheranism, or Catholicism.[47]

The growing religious diversity discovered by Glenmary Research in 1971 reflected the steady infiltration of outsiders. By 1971, more than 3,000 Roman Catholics resided in nine of the fifteen Ozark counties. Missouri Synod Lutherans also began to multiply, especially in Baxter County.[48]

Many natives of the Arkansas Ozarks witnessed the introduction of "foreign" denominations for the first time in the 1950s, 1960s, and 1970s. While exposure to new religious groups did occur, native Ozarkers maintained their old beliefs; the new, Yankee religions seldom, if ever, ventured beyond the city limits of Mountain Home, Cherokee Village, Fairfield Bay, and other thriving retirement centers.

Religious pluralism in the region expanded along with the population. By 1990 the number of adherents of nonevangelical denominations—Roman Catholicism, Lutheranism, and Episcopalianism—had surpassed 10,000, constituting 12 percent of all religious adherents in the Ozarks. Interestingly, the list of new denominations that began to appear after 1970 reflects the background of a large majority of retirees. Unlike southern Florida and other large retirement havens, the Ozarks attracted no Jews, Eastern Orthodox Christians, or other members of religious groups concentrated primarily in the Northeast. Northern retirees destined for the Ozark highlands came almost exclusively from the Midwest: Ohio, Indiana, Michigan, Illinois, Wisconsin, Iowa, Minnesota, and Missouri. Consequently, the denominations found in these states worked their way southward in moving vans and suitcases.[49]

Single families that migrate for business or career purposes, upon discovering that there are no local extensions of their native habits in their new home, often become thoroughly assimilated into the local way of life and its popular religious groups. But the northern retirees who overran the hills and mountains of the Ozarks in the 1960s, 1970s, and 1980s carefully established their own enclaves within a culturally and denominationally foreign region. They maintained their traditional customs and patterns of living, chief among them religion, and they found assimilation an unnecessary pain. Likewise, their new neighbors watched the growing enclaves curiously, and sometimes with trepidation or even resentment. These Ozark natives rigidly adhered to the faith of their forebears, perhaps even more deliberately in the face of strange new denominations.[50]

It is tempting to write off the influence the new settlers had on the traditional lives of Ozark people, since the physical manifestations of the influence, such as Lutheran churches, Formica tables, and Herb Alpert records, existed only in retiree population centers. But, as we have seen, retirement communities have not been completely isolated and devoid of contact with the native Ozarks. The Ozark way of life has experienced significant alterations in areas with large inmigrant populations. In Baxter County, where one of every five Christians is a Roman Catholic, citi-

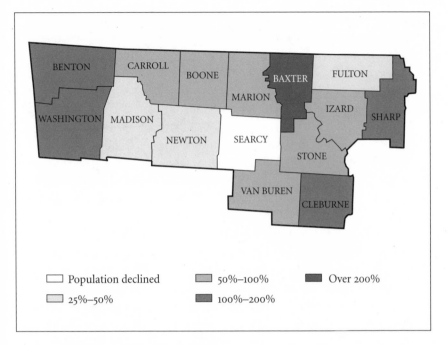

MAP 8.2. Population Change, 1960–1990

zens voted to overturn the local "dry law," which prohibited the sale of liquor. Though only three Arkansas Ozark counties were "wet" by the end of the twentieth century, other counties with large northern enclaves had only narrowly defeated similar proposals, and the visitor to the region will generally find bars and pubs only within the enclaves.

Perhaps most significant of all, the religious diversity found in certain communities in the Ozarks since the 1960s has produced important changes in the outlook of the young. Not only do professionals and retirees crop up on school boards and in parent-teacher associations, but many children of Ozark natives since 1965 have grown up with Catholic and Lutheran friends and have been exposed to a degree of religious diversity, no matter how slight, unknown to their parents and grandparents. And in a racially homogeneous region such as the Arkansas Ozarks, religion, not race, provides the young with their first tastes of multiculturalism.

The influx of midwestern retirees has also affected the Ozarks' political climate. By the late twentieth century, the Ozarks, and especially northwestern Arkansas, had become a Republican stronghold in a traditionally Democratic state. Since the late nineteenth century, areas within the region had cultivated thriving two-party systems rarely seen in most of Arkansas and the South. Bushwhacker-jayhawker feuds from the Civil War and Reconstruction eras translated into Democrat-Republican brawls for decades in remote, mountainous counties such as Newton, Searcy, and Madison. On the Springfield Plain, the post–Civil War arrival of large numbers of Lincoln Republicans posed a challenge to ruling Democratic cliques. Furthermore, the southern Ozarks was a hotbed of agrarian protest in the final two decades of the nineteenth century. The Brothers of Freedom, a farmer protest organization that eventually merged with the Agricultural Wheel, was founded by Ozone (Johnson County) farmer Isaac McCracken, and its leaders dominated the Wheel after the merger.

Despite the Democratic proclivities of the cotton counties, whose southern-style one-party politics were revealed in a Sharp County man's observation that he "saw [his] first Catholic in 1928 and [his] first Republican in 1952," the two-party system remained strong in the Ozark interior in the twentieth century. Between 1919 and 1959 five different Ozark counties, Newton, Searcy, Van Buren, Carroll, and Madison, elected at least one Republican to the Arkansas House of Representatives. In twenty-one general-assembly elections during that period, Searcy County sent a Republican to Little Rock eight times, including five consecutive sessions between 1945 and 1953, while Newton County elected a Republican representative seven times. In 1945 alone, four Ozark Republicans served in the Arkansas House. While Arkansas sent no post-Reconstruction Republicans to Congress until 1967, it was not uncommon for Republican candidates to garner more than 40 percent of the votes cast in the northwestern Third District. The arrival of thousands of retirees and younger inmigrants in the 1960s and 1970s, many of whom were midwestern Republicans, provided the swing vote in the century-old contest between native Democrats and their Republican nemeses. It is likely that the influx of newcomers proved the deciding factor in the election of Harrison's John Paul Hammerschmidt as Arkansas's first post-Reconstruction Republican congressman in 1966.[51] Thirty years after Hammerschmidt's election, Arkansas voters sent the state's first post-Reconstruction senator to Congress. Not surprisingly, Tim Hutchinson hailed from Benton County. By the turn of the twenty-first century, the combination of northern Republican inmigrants, traditional Ozark Republicans, and middle-class Christian conservatives made northwestern Arkansas a stronghold of Republicanism.

Although a strong two-party system was not universal in the Arkansas

Ozarks throughout most of the twentieth century, active local political life was common. Interest in political disputes frequently diverted interests and efforts away from other local institutions, such as schools. Schools and the underfunded education system also responded to the forces of rural modernization in the twentieth century. One-room schoolhouses, perhaps the most ubiquitous and revered institution in American lore, once dotted the rural landscape. Due to poor travel conditions created by treacherous terrain, one-room schools thrived in the Ozarks well into the depression and in the most remote areas of the region into the 1950s. In most rural Ozark communities, schools, grades 1 through 8, were in session for three to six months a year (generally two months in summer and three or four in the winter). Schools closed during spring planting and fall harvesting because children were needed in the fields. The schoolhouse was typically a local church house or community building made of crude logs or planks. Many teachers in small rural schools possessed only slightly more knowledge and education than their pupils. Passage of the state-administered teacher's certification examination qualified one to teach, regardless of educational background.

The pay and conditions for rural teachers rarely justified any attainment of higher education. Beulah Billingsley began teaching at a rural Izard County school in the early 1920s for $50 a month, and she did not obtain a high school diploma until 1929. Many teachers in one-room schools never completed high school. In 1931, after completing eight grades at a one-room Madison County school and one year of high school in Huntsville, Pauline Jackson passed the teacher's examination and at age seventeen went to work at the Henderson's Creek one-room school. She boarded with families in the community and earned $40 a month. During the depression, Van Buren County native Glenn Hackett took a job teaching the children in the isolated Cleburne County community of Wild Goose. Although he taught the children of only three families, Hackett made the twelve-mile round trip on foot every day to a rough-sawed plank building with log benches and a homemade teacher's desk. After his first year in the classroom, Hackett returned to Clinton to graduate from high school before resuming his duties at Wild Goose. At the time he left to serve in World War II, Hackett earned only $60 a month.[52]

Rural school consolidation eventually retired the one-room school in the Ozarks. A 1925 state law sparked an early round of consolidations that continued into the early years of the depression. The largest consolidation effort in the region took place on the eve of the depression, when a dozen separate one- and two-room schools were combined to form the Violet Hill school district in Izard County. In most counties rural eight-grade schools continued to be the norm until after World War II. In 1945 Van Buren County, with a population of just over 10,000, still maintained almost eighty school districts, most of them one-room schools. After Arkansas's Initiated Act No. 1 in 1948 required the discontinuation of all districts with fewer than 350 students, a vigorous consolidation campaign by the county board of education left Van Buren with only five districts in 1950, all of which survived until the turn of the century.[53] Despite the rapidity of consolidation in Van Buren County, in most areas the combination of school districts was a gradual, somewhat disorganized process.

The development of one Stone County district illustrates the process. In 1942 three rural Stone County schools, Finch, Rushing, and Fox, were consolidated to form a new Rural Special school district. Within six months, parents in the Pleasant View and Meadow Creek districts petitioned to have their small schools annexed by the Rural Special district. The new school provided nine grades instead of eight, with a converted hearse transporting children in grades 1 through 4 to Rushing and carrying the older students to the eventual site of the elementary and high schools at Fox. For four years, three teachers instructed all the students until a four-room building was completed in 1946; at the same time, a sixth one-room school, Skyland, was added to the Rural Special district. The following year brought the addition of the Turkey Creek school and the construction of a library stocked with books purchased by teachers and other local patrons. Three final one-room schools were added in 1948, Parma, Mount Vernon, and Sunnyland, as was a vocational agriculture department. It would be two more years before Rural Special students could enjoy the services of a lunchroom and a gymnasium.[54]

By the 1950s, rural school consolidation had made a high school education feasible for the vast majority of the region's children. This in turn presented an avenue to higher education for an increasing number of young Ozarkers. While the interior Ozark colleges had all closed their doors by the end of the depression, more and more of the region's youth found their way to Fayetteville, Jonesboro, Batesville, Conway, and Searcy to pursue college degrees; most of them never returned to the Ozarks, their college degrees serving as passports out of the poor region and into a more prosperous mainstream American life elsewhere. For generations Ozark education, and southern rural schools in general, had been designed to produce God-fearing, respectful, responsible, reading and writing young adults whose roles in life as hill farmers had been almost pre-ordained. There was little call for higher education, and, with the exception of the local doctor, most communities contained no college-educated resident. To most Ozarkers college was a distant dream, almost imaginary in its remoteness; only rarely would a local boy—and almost never a girl—enjoy both the spark of interest in education and the means to follow through with it. Invariably these young people, a select few, were swallowed up by college life and the outside world and seen back home only on special occasions, at weddings, funerals, and vacation visits. Although these prodigal scholars were usually welcomed and encouraged, Ozarkers in general maintained a significant degree of anti-intellectualism.

In many ways, the proliferation of high schools and the popularization of college attendance took place at an opportune time for young Ozarkers. Agricultural transformation rendered farming an increasingly precarious occupation after World War II, and manufacturing jobs remained in short supply—and in most Ozark areas completely absent—until the late 1960s. As one Ozark native recalls, high school graduates "didn't have any choice except to leave." Glenn Hackett returned to Van Buren County after World War II, only to find farming and country teaching insecure ways of making a living. Eventually he moved his young family to Fayetteville, where the GI Bill helped him earn a degree in agricultural education. Most joined the flood of outmigration to employment centers in Kansas, Washington State, California, and elsewhere, but Hackett and many others also headed to colleges and universities. Like their Ozark predecessors, they rarely resettled in their native region. Hackett was an exception to the rule—like Hackett, most exceptions were teachers—for he returned to his hometown of Shirley and eventually became superintendent of the local school district.[55]

Hackett was also somewhat of an exception by being a male teacher. In the early twentieth century women came to dominate the field of education, especially in the one-room schools of the Ozarks. In this region of small farmers and timber workers, teaching was often the only career or employment opportunity available to women. Pauline Jackson made this discovery early in life. After an unpleasant short term at a one-room Madison County school in the early 1930s, she quit only to find that "there wasn't anything else to do." Jackson passed the teacher's examination once again and eventually taught many years at schools in isolated Boston Mountain communities such as Spoke Plant and Muddy Gap. Pauline Jackson reflected a growing trend when she continued to teach even after she married Ernest Thacker in 1943 and had children.[56] Before World War II, teaching and other modes of employment had generally been reserved for young single women. Once married, women followed tradition and settled in as housewives, mothers, and farm laborers, an existence that almost always entailed more toil than any job off the farm. Developments during and after the World War II era began to chip away at the traditional roles of Ozark women.

Canning factories offered many young Ozark women their first off-farm jobs, even before World War II. As a teenager during the latter part of the depression, Irene Jackson Hunter went to work as a tomato peeler at a Madison County cannery. Eula Ferrel found seasonal employment at another Madison County cannery in the late 1930s and early 1940s after her twin sons reached school age. Ferrel, who had earlier passed her teacher's examination but found no local openings, peeled tomatoes and packed tomatoes and snap beans, and her husband drove the truck for the canning factory. It is likely that Hunter, Ferrel, and the thousands of other Ozark women who found employment in their native hills or in factories and offices far away found their new jobs both empowering for their income production and refreshing for their temporary or permanent relief from the drudgery of farm chores, as well as for the unusual opportunity for camaraderie with other women. Off-farm work became increasingly common for Ozark women during and after World War II. As a teenager, Zela Rhoads moved to St. Louis with her young husband, Guy, shortly after his medical discharge from the army in 1944. The young native of Fulton County found work in a carburetor factory and adapted well to city life. Though Zela "didn't want to come home when the war was over," Guy's desire "to hunt and fish some and be outside" brought the couple back to the Ozark countryside. Irene Hunter, who had worked in a California aircraft plant during the war, spent almost a decade as a farm wife until her husband's army disability pension and their meager farm livestock and crop sales failed to provide a living. In 1954 she went to work as the first female forestry technician in the Ozark National Forest. Her thirty-year career, first as a female trailblazer amid skeptical and sometimes malicious male coworkers, and finally as a revered veteran, would scarcely have been imaginable a generation earlier.[57]

Most women continued to find work in traditionally female-oriented jobs. The 1950s and 1960s brought a significant number of low-wage, unskilled industries to the decidedly nonindustrial region. Picking up where the canning factories had left off, poultry manufacturers employed hundreds of women and men for mundane, dirty tasks such as plucking, gutting, and skinning chickens. State legislation passed during the Faubus era made it easier for municipalities to institute bond issues and tax in-

creases for the purpose of constructing buildings for low-wage manufacturing firms. The most popular of these were shirt factories, which
sprang up in small towns throughout the region in the 1960s and 1970s:
Mountain View, Mountain Home, Marshall, Melbourne, Salem, and others. An observer at the opening of one of the region's first such plants, the
Mar-Bax Shirt Factory near Mountain Home, reported that "the money
the women earn is needed so desperately by people in the hills and valleys
that they are willing to do almost anything to accommodate the plant to
their simple lives." The people of Baxter and Marion Counties accom-
modated the shirt factory owners by voting a $535,000 bond issue and
raising taxes to cover the cost of the minuscule lease charged to the new
employer.[58] The substantial increase—more than 150 percent between
1956 and 1968—in manufacturing employment in the rural Ozark counties was in large part attributable to the proliferation of shirt factories
and other low-skilled, female-oriented industries. This growth occurred
simultaneously with the demise of row-crop agriculture and the decline
of male-dominated industries such as timber work and lumber milling,
which resulted in a growing reliance on female wage labor among rural
Ozark families.[59]

By the 1970s, shirt factories were perhaps the leading employers of unskilled women in the Arkansas Ozarks. Still other women followed even
more traditionally female activities such as cooking, sewing, and cleaning. Pauline Jackson Thacker went to work in the cafeteria of a local
school when her husband died in 1965. When Benson and Fleecy Fox sold
their Searcy County farm in 1961, they moved to Leslie, where she established a dress-making and sewing shop to support the family. After their
move from Lacrosse to Batesville in 1954, Lillie Mae Watkins supported
her family and disabled husband by cleaning houses and a nearby
church.[60]

The Watkinses' move to Batesville was part of a wholesale abandonment of one Ozark community; it also marked the end of one of the interior Ozarks' last African American communities. The limited racial diversity that had once existed in select areas of the fifteen-county region
became a memory in the 1950s and 1960s, a casualty of rural modernization and outmigration. The black population of the Ozarks was never
more than minuscule. In 1930, before the New Deal and the onset of outmigration, the fifteen-county region was home to fewer than 1,000
African Americans; only ninety-one black families worked the land, and
seventy-three of these resided in one of three counties: Izard, Van Buren,
and Washington. More than half the Ozark counties contained not a sin-

gle black farm family. The largest African American farming community was the one in which the Watkinses lived near Lacrosse in Izard County.[61]

Lillie Mae Watkins recalls the first serious outmigration from the Lacrosse community beginning in the 1930s. No one in the community owned a car, according to Watkins, making it impossible for black families to emulate their white neighbors and migrate in search of seasonal labor. Although half the black farmers in Izard County owned their land, none owned a farm substantial enough to survive agricultural modernization. The decline of cotton farming and the availability of jobs in towns and cities provided final incentives for outmigration. For generations small black farmers, just as their white neighbors, had depended on seasonal work picking cotton for extra income. Such jobs became increasingly scarce after the implementation of the New Deal allotment program. When the Watkins family moved to Batesville in 1954, they left only a handful of black families behind in Izard County. Within another decade the remaining black families would leave the land in Izard and other Ozark counties. By 1969 only three black farm families remained in the fifteen-county region. By the 1990s the Arkansas Ozark region, where whites accounted for about 99 percent of the population, was among the most racially homogeneous in the nation. Of the fewer than 2,000 persons of color in the fifteen-county region in 1990, more than 4 in 5 could be found in the university town of Fayetteville and in surrounding Washington County. Nine counties counted fewer than 10 nonwhite residents in 1990.[62]

The Ozark region, like Appalachia, continued to defy American conventional wisdom in the late twentieth century. It was one of the whitest regions in the country, yet in many areas one of the poorest. Even that observation, however, is an oversimplification. If the supreme irony of the Arkansas Ozarks' post–World War II years stems from the fact that the masses of outmigrants and inmigrants were reacting to the same modern economic and social forces, the chief paradox of the region is the continued existence of two Ozarks—the western sophisticate and the dowdy stepsister to the east. In the past half-century, the northwestern Arkansas corridor from Bella Vista to Fayetteville has become a prosperous and somewhat urbanized section in a rural region and a poor state. For the most part, this economic boom has not extended into the Ozark hinterland.

In 1966, the Ozarks Regional Commission (ORC) was created ostensibly for the purpose of rejuvenating the economy of the depressed region. The ORC never received the political and economic backing enjoyed by the more newsworthy Appalachian Regional Commission, and, although it funneled millions of dollars in grant money into its jurisdiction, it exercised very little influence in the Arkansas Ozarks. Originally composed of 125 counties in Missouri, Arkansas, and Oklahoma covering the Ozark and Ouachita plateaus and border counties, by 1974 the ORC's territory had been expanded to encompass all of five states: Arkansas, Missouri, Oklahoma, Kansas, and Louisiana. The vast expansion of territory resulted in an increasing shift of funds and projects to non-Ozark areas. Of the more than 250 grant projects undertaken between 1968 and 1974, only 20 provided financial assistance for economic development in the Arkansas Ozarks. One-quarter of these benefited the already booming area of northwestern Arkansas. Several consisted of small water and sewer improvements that ultimately had little impact on local employment opportunities. By the early 1970s Oklahoma projects, most of them outside the Ozark region, had come to dominate the attention of the ORC.[63]

The differences that existed between Bill Fulbright's Springfield Plain and Orval Faubus's interior Ozarks were still evident in the late twentieth century; in some ways they were more pronounced than ever before. Although agriculture had become increasingly homogeneous throughout northern Arkansas after World War II, the economic conditions of northwestern Arkansas and those of the bulk of the remainder of the region remained sharply divergent. By the mid-1980s, the *Forbes* magazine 400 list included three families from northwestern Arkansas. In addition, Washington and Benton Counties boasted two Fortune 500 manufacturing firms as well as the headquarters of the nation's largest retail chain and trucking company; all were located within a twenty-mile radius. These corporations and fortunes had their genesis in the Arkansas Ozarks amid the tumult of agricultural transformation and rural modernization. Unlike the corporations of Appalachia, they were not colonial in nature, but sprang from the fertile soil of the Springfield Plain and from the active, sometimes visionary minds of its residents.[64]

The emergence of the Springfield Plain as an economic oasis in the Ozarks began with the poultry industry. We have already witnessed the rise of Tyson Foods after World War II. It was the most successful of numerous manufacturing firms in the nation's center of poultry processing. By 1994, the Arkansas Ozark region contained thirty poultry processing plants owned by a dozen different corporations.[65]

The poultry industry and the rise of poultry farming indirectly and directly supported the development of northwestern Arkansas's other two giant corporations—Wal-Mart Stores and J. B. Hunt Transportation.

Wal-Mart, the Ozarks' most unusual, most successful corporation, has also exercised the greatest impact on business life in the region's and the nation's small towns and rural communities. This product of small-town America has, according to detractors, made great strides in the destruction of small-town vitality in the past three decades. The story of Wal-Mart is important for a complete understanding of Ozark modernization since midcentury. The founder of the retail behemoth, Sam Walton, like John Tyson, was not an Ozarker or an Arkansan but found his way to northwestern Arkansas in search of prosperity two decades later than Tyson. Born in Oklahoma and raised in central Missouri, Walton earned a degree in economics from the University of Missouri in 1940 and immediately took a job as a management trainee with the J. C. Penney Company. In the fall of 1945, after three years of war-industry labor and military service, he purchased a Ben Franklin variety store in Newport, a small farming town in the bottomlands of eastern Arkansas about thirty miles southeast of Batesville. Within five years, Walton built the small store into a regional leader in sales and profits. He was so successful, in fact, that the owner of his building in Newport, hoping to duplicate Walton's good fortune in his own venture, refused to renew the young businessman's lease.[66]

Unfazed by the unfortunate eviction, Walton turned his attention to northwestern Arkansas, an area near his wife's family in northeastern Oklahoma and a prime spot for quail hunting, Walton's lifelong passion. In 1950 Sam Walton purchased Harrison's Variety Store, which he rechristened Walton's 5 & 10, on the town square in Bentonville, a farmer's trading center of about 3,000 inhabitants in the middle of Benton County. Just a generation earlier, Bentonville had served as a center of fruit and truck production, but by midcentury the area's agriculturists were quickly being drawn into the poultry market. The Bentonville store, an affiliate in the Ben Franklin chain, was an immediate success, prompting Walton to open a store in Fayetteville two years later and a third in 1954 in Ruskin Heights, Missouri. By 1962 Walton and his brother, James "Bud" Walton, owned sixteen Ben Franklin stores in Arkansas, Missouri, and Kansas, including their first large variety store, Walton's Family Center, in St. Robert, Missouri.[67]

In July 1962, Walton opened his first Wal-Mart store in Rogers, Arkansas. The store itself was in no sense unique. The early 1960s were a boom time in the discount variety store industry; Walton's first Wal-Mart was built the same year that three other successful discount store chains emerged: Target, K-Mart, and Woolco. Sam Walton's contribution to the discount variety business was his geographical marketing strategy. Whereas the nation's other discount chains ignored or avoided small towns and rural trading centers, Walton anchored his company's future in these locations. (St. Robert, Missouri, home of Walton's Family Center, was a village of only 1,500 people in 1962.) When his rural strategy was rebuffed by discount franchisers Butler Brothers and Gibson, Walton had no choice but to strike out on his own. Two years after building the first Wal-Mart in Rogers, he located his second one at Harrison, an even smaller town deep within the Arkansas Ozarks and one that had practically been ignored by chain stores. By the end of 1969, when Walton began construction on a 72,000-square-foot headquarters complex in Bentonville, he had established eighteen Wal-Mart stores in Arkansas, Missouri, and Oklahoma. Only one, the North Little Rock store, was located in a town of more than 20,000 people, and more than half were found in the small Ozark towns of southern Missouri and northern Arkansas.[68]

By the late 1970s, nearly every Ozark town of 2,000 residents—and some with even fewer—was home to a Wal-Mart. The discount chain brought mixed blessings to the region. Wal-Mart stores, with their lower prices and greater variety of merchandise, hastened the demise of country stores located in rural communities within the regional orbit of one of Walton's stores. Because of improved roads, that orbit often extended for forty miles or more in sparsely settled areas. Wal-Mart stores also proved detrimental to the health of town-square businesses, especially hardware, shoe, clothing, and smaller variety stores. In recent years, Wal-Mart's expansion into the grocery market has threatened the survival of grocery stores, which only a generation or two ago had helped Wal-Mart run country stores out of business. Wal-Mart provides employment—398,000 employees nationwide in 1992—most of which is low-wage and unskilled. But, as detractors point out, in the best cases Wal-Mart's payrolls simply equal the number of jobs lost due to business closings resulting from the discount giant's arrival. Rural sociologist Gary Farley compares the "Wal-Martization of Rural America" to the expansion of railroads in the late nineteenth century. "Then . . . the town that got the railroad line prospered. The ones that didn't, died. As Wal-Mart selects a town, trade areas are redefined. Services, retail trade, and even industry is clustering in those towns."[69] In many cases, the replacement of lost jobs means replacing business owners and managers with teenage checkout girls and elderly greeters. Furthermore, corporate policy tends to distance Wal-Mart stores from their local communities by funneling money out of the region and by "discourag[ing] its store managers from civic involvement or from making significant contributions to local charities."[70]

Sam Walton's discount store empire has done much to transform the rural communities from which it sprouted. Northwestern Arkansas's other *Forbes* 400 entrepreneur, Johnnie Bryan Hunt, has had little effect on rural transformation in the region, but his fortune grew from the same foundation as did Walton's. Whereas much of Walton's early success on the Springfield Plain can be attributed in part to the infusion of cash brought about by the tremendous growth of the poultry industry and of poultry raising, J. B. Hunt owes his rise to the top of the American trucking industry completely to the northwestern Arkansas poultry industry. Hunt, the only native Ozarker of the three entrepreneurs, was born and raised in the other corner of the region on a Cleburne County farm. His parents were sharecroppers in Ozark cotton country, and his father was also a part-time timberman and lumber worker. Young J. B. first entered the latter line of work when, after completing the seventh grade, he went to work at his uncle's sawmill for $1.50 a day. After World War II, Hunt and his brothers began hauling surplus boards from the sawmill to sell in Illinois and Missouri, his first foray into the business that would ultimately make him a multimillionaire.[71]

After an abortive attempt in the cattle auction business in the late 1940s, Hunt moved to Little Rock and took a truck-driving job, which he kept for more than a decade. Inspired by his trucking visits to the poultry farms of northwestern Arkansas, in 1961 Hunt invented a machine for bagging rice hulls to be used as chicken litter, or the cover material for the floors of broiler houses, and founded the J. B. Hunt Company in Stuttgart, the center of the eastern Arkansas rice-growing region. From Stuttgart Hunt trucked his rice hulls to poultry farms across the state and especially to northwestern Arkansas. In 1969 he established his truck line at Bentonville, where Sam Walton had gone out on his own, and three years later moved his entire operation to Lowell, a rural Benton County community just north of Springdale. After the Federal Motor Carrier Act deregulated the trucking industry in 1980, Hunt was among the most successful at expanding his company on a national scale. By 1990 the J. B. Hunt Company, the nation's largest trucking firm, owned 4,700 tractors and 10,500 trailers.[72]

By the early 1990s, after expanding into urban and small-town markets around the country, Wal-Mart Stores, Inc., ranked in the top 10 American businesses in sales, net profits, and market value, and the Waltons stood as the richest family in the United States. In 1992 Wal-Mart recorded more than $55 billion in sales and almost $2 billion in net profits. Meanwhile, Tyson Foods, the nation's largest poultry producer with sales of over $4.1 billion in 1992, was the leader of a half-dozen large poultry processing firms headquartered in northwestern Arkansas. Hudson Foods in Rogers joined Tyson on the Fortune 500 list in the early 1990s, and Peterson Industries almost completely dominated economic life in the small Benton County town of Decatur.[73]

Nevertheless, the atmosphere of prosperity and potential in evidence in northwestern Arkansas was rare elsewhere in the Ozarks, especially in the sparsely settled hinterland. Only a few other Ozark towns and areas have enjoyed even a fraction of the economic success of Springdale, Fayetteville, and the other northwestern towns. In the southeastern corner of the region, Batesville has become an employment center for an area extending thirty miles or more in all directions. Industries in the Independence County seat range from low-wage poultry processors to Arkansas Eastman, a chemical manufacturer that has served as the centerpiece of Batesville's resurgence over the past quarter-century and an employer whose wages and benefits attract significant numbers of professionals and college graduates. Mountain Home has also developed a small but significant manufacturing base that balances out its image as a haven for midwestern retirees. Beginning with the arrival of Baxter Laboratories in the late 1960s, this tourist and recreation center has collected enough small industries to provide almost 3,000 manufacturing jobs, the third most in the fifteen-county region.

After almost 150 years, there continue to be great disparities between the fortunes of northwestern Arkansas and the rest of the Ozark region. While the Springfield Plain has always been the most prosperous area of the northern Arkansas hill country, its appearance as an oasis is perhaps more pronounced now than at any time before. In many respects, nevertheless, the Arkansas Ozarks is more homogeneous now than it was at midcentury. The forces of outmigration, migratory labor, agricultural transformation, rural modernization, and inmigration by retirees and other groups of non-Ozarkers have affected even the most remote Ozark communities. The modern Ozark region no longer relies on farming for its livelihood, and the limited manufacturing base frequently takes a backseat to the region's most popular industry, tourism. The modern Arkansas Ozarks bears little resemblance to the region before World War II. Forced isolation has been erased by automobiles, paved roads, television, and the Internet. Materially, Ozarkers' lives differ little from those of rural Americans in other regions. The national image of the region and its people has remained remarkably stagnant, however, in the face of tremendous change. The Ozark community has undergone a tremendous and modernizing transformation, but its reputation and representation have not kept pace. Instead, the region's image remains bogged in the nostalgia and occasional derision of pre–World War II romanticism.

From the Smokehouse to the Stage

HAROLD SHERMAN was nothing if not opportunistic. He was also incredibly industrious, surprisingly unambivalent, and often naive—a born romantic turned promoter, a rootless, curious fellow possessed of unbridled energy and inestimable confidence. As such, he represented well his ilk in the post–World War II Ozarks—the surreal Ozarks of craft shows and public jig dances, of theme parks and mountain music, of log cabin folks and storefront whittlers—the Ozarks, in other words, of popular imagination and national consciousness. Like most public purveyors of traditional cultures, or as Robert Cochran labels them, "heritage hustlers," Sherman was not an Ozarker, not an Arkansan, not even a southerner or a mountaineer. He was a midwesterner, not the kind who retreated to the hills to live out his final days on golf courses, at yard sales, and in the comfort of his A-frame, suburban house in rocky, rugged Arkansas, but a midwesterner by way of New York and Hollywood, a mover and shaker accustomed to making things happen—loud, successful things.

Born and raised in Traverse City, Michigan, Sherman married Martha Bain in 1920. Four years later the young couple left Marion, Indiana, the small town where Harold had begun his newspaper reporting career, and moved to New York City, where Sherman spent the Roaring Twenties and depression years as a freelance writer, novelist, and CBS radio commentator. In 1942, on his way to Chicago from Hollywood, where a brief sojourn had satisfied his screenwriting ambitions, Sherman took a friend's advice and made a scenic detour through northern Arkansas. The Sherman family's first encounter with an Ozarker, a friendly man who made several trips to the creek to fill his hat with water for the city folks' overheated car, left the now middle-aged Harold with a sudden feeling of "revulsion against the sham of civilization." Inspired by the hill man's hospitality, and perhaps equally so by the pitifully low land values of a region on the brink of rapid depopulation, Sherman immediately purchased a 120-acre farm with a house south of Mountain View in Stone County. After settling permanently in the Arkansas Ozarks five years later, he quickly made his presence known by heading up local efforts to obtain electricity and paved highways for his adopted county and region. Sherman would spend the last forty years of his life in the Ozarks, much of it engaged in promoting tourist enterprises and economic development in Stone County.[1]

Sherman's Ozark interests and activities embodied the ambiguity, irony, and often dishonest posturing of the Ozarks' most important post-Eisenhower industry, tourism, and the related business of image development. In the midst of the region's most sudden and dramatic transformation, amid an era of rural modernization, the Ozarks maintained the ambiguous image that had been crafted in the years before World War II. In spite of the exodus from farms and backcountry communities, the homogenization of agriculture, the growth of small-scale manufacturing, and the blossoming of retirement villages and wealthy indigenous corporations, the Ozarks and its inhabitants—its native residents, at least—remained in the minds of Cold War Americans isolated, independent, contemporary ancestors, America's "Yesterday Today." Only at a point in time when this image, now myth, had become even less applicable than ever before did it promise, or threaten, to bring economic salvation to a region whose dependence on outside aid was well established but whose plight had escaped the eyes and ears of the national warriors against poverty. One solution, it seemed, would be to embrace the anachronistic image and put it to work for the Ozarks. And there were plenty of people, natives as well as Sherman and his army of fellow invaders, willing to seize the opportunity.

The Arkansas Ozarks was a place without a history. The region has never had a serious historian. Vance Randolph and his folklore successors and Otto Ernest Rayburn and his cadre of travel writers have so dominated the region's perception that historians have maintained their distance, perhaps in the belief that any region whose life and people are this static lacks the transformations, dialectics, or basic struggles that form the backbone of social history. As we have seen, such an assumption is mistaken, even if understandable. The lack of historical treatment underscores a key feature of the Ozarks' place in the American consciousness. The Ozark region has been sacrificed at the altar of American nostalgia and uneasiness over the loss of a rural past and over the decidedly unprogressive and backward nature of that past. In many ways, the region has scaled the sacrificial heights as a willing if anxious Isaac. The Ozarks is in some real sense post–World War II America's symbolic scapegoat. Within its ambivalent image, the region bears the sins—in this case the hopeless, timeless, backwardness of the hillbilly—of this frontier nation and simultaneously offers salvation from the sins of modernity, both physical salvation within the picturesque, untamed yet embosoming hills and cultural salvation through the worship of a traditional way of life supposedly maintained in conscious isolation. Treated as playground and refuge, the Ozark region and its people have never been taken seriously. The people are so different from the norm of modern, urban America that they cannot possibly possess a tangible past, for they are one with their ancestors. They are *our* ancestors.

Unlike Appalachia, which became a cause célèbre during the 1960s war on poverty, the Ozarks never entered the mainstream consciousness as a region racked by unbelievable poverty and distress. Reporters and politicians preferred their poverty in neat clusters, in neighborhoods of clapboard mining shacks and in rows of millworker houses. Even in Appalachia, the backwoods poor generally escaped the compassionate eye of the muckraker. The plight of the Ozarks was just as isolated from the nation's view as the Ozarkers had been. While the *New York Times* and *Newsweek* ran articles decrying Appalachian poverty during the Johnson administration, the Ozarks rarely advanced beyond the pages of *Holiday* and the funny papers. Whether consciously or unconsciously, the Ozark region had been relegated to almost pure image, a land that apparently embodied the rural and pastoral virtues of a largely mythological American past yet one not worthy of serious thought or respect. The Ozarks was, ultimately, a land apart, a world of hillbillies, be they ennobled contemporary ancestors, clowns, monsters, or "mama's boys."[2]

Ironically, America's complex reaction to the hillbilly and his ways presented an avenue out of poverty and backwardness for some Ozark communities. The same economic forces that first depopulated the Ozark countrysides and then refilled them with retiring outlanders also created an industry of leisure and tourism. Tourism has exalted what historian Daniel J. Boorstin calls the "pseudo-event" to a position of prominence in the Ozarks.[3] The past four decades have brought about the active and anachronistic application of the Ozark image to enterprises within the region aimed at an outside audience. The images of the poor mountaineer in black floppy hat, the quilt-making grandmother, the moonshiner, the fiddler, products of anachronism and nostalgia even when introduced in predepression days, lingered in the American consciousness a generation or two later. Although the era of the mountaineer had long since passed by the 1960s, it did not matter. Just as the back-to-the-land homesteaders had fled to the Ozarks of their fantasies in the early twentieth century, the "pseudo-events" of the modern Ozarks, based on the region's static image, were always undertaken with one eye closed, diminishing the dimensions of mountain complexity and winking at the doubly false nature of it all.

The image of the Ozarks in the popular press has undergone subtle changes. Travel writers and folklorists could not and did not deny the obvious changes in the region's material culture. Nevertheless, amid Cold War anxiety in the decade and a half after World War II, portrayals of the Ozarks tended to mimic the romantic stories of Appalachia. In his study "The Southern Mountaineer in Fact and Fiction," Cratis D. Williams observed that the writers of the late 1940s and 1950s treated "the mountains as a kind of Shangrila in which men harassed by the pressures and frustrations of contemporary life find peace and contentment. The slow tempo and comfortable patterns of the life of the natives are set in contrast with the rush and uncertainty of the social and economic ferment of life in the cities with the result that a new kind of romantic glamor [was] flung over the loitering mountain folk and their innocent ways."[4]

The presentations of Ozark life in mass-published national magazines and books during World War II and in the decade and a half following the conflict generally consisted of two types, both of which either explicitly or implicitly established connections with prewar romantic literary visions of the region and maintained the bucolic, static image of the hill country with only subtle adjustments. Most articles and books on the region could be classified as examples of either folklore or travel writing. Most travel writers consciously cultivated an Ozark image of backwardness, innocence, and physical beauty. While folklorists may not have consciously promoted a contemporary ancestor theme, the very nature of their quest was rooted in the desire to preserve something valuable from a quickly disappearing past; consequently, their books and articles of ballads and tall tales suggested a people unaffected by progress and modernity.

America's first wartime glimpse of the Ozarks in a 1943 *National Geographic* article entitled "Land of a Million Smiles" was for the most part an example of the former, though the propagandistic demands of the war era and the unique approach of the magazine rendered it a less-than-perfect example. Typical of the magazine's American regional portraiture of the era, author Frederick Simpich attempted to cover the gamut of Ozark life from isolated mountain retreats and prosperous valley farms to tourist attractions and revival meetings. The title—the slogan of the Ozark Playgrounds Association—provided a link with prewar Ozark treatments, and much of the article's text covered physical features and other usual Ozark fare: razorback hogs, hillbilly music, and Elizabethan dialect. Above all, "Land of a Million Smiles" was a patriotic booster piece that started off by discussing military training sites, war factories, and lead and zinc mines in southern Missouri. The Anglo-Saxon purity line came across as especially Anglocentric. As with most *National Geographic* articles, the pictures are more telling: a female worker in a corncob pipe factory, teenage penitents at homemade altars at a country revival, an old woman in a sunbonnet, river baptizing, a crusty old blacksmith, "shape-note" singers, even obviously staged photographs of a pretty, impeccably dressed young woman with painted fingernails ostensibly gathering corn and a fisherman in overalls with a modern casting reel and a hat full of store-bought jigs and lures. The message was clear: This may be an arrested frontier, a place of unconscious innocence and traditional life, but it is modern enough to be safe and appealing to the urban traveler.[5]

Two months after the appearance of Simpich's article, Otto Ernest Rayburn published the first issue of *Rayburn's Ozark Guide*, the magazine that would lure more tourists and newcomers to the Ozarks than any other publication until Rayburn's death in 1960. Almost no one in the Ozarks—especially not Ozark natives—read *Rayburn's Ozark Guide*. It was never designed for such an audience. Rayburn embodied the subtle change in approach among chroniclers of the Ozarks. His 1941 *Ozark Country* had been, like most works of the previous decade and a half, romantic, nonjudgmental, and relatively free of boosterism.[6] (Vance Randolph, for one, was even antiboosterish, remarking on one occasion to Rayburn that "every statement a writer makes about illiteracy, poverty, and backwardness in the Ozarks is challenged by the village patriots.")[7] The writers and village patriots gradually mended their broken fences after World War II in a coordinated attempt to build a tourist and retirement industry. This was especially true of the ailing resort town of Eureka Springs, to which Rayburn moved in 1946 and Randolph the following year.[8]

By the 1950s, *Rayburn's Ozark Guide* was a manual for tourists, retirees, and others seeking temporary or permanent refuge in the hills of northern Arkansas and southern Missouri. Rayburn surrounded articles on folk culture and Ozark life with advertisements for resorts, hotels,

Vance Randolph (left) and Otto Ernest Rayburn (right) watch Ozark musicians Opal Arnold and Lou Goddard perform, ca. 1953. Courtesy of Ernie Deane/Shiloh Museum of Ozark History.

fishing services, and other attractions. He also used his quarterly magazine to further his real estate business. But Rayburn faced a sometimes daunting task. He had to maintain a fine line between the image of Ozark frontier backwardness and the increasing reality of modernization. Rayburn and other travel writers had to present the Ozarks as fundamentally different from mainstream America, as isolated, backward, and innocent, yet not so different as to reduce the region to an unappealing, uncomfortable, even dangerous backwater. This was accomplished by portraying the region as a benign, safe place, a land of contemporary ancestors and contemporary American conveniences. So moving were Rayburn's and other writers' descriptions of the Ozarks that the publisher received numerous inquiries from readers interested in settling near Eureka Springs. One especially revealing letter came from a California man in 1957. The earnest man sought a home in the Ozarks of an earlier day, the Ozarks of national consciousness. "I'm interested in living in or *near* a small *one-horse village* in Ozarks. . . . I like old-fashion folks who live in cabins, drive model-T's, take corn to grist mill, etc."[9]

Other travel writers walked Rayburn's tightrope between moderniza-tion and traditionalism. In one of the era's first travel pieces on the re-gion, a writer in *House Beautiful* remarked: "Even more than most places, the Ozark Mountains are all things to all people." The article touted the region as a perfect place for "an inexpensive summer vacation, just a piece away from some of the Midwest's larger cities and complete with dance bands, safe horses, and staged mountain music." But to assure readers that they would indeed be venturing into a place of legend, the writer promised tourists that "typical Ozark people still come up now and then with speech somewhat Elizabethan and consider it only good manners to have a pleasant 'Good-morning' for all comers."[10] Five years later, in an *American Magazine* article, Don Eddy played down the hill-billy image in an attempt to attract visitors. The Ozarkers who awaited tourists in Eureka Springs were not "hillbillies with floppy hats and long white whiskers" but rather "well-informed, sociable souls with all mod-ern conveniences."[11]

The decade after World War II produced several popular magazine ar-ticles on the Ozarks that fit Cratis D. Williams's Shangri-la theme and fu-eled the interest of readers looking for "real hillbillies." The authors of a *Better Homes and Gardens* article lured readers to the "homey . . . quaint" Ozarks by promising them they would "find nothing but 9 o'clock towns where real hillbillies sit on curbs and chew 'snoose.' . . . And when you get back into the hills, you're apt to run across a church chock-full of overall-clad people earnestly singing hymns."[12] Like his predecessors in the 1930s, Hartzell Spence headed for rugged Newton County for his *Saturday Evening Post* feature. Spence found the county's inhabitants isolated be-yond expectation. "Electricity and automobiles are found only along the roads. . . . The tiny store on Mount Sherman sells snuff, coal oil and am-munition as its staples." But Spence's subject lent little insight into the lives of Ozarkers. Ted Richmond, a favorite of Ozark writers and dubbed a "Modern Shepherd of the Hills" by Spence, was a former teacher and freelance writer from Iowa who in 1931 had moved into a Newton County log cabin, from which he delivered books to mountaineers and raised goats to provide his modest cash needs.[13] One author of a *Collier's* piece on Leslie, the old railroad-lumber town left relatively isolated and stranded when the M&NA shut down in 1947, approached his first trip into the re-gion as if he were bound for never-never land. "From my earliest child-hood I had heard about the people of the Ozarks and listened to many stories of their strange and fabulous ways." Although he was dissuaded by Little Rockers who assured him that southern Ozarkers were no different from anyone else, he found, to his delight, a unique region of moonshiners, foxhunters, whittlers, and beekeepers. Even Charles Morrow Wilson, that pioneer of Ozark chronicling, contributed to the genre with his *The Bodacious Ozarks: True Tales of the Backhills.* Even though the old romantic admitted that the "Ozarks backhills are not nearly so far back as they used to be," he believed the region still to be "a land of yesterday and tomorrow in unbreakable wedlock. They are still a frontier of tangible land and intangible spirit; of people who come in and go out."[14]

Two 1955 articles stressed the "otherness" of the region in comparison with urban America. *Americas* carried an unlikely feature on the region written by Pearl Anoe. As romantic and daffy as any of the postwar Ozark treatments, Anoe's article almost comically described a land of "Blue Skies and Laughing Waters" and a race of "hillbillies [who] adapt easily to change." Anoe approached this Third-World American region with about as much respect and serious analysis as one could expect from the magazine's examination of Bolivian mountaineers.[15] Even more verbose and strangely hyperbolic was Julia McAdoo, a former psychiatrist who had recently settled on a small tract in the Arkansas Ozarks. Within McAdoo's hills lived "a race, a people, quite different from most. Unimpressed by riches, unafraid of poverty, serene, not humble and not proud. These 'hillbillies,' these woodsmen, have no set standard of living, no respect for money, nor fame, nor caste. They know no greed, no envy, no subserviency. These unimpressive men in unimpressive garb, though poor they seem, are immensely rich." The honesty of one neighbor rendered McAdoo "a little humble, a little awed, and very grateful and very glad, as in a great cathedral." Nevertheless, in an ironic example of restoring the ambiguous nature of the Ozark image, the editor, in a move probably unforeseen by McAdoo, filled the empty space at the bottom of her final page with a hillbilly joke.[16]

In a *Holiday* article, Phil Stong summed up twenty-five years of Ozark literary imaging: "This is the land of lakes and hills—of rugged and gentle scenery; the land of the square dance, the Elizabethan ballad and the Walker hound." Stong immersed the reader in a sparkling mountain pool of stereotype and cliché. On Anglocentric contemporary ancestor worship, he wrote: "Not only are these mountains old but the way of life is old, too—a survival of young America, with the almost unadulterated Anglo-Saxon stock, the speech, the attitudes, the values, the music and poetry and imagination of the first English settlers of this continent." On the Ozarks as "other" or apart: "You may not know much about hound-dogs and square dancing, and you may be heartily sick of hillbilly ballads; but you'll know you have crossed a border when you enter this country." On idiot-savant, innate mountain musical ability: "Don't ask me how they do it—'fiddling' just comes natural down there. If the leader decides on a 'blues' minor, the others follow before Toscanini could say '*Santissima!*'" Interestingly, Stong also made an early attempt to draw a distinction between the Appalachian mountaineer and the Ozarker. "The Ozarkian hillbilly is not related to Li'l Abner and his Eastern hillbilly kin. . . . They [Ozarkers] are not lanky and bearded." In other words the Ozark highlander was not the clown-monster of stereotype. He was perfectly harmless and even noble in his unconscious innocence.[17]

The most enduring products of Ozark writers in the post–World War II years were not the whimsical, commercial travel stories but the folk song and folklore collections. Although probably less familiar than the travel stories to the reading public of the era, folk writings were equally powerful in promoting a static image of backwardness and quaintness. Vance Randolph emerged as the voice of the Ozarks through his massive collections of folk material published after the war. Unlike the tourist baiters and "heritage hustlers" who maintained the rustic, innocent Ozark image for the commercial benefit of themselves and their entre-preneurial supporters at travel agencies and resorts, Randolph did not set out to freeze the region in a timeless vacuum. Whenever possible he eulogized the disappearance of traditional life and culture in the Ozarks. The travel writers were inspired by nostalgia and the potential of the very modern tourist industry to re-create the past or at least present the illusion that it never passed. Randolph, on the other hand, was driven by a romantic spirit and strong sense of cultural loss to preserve the remnants, in songs and stories, of a past that he realized all too well had already passed. Furthermore, Randolph's work was decidedly uncommercial and unexploitative in nature. He did not refuse the profits from later popular works and he did approach his projects shrewdly, but Randolph maintained his distance from the tourist hawks and hillbillyizers. He felt that the purest humor of Ozark stories was lost on urban audiences, and he expressed that belief in an article he wrote for *Rayburn's Ozark Guide*, a publication targeting those very readers. Randolph chastised writers and folklorists who overromanticized Ozarkers and were "interested in folktales to the exclusion of the folk who tell them."[18] Despite his calls for more serious, perhaps even historical, treatment of the region, Randolph's own mass of folk publications contributed to the lingering image of Ozark backwardness and would probably do more than anything else to shoo away from the hills historians and social scientists, wrapping the region instead inside the protective coat of nostalgia and romance.

Randolph first achieved commercial and critical success with two works completed as the smoke from the war cleared. *Ozark Folksongs*, "a monumental work, awesome in its scope and attention to detail," was published in four volumes between 1946 and 1950 by the State Historical Society of Missouri. The collection of 1,644 texts for 882 titles covered a full range of Ozark mountain music, from old ballads to humorous songs to religious music.[19] He followed that up with the equally influential *Ozark Superstitions*, published by Columbia University Press, a collection of folk beliefs that included previously published and new material. The 1950s brought a flood of Randolph works, including dozens of folk song and folktale articles in the *Journal of American Folklore*, the *Southern Folklore Quarterly*, *Midwest Folklore*, and other respected journals and magazines, as well as five books, including *We Always Lie to Strangers: Tall Tales from the Ozarks* (1951) and *Who Blew Up the Church House? and Other Ozark Folk Tales* (1952).[20]

Randolph was at the forefront of an increasingly intense movement to collect folk material after World War II. John Quincy Wolf Jr. returned to the backwoods of his native region during and after the war to record traditional Ozark music, although his focus gradually shifted to black blues singers in the Mississippi Delta region and white shape-note singers in northeastern Mississippi. Even Pulitzer Prize–winning poet John Gould Fletcher immersed himself in the folk culture of his native state. It was Fletcher, with assistance from the University of Arkansas's English department and such folk luminaries as Randolph, Rayburn, and Wolf, who launched the movement that resulted in the founding of the Ozark Folklore Society in 1949. The society secured a course in American folklore at the university in the fall of 1949, and the library there initiated a program to collect and store folklore records and materials. Fletcher served as the society's president until his death the following year. In his history of Arkansas he had revealed his interest and foretold the society's emergence two years before its founding: "A real revival of Ozark folk skills and arts is profoundly necessary, economically as well as morally, today; but the State of Arkansas has still to wait, apparently, till such skills and arts have completely disappeared before anyone can want to bring them back."[21]

While Fletcher was certainly unique among the Ozark folk enthusiasts at midcentury, his journey into that world provides insights into the movement's most powerful stimuli, namely, romanticism, nostalgia, and intellectual concern for the preservation of a dying way of life. On the surface Fletcher seemed an unlikely candidate for folk culture circles. The only son of a prominent and prosperous Little Rock family, privately educated and Harvard-trained, he spent most of his adult life in Europe moving in the circles of Imagist poets. After rejuvenating his American and southern juices through his contribution to the agrarian-themed *I'll Take My Stand*, Fletcher ended his twenty-five-year expatriation in 1933 and moved back to Little Rock. After visiting Eureka Springs that same year, Fletcher accompanied University of Arkansas music professor and composer Laurence Powell into the Ouachitas to visit Emma Dusenbury and record her songs. Even though the seventy songs obtained on this and subsequent visits were never published, according to Van A. Tyson, "the experience fired his enthusiasm for preserving the traditional materials of Arkansas." Fletcher received a more thorough introduction to the Ozarks from Charlie May Simon. After reading her account of Ozark homesteading in *Scribner's*, Fletcher invited Charlie May and her husband, Howard Simon, to his Little Rock mansion in 1934. He was immediately taken with the attractive young artist-writer. On a trip to the Simons' homestead, Fletcher obtained his first brief view of Ozark highland living. "A glimpse or two into a mountain cabin by the way sufficed to show me that these people lived in conditions of almost unbelievable primitiveness." A year and a half later, both recently divorced, John Gould Fletcher and Charlie May Simon married.[22]

In the following years, Charlie May Simon (she retained Simon as a pen name) introduced Fletcher to her ancestors' highlands. The couple attended the 1941 folk festival in Searcy County and made numerous other journeys and jaunts into the hills north and west of Little Rock. After the publication of *Arkansas* in 1947, Fletcher used his considerable influence and reputation to bring organization and focus to the still-young folk collection movement in the Ozarks and in all Arkansas. He had been envisioning some sort of state folklore society since the 1930s, but it was only in 1949 that Fletcher, as artist-in-residence at the University of Arkansas in Fayetteville, was finally successful in organizing such a group. Fletcher, Vance Randolph, and four other men associated with the university formed the Ozark (later Arkansas) Folklore Society in April 1949. By the end of the year, the society counted 149 members. Perhaps Fletcher's greatest contribution to folk preservation was his success in persuading the University of Arkansas to oversee and fund the collection of folk songs and materials. By 1950 the university's first folklore gatherer, a graduate student from Texas named Merlin Mitchell, was in the field. Fletcher also organized the first folk festival on the university's campus in July 1949 and began work on a folklore-themed issue of the *Arkansas Historical Quarterly*. He would not live to see the publication of this last project, however. Overtaken by a recurrent bout of depression, Fletcher drowned himself at Johnswood, his and Charlie May's estate west of Little Rock, on 10 May 1950.[23]

According to his peers, Fletcher's value in the folk preservation movement rested not in his own collecting efforts, although he did venture into Arkansas's hinterlands with tape recorder in hand on occasion, but in his ability to promote cooperation and inspire other, more able collectors to greater efforts. Like so many collectors of folk materials, Fletcher never achieved a full, personal understanding of hill people. Because he lacked Randolph's ability to communicate one-on-one with his subjects, Fletcher often accompanied other collectors on field trips and remained a mostly silent observer. Furthermore, according to Francis I. Gwaltney, who as a university student often served as Fletcher's driver and translator, the poet's formal speech and demeanor frequently intimidated mountain people and rendered them less natural and authentic in his presence.[24]

Fletcher's incomplete understanding of Ozark people and their lifestyles combined with his antimodernism and his romantic appreciation of hill culture to produce analyses of Ozarkers that were at once both poignant and deeply ambivalent. Fletcher attributed Ozarkers with universal dignity and even went so far as to record his generalizations regarding the physical appearance of the "average" hill person; he obviously sympathized with "the most independent, and yet the most hidebound of all people, these Puritans of the Upper South." In one particularly stirring account of an imaginary hill family's trip to town, he wrote: "The people in the cities—smart as steel traps, one could see, one and all—stared at him, his uncouth ways, his blue jeans, his wife's calico, his limp and spiritless children. He was nothing but an old hayseed, a 'rube,' a yokel. Small boys gathered on street corners and mocked at him, as his wagon creaked drearily past." Perhaps Fletcher yearned to save the hill man and his family, the representatives of America's and the Upper South's agrarian tradition, from the American materialism and homogeneity embodied in the mocking boys. Fletcher appreciated the folk culture of the Arkansas hills but realized that most others would not share this appreciation. "As the population has been drained off, people from without have come in; to them the Ozark lore is only cute and quaint."[25]

Fletcher's aloofness and innate discomfort in personal contact with Ozarkers reflect another dimension of the development of the Ozark image. The primary lure of the Ozarks for travel writers, as well as many folk collectors, was the region's physical beauty. Fletcher was among these admirers of the Ozark aesthetic. His first Ozark infatuation was with the northern Arkansas hills, not the hill people. "I felt a great kinship of spirit stirring in me at the sight of these long wooded ridges, these dense forests, and these lonely mountain settlements and their unspoilt people."[26] To many visitors, the Ozark people were at best simply an extension of the physical region—untamed, picturesque, ancient, but rarely threatening—or at the worst an unfortunate and inconvenient blemish on an otherwise splendid landscape. It is interesting to note that the term "Ozarkia," or some other connotation for the community of people in the region, never achieved popular usage as did "Appalachia." In the Ozarks, interest in the people has always been secondary.

The Ozarks' identification as a physical region first and as a community of people second contributed to the growing divergence between the images of Appalachia and the Ozarks in the 1960s. Cratis D. Williams's Shangri-la portraits adequately described the images of both regions in the 1950s. Nevertheless, at the very moment Williams decried the lack of authenticity in Appalachian writings in the 1950s, his Appalachia stood on the threshold of rediscovery and revision. During the 1960 Democratic presidential primary, John F. Kennedy and Hubert H. Humphrey "out-liberaled" one another in the campaign to secure the votes of West Virginia. Campaign speeches and debates brought national attention to the economic distress of southern Appalachia.[27] Three years later, Harry Caudill's *Night Comes to the Cumberlands* almost single-handedly inspired a generation of reporters, social scientists, and historians to reevaluate the myths and images of the eastern mountaineers, to make public the romantic fallacies of the post–World War II chroniclers, and to expose the impoverished and wretched existences of the lowly masses of mountain people. The Ozarks experienced no such rediscovery, no revision. In fact, the flood of "Third-World" reports from the recesses of eastern Kentucky, southern West Virginia, and other Appalachian areas almost eclipsed any vision of the Ozarks.

The *Reader's Guide to Periodical Literature* covering the two-year period between March 1963 and February 1965 recorded eighteen article titles under the heading "Appalachian Region." Of those, fifteen were "realistic" or "proletarian" pieces dealing with poverty, government aid, and dam building; the other three discussed the establishment of the Appalachian Trail. The same volume contained only three mentions of the Ozarks, none of them indicative of the reformist reporting that was beginning to dominate Appalachia's treatment in the press. While Appalachia inspired articles in *U.S. News and World Report, Newsweek,* and other national publications with titles such as "Antipoverty Plan for Appalachia," "Poverty, U.S.A.: Appalachia," "Mountains of Poverty," and "Tragedy of Appalachia," *Holiday* treated its readers to "Autumn in the Ozarks," and *National Parks Magazine* featured an article on the Ozark National Scenic Riverways in southern Missouri. *Life* ran pictorial stories on both regions: "Valley of Poverty" and "Wonders of a Cave Find."[28] No clearer example exists of the divergent perceptions of the two regions, one suddenly a people bowed low before the onslaught of modernization and rampant, exploitative capitalism, and the other an escapist's dream of untold natural beauty and mystery.

The reasons for the sharp divergence between the national images of the two southern mountain regions are numerous. First, the smaller and much less politically important Ozark region, which had a minuscule representation in Congress, inspired no national political fracas over white poverty. Second, the Ozarks was home to no Harry Caudill. The first shot was never fired, thus maintaining the truce between the Ozarkers and their writing observers. The Appalachian region also tended to eclipse its smaller offspring. New York reporters and writers and Washington politicians could not see beyond the highlands in their backyards. The Appalachians were three times as high as the Ozarks and must have seemed three times as poor. Another point of difference was urbanity. Most poverty stories concerned the landless, gardenless poor of the towns and cities of industrial Appalachia. The Ozarks contained few examples of such magnified squalor. The region's largest city, Springfield, Missouri, was by the 1960s a farm trading center turned college town and retiree destination on the verge of dynamic expansion and prosperity, and the Arkansas side's chief town, Fayetteville, was a college town at the southern end of the region's most prosperous area. Neither place, nor most other Ozark towns for that matter, contained any signs of desolation and desperation remotely resembling a coal or mill town.

In the Ozarks it appeared that Darwinian forces would solve the problems of poverty and displacement. The overwhelmingly rural, land-based population would make its own adjustments. Thousands of landless, poor, and young had deserted and would continue to desert the region, the strongest and the oldest would stay on the farms, and others would perhaps farm and work in town. But many of the poor remained. In fact, according to economist Joseph Frank Singer, outmigration failed to improve economic opportunities for many nonmigrants because of the simultaneous rush of inmigration, which flooded some Ozark areas with young and middle-aged workers whose better educations and skills made them more employable than most Ozark natives. By 1970 the average family income of rural, inmigrant families exceeded that of their nonmigrant neighbors by 25 percent.[29]

According to some measuring sticks, the Ozarks was actually a more depressed region than Appalachia. A study conducted by the Economic Research Service of the U.S. Department of Agriculture found that the per capita income in rural hill counties of Arkansas in 1959 was barely two-thirds of Appalachia's per capita income. Furthermore, median family income in these same Arkansas counties only slightly exceeded one-half of that in Appalachia. The Ozarks' unemployment rate nearly matched that of the eastern mountainous region, and the Arkansas hill people probably suffered a greater degree of underemployment. A 1961 cooperative extension service report for north central Arkansas found that 85 percent of Stone County's residents received cash payments from the state welfare department, and half the citizens there received surplus commodities. The same report noted the reluctance of many to leave their homes for work elsewhere, which, when combined with the scarcity of employment in the region, resulted in a large group relying on part-time timber work and unskilled, nonfarm labor. As late as 1969 the Economic Opportunity Information Center found a 45.1 percent poverty index in Newton County, a mountainous area with no settlement of more than 500 people.[30]

Perhaps the most important forces in the maintenance of the bucolic, innocent image of the Ozarks, however, emanated from within the region. The rural Ozarks by the early 1960s had reached low ebb in terms of economic status and population. Many of the more able and better educated leaders had abandoned the region in the two decades following the United States' entry into World War II. The expansion of the poultry industry and the growth of the university spurred economic development in northwestern Arkansas, but most of the Ozark region remained rural, poor, and bereft of opportunity. Tourism would come not as an economic savior to these areas—or at least the ones with such potential—but as a last resort. This new industry in northern Arkansas would be built in large measure upon the Ozark image formulated during the depression and perfected in the 1950s.

Most tourist attractions in the Arkansas Ozarks fall into one of three broad categories: water, Ozark heritage, and general, non-region-specific attractions. The water attractions include the region's four man-made reservoirs and rivers popular for fishing (the White and the Little Red Rivers) and floating (the Buffalo and the Spring Rivers). Other attractions, both Ozark-themed and general, are for the most part located within a twenty-five-mile radius of one of three tourist centers: Mountain View, Eureka Springs, and Hardy.

By the mid-1950s the most popular tourist destination in northern Arkansas was the twin lakes area near Mountain Home. Norfork and Bull Shoals Lakes provided fishing and water recreation, while the cool, dam-generated waters of the North Fork and upper White Rivers became prized spots for trout fishermen from around the South and Midwest. Dozens of small motels and resorts sprang up around the lakes to cater to summer visitors. By the mid-1950s, Baxter County boasted more than 150 resorts, lodges, restaurants, and hotels; dozens of small businesses and service companies grew to depend on tourism dollars. A select few tourist destinations, such as Gaston's White River Resort below Bull Shoals Dam, eventually achieved regional or even national status as the area's popularity expanded in the 1960s and 1970s. The process was repeated for the environs of Greers Ferry and Beaver Lakes after their completion in the 1960s.[31]

Arkansas's most popular free-flowing stream, the Buffalo River, was almost turned into a series of reservoirs like the White River and owes its preservation to the growing disenchantment with the Army Corps of Engineers' dam building. The story of the nationalization of the river reflects common tourism themes—influence by outsiders and limited financial benefits—and serves as another example of Ozark otherness. The Flood Control Act of 1938 that provided for the construction of Norfork and Bull Shoals Dams also authorized the building of Lone Rock Dam on the lower Buffalo River in Searcy County. With the Korean conflict uneasily settled and Bull Shoals completed, the Army Corps of Engineers turned its attention to the Buffalo River and recommended the construction of two dams in 1954. These dams were placed on a new flood control bill that Eisenhower vetoed in 1956 and again in the following year. The president's opposition disgusted Governor Faubus and Senator Fulbright as well as dam advocates, who comprised the majority of the local population—or at least those who did not own land that stood to be inundated. This delay proved crucial for the incubation of an infant conservation movement. In 1958 Kenneth Smith, a University of Arkansas student and floating enthusiast, began describing Lost Valley, a particularly scenic stretch of the Buffalo River near Ponca in Newton County, for the readers of the *Arkansas Gazette*. By the time northwestern Arkansas congressman James W. Trimble proposed a comprehensive hydroelectricity and flood control plan for the White and Buffalo River valleys in 1961, a small but vocal group of concerned citizens had followed Smith into the deepest reaches of the upper Buffalo River and were willing to oppose Trimble's plan.[32]

Two months after Trimble's proposal became public, Neil Compton, a physician from Bentonville who had long floated the streams of the Ozarks, led a group of mostly northwestern Arkansans in founding the Arkansas Nature Conservancy, which called for the government to purchase Lost Valley and create a national park on the upper and middle reaches of the river. With its strong Fayetteville membership, the Arkansas Nature Conservancy succeeded in convincing Fulbright to suggest a National Park Service survey of the proposed dam basin area. Fulbright arranged for such a survey, officially sparking the "Battle for the Buffalo." In early 1962, business owners and other prominent citizens of Marshall, the town nearest the proposed dams and most likely to prosper in the way Mountain Home had in the previous two decades, formed the Buffalo River Improvement Association (BRIA) for the purpose of promoting the dams. After the BRIA dominated a January 1962 public meeting in Marshall to discuss the proposed dams, Compton and his preservationists formed the more narrowly focused Ozark Society. A group of local landowners who opposed both inundation and the Ozark Society's plan for nationalization founded a third group, the Searcy County (later Buffalo River) Landowners' Association (BRLA). In April 1962, Supreme Court justice William O. Douglas, a noted conservationist, floated the river and publicly gave his support to the nationalization plan. Soon the tide began to turn against the dam proponents. Later in 1962 the *Arkansas Democrat, Arkansas Gazette*, and several smaller in-state papers began denouncing the Army Corps of Engineers' plans. After a second public hearing in Marshall in late 1964, the *Kansas City Star* and several national outdoor magazines called for preservation of the river. According to participants in the battle, the most crucial event was Governor Faubus's public conversion to the preservationist cause in December 1965. Plans for dam construction on the Buffalo River were withdrawn the following year.[33]

With the Army Corps of Engineers out of the picture, the battle for the river continued for six more years, pitting prominent politicians, conservation groups, and the outsider-dominated Ozark Society against local

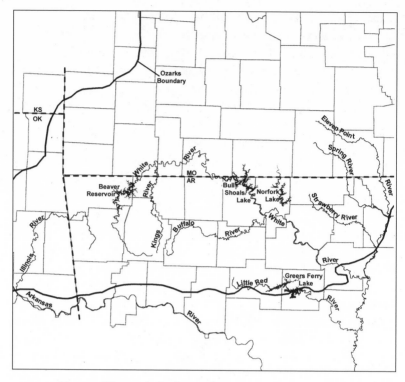

MAP 9.1. Rivers and Reservoirs in the Ozarks

landowners in the BRLA. The feud between the BRLA and preservationists became particularly heated in the late 1960s. The preservationists' use of frontier images of the Buffalo River valley angered local residents. In a heated rebuttal to an article written for the *Kansas City Star* by John Heuston, first vice president of the Ozark Society Canoe Floaters Club— in which he described the area under question as "A Magic World Nobody—Almost—Knows" and a "Wilderness . . . Waiting for It's Rediscovery"—one member of the BRLA warned canoeists and hikers that they "should also be able to run, in addition to walk, climb, crawl and scramble, if they decide to visit the Big Buffalo River again any time soon." Four months later a group of Newton County Buffalo River landowners felled 200 trees across the upper part of the river in protest to the federal government's efforts to nationalize the stream.[34]

Despite the strident opposition of farmers and landowners, Congress passed a bill in 1972 creating the Buffalo National River, the country's first river to receive that designation. The very farmers who had been influential in halting the progress of the Corps of Engineers were now quietly

ENDINGS AND TRADITIONS

pushed aside by their preservationist partners. The Buffalo River had been the lifeline of Boston Mountain farmers for almost 150 years. The government's acquisition of its narrow but fertile bottoms placed the official stamp of approval on the extension service's longtime estimation of the region: this was no place for farming. Unfortunately, for those lucky enough to own the river bottomlands it was the only place worth farming. By the 1990s, Buffalo River tourism, which attracted more than a million visitors to the stream annually, sustained seventeen canoe rental businesses and a few camping outfitter shops and scattered rural stores but little else. As it turns out, canoeists have shown less concern for the valley's and the river's health and pristine preservation than did the landowners. By the early 1990s overuse of the stream had produced occasional canoe jams, littering, and pollution on the most frequently traveled stretches, prompting the Ozark Society to lobby the National Park Service for the implementation of restrictions on use of the river.[35]

The Buffalo River story also provides another contrast between the Ozarks and Appalachia. At the same time that politicians, landowners, and conservationists fought over the Ozark stream, a similar battle raged in eastern Tennessee over the Tennessee Valley Authority's (TVA) proposed construction of Tellico Dam. Landowners and environmentalists were unsuccessful in eastern Tennessee; the TVA closed the floodgates on the dam in 1978. The two events deserve comparison. It is quite likely that the Ozark image saved the Buffalo River. In a region valued more for physical beauty than for community welfare, it was a natural step to halt the useless harnessing of free-flowing streams, especially one as small as the Buffalo. Of course, the victory was not for the landowners threatened with inundation. Their numbers were minuscule when compared with the displaced from any of the previous four reservoir projects, and they eventually lost the use of their lands anyway. By the 1970s the idea of "progress" was so embedded in the rhetoric of rescuing Appalachia and in the machinery of the TVA that preservation of the natural landscape was merely an afterthought. Nevertheless, in both instances local ways of life meant little to the outsiders who controlled the rivers' destinies.[36]

The influence of non-Ozarkers and outside forces is a recurring, almost constant, theme in Ozark history and especially in the development of tourism. Only in rare instances has a project been conceived and carried to fruition by Ozark people. Most tourism projects have been linked in some way to the principal characteristics or the popular image of the region, but certainly not all have been. The best example of the superimposition of a generic tourist concept onto the region is also the driving force behind the Ozarks' chief tourist center, Eureka Springs. The Passion Play and its Christian-themed accoutrements in northwestern Arkansas could have been built anywhere, but it is quite fitting that this most un-Ozarkian attraction would spring from the hills of this most un-Ozarkian community.

From its inception, Eureka Springs was a novelty in the Arkansas Ozarks. Built on hucksterism and mineral-water peddling, the Victorian-Swiss architecture could not have been more foreign to the hills where it was built in the late nineteenth century. Furthermore, no ambitious Ozark settler worth his salt would have chosen the town site itself, with its steep, curving streets and granite ledges. After World War II, Eureka Springs became a haven for regional and second-rate writers and artists, a place where the Ozark image was crafted within a modern protective enclave quite leery of the poor hill folks lurking in the hinterland. After the depression put a halt to the resort business, Eureka Springs began to refocus its efforts in the 1940s and 1950s in an attempt to attract modern midwestern tourists. In 1946, Chicagoan Dwight Nichols purchased and renovated Eureka Springs' Crescent Hotel and initiated a package vacation program. In the early 1950s, at a price of $52.50 per week, Nichols transported guests to and from the nearest railroad depot fifty-seven miles away (the M&NA ceased operations in 1947) and provided rooms, meals, games, sightseeing, lake cruises, dances, hayrides, swimming, and other activities.[37]

By the 1950s Eureka Springs had begun to make a disturbing discovery: the town was too modern for its own good, too dehillbillyized. The vacationers who had been promised electric lights and hot showers in their mountain bungalows had also been promised real hillbillies by the travel writers and, incidentally, by the folk tales and songs in *Rayburn's Ozark Guide*. They received only the former. In 1948 Eureka Springs revived its Ozark Folk Festival to recapture the hillbilly spirit that the town had never possessed. But the staged musicals and dances—some of the performers were not real Ozarkers—and the Indian relics and factory-made corncob pipes were less than authentic. Even most visitors could tell that. The tourists who did manage to spot a stereotypical hillbilly on the outskirts of town probably fell prey to the area's resident fake anachronism. When he visited Eureka Springs in the postwar years, Paul Faris found what appeared to be a classic, stereotypical mountaineer on a hill outside of town. By Golly was an old, bearded man who slept in a tent behind a highway billboard, tended to his donkeys and goats, sketched portraits of tourists to sell, and posed for photographs. In reality By Golly was Ernest

Schilling, a former Barnum and Bailey's circus performer born to Swiss immigrant parents in New York City. Schilling, like so many others in the twentieth century, had settled on a plot of land near Eureka Springs before World War I to pursue an alternative lifestyle. Untold tourists returned to their homes in Chicago or St. Louis with authentic pictures of a real New York hillbilly.[38]

What the old resort town needed was a good dose of such Ozark stereotype. One visitor from California suggested as much in a letter to Rayburn: "Do away with the modern store windows, signs, et al. In this way, I think, Eureka Springs will again be the sought after area." A local resident with origins outside the region suggested improving Eureka's Ozark image by staging appearances by hillbilly stereotypes based on an artist's representation. "You know . . . the girl with the daisy on her hat, the boy with the toothless smile, Pa with his battered hat, red necktie and the stickpin. I think those should be played up more in this region. . . . The tourist is always looking for a hill-billy." The recipient of all this advice, Rayburn, knew the last statement was unfortunately—for Eureka Springs at least—correct. "I soon discovered what the tourists from the North want to see in the Ozarks. They are interested in log cabins and the old crafts such as spinning, weaving, woodcarving, blacksmithing, and basket making. They want to see real hillbillies who pick the guitar, play the fiddle, and sing the old traditional ballads that grandfather sang. These tourists are usually disappointed in Eureka Springs, for we have only a few hillbillies to show them. We have killed the goose that laid the golden egg."[39]

Indeed, modernization had killed the hillbilly, and Eureka Springs suffered the false advertising of travel writers. The Ozark image no longer described the region by the time of Rayburn's lament in 1957. Actually, the image had represented only a distinct, isolated few, and exaggeratedly so, even when first developed almost thirty years before. By the late 1950s, even the Hemmed-in Hollers were not so hemmed-in any more. The only solution, as at least a few saw it, was to make the town conform to the image. As Rayburn suggested, that would not work for Eureka Springs, and he would not live to see that solution put to work in Mountain View. Instead, Eureka Springs' economic salvation would come from a more unlikely source, though perhaps one more fitting for the old resort town.

The man who single-handedly revitalized the slumping Swiss village was Gerald L. K. Smith, an ultra-right–wing newspaper publisher. Born in Wisconsin in 1898, Smith enjoyed a varied career as a political organizer for Huey Long in the 1930s, an anti-Communist speaker in the 1940s, and founder of the racist, anti-Semitic *Cross and the Flag* in California. In 1964, in hopes of establishing a pioneer farm with an authentic log cabin, furnishings, and frontier farming implements—a sort of museum to America's nostalgic past as interpreted by Smith—he dispatched his assistant Charles F. Robertson to find such a farmstead. Robertson, apparently familiar with the popular image of the arrested frontier Ozarks, journeyed to Eureka Springs. He found no log cabin fitting Smith's description, but he did take a fancy to a Victorian mansion there, Penn Castle. Robertson purchased the mansion as a retirement home for the Smiths, who were themselves familiar with and fond of Eureka Springs. At the time of Smith's arrival in Eureka Springs in late 1964, Rayburn, the heart and voice of the village, had been dead four years; the town's population had dropped to below 1,500 inhabitants, mainly retirees with a sprinkling of writers, artists, and craftspeople.[40]

The wealthy Smith had big plans for his new hometown. He bought 167 acres east of town on Magnetic Mountain and announced plans to construct on that site a statue of Christ. For this project Smith commissioned the elderly Emmett Sullivan, a former South Dakota cowboy and attorney who had settled in Eureka Springs to pursue his love of painting and sculpting. Two years later the "Christ of the Ozarks," a 70-foot-tall concrete behemoth, was dedicated by Smith, Sullivan, and local dignitaries. The statue, almost hideously disproportionate and sadly foreign on the rocky, brushy ridge, stood "masquerading as a monument to Christ . . . intended . . . in reality as a monument to [Smith]." The "Christ of the Ozarks" was the first part of Smith's dream of a sort of Christian theme park at Eureka Springs. His most ambitious project, the Passion Play, followed.[41]

The Passion Play transformed Eureka Springs into a thriving tourist town. Smith conceived the idea of staging a Passion Play, which chronicled Jesus' last days on earth from Palm Sunday to the Ascension, and named another South Dakotan, Robert Hyde, to oversee its production. Hyde, who had most recently achieved a small measure of notoriety as a scriptwriter for the television Western *The High Chaparral*, wrote the play, designed the 6,000-seat amphitheater and set, directed the play, and portrayed Jesus. Two hundred additional actors, both professional and amateur, were brought in for the 1968 opening. By the mid-1970s the Passion Play had become the largest outdoor pageant in the United States. In addition, Smith had overseen the establishment of two more attractions, the Christ Only Art Gallery and the Bible Museum. He also had in the works a Christian amusement park containing replicas of shrines and landmarks from the Holy Land. By bringing in tens of thousands of tourists each year, Smith's Passion Play revitalized the Main Street business district of Eureka Springs. Gift shops opened, hotels sprang up along all the roadsides leading into town, and, ironically, Eureka Springs began to gain a reputation as a center of Ozark craft making.[42]

Paradoxically, at the same time that Eureka Springs was growing famous and prosperous for its Passion Play, it was also becoming an Ozark center of the counterculture movement. Back-to-the-landers flocked to the area in the early 1970s, many attracted by a desire to learn and practice traditional Ozark crafts or to simply live off the land in conscious rejection of mainstream American life. Smith and the young hippies distrusted one another. Smith generally enjoyed rocky relations with the rest of the town, although his position as the engineer of prosperity shielded him from serious blasts. Between 1964 and 1972, the gross municipal product of Eureka Springs increased from less than $1 million to almost $15 million. Smith's tourist attractions transformed the town into the most popular tourist destination in the Arkansas Ozarks and the leading tourist municipality in the state.[43]

By the 1990s, Eureka Springs was in many respects a typical late twentieth-century tourist town. Downtown shops and restaurants offered goods and dishes found elsewhere around the country. The crafts were frequently passed off as authentic Ozark products, but their makers were almost never natives of the region. Eureka Springs' success had been at best indirectly related to the region's image; consequently, it offered little in the way of Ozark heritage and tradition. The tourist now searching for attractions built on this heritage (or the inherited image of the Ozarks) found them in abundance in places that were both distinctly Ozarkian and generically, buffoonishly nonregional.

The recognized center of heritage-based tourism in the Arkansas Ozarks was Mountain View, the once-isolated Stone County seat perched atop the heights where the Boston Mountains collide with the White River Hills. Mountain View and its environs had long been unique in the interior Ozarks as decidedly nontouristy yet inviting to outsiders. Before World War II, the Sylamore District of the Ozark National Forest north of the village had served as the state's last best refuge for whitetail deer; consequently, the area around Big Flat became a prime deer-hunting destination. In 1937 more than two in five whitetails harvested in Arkansas were killed in Stone and Baxter Counties, and after World War II the Arkansas Game and Fish Commission used deer captured in the Sylamore District to bolster depleted deer populations in other parts of the state.[44] The work completed by CCC crews in the district laid the physical foundation—roads, parks, buildings—for a small camping and resort business in the postwar years. It was only in the late 1950s and early 1960s, however, that Mountain View and surrounding areas began to be transformed into popular tourist destinations.

A close look at the evolution of the tourist industry around Mountain View, the industry's reliance on both nature- and heritage-based attractions, and the inner workings of various key individuals and groups presents an Ozark case study in what David E. Whisnant has termed "the politics of culture." The odyssey that eventually produced northern Arkansas's second most popular tourist destination involved government agencies and private groups, outsiders and native Ozarkers, Washington politicians and mountain musicians. As has most often been the case, it was an outsider who set in motion the forces of change and the wheels of tourism in Stone County. Harold Sherman arrived in 1947 to find a region quite unlike Hollywood or Chicago. Most of the county's residents lacked electricity and running water, and Stone County was one of the few in the state with no paved highway running through it. Sherman led local efforts to obtain electricity in the early 1950s and later headed up a group of locals who succeeded in getting key highways paved. Like John Gould Fletcher, Harold Sherman never truly understood his Ozark neighbors, but unlike Fletcher, he never really sought to.

From the time of his arrival Sherman looked upon his new home region as a project. He would lead the silent and thankful natives out of the wilderness in a play scarcely believable outside Hollywood. And he would do so by making Stone County the playground of the rich from Michigan to Texas. Sherman was an ardent supporter of local issues and projects when they were also his issues and projects and a harsh and spiteful critic when local groups failed to share his visions. In a 1957 letter to First District congressman Wilbur D. Mills, Sherman complained about the state highway commission's decision to pave a twelve-mile stretch of highway in western Stone County rather than his proposed stretch, a road in sparsely settled southern Stone County that was frequently traveled by tourists from Little Rock. In complete earnestness he quipped: "Such a road, serves only the local needs." By the 1960s, after more than a decade of his meddling and cajoling and after local residents learned of his interest in extrasensory perception and other eccentricities, he could be a liability to his own favorite causes or a skillful promoter of other projects.[45]

Sherman's urgency in the spring of 1957 was motivated largely by self-interest, by his concern for a project that, he assured Mills, "HAS to be done." That project was an archery range and hunting resort conceived in 1954 and called the "Land of the Cross-Bow." Sherman's grand plans for the resort encapsulated most of the elements of the postwar Ozark image. The Land of the Cross-Bow carried the Anglo-Saxon seedbed theory to its most absurd extreme. The resort, situated in an isolated, barely accessible area of Stone County, would sport "taverns of early England," bowling greens, and "signs constructed in the old English style to create for tourists an atmosphere of medieval times." Furthermore, the attendants would all adorn the garb of some unspecific early English era. The press release for the resort repeated the by now popular mantra of travel writers and folk-lorists alike, assuring readers that "the rugged country in which it lies is one of the last refuges of original Anglo-Saxon stock which first colonized this country." Visitors were promised native fishing guides, and in case the park sounded too upscale, Sherman assured readers that "there is no question at any time but what you have 'gotten away from it all.'"[46]

Sherman's project looked promising in 1957. That summer he and the Stone County Lions Club, which held the original lease granted by the U.S. Forest Service, began negotiations with a Pine Bluff firm, Ben Pearson, Inc., that promised to develop the resort and surrounding region and protect the Blanchard Springs area "from any Honky tonk interests moving in." The Lions helped construct a small airstrip so that Pearson could "fly in wealthy archery club members from all over the country." Sherman wrote optimistically to Mills: "This latest development is really going to be IT." After a successful archery tournament and deer hunt in the fall of 1957, the Lions Club turned over its lease on the forest land to Pearson, and Sherman hatched a plan for a television show to be filmed at the Land of the Cross-Bow. In early 1958 he formed Mountain View Productions, Inc., for the purpose of filming a pilot segment, "The Amazing Adventures of My Dog Kelly," a title later changed to "My Dog Sheppy." But Sherman's dream of a prosperous resort and successful tel-evision program unraveled in the first half of 1958. In May he informed Mills that he had "unwittingly played into the hands of a company which . . . intends to convert the Land of the Bow and Arrow into what will amount to a private archery operation." It would not become even that. Just before Christmas, Pearson pulled out of the project and turned the lease back over to the U.S. Forest Service. In the meantime, Sherman's pilot, filmed on location in the Blanchard Springs area using B-list Hol-lywood television talent and a few locals, including country music star

Jimmy Driftwood, was flatly rejected by NBC. By 1959 the Land of the Cross-Bow was simply an unpleasant memory for Sherman and the locals involved.[47]

The concept had been far-fetched to start with and, like Gerald L. K. Smith's Eureka Springs projects a decade later, wholly divorced from the tradition and history of the region. The failure of the Land of the Cross-Bow further exacerbated political divisions in a county already notorious for its infighting. It was clear that such a project offered no economic salvation for the depressed people of north central Arkansas and that such schemes should be avoided in the future. It was also clear, to most locals at least, that Sherman was either a con man or a kook, perhaps both, and certainly a damn Yankee. As the business and political leaders of Mountain View would soon discover, salvation, if any were to be had, could come only through utilization of the region's physical attributes and through heritage hustling, through playing up the static image of the Ozarks at the very moment Appalachia's image was experiencing a fundamental makeover.

Sherman's next and most important project held better promise for promoting tourism in north central Arkansas. In the early 1960s, he was unofficially appointed by local leaders to oversee the development of Blanchard Springs Caverns. According to one participant, his active direction of the caverns project served to rid the more important folk center movement of his less-than-welcome assistance and negative reputation among many local residents. Nonetheless, Sherman used his media savvy and his friendship with Congressman Mills to guide the project to completion. The project involved the use of a cave (eventually discovered to be a maze of caverns) in the Sylamore District that was first explored in 1934 but only recently seriously mapped and charted by Batesville spelunkers Hugh Shell and Hail Bryant. In 1963, at a Stone County press conference conducted by Sherman, the U.S. Forest Service announced plans to set aside Half-Mile Cave for recreation purposes. Although Sherman's original plan called for private development of the cave, he soon acquiesced to Forest Service control. The Forest Service began construction on a visitors' center in 1970 and opened Blanchard Springs Caverns to the public in the summer of 1973, less than a month after the grand opening of the Ozark Folk Center.[48]

Blanchard Springs Caverns was, like the spring dogwood blooms and autumn leaves, a tourist attraction based solely on the region's physical beauty and uniqueness. The real growth of tourism in the Mountain View area would come to depend on the people, or at least on Americans' image of the people. The growth of heritage tourism and the transformation of Mountain View and its environs can be traced back to 1959. In November the Arkansas Cooperative Extension Service established its first Area Rural Development district for the purpose of formulating plans to address the economic needs of four north central counties, Stone, Independence, Izard, and Sharp. Fulton was added in February 1961. Because the Area Rural Development Committee was under the extension service, the original focus was on improving agricultural methods and marketing and on developing small industry. By the time Leo Rainey arrived in September 1961 to replace Everette Sanders as rural development director, the extension service had begun to shift its focus to tourism. Rainey noted in his annual report the following June: "It is true that more emphasis has been placed upon tourism this year as well as crafts. Economists state that tourism probably offers the greatest hope for economic development in the rugged areas of this section."[49]

Only twenty-nine when he arrived in Batesville with the daunting task of practically orchestrating the economic revitalization of an area never known for its financial prosperity and even further removed from the American economic mainstream in the early 1960s, Rainey would soon find himself in the center of a burgeoning tourist industry and heritage revival, a movement that would ultimately revitalize sections of his region but pass over others. Although he was not an Ozarker, Rainey was closer than most who were so intimately involved in the development of the modern tourist industry in northern Arkansas. He was born at Center Ridge, a small community situated on the rolling uplands of the Arkansas River valley near the southern terminus of the Ozark plateau, raised near Morrilton, and educated, like most extension agents, at the University of Arkansas in Fayetteville. A sturdily built, devoutly Christian man, Rainey was possessed of unlimited energy and an Eisenhower-era, capitalistic, boosterish mentality that considered any progress good progress. He would be willing to tolerate, perhaps even perpetuate, the negative aspects of a tourist industry based on a regional image in the confidence that the economic benefits would outweigh, or at least offset, the more unflattering images absorbed by visitors to the region. Rainey was actually quite cognizant of the fact that the Ozarks of legend existed only in legend, but he also realized that he had a responsibility to take whatever steps were necessary to pull the eastern Ozarks out of economic quicksand.

Rainey helped launch the tourist movement in September 1961 when he accompanied three other extension service employees and thirty-six community leaders from north central and northwestern Arkansas on an information-gathering trip to the fall fair of the Southern Highlands Handicraft Guild in Gatlinburg, Tennessee.[50] The trip was organized by the extension service and funded by rural electric cooperatives in Clinton, Salem, and Berryville. While no Ozark town enjoyed Gatlinburg's unique geographic advantage—it is located on the main thoroughfare leading into the Great Smoky Mountains National Park—the agents and community leaders hoped to emulate the eastern Tennessee city's success as a center of mountain handicraft production. Upon the group's return, Rainey promptly organized the Area Tourist and Recreation Committee and Area Craft Subcommittee. In the spring and summer of 1962, the craft subcommittee oversaw craft fairs in Rainey's five counties as well as in Van Buren and Cleburne Counties as a way of finding native talent. To their dismay, Rainey and his fellow subcommittee members found a severe shortage of native crafters in the Ozarks. Based on the subcommittee's preconceptions of what constituted mountain crafts, preconceptions largely formed during the visit to Gatlinburg, fifty-five craftspeople were chosen from the seven-county region, all of whom were invited to display and sell their wares at a regionwide fair in Batesville in August. The craft subcommittee selected craftspeople, most of whom were native Ozarkers, on the basis of both authenticity and quality. Crafts displayed in Batesville ranged from wood carvings to handwoven rugs and from corncob dolls to cornshuck hats. In November the fifty-five craftspeople formed the Ozark Foothills Craft Guild and made plans for the establishment of craft shops. By 1965, with the help of a loan from the Small Business Administration, the guild operated small seasonal shops at Mountain View, Clinton, Heber Springs, and Hardy.[51]

In addition to its work with the craft guild, the Area Tourist and Recreation Committee organized the first Dogwood Drive automobile tour for the spring of 1962 to capitalize on Stone County's scenic beauty and its recently paved highways. The committee printed 20,000 color brochures advertising the drive and distributed them at the Dallas Sports and Vacation Show and the Arkansas Livestock Show. The committee also organized a series of tourist service and information courses that were offered in towns around the region in 1962. Designed for "persons who have contact with tourists" and taught in three two-hour increments by representatives of the State Department of Vocational Education, the course offered instruction in Ozark history and legend, fishing, and hunting and provided information concerning tourists' needs and expectations.[52]

In 1963 Rainey attempted to revive an earlier "Farm Vacation" program that had failed to attract interest. As early as 1959, Ozark businessmen and extension agents had urged area farmers to "halt the exodus from Arkansas farms" by turning their farms into "holiday and vacation resorts for city folks." By the early 1960s, the Farmers' Home Administration offered loans for the construction of recreation facilities on farms, such as cabins, ponds, riding stables, trails, picnic grounds, and shooting preserves. After a tour of Ohio farms that successfully hosted summer guests, Rainey organized the Farm Vacation Program with fifteen families from six different Ozark counties and printed 6,000 brochures to distribute in cities around the region. The Farm Vacation Program failed in the Arkansas Ozarks. Farmers were leaving their lands as quickly as tourists were discovering the area. Those who stayed worked part-time off the farm, thus failing to satisfy vacationers' preconceptions of the American family farm, or transformed their homesteads with nontraditional and aesthetically displeasing agricultural practices such as poultry raising. As Rainey recalls, there were also two greater disadvantages that doomed the program. Most Ozark farmhouses were not spacious and modern enough to serve as bed-and-breakfast inns, and the majority of the residents of Little Rock, Memphis, and other nearby cities were not so long removed from an agrarian past that such a vacation held allure and enchantment for them.[53]

The Farm Vacation Program would prove to be a rare misstep in north central Arkansas's, and more specifically Stone County's, march toward the heights of tourism. The year 1963 also witnessed the genesis of three separate but interrelated projects that would transform the county into a traveler's destination. Local craft guild members, Jimmy Driftwood, Rainey, and other leaders organized Mountain View's first Arkansas Folk Festival, which would become a popular annual event. Harold Sherman began efforts to transform Half-Mile Cave into a federally operated tourist site. Local and federal officials also launched the movement that eventually produced the state-operated Ozark Folk Center.

The Arkansas Folk Festival first attracted large numbers of visitors to Mountain View and directly or indirectly spurred the completion of the other two projects. The 1963 festival shared only a tenuous link with Stone County's original festival in 1941 or with the annual Ozark Folk Festival in Eureka Springs. Mountain View's Arkansas Folk Festival was a straightforward attempt to revive the depressed area's fortunes and funnel tourist dollars into local businesses and into the empty pockets of craft guild members. It was conceived in relative haste and rolled along willy-nilly into snowballing success. In October 1962, even before the establishment of the Ozark Foothills Craft Guild, Rainey, three district extension service employees, and Stone County extension agent Lloyd Westbrook met to plan a craft fair scheduled for April 1963. W. H. Freyaldenhoven, district extension agent, suggested incorporating local musical talent as a complement to the craft sale. Westbrook, the lone Stone County resident of the five, was given the task of convincing the county's most famous citizen, Jimmy Driftwood, to organize musicians for the fair. Driftwood agreed to serve and came on board in January 1963.[54]

Born James Corbett Morris in a Stone County community south of Mountain View in 1907, Driftwood grew up in an atmosphere rich in mountain musical heritage. Neal Morris, Jimmy's father, was a locally prominent folk singer who had learned more than one hundred old ballads from his mother, and Driftwood's maternal grandfather was a traveling merchant who regaled customers with his renditions of ballads both recent and ancient. Driftwood and his wife Cleda spent their young adult lives as country teachers. Jimmy served for thirty-four years as a teacher and principal at the little three-room school in Timbo. It was as a teacher at the tiny Snowball school during the depression that Driftwood, to aid his students' mastery of American history, wrote the words to his famous "Battle of New Orleans" and set them to the melody of an old Irish fiddle tune, "Eighth of January."[55]

On a folk song–gathering trip to the 1941 folk festival in Stone County, Southwestern (now Rhodes) College English professor John Quincy Wolf Jr. "discovered" Driftwood. In succeeding years Jimmy Driftwood became something of a "professional hillbilly" and an unofficial Ozark spokesman. Wolf directed folklorists to Timbo, where they would meet Driftwood and through him locate sources of folk songs. But underneath the facade of the country teacher-farmer-troubadour with the squatting black hat, and in later years the black-rimmed glasses, was a shrewd, college-educated man whose world was not circumscribed by the Boston Mountains. Driftwood's experiences with folklorists and other visitors to the region taught him their images of the Ozarks and revealed to him the hills' most sought-after commodity, its dying folk culture. Consequently, by the late 1950s Driftwood was a conscious Ozarker. Unlike most of his neighbors, he had viewed himself and his people through the eyes of his visitors and by so doing had developed an even greater appreciation for the Ozarks' heritage and folk culture. His efforts to revive folk music through the Arkansas Folk Festival and Ozark Folk Center grew from a conscious understanding of Ozark folk tradition and both an academic and nostalgic desire to preserve a piece of his own heritage.

At middle age, Driftwood followed the advice of Wolf and took his act to Nashville. In 1957 Jimmy and Cleda wound their way out of the hills and across the Mississippi to the nation's center of country-and-western music. After an informal session sitting on the bed of a two-dollar Nashville hotel room with producer Don Warden, Driftwood was invited to reprise his "Battle of New Orleans" for RCA's chief talent scout, Chet Atkins, the following morning. The Driftwoods left Nashville with no contract and promises of future contact with RCA, perhaps the same promises made to every two-bit act that passed through town. After a short time, Don Warden appeared at their farm with a contract. Within a year and a half Jimmy Driftwood would be a Nashville star. "Battle of New Orleans," recorded by Johnny Horton, reached number 1 on both the country and pop charts and won Driftwood a Grammy Award in 1959. He followed that with a string of history-lesson hits recorded by himself and others: "Billy Yank and Johnny Reb," "The Wilderness Road," and "Tennessee Stud." In mid-September 1959, six of Driftwood's songs were in the country Top 40. In subsequent years he performed regularly at the Grand Ole Opry, played Carnegie Hall and the Newport Folk Festival, and traveled to Europe and Asia on tours sponsored by the U.S. State Department.[56]

From the moment Driftwood entered the picture, the project took an unexpected and monumental turn that would alter the destiny of Mountain View and Stone County. Although it is likely that music would have been considered part of the Arkansas Folk Festival even without Driftwood's input, it is almost certain that the outcome would have been different. The festival's planners had envisioned something along the lines of a small country-and-western music program featuring Driftwood and a few of his fellow musicians from the Grand Ole Opry in Nashville. Driftwood had other visions. Concerned over the almost complete disappearance of traditional, pre–country-and-western, mountain folk music in his home county and region (and perhaps equally dismayed by the prospect of getting second or third billing to more popular Grand Ole Opry performers), Driftwood, quite oblivious to the objections of his fellow festival planners, decided to use the Arkansas Folk Festival as both a platform for personal notoriety and a project for the resuscitation of his musical heritage. Driftwood's vision for the Rackensack Folklore Society exceeded any plan of the Ozark Foothills Craft Guild or the Area Tourist and Recreation Committee.

Driftwood was not wholly without a foundation on which to build. For more than a decade John Quincy Wolf Jr. had been scouring the eastern Ozarks for folk singers and their songs. Having gained an appreciation for his region's folk music while a student at Batesville's Arkansas College just after World War I, Wolf left Arkansas to earn a master's degree from Vanderbilt and a Ph.D. in English from Johns Hopkins University. The 1941 festival in his father's native Stone County rekindled his interest in Ozark folk culture. After World War II, Wolf began scouting for folk singers by making personal journeys through north central Arkansas and by submitting folk song requests to local newspapers. Among his most notable "discoveries" were Aunt Ollie Gilbert, a Stone County grandmother whose phenomenal repertoire of British ballads was eventually displayed at the Smithsonian Folk Festival in Washington, D.C., and other festivals around the country, and Almeda Riddle of Cleburne County, whose endearing stage presence and artistic capabilities made her the region's most prominent folk singer and, next to Driftwood, the chief celebrity of the Ozark folk revival. Wolf particularly relished the thought of Riddle's concert on the campus of Harvard. "The most prestigious campus in the United States listening to Almeda Riddle. That's an incongruity." By the early 1960s both women had gained national publicity; Gilbert would become a founding member of the Rackensack Folklore Society.[57] Nevertheless, the Arkansas Ozarks continued to lack a concerted focus around preserving and passing on its musical heritage.

In early 1963 Driftwood, who had maintained his Stone County residence even during the heyday of his national fame, contacted a few old musicians whose instruments had rarely been played in the postwar years. His search was aided by a recent local development; Dr. Lloyd Hollister, a Mountain View physician, had only months earlier begun conducting informal weekend musical gatherings at his office in town. Only a handful of old musicians showed up at the initial sessions, but within two months the weekly gatherings had outgrown the tiny office, and the informal group had assumed a new identity as the Rackensack Folklore Society. By spring the musicians had moved their weekend sessions to the courthouse lawn. As was Driftwood's style, he quickly assumed leadership of the society and began planning a spring musical. Rainey and the festival's organizers decided to schedule the craft fair and musical to coincide with the second annual Dogwood Drive automobile tour. Mountain View hosted its first Arkansas Folk Festival on the weekend of 19–21 April 1963. In spite of a general pessimism among the town's business leaders regarding the festival's reliance on unknown local musical talent, approximately 10,000 visitors passed through town that weekend, and 4,500 jammed themselves into the tiny high school gymnasium to watch the performances of Driftwood's "timber cutters, farmers, housewives, and all plain people of the hills." The craft fair, limited to guild members only, generated more than $2,000 for forty-five craftspeople.[58]

Through word of mouth and promotion by Driftwood and the craft guild, the Arkansas Folk Festival expanded into the state's biggest annual tourist event. By the late 1960s, every inch of Mountain View was devoted to the April festival, and for a few years beginning in 1975, festival organizers scattered events over a three-weekend period to maintain enthusiasm, draw larger crowds, and prevent single-weekend traffic jams. By the early 1970s, crowds regularly exceeded 100,000 people. The thousands of automobiles and tour buses clogged Mountain View's tiny town square, the side streets, and all four roads leading into and out of town. Like Eureka Springs, Mountain View attracted large numbers of young counterculture denizens, many of whom sought the solitude of the Ozark National Forest for activities both legal and illegal. Their presence frequently created havoc as local law enforcement officials neglected traffic control to round up dozens, even hundreds, of hippies in Mountain View's hinterland. In 1975 local law enforcement officials, assisted by twenty-two state troopers and fourteen narcotics officers from the state police, arrested more than 400 people during the three-weekend festival. Over time, the festival also grew beyond the control of its original planners, the members of the Arkansas (formerly Ozark Foothills) Craft Guild. Faced with declining sales due to the proliferation of independent craft dealers who set up tables and booths on every street corner in town, the guild ceased its sponsorship of the Arkansas Folk Festival.[59]

The Arkansas Folk Festival, still conducted each April in conjunction with the Ozark Folk Center, was perhaps the purest and most earnest example, at least in its early years, of Ozark heritage tourism. The driving force was economic revitalization for a poor town and county, and most of the original craftspeople and musicians were native Ozarkers if not residents of Stone County.[60] As the native craftspeople and musicians have died, lost interest, or grown too old to participate, they have often been replaced by non-Ozarkers, many of them counterculture holdovers or urban escapists who came to the Ozarks in the 1960s and 1970s to learn traditional crafts. Most often this process of replacement is by necessity. Few modern Ozarkers are interested in the handicraft and musical skills of their forebears, and fewer still are recipients of such traditional folk knowledge handed down through the generations. Of course, such cultural and generational apathy is not unique to the Ozarks but is common in any modern culture. Ozarkers are no longer bound by isolation and poverty to carry on the unconscious traditions born of necessity, place, and want. The Ozarkers of 1963 were not bound to their heritage, either, which explains the paucity of native craftspeople and the musicians' need to dust off their instruments. The later years of the festival also brought an influx of hillbilly stereotypes into the picture. The wood-and-plastic caricatured moonshiners and "Daisys" obscured the original goals and products of the Arkansas Craft Guild, which in part explains the guild's ultimate disassociation from the event. Furthermore, by focusing so intently on one phase of the region's past, a period assumed to adequately represent the whole of the Ozarks' static history, the festival tended indirectly to perpetuate the image of Ozarkers as "a people without factories, who made everything they used with their own hands and who sang 'Barbara Allen' and other British ballads as in the days of Elizabeth and James I."[61]

The spirit of the Arkansas Folk Festival had its physical manifestation in the Ozark Folk Center. Nevertheless, the Ozark Folk Center grew out of a separate cause, one infused with more political overtones and less folk earnestness. The Ozark Folk Center was a decade in the making and for a dozen years racked with political turbulence. The folk center idea came from a young bureaucrat named John Opitz. Opitz, a Conway native and veteran of Korea, first mentioned his idea for a cultural center in 1963 in his capacity as regional director of the Area Redevelopment Administration (ARA), a federal agency created by Congress in 1961 for the purpose of funneling loan and grant monies into rural areas for industrial development, public facilities, technical assistance, and training programs. Personally interested in the folk movement himself, Opitz had two goals in mind: the construction of a new water and sewer system for Mountain View, a popular cause in town, and the establishment of a folk culture center for the preservation of traditional music and handicrafts. In order for the town to receive the water and sewer system, Opitz proposed to Jimmy Driftwood and local leaders the building of a music auditorium with ARA assistance. The auditorium would have to come equipped with a new system to pump water from the nearby White River, and, he suggested, the town of Mountain View could hook up to the auditorium's system. Thus began the movement to preserve the Ozarks' culture and dying traditions.[62]

Opitz's offer came as a welcome project, one whose direction Driftwood happily assumed and often selfishly maintained. In the dozen years after 1963, Driftwood would adopt the center as his personal project. Already recognized around the nation as a leading practitioner of traditional mountain music and a self-taught expert on Ozark culture, he served as a go-between, though certainly not a universally popular or uncontroversial one, in the drawn-out negotiations between Washington politicians and bureaucrats and local officials. In October 1963, a group of more than a dozen Stone County residents, including Driftwood, Harold Sherman, and craft guild president Edwin Luther, traveled to Washington, D.C., to seek financial assistance from the ARA. That request and subsequent pleas for financial assistance fell on deaf ears. After the ARA's suggestion that lobbying by a group of folk center supporters who represented a wider range of the state's interests (that is, Arkansans with more power and wealth than could be found in Stone County) would help the cause, the center's backers created such a group. In May 1965 the city council of Mountain View, under power of a state enabling act, formed the Ozark Folk Cultural Commission and elected as its chair Bessie Moore of Little Rock, a former Stone County resident who had gained statewide and national publicity as a crusader for educational and economic causes. Of the commission's eight members only one, automobile dealer Guy Lackey Jr., was a Stone County resident. Even with Driftwood marshaling the local troops and carrying the campaign on his folk-singing tour of universities, and with Moore exercising her considerable personal charms and political skills, the project ground to a halt. Orval Faubus, perhaps the country's most notorious hillbilly clown, pumped life back into the floundering commission when, as his last official gubernatorial act in early 1967, he granted the folk center supporters $25,000 out of the governor's emergency fund. Ultimately, the commission's victory relied on national political power. Wilbur D. Mills, who represented Stone County and much of the eastern Ozarks in the House, used his considerable clout as chairman of the Ways and Means Committee to coax a favorable reevaluation of the project out of the Economic Development Administration (EDA), successor to the ARA. In September 1968, the EDA approved the folk center project and set aside more than $3 million, 20 percent of which was to be paid back by the city of Mountain View over a fifty-year period.[63]

The original folk center concept called for a center for both preservation and training. The center's leaders soon discovered, as had Driftwood five years earlier, that the traditional crafts and music to be preserved had not been bequeathed to recent generations of Stone Countians. Ozarkers would have to be taught the folk skills and activities that visitors to the Arkansas Folk Festival assumed they already possessed. Consequently, in November 1969 the State Department of Vocational Education agreed to establish a branch of Searcy's Foothills Vocational–Technical School at the Ozark Folk Center for the purpose of instructing local young people in the forgotten music and crafts of their heritage. The irony explicit within the nature of the center was compounded in succeeding years. When the Advanced Project Corporation of New York, the firm awarded the original contract to build and operate what was to be a privately controlled folk center, went bankrupt in 1972, the state Parks, Recreation and Travel Commission purchased the operating lease at the behest of Ozark Folk Cultural Commission leaders and Governor Dale Bumpers. The Department of Parks and Tourism had no need for another expensive, unprofitable project and agreed to operate the Ozark Folk Center as a state park only when the Ozark Folk Cultural Commission agreed to scrap the original vocational training mission and convert the center into an outdoor museum that would charge admission.[64]

When the Ozark Folk Center was officially dedicated in May 1973, the 300-acre complex, only 80 acres of which were developed, contained a 1,060-seat auditorium, sixteen craft shops, a tourist reception center, a conference center, a restaurant, a fast-food counter, and a sixty-room lodge. The first couple of years of the Ozark Folk Center's existence were racked by numerous problems. Among the shortcomings noted by Leo Rainey in a 1973 letter to a guild member were "inadequate time to prepare for opening, inexperienced personnel in all phases including Parks employees, craft sales and demonstrations, adverse local political climate, no written guidelines on eligible products and demonstrations." The two activities of the center, music and handicrafts, were originally undertaken by locally based groups. The Department of Parks and Tourism contracted with the Ozark Foothills Craft Guild to supply Ozark crafts and craft demonstrators. The members of the guild received no salaries or wages, relying instead on sales of their crafts. Because the original center had no gift shop, craft sales were conducted at the individual shops scattered around the compound. This system proved unwieldy for the craft guild and unprofitable for its members, prompting the guild to pull out of the project and open its own craft shop near the folk center in 1975. The Department of Parks and Tourism began contracting directly with individual craftsmen, most of whom were guild members.[65]

Likewise, the Department of Parks and Tourism originally relied on Driftwood's Rackensack Folklore Society to provide musicians. By doing so the Department of Parks and Tourism, perhaps unwittingly, placed the Ozark Folk Center in the middle of a fierce local political and personal conflict. Driftwood and a core group of his original Rackensackers had long demanded that the society's song selection and musical presentations be free of any modernizing influence. Much of Driftwood's obstinacy in this regard can be attributed to his friendship and professional relationship with John Quincy Wolf Jr., a self-taught, accomplished academic folklorist who in June 1969 conducted Arkansas College's first summer Ozark Folklore Workshop.[66] The Arkansas Folk Festival in 1963 had made only one concession to modernity; a sound system and microphones were utilized because of the unexpectedly large crowd. Driftwood and Wolf relied on musicologists' definition of southern mountain folk music as premodern country music, which prevented the group from performing any song composed later than 1940 and from using electric or electrically amplified instruments. His enemies, however, challenged Driftwood's authenticity and claimed that his definition of traditional music often depended upon his personal appraisal of the musician. In the late 1960s Driftwood's hard-line, traditional approach and his sometimes abrasive leadership resulted in a split within the Rackensack ranks. His opponents, most favoring a more liberal presentation of both traditional and modern sounds, formed the Mountain View Folklore Society and began playing on the courthouse lawn on a different night of the week. According to a study by Diane O. Tebbetts, the two groups proceeded to align themselves with existing political factions within the county.[67]

By the time the Ozark Folk Center opened in 1973, Stone County's musical scene was a fragmented mess, with numerous tastes based on socioeconomic and political differences at odds with each other. Among the different groups identified by H. Page Stephens were older merchants who were attuned to contemporary national styles and for whom the traditional Ozark music represented the hillbilly stereotype that they had spent their lives outrunning; younger merchants who accepted their musical origins but were, nonetheless, more likely to prefer contemporary country-and-western sounds; Driftwood's small cadre who were aware of the nation's interest in folk culture, knowledgeable of academic definitions of folk music, and cognizant of the economic potential of mountain music; and finally, a shrinking community of older farm and rural residents whose maintenance of traditional songs and lack of exposure to national musical trends made it an attractive and valuable reservoir for performances of Ozark folk music. When the Department of Parks and

Tourism contracted with the Rackensack Folklore Society—a foregone conclusion, according to critics, because of Driftwood's membership on the Parks, Recreation and Travel Commission that controlled the department—it implicitly adopted the policies of Driftwood and the minority of traditionalists on Ozark music, further exacerbating a local rift and alienating a large number of Stone County natives. The center's opponents later accused Tommy Simmons, former Mountain View mayor and first director of the Ozark Folk Center, of awarding jobs on the basis of political motives. This multilayered division, at least initially, could be reduced to two sides: those who opposed performances of contemporary country-and-western music alongside traditional folk music versus those who accepted it. According to Stephens, the Mountain View Folklore Society and others whose musical tastes were not limited to the songs of their ancestors "remained in the mainstream" of the county's musical tastes, "while those musicians who were recreating older styles of music for a broader market were outside the current local traditions." Thus, states Stephens, "the local revival was not indigenous . . . but a reaction to national trends."[68]

Ironically, the Ozark Folk Center, by virtue of its affiliation with the Rackensack Folklore Society and that society's definition of folk music, excluded a large number of native Ozarkers and Stone Countians whose contacts with wider American culture had rendered them less "authentic." Their unself-conscious and extemporaneous melding of the indigenous and inherited with the external made them in some ways more natural and historically accurate representatives of contemporary Ozark life. They more fully reflected an Ozark heritage of experimentation, change, and adaptation than did Driftwood and the Rackensackers. Ozarkers, though certainly behind the curve of American modernization, had never lived in a timeless vacuum. Ozark farmers had long ago sought markets for their goods and goods for these markets. Their practices and lifestyles were not those of their early nineteenth-century forebears in western Virginia or the Carolinas. Their music was not either, really. Many of the songs were ancient, and many were not. Many bore the stamp of the Arkansas hills and of the twentieth century. They had been altered both subtly and completely over the generations so that drawing a boundary in the web of the past was an arbitrary exercise, one that reflected the standpoint of those outside the folk tradition.

The bottom line was that no one cared to listen to a middle-aged man from Fifty-Six play the guitar and sing about his Ozark life in a style too closely resembling that of George Jones or Merle Haggard. People would listen, and pay to listen, to an Ozarker sing folk songs. But ultimately they were not the songs of the Ozark folk. They were the songs of America's past, of its British heritage forged in wood on the southern frontier and preserved by our contemporary ancestors in this forgotten region, this "Land of a Million Smiles." This would soon become apparent to the residents of Stone County. In September 1975, after two years of political sniping in Mountain View, Governor David Pryor fired Simmons and Driftwood and completely removed any local influence from the administration of the center.[69]

Pryor's actions stemmed from a feud that had further splintered the Stone County musical community. In early 1975 Driftwood was appointed as the unsalaried musical director of the Ozark Folk Center. By this time there were, in effect, three competing groups in Mountain View. In order to contract with the Department of Parks and Tourism in 1973, the Rackensack Folklore Society had formed a nonprofit corporation, Rackensac, Inc. By 1975 the members of Rackensac, Inc., the only musicians allowed to play at the center, had split into two camps largely based on the by now larger-than-life personality of Driftwood. Driftwood's opponents within Rackensac, Inc., complained that his appointment as director posed a conflict of interest because of his position on the Parks, Recreation and Travel Commission. Several vocal members of the group resented Driftwood's dictatorial policies and most likely envied his success and fame. Driftwood feared that he and his aging original performers were being denied stage time to make way for younger talent. The conflict came to a head at the Arkansas Folk Festival in April when Driftwood, deprived of his promised thirty minutes of performance time, apologized to the audience and claimed that other members of Rackensac, Inc., were attempting to crowd him out. Rackensac, Inc., board members promptly issued a formal complaint to the Department of Parks and Tourism, asking that Driftwood be removed. When no action was taken, Rackensac, Inc., led by president and Stone County native Buddy Lancaster, terminated its contract with the folk center in May and began giving free Friday night performances on the court square.[70]

In July 1975 Driftwood instituted an individual contract system, similar to the one employed in the crafts section, whereby fifty-five musicians signed contracts to play three nights a week for $5 per night. This time Driftwood's policy of no electrical instruments or amplified music was written into the contracts. Most of those who signed to perform at the center were members of the old Rackensack Folklore Society. The furor continued, however, fueled by events that were almost comical and certainly unlikely to erase the images of feuding hillbillies in the minds of bureaucrats and politicians in Little Rock and elsewhere around the nation. In mid-July a fight broke out backstage of the auditorium between two women square dancers representing opposing sides of the Rackensac-Driftwood feud. The next week Rackensac, Inc., threatened to build its own auditorium to compete with the Ozark Folk Center. When Governor Pryor removed Simmons and Driftwood in September, he offered a compromise to the competing factions. Each of the three groups—the Mountain View Folklore Society, Driftwood's old Rackensack Folklore Society, and Rackensac, Inc.—could play two nights a week. Only Rackensac, Inc., accepted, although a few members of the Mountain View Folklore Society signed contracts late in the season. Driftwood and his Rackensackers moved to the old Uptown Theater before building the Jimmy Driftwood Barn in 1979.[71]

Increasingly in subsequent years, aging and dying native Ozark musicians and craftspeople came to be replaced by performers and demonstrators from outside the region. Some Stone Countians who "felt the idea of helping the local work force should come first" grew disillusioned in the process. A 1975 *Stone County Leader* editorial sarcastically verbalized the sentiments of many local people who felt alienated by folk center decisions. "Only a couple of weeks ago it was announced that a lady from the southern part of the state was hired to cook old-fashioned bread; of course everyone knows none of the unemployed or underemployed local hillbillies can bake those old-time biscuits."[72]

The center was also susceptible to charges of artificial preservation. As Diane O. Tebbetts stated in her study of perceptions of the Ozark Folk Center, a major concern was to avoid a situation in which the presentation of Ozark culture was "related to the real culture in the same way a mounted butterfly collection relates to a living swallowtail." Nevertheless, artificial qualities were inherent to the project. John Gould Fletcher was correct: The revival had come too late to avoid the hint of insincerity. The era in which the handicraft skills and music represented at the center were prevalent in the region had long since passed, forcing a re-creation of a past to be preserved. The lack of training funds or local interest, especially in craft making, bred an early reliance on nonnative demonstrators —women from New England and men from the urban Midwest emulating Ozark pioneers. Perhaps most important, the central purpose and function of the center, the public performances and demonstrations, ran counter to the fundamental tenets of folk culture. Folk ballads, white oak baskets, and cornshuck dolls were the products of an inward-looking, enclosed, unself-conscious people. The folk arts were not performance arts. They were part and parcel of an era of Ozark experience, integral to survival, the maintenance of tradition, and the ordering of life. Mildred Paysinger had sung ballads in the cotton fields of Sharp County to divert the young minds of her children from the painful, stinging monotony of cotton picking. Rex Harral had created cedar chests and carving tools as a creative outlet from the arduous labor of the farm and the blacksmith shop and as a valuable source of income. By making the implicit explicit, the unself-conscious self-conscious, the meaning of the folk art was altered. Each was compartmentalized and categorized into quaintness and novelty. Just as the purest Ozark humor was lost in translation, misunderstood outside its proper context and natural audience, Ozark music and craft making were inherently staged and removed from their natural environment in demonstration.[73]

Several observers recognized the discordance involved in the public presentation of folk culture. Jim Buchanan, director of publicity for Arkansas College, observed: "No longer does a wood carver sit in the shadows of the front porch to whittle out shapes from native woods. Instead he sits in the air-conditioned building in the craft area of the Folk Center with interested tourists peering at his aged hands as they go about their work."[74] John Gould Fletcher discovered quite early that Ozark music and craft making did not transfer easily into public demonstration. "The difficulty with all such attempts to get the Ozark people to display their vanishing talents is, first of all, that the people themselves are shy and do not much care to show off in front of strangers; and second, that so much fun has already been made of their supposed coarseness and quaintness, in comic strips and elsewhere, that the mountaineers have even begun to accept much of it themselves." No better example of the Ozarkers' recognition of the incongruity of public performance exists than one recounted by a contemporary of Fletcher. In 1949, while at the University of Arkansas in Fayetteville, Fletcher arranged for a local banjo player and his friends to perform for about thirty university faculty members and students. The musicians, accustomed to playing in private on Saturdays while relaxing and drinking beer, suffered stage fright and performed from inside a smokehouse. "From time to time they could be heard whispering among themselves; then they would burst into song."[75]

Despite the inherent contradictions involved in the conscious display of Ozark folk culture by non-Ozarkers, the Ozark Folk Center stands as a monument to the dream of Jimmy Driftwood and to the academic integrity of John Quincy Wolf Jr. and the center's administration. For more than a quarter-century the Ozark Folk Center has by and large maintained the original historical and cultural integrity of its visionaries, regardless of the vision's unrepresentativeness in the 1960s and 1970s. This was after all a cultural preservation that first relied on re-creation. The center achieved an even greater degree of academic integrity in 1976 when it hired professional folklorist and musicologist W. K. McNeil as full-time researcher and consultant. The Ozark Folk Center has successfully avoided the "fast-buck artists" who "jam the streets with gimmicks, Hong Kong trinkets, mass-produced glasswares, and the like."[76] The town of Mountain View and surrounding areas have been less successful in that regard.

Many local residents still harbor ill will against the center, if not for the three-decades-old political squabble, then for the center's indirect role in attracting the typical tourist town's "stall-run of roadside catering goods, which along with factory-made quilts and rugs and corn-cob pipes made in Japan, include Chinese temple bells and Alaskan totem poles."[77] Perhaps the most common complaint is that the Ozark Folk Center has not been the economic savior promised by its supporters. By the mid-1980s, the center was the county's largest employer, but of its 300 workers only 23 were full-time employees. Two-thirds of the center's workforce was comprised of seasonal contract craftspeople and musicians. Furthermore, the success of Branson, Missouri, which was blamed in part on a slumping 1990s tourism market in northern Arkansas, has rekindled old animosities toward Driftwood and the folk purists whose shortsighted meddling in local musical circles, so goes the argument, prevented Mountain View from achieving the same broad-based, musical, family-oriented success enjoyed by Branson. Nevertheless, it is probably the lack of blatant commercialism that continues to make Mountain View eminently more visitor friendly and livable.

The folk culture craze in Mountain View inspired related activities around north central and northwestern Arkansas and sparked a renewed academic interest in folklore. Three years after the first Arkansas Folk Festival, Leo Rainey helped organize the Greers Ferry Lake and Little Red River Association in Cleburne and Van Buren Counties. The organization sponsored the first annual Ozark Frontier Trail Festival at Heber Springs in 1966. In October 1972, Heber Springs held its first annual Arkansas Blue Grass Festival, which featured Bill Monroe and Lester Flatt.[78]

Three other entertainment attractions arose in the late 1960s to capitalize on the region's growing popularity and on the images of the Ozark folk, both positive and negative. Though not immediate products of the folk culture movement in the Ozarks, all three owed their existence at least in part to the heightened interest in the region brought about by the movement. One of the three disappeared almost as quickly as it was conceived. Ozarkland, a small theme park complete with a frontier homestead, was hastily erected in the retirement village of Horseshoe Bend in 1969, primarily to serve as a filming location for the short-lived syndicated *Ozarkland Jamboree*. The company's creator, Albert Gannaway, an Arkansan who undertook the project at the urging of the Ozarks Regional Commission, hoped to re-create the success he had enjoyed with his earlier *Grand Ole Opry* television program in the 1950s and 1960s. Like the retirement community in which it was built, Ozarkland and the *Ozarkland Jamboree* had almost no connection to the local area or to the region. The regular musicians hired for the show were recruited from Nashville and from a West Virginia television program, the *Wheeling Jamboree*. Despite a flurry of activity in the summer of 1969—Ozarkland even constructed an exact replica of *Gunsmoke*'s Dodge City set, called Starr City, in hopes of luring that production to Arkansas for an episode or two—by the end of the year *Ozarkland Jamboree* had folded and Gannaway had left. In the early 1970s, small-time country music producer and promoter Gene Williams of West Memphis tried to attract visitors to the facilities Ozarkland left behind by presenting musical events and refurbishing the homestead and Starr City into an amusement park called Frontierland. Despite these efforts, Horseshoe Bend proved to be a poor location for such generic tourist attractions.[79]

Horseshoe Bend might have been less than ideal for a theme park and television studio, but one other retirement community proved an ideal location for a more Ozark-themed attraction. In 1968 Leo Rainey decided to put his hard-earned tourism expertise to the test by opening up the Arkansaw Traveller Folk Theatre just below Hardy and near the entrance to Cherokee Village. He and James Bobo came up with the idea for a humorous, musical play based on the nineteenth-century legend after a 1967 trip to Gatlinburg, Rainey's first journey to eastern Tennessee since 1962. Rainey's involvement in the folk culture movement had spurred his own interest in folk music and had introduced him to enough talented eastern Ozarkers, including Cave City musicians Olaf and Orilla Pinkston, to fill out the cast of a dinner theater troupe. For several years the Arkansaw Traveller Folk Theatre flourished with a captive audience. In the summers of the late 1960s and 1970s, Cherokee Village entertained hundreds of guests each weekend, most of them midwesterners attracted by the free lodging provided as a marketing tool. Most often Rainey's theater was the only entertainment Sharp County's nights offered. The Arkansaw Traveller Folk Theatre was indicative of the Ozark tourist industry in general in that it capitalized on Ozark stereotypes but attempted to redeem the hillbilly. Tourists from Illinois and Ohio got to hear real hillbilly music played by real Ozarkers, and the natives in the play delighted in the assurance that the poor, slovenly squatter outsmarted the city fellow every time. Rainey sold the theater in 1990 after several years of declining attendance. The new owner, from northeastern Arkansas, attempted to revive interest by intensifying the hillbilly quotient. She brought to the stage the barefoot, slack-jawed frontiersmen found on postcards in every convenience store and tourist trap in the Ozarks, but the buffoonish Ozarkers could not bring back the crowds, forcing the theater to close its doors in the mid-1990s.[80]

The Arkansas Ozarks' most ambitious tourist project relied from its inception on the cultivation of the more negative aspects of the Ozark image. Dogpatch, U.S.A., was the largest theme park ever developed in northern Arkansas and the most exploitative of American stereotypes of mountain people. The idea for the park originated with a group of Harrison businessmen in 1967. A generation earlier, Randolph's "village patriots" would have fainted at the prospect of spending hundreds of thousands of dollars to build a small city whose basic purpose was to empty tourists' pockets by reinforcing their stereotypes of Ozarkers. By 1967, amid the rediscovery of the region sparked by the folk culture movement, middle-class Ozark town dwellers had begun to see dollar signs in the region's image, regardless of the interpretation. There were concerns about the image Dogpatch, U.S.A., would project, but the most vocal opponents were state publicity employees who feared the park would revive Arkansas's "Bob Burns image."[81]

Dogpatch, U.S.A., was based on the long-running Al Capp comic strip "in which rustic yokels cavorted in a manner supposed to have originated in backwoods Kentucky, not Arkansas."[82] The New England–born cartoonist granted permission to use his characters; he was even among the eleven original stockholders of Recreation Enterprises, Inc., the Harrison-based parent company of the park headed by realtor O. J. Snow. Recreation Enterprises, Inc., chose its location on Arkansas Highway 7 midway between Harrison and Jasper, near the Boone-Newton county line. The 825 acres in the Boston Mountain region lay in one of the most rugged and sparsely settled areas of the Ozarks; nevertheless, Highway 7 was a favorite route for motorists who were absorbing some of Arkansas's most scenic vistas, and the park site lay only a few miles from the Buffalo River.

Despite its isolation, the site seemed a perfect place for the theme park. The land contained two natural attractions, Marble Falls and Mystic Cave. Furthermore, the post office and deserted general store from the old hamlet of Marble Falls (formerly Wilcockson) stood as a reminder of the small but nearly vanished farming community that once scraped life from these hills and hollows.[83]

Recreation Enterprises, Inc., hired local farmers and carpenters to erect the log and plank buildings of Dogpatch, U.S.A., using old lumber and logs snatched from deserted neighborhood buildings. When the craftsmanship of the Newton and Boone Countians turned out to be too superior for the hillbilly image depicted in Capp's fictional Dogpatch, management called the workers back to "smash the ridgepoles and make the roofs look slovenly."[84] Capp made his first visit to Newton County in the fall of 1967 for Dogpatch, U.S.A.'s, dedication. When asked by a wary reporter if he thought the new park would hurt the state's image, Capp wryly replied that it certainly could do nothing more to hurt the image and, most important, it would bring money to the depressed area. In fact, officials of Recreation Enterprises, Inc., believed they knew just how much money it would bring. A Los Angeles–based firm they commissioned to conduct an economic impact study promised that within ten years Dogpatch, U.S.A.'s, annual attendance would exceed 1 million, which would translate into the addition of $5 million to the local economy each summer. Dogpatch, U.S.A., officially opened on 18 May 1968, again with Capp on hand. Capp's whole crew—Li'l Abner, Daisy Mae, Mammy and Pappy Yokum—were on hand as well to witness the beginning of what he called the "greatest Urban renewal project I've ever seen." As Capp addressed the audience, Mammy Yokum hollered from the roof of the country store, and an angry hillbilly with a shotgun chased his daughter and her young suitor across the roof of the railroad station. Most of the other roofs were adorned with statues of goats. Clearly, this was no cultural celebration, but blatant exploitation, and most of the local people knew it. The park's demonstration of Ozark fiddling, singing, dancing, and wood carving did little to assuage local suspicions.[85]

Dogpatch, U.S.A., underwent a transformation in late 1968 and early 1969 from the merely corny to the bizarre. In October 1968 Little Rock businessman Jess P. Odom, fresh from the $11.5 million sale of his interest in National Investors Life Insurance Company, purchased Recreation Enterprises, Inc., for $750,000 and immediately announced plans to spend $5 million in an effort to bring Dogpatch, U.S.A., to the level of other successful amusement parks such as Six Flags and Disneyland.

(During the 1968 summer season, the small park had managed to attract 300,000 visitors despite its lack of Disneyland-type rides and its relative isolation.) Three months later Odom hired former governor Orval Faubus to run Dogpatch, U.S.A.—the most caricatured Ozarker alive overseeing an entire estate of hillbilly stereotypes and caricatures. Faubus had his own reasons for accepting the offer. Primarily, he needed the money. Faubus had foolishly begun construction on a veritable mansion back home in Madison County, although his $10,000 a year former governor's salary and his lack of financial acumen had left him only slightly better off than he had been before his twelve-year reign of Arkansas. To make matters worse, he was in the process of losing the house in a divorce from his first wife. So in early 1969 Faubus and his new bride, almost thirty years his junior, settled in Harrison to be nearer his new project. Odom also brought in a creative director to oversee the actors portraying Capp's characters, added several amusement park attractions such as a roller coaster, railroad, and other rides, and antagonized local residents of Marble Falls by constructing a new post office on park grounds and by officially changing the community's name to Dogpatch. Odom and Faubus advertised nationally and held the first Miss Dogpatch Pageant in June in front of the "Korn-vention Hall," with college student contestants from as far away as Florida.[86]

As it turned out, Dogpatch, U.S.A., was the first acquisition in Odom's Ozark spending spree. In June 1969 the millionaire purchased the 14,000-acre Ozark Wildlife Club in the remote eastern Newton County community of Bass. Faubus was also placed in charge of this resort area, which at the time already contained a small hotel, swimming pool, hunters' bunkhouse, five lakes, riding stables, and rifle and archery ranges. Odom viewed the club, renamed National Wildlife, Inc., as a complement to Dogpatch and arranged for the sale of lots at Bass. Three years later, Odom established Marble Falls Estates across the highway from Dogpatch. Billed as Arkansas's first winter sports resort, Marble Falls Estates boasted three ski slopes, a three-story Alpine lodge, an indoor skating rink, and a 17,000-square-foot convention center and hotel fashioned from native stone and wood. Odom also offered to sell estates adjacent to the resort and planned to construct chalet rentals and an antique automobile museum.[87]

Faubus eventually left Dogpatch, U.S.A. The park, moderately successful but never in danger of threatening Disneyland (or most other American amusement parks for that matter), changed hands a few times before it closed in the early 1990s. Dogpatch, U.S.A.'s, various managers could never decide if they wanted a Six Flags over the Ozarks or a New-ton County version of Silver Dollar City.[88] The park was too far from the currents of American mainstream tourism to succeed as the former, and Dogpatch, U.S.A., was from the beginning too hokey and insincere to emulate the latter. Odom's other Ozark ventures proved even more fleet-ing. In 1997 residents of Dogpatch, Arkansas, many of them newcomers to the area, perhaps officially brought an end to the Dogpatch saga when the U.S. Postal Service granted their petition to change the name of the post office to Marble Falls. The amusement park still sprawls in the hol-low as a reminder of failed dreams. It is a testament to America's willing-ness to exploit the images of an entire culture and of many Ozarkers' will-ingness to poke fun at themselves. By the late 1990s Dogpatch, U.S.A., once a giant living stereotype of mountain life, had become a tawdry symbol of man's struggle in the hills of northern Arkansas. This multi-million-dollar caricature of a region and its image had suffered the same fate as scores of the Ozarks' promising settlements over the past 175 years.

With the exception of the Passion Play and the Ozark Folk Center, the most ambitious tourism projects in the Arkansas Ozarks eventually failed. By the late 1990s even these two enterprises had begun to feel the effects of Branson's rise to national prominence and the growing popu-larity of casinos in Missouri and Mississippi. Furthermore, tourism is a precarious business. The tastes of travelers are finicky and can change on a whim. By the 1990s, the nation's interest in southern mountain folk music had clearly subsided. Many Ozark tourist towns, such as Hardy, Mountain View, and Eureka Springs, had come to rely increasingly on a renewed interest in Ozark crafts, both the tacky factory-made glasswares and corncob pipes and the high-quality handicrafts of artisans in the Arkansas Craft Guild. Just as outsiders interested in preserving folk music have replaced native Ozark performers at the Ozark Folk Center, newcomers have achieved an almost complete dominance of the handi-craft industry. Arkansas Craft Guild members and independent crafts-people in the Ozarks produce some of the finest ironworks, pottery, can-dles, dulcimers, and wood carvings found anywhere in the United States. Most are not particularly Ozarkian, and almost none are handcrafted by Ozark natives.

Tourism has not been a panacea for northern Arkansas's economic woes. Northwestern Arkansas, easily the region's most prosperous area, owes little of its success to the tourism industry. Influential residents and government officials in north central Arkansas, however, consciously hitched their financial wagons to tourism when it looked as if no other approach was feasible. The results have been bittersweet. Certain areas, Mountain Home, Mountain View, Hardy, and Eureka Springs among them, have experienced economic revitalization and tremendous business growth. But this has rarely worked for the benefit of the natives whose depressed status in the early 1960s had originally prompted efforts to lure tourists to the Ozarks. The tourism industry has generated for Ozarkers unskilled, seasonal, minimum-wage, usually retail employment that barely lifts workers above poverty level. Skilled occupations such as folk music and handicraft jobs have been assumed by newcomers drawn to the region by nostalgia for the old days or by currents of the counterculture movement. The Parks, Recreation and Travel Commission's decision to drop the Ozark Folk Center's original and costly mission of training local young people in the arts and music of their ancestors helped assure this development. Furthermore, the government-operated and private small businesses created by tourism contribute relatively little to local tax bases that support schools, hospitals, and other services.

Perhaps the most ironic, and the most predictable, result of the post–World War II tourism boom has been its modernizing influence. The Arkansas Ozarks' popularity in the 1960s and 1970s grew both from its image of isolated innocence and from the survival of British folk ballads and remnants of a frontier existence long vanished in most parts of urbanized America. The very unconscious quaintness and uniqueness that first attracted visitors and tourists to places like Mountain View and Hardy quickly disappeared in the wake of waves of tourism in the late 1960s and 1970s.

Anthropologists Charles F. Keyes and Pierre L. van den Berghe have addressed this phenomenon. The presence of the tourist "transforms the native into a 'touree,' that is, into a performer who modifies his behavior for gain according to his perception of what is attractive to the tourist. ... The tourist quest for authenticity is, thus, doomed by the very presence of tourists."[89] One writer for the St. Louis Post-Dispatch noted this development during a trip to the 1974 Arkansas Folk Festival. "The Folk Festival was founded ostensibly to preserve the old mountain ways, but it is very much the child of change. ... The Arkansas Ozarks are becoming more and more a bustling, 'progressive' place."[90]

By the 1990s, visitors were still invited to "step back in time to the Arkansas that used to be" in Mountain View, but they could also expect to find the same fast-food franchises, convenience stores, and traffic jams that they had left behind. And they were just as likely to buy an Ozark handicraft made by someone from their hometown or state as they were one made by a native Ozarker. One result of this modernizing phenomenon is that the areas of the region infrequently visited by tourists, the locales whose lack of scenic vistas, folk singers, or log cabins rendered them somehow less Ozarkian and therefore less appealing in the 1960s and 1970s, had become by the 1990s the truest bearers of unself-conscious Ozark tradition and life. Towns such as Huntsville, Berryville, Marshall, Salem, and Melbourne and their rural hinterlands were purer, less adulterated representatives of the modern Ozarks and its agricultural past than were Mountain View, Hardy, and Mountain Home, and certainly more so than Eureka Springs or Dogpatch.[91]

In many ways the Ozark image has changed less than the tourist towns that live off that image. Appalachia lost its innocence in the eyes of the nation during the 1960s. There were still pockets of territory in the eastern mountains untouched by the miner's pick and as seemingly bucolic as any in the Ozarks. But the mountains of articles about poverty and the political battles of the Appalachian Regional Commission had altered Americans' perceptions of the region. Most treatments of the Ozarks over the past three decades, however, have continued to perpetuate myth and legend either directly or indirectly by relying on tried and tested methods of Ozark portraiture. In the first year of the Reagan era, *Reader's Digest* carried a romantic, nostalgic article on the region in which the author claimed: "Life in the Ozarks is notably like life in the rural past. Stacked beside cabins with wood stoves for heating rise hand-hewn walls of cordwood. Few of those cabins have phones; some have only kerosene lanterns for light."[92] In 1970 *National Geographic* featured a story on the region, "Through Ozark Hills and Hollows," that was in essence an update of the magazine's 1944 article. Except for photos of a modern resort, a traffic jam, and a nuclear testing facility, the pictorial essay was almost interchangeable with the earlier piece, featuring jig dancing old men on the Stone County courthouse lawn, an antique water mill, canoeists, fishermen, rifle-toting town marshals, an aging farmstead with its elderly tenders, folk musicians, craftspeople, and a tent revival. The article featured foxhunting, storytelling, and other typical topics from the 1950s, but the writer's theme stressed recent transformations in the region and their positive effects. The Ozarks may have been poorer than Appalachia, but prosperity was around the corner in the form of tourism and retiree settlement.[93]

Most post-Watergate popular treatments of the region reflected a subtle change in the image. Most, in the words of Paul Faris, "have avoided the word 'hillbilly,'" although realism has been shunned in favor of nostalgia and romance.[94] The most common portrait of the region in the past quarter-century, the photographic book or essay, has transformed the feelings of romance for the Ozarks as a land of contemporary ancestors to feelings of nostalgia for the Ozarks and Ozarkers as they used to be. Whereas travel writers once mourned the loss of rural America by wrapping their arms and cameras around the picturesque elements of the Ozark backcountry, by the 1970s writers and photographers were lamenting the demise of the last American stronghold of the "log cabin folks." With the exception of the *Reader's Digest* article mentioned above, most writers in this era did not try to pass the region off as a modern Shangri-la. They did, however, suggest that the "hills continue to provide a haven for those who wish to leave time be" and that the remote Ozarks was a place "where a woman may still cook over a wood-burning stove and a man may still plow with a team of mules."[95]

By the 1970s the Ozarks had lost its value as a land of contemporary ancestors. It had lost its value as a contemporary culture altogether. The image that had for so long represented the region was no longer tenable. The only thing left to do was reminisce nostalgically about the loss of the Ozarks', and hence America's, innocence as a place at one with nature, as a land unspoiled by the encroachment of modernity. In some sense this reaction reflected not only the realization that the Ozarks of popular image had disappeared but also the benediction of the failure of the back-to-the-land movement and the ultimate American triumph of technology, industry, and the marketplace. And in the tradition of popular Ozark chronicling, the presentations of the region in the 1970s and 1980s demonstrated ambivalence; the photographs and texts often told two different stories. The four best representatives for this era of popular Ozark interpretation appeared in an eight-year span between 1975 and 1983. All of them relied heavily on the power of photography to invoke romantic appreciation for the majesty of nature and nostalgia and regret for a lost Arcadia.

C. W. Gusewelle's article in *American Heritage* was indicative of the modern, popular Ozark interpretation. Amid dominating color photographs of mountains and rivers, the *Kansas City Star* editorial writer interjected a brief but generally accurate history of the region, with the usual concentrations on free-flowing streams and an isolated Newton County community. Gusewelle recognized that the primary attraction of the Ozarks had always been its natural gifts. Interestingly, his only photo involving people captured a picking and grinning musical session on the large wraparound porch of an old white house. Within his text Gusewelle was careful to inject a dose of reality as a counterpoint to the romance and nostalgia of the photographs. Although readers never viewed the "hardship and disappointment and pain," they were assured it existed. Furthermore, readers were reminded that "a region and its people cannot be kept as a living museum. Even if that were possible, it would be wrong."[96]

There were, of course, those who would have been content with a living Ozark museum. Many tourism entrepreneurs depended upon it, or at least upon the perpetuation of that museum in image. Others sought to perpetuate the static Ozark image in print. Whereas some writers and photographers searched the remote Boston Mountains for relics of generations past, Helen and Townsend Godsey declined to search for anachronisms. Instead their *Ozark Mountain Folk: These Were the Last* consisted of photographs depicting northern Arkansas and southern Missouri at midcentury. Their failure to indicate dates for the pictures invoked once again, perhaps intentionally, the old static image of the Ozarks. Another work of Ozark photography, Paul Faris's *Ozark Log Cabin Folks: The Way They Were*, also made use of midcentury photos, though they were less staged than the Godseys'. Faris's work was also the most realistic of the four treatments in both its text and pictures. Although obviously presented in a spirit of nostalgia, *Ozark Log Cabin Folks* offered the reader a more accurate presentation of Ozark social change. Faris based his book on the pictorial contrasts between log cabin farmsteads as they were when he first visited them between 1949 and 1952 and as they appeared when he returned in 1969. The people Faris visited after World War II "were mostly Ozark log cabin folk in the last of their years. Even for them the conditions typical of their earlier years were largely gone." By 1969 the cabins themselves were gone or had been turned into storage sheds and barns.[97]

The first of the four, and the most sentimental and artistic, was Roger and Bob Minick's *Hills of Home*. The subjects of Roger Minick's photographs from the late 1960s and early 1970s were the relics of the region's past, both recent and distant: Stone County musicians, Leslie store-porch whittlers, leather-skinned octogenarians, mule-plowing farmers. Poignant and beautiful photos all, they were nonetheless the Ozarkers of the Minicks' nostalgic yearning. They were representatives of a past whose vision was clouded by the uncertainty of the future. The black-and-white, wintery backdrops of most photographs heightened nostalgic intensity while they also reinforced the vision of finality within seasonal perpetuity.[98] *Hills of Home* is a sad book, haunted by modernization and the inevitable march of time. We learn in the introduction that the Stilleys, the young family featured so prominently throughout the book as an anachronism in a region that breeds and thrives off anachronisms, had, like their Ozark predecessors, succumbed in part to the forces of the modern world by the time the book was published in 1975. Unable to meet the demands of the local dairy company that had been purchasing the family's milk, the patriarch of the Stilleys, a prematurely gaunt and toothless man, had been forced to find work in a nearby town. It was a story so old and so common in the Arkansas Ozarks and in rural America as to be almost mundane and hardly newsworthy. The immediacy of this one final instance bore the despair and resilience of generations of Ozarkers, the antidote, but a nostalgically addictive one, to an Ozark image nearing a half-century in age. The faces of the old foretold the Stilleys' demise. Staring from colorless porches on two-dimensional houses, their eyes exhausted from viewing a lifetime of change and their shoulders stooped beneath the memories of unseen hardships and joys, the elderly Ozarkers would soon be gone and with them all traces of a past so revered and romanticized, yet so misunderstood.

CONCLUSION

IN THE SUMMER OF 1993, I took a three-month position as oral historian and director of the Ozark Oral History Program at the Ozark Folk Center in Mountain View. To familiarize myself with the center, I spent one June morning touring the grounds and shops of the craft section. When I introduced myself and explained my purpose at the center to one young craftswoman, whose accent revealed that like most of her fellow craftspeople she was a newcomer to the Ozarks, she assured me that there were pockets of the region, some not far from the Folk Center, where the natives still spoke with a style of English nearly Elizabethan. I was shocked and somewhat disturbed to hear this statement, by now a company line for the preservers and purveyors of Ozark culture, that I had read time and time again in magazine articles and books dating to the 1920s. One year later, writer and humorist Andrei Codrescu informed readers of *Travel Holiday* magazine that "going to the Ozark Mountains is like visiting your grandmother, provided your grandmother was an old-fashioned, pie-baking, herb-growing pioneer who used homemade brooms and poured ice cream from a dented churn."[1] Codrescu's tongue-in-cheek style may have undermined the sincerity of his observation; it also subtly let the reader in on the joke. Everyone knew that such a frontier wonderland could scarcely be possible inside the modern American society of fax machines, computers, and cross-country flights, even in the Ozarks. But it certainly did not hurt to dream of a simpler, more romantic past, and the Ozarks' static image continued to provide a tenuous link to such a past. Old images die hard, if in fact they ever do.

By the 1990s the Arkansas Ozark region was a vastly different place than it had been in the 1890s or even in the 1950s. The region's image, however, maintained many of the elements that had first been incorporated into Americans' visions of the "Land of a Million Smiles" more than half a century earlier and cultivated by folklorists and tourism entrepreneurs in succeeding decades. For many urban dwellers around the

Midwest and the middle South, the Ozarks remained a clean, rural get-away far removed from the hustle and bustle of the modern world and reminiscent of an earlier, more simple and innocent way of life. In fact, the Arkansas Ozarks in the 1990s was still, by American standards, very rural. Over half the region's counties contained no town of at least 2,500 inhabitants, and only in northwestern Arkansas—where Fayetteville, Springdale, Rogers, and Bentonville had practically grown together to form "Northwest Arkansas City"—were there concentrations of people substantial enough to qualify as metropolitan under U.S. Census Bureau requirements. The Ozarks continued to offer the traveler scenic autumn vistas of forested hillsides ablaze with color, free-flowing streams beneath sheer granite bluffs, and quaint town squares of native sandstone and whitewashed buildings.

Beyond the aesthetic qualities of the region lay the signs of rural modernization, economic and agricultural transformation, and demographic change. Intraregional divergence was as visible as ever before. The University of Arkansas and a handful of Fortune 500 companies had lifted the northwestern corner of the state to a position of economic and cultural prominence. By the 1990s the "Northwest Arkansas City" corridor was the fastest-growing and most prosperous section of the state. The interior of the Arkansas Ozarks, nevertheless, was marked by pockets of poverty and large expanses of rural landscape offering little hope for economic betterment and lifestyle improvement. (A 1998 study conducted by the state education department revealed that more than 90 percent of the students at the smallest and most isolated school in Arkansas, Witts Springs, lived in families considered impoverished by the federal government.) Within the Ozarks outside of the Springfield Plain, a few municipalities had experienced economic growth and modernization through the tourism industry and fewer still through the development of a small manufacturing industry. These striking disparities within the Arkansas Ozarks were not new to the late twentieth century, but had been evident since antebellum times.

The price of modernization, even in the most rural backcountry areas of the region, had been the demise of the local community and the loss of a traditional culture and way of life fashioned by frontier demands, isolation, and hardship. By the late twentieth century, VCRs, cable and satellite television, paved roads, automobiles, and the Internet had in many ways brought homogenization to disparate American communities and regions by leveling cultural differences. Ozark children in the 1990s were eminently more familiar with the lyrics of songs by Mariah Carey and

Garth Brooks than with the words to "Barbara Allen." Some in the Ozarks had even benefited from the loss of traditional culture. The demand for folk music and Ozark crafts relied heavily on nostalgia, usually by non-Ozarkers, for this lost culture and its bygone, romanticized era. This nostalgia most likely will intensify in the twenty-first century. But the demands of travelers and tourists searching for the physical manifestations of the American rural past, searching for their contemporary ancestors, must increasingly be met by the artificial and the staged. By the late twentieth century that is probably what most Americans had come to expect, perhaps even to desire.

Even the people inhabiting the Ozark region in the late twentieth century were becoming less Ozarkian in the sense of their possessing an ancestral link with the region. The last half of the twentieth century brought about a monumental demographic shift in the Arkansas Ozarks that witnessed a mass exodus of rural families whose forebears had found the region in the nineteenth century and an equally significant inmigration of people whose heritage lay outside the northern Arkansas hills. By the 1990s, newcomers to the Ozarks outnumbered natives in several areas around the region; even the most remote, dirt-road sections of northern Arkansas had been affected in some way by this twentieth-century invasion. In a 1998 *National Geographic* feature, writer Lisa Moore LaRoe observed this demographic development and revealed a key component of the modern Ozarks' allure to nonnatives: "I felt at home in Jasper. Nearly everyone I met was from somewhere else."[2] And, although the majority of these newcomers were white Americans from midwestern states, the 1990s witnessed the arrival of some 20,000 Hispanic immigrants (many of them illegal aliens) in northwestern Arkansas, most of them lured to Washington and Benton Counties by the promise of low-income labor in poultry processing plants. By the beginning of the twenty-first century, one could find on the Springfield Plain Spanish-language newspapers, radio, and church services.[3] This latest wave of immigration into the region may achieve the most significant and lasting demographic alterations of any such development in the Arkansas Ozarks.

Although the Arkansas Ozarks in the late twentieth century was largely a rural region, it was no longer an agricultural one. The cattle, poultry, and dairy farmers whose barns and animals inhabited the hills and hollows were only a sparse remnant of the tens of thousands of agriculturists who once farmed the rocky hillsides and fertile bottoms. The intraregional diversity that had once described the region's agriculture —cotton in the east; grain, dairy, and fruit in the west; and general semisubsistence farming in the mountainous interior—had been replaced by a generally homogeneous system of small, part-time commercial cattle raisers and contract poultry farmers. The vast majority of Ozarkers made their livings in the region's towns, where small factories, wood and agricultural processing plants, and low-paying government and service jobs had largely transformed the last two generations of Ozarkers from farmers and farm laborers into blue-collar workers. The development of small-scale industry and the expansion of service employment had helped stem the tide of young people leaving the area. Nevertheless, most areas of the Arkansas Ozarks continued to offer little promise for college-educated and highly skilled workers. Most of the young leaving for college in the late twentieth century could still expect to be swallowed up by the world outside their home counties and region.

The Arkansas Ozarks entered the twenty-first century as a region of paradox and change. The Ozark region produced Orval Faubus and J. William Fulbright. It is the home of Fayetteville and Hemmed-in Holler, of Mountain Home and Mt. Judea. It is a former domain of the crossroads merchant and the birthplace of Wal-Mart. It has inspired images of backwardness and bucolic innocence, which in turn have spawned Dogpatch, U.S.A. and the Ozark Folk Center. It has been vacated by thousands of its children in poverty and despair and coveted by thousands of others for its beauty, serenity, and isolation. Its soil has provided life and little else for generations of agriculturists; now it rests beneath pastured fields, terraced and gullied hillsides, manicured golf courses, and blackjack scrub thickets. It is a "land of yesterday and tomorrow in unbreakable wedlock."[4] It is an image and a people, an experience of reality shrouded by myth. The Ozarkers are its offspring. Their ridges and mountains have wrapped them at times in isolation, at times in poverty, at times in shelter, and almost always in stereotype and in the shadows of the past.

NOTES

Abbreviations

AAES	Arkansas Agricultural Experiment Station, Fayetteville
AHC	Arkansas History Commission, Little Rock
AMS Census	Agricultural Manuscript Schedules of the U.S. Census
FESRA	Federal Extension Service Records—Arkansas, National Archives and Records Administration, Southwest Region, Fort Worth, Texas
LCA	Lyon College Archives, Batesville, Arkansas
SHC	Southern Historical Collection, University of North Carolina, Chapel Hill
UASC	University of Arkansas Special Collections, Fayetteville
UCAA	University of Central Arkansas Archives, Conway

Introduction

1. Randolph, *The Ozarks*, v, 21, 4, 5.

2. Ibid., 4.

3. Shapiro, *Appalachia on Our Mind*; see also Whisnant, *Modernizing the Mountaineer*, and Whisnant, *All That Is Native and Fine*.

4. I do not propose that other regions in the United States did not embody the traits of innocence and isolation after World War II. Appalachia contained pockets of society untouched by the lumberman's saw or the miner's pick. Americans also found tradition and folk life alive in communities from New England to the West Coast. But as an entire region, the Ozarks best exemplified the nostalgic ideal.

5. Louisa Comstock, "How to Leave Home and Like It," *House Beautiful*, March 1949, 190. The term "contemporary ancestors" dates to the turn of the century and has become a key element of any discussion of southern mountain image. William Goodell Frost, "Our Contemporary Ancestors in the Southern Mountains," *Atlantic Monthly*, March 1899, 311–19.

6. The Ozark region has been difficult for writers and government officials, and sometimes even geographers, to pin down. Boundaries fluctuate according to their purposes: geological, cultural, political, or socioeconomic. The term "Ozark" is often erroneously applied to sections of the Ouachitas, a separate and distinct upland region in southwestern Arkansas and southeastern Oklahoma. While my Ozark bound-

aries for this study may initially appear arbitrary, I have made use of a combination of the above boundary determinants to establish a fairly homogeneous sociocultural area sharing basic economic and political characteristics. The physiographical and topographical characteristics of the Ozark plateau completely encompass thirteen counties in north central and northwestern Arkansas and account for significant portions of several "border" counties. Although the similarities of rural lifestyles in southern Missouri and northern Arkansas are great, the political boundaries have produced both subtle and obvious differences that prevent automatic comparisons. For general statistical purposes I will cite census data only from the thirteen counties completely within the Ozark plateau in addition to Cleburne and Van Buren Counties. My reason for this is quite simple. Whereas the majority of border counties, such as Franklin, Randolph, and Independence, are comprised at least in small part of flatlands distinguishable from the Ozarks—the Arkansas River valley in the south and the Mississippi alluvial plain in the east—Cleburne and Van Buren are entirely made up of upland topographical features. Although the southern stretches of both counties are technically a part of the extended uplands of the Arkansas River valley, any physical and cultural dissimilarities between the northern (Ozark) and southern (Arkansas River valley) sections of these counties are indistinguishable to the naked eye, and the history and development of these two counties has in almost every way been consistent with the history and development of the other Ozark counties.

7. Although my work is not a revision of historical interpretations of the Ozarks, it is consistent with a growing body of works in the field of Appalachian studies that downplays exceptionalism and stresses intraregional diversity. See Pudup, Billings, and Waller, *Appalachia in the Making*; Dunn, *Cade's Cove*.

Chapter One

1. Schoolcraft, *Rude Pursuits*, 44, 51; Rafferty, *The Ozarks*, 17, 18. For a detailed analysis of the diversity of soil types and fertility in the Ozark region, see Sauer, *Geography of the Ozark Highland*.

2. Schoolcraft, *Rude Pursuits*, 76; Rafferty, *The Ozarks*, 16, 17.

3. Schoolcraft, *Rude Pursuits*, 95–96.

4. Ibid., 82; Rafferty, *The Ozarks*, 14.

5. Rafferty, *The Ozarks*, 18, 19.

6. Schoolcraft, *Rude Pursuits*, 78; Ingenthron, *Indians of the Ozark Plateau*, 60, 105, 100; Rafferty, *The Ozarks*, 35; Lankford, "'Beyond the Pale,'" 63. See also Lankford, "The Cherokee Sojourn."

7. Rafferty, *The Ozarks*, 51; Jeffery, *Historical and Biographical Sketches*, 1, 2; Lafferty, "The Lafferty Family," 4–5; Lankford, "'Beyond the Pale,'" 64; Shinn, *Pioneers and Makers*, 291–93. According to some accounts, the Laffertys were accompanied by a family named Creswell or Criswell.

8. Huddleston, Rose, and Wood, *Steamboats and Ferries*, 3–6; Lankford, "Shawnee Convergence," 392; Schoolcraft, *Rude Pursuits*, 110, 111.

9. Jeffery, *Historical and Biographical Sketches*, 9.

10. Baker, "Jacob Wolf," 182–92; Schoolcraft, *Rude Pursuits*, 109. The Wolf house,

widely believed to be the oldest surviving two-story log house in Arkansas, still overlooks the White River.

11. Schoolcraft, *Rude Pursuits*, 67, 62; Keefe and Morrow, *The White River Chronicles*, 16–17.

12. Pitcaithley, "Buffalo River," 70–71.

13. Worley, "Story of an Early Settlement," 122–23; Evalena Berry, *Time and the River*, 19.

14. Schoolcraft, *Rude Pursuits*, 113–14; Dougan, *Arkansas Odyssey*, 63. According to Rafferty, the editor of Schoolcraft's journal, the site of the hamlet on a tributary of the Strawberry was probably at or near the present-day community of Calamine.

15. Goodspeed, *Northwestern Arkansas*, 142–43.

16. Shiloh Museum, *History of Washington County*, 91–92.

17. Ibid., 94; Ted J. Smith, "Slavery in Washington County," 14.

18. Walz, "Migration into Arkansas," 74; Owsley, *Plain Folk*, 52. In addition to the Ozark counties of Benton, Carroll, Fulton, Izard, Madison, Marion, Newton, Searcy, Van Buren, and Washington, Walz includes in his calculations the border, but majority Ozark, counties of Independence and Lawrence.

19. Gerlach, "Ulster Influence," 34–35. Another factor is that almost any family native to the Ozarks today lays claim to at least one Native American ancestor. While it is possible and even likely that some of the Appalachian settlers in the region had intermarried with the Cherokee or other tribes, it is unlikely that it was as common as eager genealogists would have us believe.

20. Shiloh Museum, *History of Washington County*, 93–94; Huddleston, "The Early Jefferys," 3–4; Baker, "Jacob Wolf," 182; Goodspeed, *Northwestern Arkansas*, 974, 1005.

21. U.S. Department of State, Agricultural Manuscript Census Schedules, Newton, Izard, and Fulton Counties, Arkansas, 1860; Sistler and Sistler, *1850 Census—Tennessee*.

22. Goodspeed, *Northeastern Arkansas*, 938–39, 975; Goodspeed, *Northwestern Arkansas*, 984–85.

23. Turner, "Significance of the Frontier," 206–8; Schoolcraft, *Rude Pursuits*, 52, 60, 62–63. Although Schoolcraft refers to the them as the McGary family—probably a phonetic spelling mimicking the family's pronunciation of their name—Rafferty identifies this family as the same McGarrahs who eventually made their way to northwestern Arkansas.

24. Schoolcraft, *Rude Pursuits*, 114; Turner, "Significance of the Frontier," 199–227; Sauer, *Geography of the Ozark Highland*, 113. Turner's trappers and herders were transient individuals and families who were eventually supplanted by yeoman farmers.

25. U.S. Department of State, *Sixth Census*, 94–95, 323–33. For an examination of Arkansas's colonial and antebellum years, see Bolton, *Arkansas, 1800–1860*.

26. U.S. Department of State, *Sixth Census*, 94–95, 323–33.

27. Ted J. Smith, "Slavery in Washington County," 1, 9, 17, 43, 46, 48. In many ways the settlement and development of the Arkansas Ozarks resemble those of Appalachia. Historian Paul Salstrom argues that Appalachian diversity was shaped by three distinct settlement subregions: older, intermediate, and newer Appalachia. As in the Ozarks, Appalachia's "settlement sequence was prompted primarily by topography, by the lay of the land" (Paul Salstrom, "Newer Appalachia as One of America's

Last Frontiers," in Pudup, Billings, and Waller, *Appalachia in the Making*, 77). Using Salstrom's model, we can identify the Springfield Plain and the fertile stretches of the White River valley in the vicinity of Batesville as the "older" Ozarks. These areas have consistently maintained a relative degree of prosperity and have avoided overpopulation in much the same manner as have the valleys of "Older Appalachia." Although the Ozark region, of course, is much smaller than Appalachia, we can also identify at least one other distinct wave of topographically influenced settlement, and perhaps two. After the Springfield Plain and White River valley had experienced substantial settlement, newcomers began to inhabit the rolling, less fertile hills of the Salem Plateau and the more manageable elevations of the White River Hills and Boston Mountains. If there was a distinct third sequence—and, again, the relative smallness of the northern Arkansas hill region presents challenges in delineating such distinctions— it occurred in the most inaccessible and rugged reaches of the Boston Mountains.

28. U.S. Department of State, Agricultural Manuscript Census Schedules, Izard County, 1850; *Population Schedules of the Seventh Census (Slave Schedules)*, Izard County.

29. U.S. Department of State, *Seventh Census*, 535.

30. Lindley, "The Watkins Brothers," 8. For studies of economic and class diversity within highland communities and regions, see Waller, *Feud*; Hsiung, *Two Worlds in the Tennessee Mountains*.

31. Lindley, "The Watkins Brothers," 10, 12, 14; U.S. Department of State, Agricultural Manuscript Census Schedules, Izard County, 1850; *Population Schedules of the Seventh Census (Slave Schedules)*, Izard County, 1850. Only one of Watkins's twelve slaves was an adult male, which appears to have been common among Ozark slaveholdings. Jacob Wolf likewise owned only one adult male in 1850 out of a total of fifteen slaves. Marion County's largest slave owner, Joseph Coker, owned eighteen slaves but only one adult male. One can only speculate about the reasons for this practice. Perhaps the lack of a cash crop economy left these slaveholders with little need for field laborers. Perhaps Coker, Wolf, and other slave owners opted to sell males once they reached a profitable age. Perhaps these white men feared the possibility of sexual encounters between adult male slaves and female members of the slaveholding families. Whatever the reason for the paucity of adult male slaves, one noticeable result was the prominence of mulattoes among the Ozark slave population. In Marion County over half of the forty-two slaves owned by the extended Coker family were listed as "mulatto" in the 1850 census. Many of the mulattoes were listed as "servants" instead of as slaves.

32. U.S. Department of State, Agricultural Manuscript Census Schedules, Izard County, 1850, 1860.

33. Craig and Lankford, "Letters from a Steamboat Passenger," 9, 11; Baker, "Jacob Wolf," 187; Ted J. Smith, "Slavery in Washington County," 31.

34. U.S. Department of State, *Sixth Census*, 324; U.S. Department of State, *Seventh Census*, 556; U.S. Department of State, Agricultural Manuscript Census Schedules, Izard County, 1850, 1860; Lindley, "The Watkins Brothers," 15; *Population Schedules of the Seventh Census (Slave Schedules)*, Izard County, 1860.

35. Ted J. Smith, "Slavery in Washington County," 41; Sauer, *Geography of the Ozark Highland*, 121–22.

36. U.S. Department of the Interior, *Eighth Census*, 7; U.S. Department of State, *Sixth Census*, 329.

37. Lindley, "The Watkins Brothers," 15; Sauer, *Geography of the Ozark Highland*, 141; U.S. Department of the Interior, *Eighth Census*, 6, 7.

38. Goodspeed, *Northwestern Arkansas*, 983; Ted J. Smith, "Slavery in Washington County," 47; Denton, *Old Brands and Lost Trails*, 64, 79.

39. For a study of economic diversity within and between communities in Appalachia, see Ralph Mann, "Diversity in the Antebellum Appalachian South: Four Farm Communities in Tazewell County, Virginia," in Pudup, Billings, and Waller, *Appalachia in the Making*, 132–62.

40. U.S. Department of State, Agricultural Manuscript Census Schedules, Fulton, Benton, and Newton Counties, 1860; Liles, *Old Folks Talking*, 10.

41. Ted J. Smith, "Slavery in Washington County," 51.

Chapter Two

1. W. L. McGuire Journal, 1862–1863, Box 1, Folder 3, McGuire Family Papers, LCA; Britton, "W. L. McGuire Journals," 23, 3.

2. Britton, "W. L. McGuire Journals," 3–4, 18–23.

3. Several works deal with Arkansas's experience with secession, war, and reconstruction. Every Ozark county sent an antisecessionist delegate to the state's first secession convention; after Fort Sumter, the only negative vote was cast by an Ozark representative who would later become Arkansas's first Republican governor, Isaac Murphy of Madison County. For the Ozark region's role in secession and war, see James M. Woods, *Rebellion and Realignment*; Dougan, *Confederate Arkansas*; Ingenthron, *Borderland Rebellion*; Christ, *Rugged and Sublime*; Shea and Hess, *Pea Ridge*; and Steele and Cottrell, *Civil War in the Ozarks*. For the effects of Reconstruction on Arkansas, see Moneyhon, *Impact of the Civil War and Reconstruction on Arkansas*; George H. Thompson, *Arkansas and Reconstruction*; and John I. Smith, *Forward from Rebellion*. See also John I. Smith, *Courage of a Southern Unionist*.

4. Walz, "Migration into Arkansas," 109–13; U.S. Department of the Interior, *Ninth Census*, 102; U.S. Department of the Interior, *Tenth Census*, 214. See also Moneyhon, *Arkansas and the New South*, and Hahn, *Roots of Southern Populism*.

5. *Arkansas Times* (Batesville), 2 January 1869, 11 December 1869; *Batesville Guard*, 18 January 1877, 25 January 1877, 5 May 1877, 15 November 1877; and other issues of the *Arkansas Times* and the *Batesville Guard* in the Fred P. Kealer Papers, SHC.

6. Goodspeed, *Northeastern Arkansas*, 262; Santeford et al., *Empty Rooms and Broken Dishes*, 64. The St. Louis & San Francisco Railroad acquired the Kansas City, Fort Scott & Memphis Railroad in 1901, and was in turn bought by Burlington Northern in 1979.

7. U.S. Department of State, Agricultural Manuscript Census Schedules, Fulton County, 1860, 1870; Izard County, 1880.

8. U.S. Department of State, Agricultural Manuscript Census Schedules, Izard County, 1880.

9. Bradshaw, *My Story*, 23–24.

10. Wolf, *Life in the Leatherwoods*, 32–33.

11. Goodspeed, *Northeastern Arkansas*, 922, 264–65; U.S. Department of the Interior, *Eleventh Census: Agriculture*, 393; Pitcaithley, "Buffalo River," 123; *Harrison Times*, 19 June 1886, 27 November 1886; Walter F. Lackey, *History of Newton County*, 364.

12. U.S. Department of the Interior, *Eleventh Census: Agriculture*, 393; U.S. Department of the Interior, *Twelfth Census*, 430.

13. Sauer, *Geography of the Ozark Highland*, 119–20; U.S. Department of State, Agricultural Manuscript Census Schedules, Fulton County, 1860, and Izard County, 1880; U.S. Department of the Interior, *Eighth Census*, 7; U.S. Department of the Interior, *Ninth Census*, 102; *Arkansas Gazette*, 25 February 1874, 3; 7 July 1877, 3; U.S. Department of the Interior, *Eleventh Census: Agriculture*, 423; Moneyhon, *Arkansas and the New South*, 68.

14. Walz, "Migration into Arkansas," 107–13; U.S. Department of the Interior, *Ninth Census*, 102; U.S. Department of the Interior, *Tenth Census*, 214; U.S. Department of the Interior, *Eleventh Census: Agriculture*, 393.

15. U.S. Department of the Interior, *Tenth Census*, 143, 179.

16. Ibid., 105; U.S. Department of the Interior, *Eleventh Census: Population*, 10.

17. Goodspeed, *Northwestern Arkansas*, 817, 811, 1091, 935–36, 941–42, 959, 1001–2; U.S. Department of the Interior, *Eleventh Census: Agriculture*, 278.

18. *Arkansas Gazette*, 4 February 1868, 3; U.S. Department of the Interior, *Eighth Census*, 7; U.S. Department of the Interior, *Ninth Census*, 102; U.S. Department of the Interior, *Tenth Census*, 290.

19. *Arkansas Gazette*, 20 June 1869, 3; 30 July 1869, 4; 9 April 1871, 3; 11 June 1871, 1; 24 July 1873, 3; 22 January 1874, 3; U.S. Department of the Interior, *Ninth Census*, 102.

20. U.S. Department of the Interior, *Tenth Census*, 25–29, 254.

21. Ibid., 26; U.S. Department of the Interior, *Eleventh Census: Agriculture*, 423.

22. Shiloh Museum, *History of Washington County*, 234, 232, 236; J. Dickson Black, *History of Benton County*, 84; Stewart-Abernathy, *Independent but Not Isolated*, 18; U.S. Department of the Interior, *Eighth Census*, 8; U.S. Department of the Interior, *Ninth Census*, 100; U.S. Department of the Interior, *Tenth Census*, 255, 257; *Arkansas Gazette*, 31 December 1872, 2.

23. Shiloh Museum, *History of Washington County*, 236, 248; Stewart-Abernathy, *Independent but Not Isolated*, 18. The Kansas City Southern Railroad also crossed the extreme northwestern corner of Benton County in the 1880s on its way to Texas.

24. Strausberg, *Century of Research*, 5, 6, 14, 16, 19.

25. U.S. Department of the Interior, *Eleventh Census: Agriculture*, 501–2; J. Dickson Black, *History of Benton County*, 86, 87, 77; Goodspeed, *Northwestern Arkansas*, 824, 815, 913–14, 1013; Benton County Heritage Committee, *History of Benton County*, 107.

26. J. Dickson Black, *History of Benton County*, 86, 87; Benton County Heritage Committee, *History of Benton County*, 107; U.S. Department of the Interior, *Twelfth Census*, 622, 624.

27. Goodspeed, *Northwestern Arkansas*, 805, 923–24; Shiloh Museum, *History of*

Washington County, 250; U.S. Department of the Interior, *Twelfth Census*, 713–14.

28. Shiloh Museum, *History of Washington County*, 249, 252; Lewellen, "'Sheep amidst the Wolves,'" 19–40; U.S. Department of the Interior, *Twelfth Census*, 625.

29. Goodspeed, *Northwestern Arkansas*, 109.

30. Hogue, *Back Yonder*, 260; Stapleton, *Moonshiners in Arkansas*, 18. See also Miller, *Revenuers and Moonshiners*.

31. U.S. Department of State, Agricultural Manuscript Census Schedules, Newton County, 1880.

32. Walter F. Lackey, *History of Newton County*, 404, 408–9; Hogue, *Back Yonder*, 16, 17, 19, 41, 59, 155.

Chapter Three

1. Goodspeed, *Northeastern Arkansas*, 952; M. Shelby Kennard to George S. Kennard, 30 June 1892, 22 October 1893, 12 April 1896, 22 June 1900, 23 July 1900, Box 1, Folders 6–9, Kennard Papers, LCA. See also Griffith, "Michael Shelby Kennard"; Kennard, "Michael Shelby Kennard."

2. Wolf, *Life in the Leatherwoods*, 37.

3. John B. Thompson interview.

4. Allured, "Ozark Women and the Companionate Family," 232, 256.

5. Ashcraft et al., *Pioneer Faith*, 19.

6. Shiloh Museum, *History of Washington County*, 93–94, 132; Thomas H. Campbell et al., *Arkansas Cumberland Presbyterians*, 17.

7. David Edwin Harrell, "The Evolution of Plain-Folk Religion in the South, 1835–1920," in Hill, *Varieties of Southern Religious Experience*, 24.

8. Boles, *The Great Revival*, 144.

9. Vernon, *Methodism in Arkansas*, 185.

10. Bolton, *Arkansas, 1800–1860*, 111; Britton, *Two Centuries of Methodism*, 21–22.

11. Hinson, *History of Baptists in Arkansas*, 4–5; Ashcraft et al., *Pioneer Faith*, 32.

12. Hinson, *History of Baptists in Arkansas*, 5; Ashcraft et al., *Pioneer Faith*, 90.

13. Hinson, *History of Baptists in Arkansas*, 47.

14. Ibid., 36.

15. McAllister, *Arkansas Disciples*, 10, 11, 15, 29–30; Goodspeed, *Northwestern Arkansas*, 302–3. For a thorough examination of the rise and development of the Christian movement, see Harrell, *Quest for a Christian America*.

16. Thomas H. Campbell et al., *Arkansas Cumberland Presbyterians*, 5–6; Boles, *The Great Revival*, 162–63.

17. Thomas H. Campbell et al., *Arkansas Cumberland Presbyterians*, 22–23.

18. Goodspeed, *Northeastern Arkansas*, 734–35, 920; Goodspeed, *Northwestern Arkansas*, 131.

19. Goodspeed, *Northeastern Arkansas*, 263–64; Goodspeed, *Northwestern Arkansas*, 131, 480–81; Britton, *Two Centuries of Methodism*, 161–63.

20. Hinson, *History of Baptists in Arkansas*, 45.

21. Womack, *Reminiscences*, 58; *Arkansas Gazette*, 8 May 1870, 3.

22. Goodspeed, *Northwestern Arkansas*, 474–75; Goodspeed, *Northeastern Ar-*

kansas, 921, 734, 263; Wolf, *Life in the Leatherwoods*, 139–40; Womack, *Reminiscences*, 7, 15.

23. McAllister, *Arkansas Disciples*, 29, 30, 32.

24. Leflar, *The First 100 Years*, 7, 9, 10, 19, 23, 67.

25. McGinnis, "Arkansas College," 21, 28.

26. *Batesville Guard*, July 1901, newspaper clipping, Box 1, Folder 1, Kennard Papers, LCA.

27. M. Shelby Kennard to George Kennard, 30 June 1892, Box 1, Folder 6, Kennard Papers, LCA.

28. M. Shelby Kennard to George Kennard, 22 October 1893, Box 1, Folder 7, Kennard Papers, LCA; Morton, *History of the Ozark Division Mountain Mission Schools*, 39; Hinson, *History of Baptists in Arkansas*, 140; Messick, *History of Baxter County*, 144.

29. M. Shelby Kennard to George Kennard, 12 June 1896, 21 November 1896, Box 1, Folder 8, Kennard Papers, LCA.

30. Douglas Ensminger and T. Wilson Longmore, "Rural Trade Areas and Villages," in Taylor et al., *Rural Life in the United States*, 79. Ensminger and Longmore define the term "hamlet" as a settlement of fewer than 250 people, a "village" as one containing between 250 and 2,500, and a "crossroads store center" as simply an isolated mercantile establishment in an otherwise rural, farming area.

31. Ibid., 83.

32. *Arkansas State Gazetteer and Business Directory, 1898–1899*, 284, 502.

33. Ibid., 360, 266.

34. Wolf, *Life in the Leatherwoods*, 36.

35. Ensminger and Longmore, "Rural Trade Areas and Villages," 82. See also Thomas D. Clark, *Pills, Petticoats, and Plows*.

36. Rand, "Edward Nicholas Rand," 14, 17, 19.

37. Ibid., 19–20; *Arkansas State Gazetteer and Business Directory, 1888–1889*, 637.

Chapter Four

1. Goodspeed, *Northwestern Arkansas*, 243–44.

2. Ibid., 244.

3. U.S. Department of the Interior, *Eighth Census*, 15–20.

4. Pitcaithley, "Buffalo River," 131; Orville J. McInturff, "Floating Timber down the Buffalo River—1890s," *Mountain Wave*, 25 May 1972, 8–9; Jones, "The National Forests and Arkansas," 1.

5. Shiloh Museum, *History of Washington County*, 245.

6. Ibid., 247.

7. Fair, *The North Arkansas Line*, 8; Santeford et al., *Empty Rooms and Broken Dishes*, 64; Goodspeed, *Northeastern Arkansas*, 262.

8. Hull, *Shortline Railroads of Arkansas*, 68; Fair, *The North Arkansas Line*, 25, 49, 81.

9. *Mountain Echo*, 12 March 1886, 2.

10. *Arkansas State Gazetteer and Business Directory, 1888–1889*, 383, 431, 438, 515, 547, 554, 590, 591, 592.

11. Daniel Boone Lackey, "Cutting and Floating Red Cedar Logs," 361; McInturff, "Floating Timber down the Buffalo River," 9.

12. Daniel Boone Lackey, "Cutting and Floating Red Cedar Logs," 361; Handley, "Settlement across Northern Arkansas," 278–79; Fair, *The North Arkansas Line*, 91. Before 1887, Leslie was called Wiley's Cove.

13. Handley, "Settlement across Northern Arkansas," 278, 280.

14. Fair, *The North Arkansas Line*, 81; Handley, "Settlement across Northern Arkansas," 280, 290.

15. Handley, "Settlement across Northern Arkansas," 279; Morgan, *Black Hillbillies*, 128, 122.

16. Benson Fox interview, Glenn Hackett interview, OOHP; Daniel Boone Lackey, "Cutting and Floating Red Cedar Logs," 365.

17. Page, *Voices of Moccasin Creek*, 103–4.

18. Walter F. Lackey, *History of Newton County*, 365, 150.

19. Glenn Hackett interview, OOHP.

20. Shaddoxx, "Sawmills in the Ozark National Forest," 11, 12, 18; Jones, "The National Forests and Arkansas," 3.

21. WPA Federal Writers' Project Files, Boone, Newton, and Cleburne Counties, AHC.

22. John Quincy Wolf, "Spring Creek in the Long Ago," typescript, Box 1, Folder 16, John Q. Wolf Sr. Papers, LCA; Tom Ross interview, Ray Watts interview, OOHP; Aaron Stevens interview, OHI/OOHO; Hanks, "Mount Olive," 3; Harris, "History of the Town of Guion," 11; WPA Federal Writers' Project Files, Baxter County, AHC.

23. Miser, *Manganese Carbonate in the Batesville District*, 1, 3, 4; Wood and Smith, *The Batesville Manganese District*, 4; *Baxter Bulletin*, 28 June 1940, 3.

24. Spier, "Social History of Manganese Mining," 131; *Baxter Bulletin*, 28 June 1940, 3; Santeford et al., *Empty Rooms and Broken Dishes*, 66; Spier, "Farming and Mining Experience," 81–82; Wood and Smith, *The Batesville Manganese District*, 4, 6, 8, 25, 33.

25. U.S. Department of the Interior, *Eleventh Census: Report on Mineral Industries*, 288, 292–93; Wood and Smith, *The Batesville Manganese District*, 25, 26, 29, 30; Miser, *Manganese Carbonate in the Batesville District*, 1; Spier, "Farming and Mining Experience," 84; Spier, "Social History of Manganese Mining," 132.

26. Wood and Smith, *The Batesville Manganese District*, 31, 34.

27. Spier, "Social History of Manganese Mining," 132, 134, 135, 136; Spier, "Farming and Mining Experience," 84, 87, 97; Wood and Smith, *The Batesville Manganese District*, 28.

28. Adams, *Zinc and Lead Deposits*, 13, 14; Pitcaithley, "Buffalo River," 162; Pitcaithley, "Zinc and Lead Mining," 296, 297. See also Earl Berry, *History of Marion County*, 461–71. The smelting operation at Lead Hill may be the one that Batesville humorist C. F. M. Noland referred to in one of his "Colonel Pete Whetstone" letters in early 1850; Noland, *Pete Whetstone of Devil's Fork*, 115.

29. Adams, *Zinc and Lead Deposits*, 14, 18; Pitcaithley, "Buffalo River," 297–98; Pitcaithley, "Zinc and Lead Mining," 162–64.

30. Adams, *Zinc and Lead Deposits*, 15, 14; Frances H. Shiras, *History of Baxter*

County, 77; Messick, *History of Baxter County*, 292; Pitcaithley, "Buffalo River," 170, 172, 175; Pitcaithley, "Zinc and Lead Mining," 302–3.

31. Goodspeed, *Northeastern Arkansas*, 265; Glenna Garner interview, OOHP; Rafferty, *The Ozarks*, 136; WPA Federal Writers' Project Files, Benton County, AHC; Pace, Swope, and Simers, "Mammoth Spring," 34.

32. "Chronologies," Box 1, Folder 3, Arkansas Lime Company Records, LCA; Fair, "The Batesville White Lime Company," 7, 9, 11; Larry Stroud, "Arkansas Eastman Grows Steadily; Limestone Companies Prosper," *Batesville Guard*, 9 May 1985, 4-f.

33. Eller, *Miners, Millhands, and Mountaineers*.

Chapter Five

1. Randall Bennett Woods, *Fulbright*, 4, 6.

2. Lee Riley Powell, *J. William Fulbright and His Times*, 2, 5.

3. Ibid., 8, 12, 15, 19, 25.

4. Faubus, *Faraway Land*, 4; Reed, *Faubus*, 25–26.

5. Faubus, *Faraway Land*, 7–11, 14; Reed, *Faubus*, 51.

6. Faubus, *Faraway Land*, 15–17; Reed, *Faubus*, 36, 49, 56, 61.

7. In his study of the Missouri Ozarks, Edgar D. McKinney found traditional, subsistence farming to be rare indeed by 1920, though "significant portions of the Ozarks upland . . . had evolved into a traditional economic system at some point between the poles of subsistence and a cash economy." McKinney, "Images, Realities, and Cultural Transformation," 125.

8. *Mountain Echo*, 11 August 1911, 1.

9. *Melbourne Times*, 27 June 1912, 1; 15 August 1912, 1; Gow, *Tick Eradication*, 6, 10–13. For more detailed accounts of Texas fever tick eradication, see Dethloff and Dyal, *Special Kind of Doctor*, and Hutson, "Texas Fever in Kansas."

10. *Melbourne Times*, 30 May to 25 June 1912; Gow, *Tick Eradication*, 6; Mosier, "The 1922 'Tick War,'" 7.

11. Strausberg, *Century of Research*, 19; Jansma, "The Benton County Horticultural Society," 127, 131, 132.

12. J. Dickson Black, *History of Benton County*, 87.

13. Ibid., 88–90, 96–97; U.S. Department of Commerce, *Fourteenth Census*, 575, 581.

14. Mrs. E. S. Warren to Mrs. Betty Brown, Fall 1907, printed in the *Daily News*, 1 July 1950, and reprinted in J. Dickson Black, *History of Benton County*, 98–101; Black, *History of Benton County*, 97–98.

15. Shiloh Museum, *History of Washington County*, 299; U.S. Department of Commerce, *Fourteenth Census*, 575, 581.

16. U.S. Department of Commerce, *Fourteenth Census*, 575, 581; Shiloh Museum, *History of Washington County*, 285, 299.

17. Shiloh Museum, *History of Washington County*, 300–301; Frances B. Baldwin, "Benton County Industrial and Commercial," Folder 1, "Carroll County Industrial and Commercial," Folder 2, "Madison County Industrial and Commercial," WPA Historical Files, AHC; "Narrative Report of County Extension Workers—Madison

County, 1925," Box 19, FESRA. For a discussion of canneries (especially tomato) in the Missouri Ozarks, see Edgar D. McKinney, "Images, Realities, and Cultural Transformation," 292–96.

18. "Narrative Report of County Extension Workers—Carroll County, 1925," "Newton County, 1925," "Madison County, 1925," Box 19, FESRA. The M&NA did not traverse Newton County, but farmers in the community of Western Grove enjoyed easy access to the railroad just across the line in Searcy County.

19. "Narrative Report of County Extension Workers—Newton County, 1925," "Washington County, 1925," "Carroll County, 1925," Box 19, FESRA.

20. Salstrom, *Appalachia's Path to Dependency,* xvii; U.S. Department of the Interior, *Twelfth Census,* 154, 155, 418, 419, 420, 421; U.S. Department of Commerce, *Census of Agriculture, 1935,* 683, 689.

21. *Harrison Times,* 2 May 1924, 1.

22. "Narrative Report of County Extension Workers—Madison County, 1925," Box 19, "Stone County, 1925," Box 18, "Newton County, 1925," Box 19, FESRA.

23. "Narrative Report of County Extension Workers—Carroll County, 1925," Box 19, FESRA.

24. U.S. Department of the Interior, *Twelfth Census,* 267–68, 418–21; U.S. Department of Commerce, *Census of Agriculture, 1935,* 681, 684; *American Aberdeen-Angus Herd-Book* 37 (1930): v; Irma Giffels interview, SMOHC.

25. *Benton County Democrat,* 22 January 1942, 4; Frances B. Baldwin, "Carroll County Industrial and Commercial," Folder 2, "Madison County Industrial and Commercial," WPA Historical Files, AHC; U.S. Department of Commerce, *Census of Agriculture, 1945,* 96, 109, 105; U.S. Department of Commerce, *Fourteenth Census,* 574.

26. Strausberg, *From Hills and Hollers,* 12–13.

27. Shiloh Museum, *History of Washington County,* 311–14; Strausberg, *From Hills and Hollers,* 15; *Benton County Democrat,* 22 January 1942, 1; U.S. Department of Commerce, *Fourteenth Census,* 568, 574; U.S. Department of Commerce, *Census of Agriculture, 1945,* 96, 109.

28. Aaron Stevens interview, OHI/OOHO.

29. Doyle Webb interview, OOHP.

30. Kennard Billingsley interview, OOHP.

31. U.S. Department of the Interior, *Twelfth Census,* 430; U.S. Department of Commerce, *Census of Agriculture, 1935,* 685–91.

32. U.S. Department of the Interior, *Twelfth Census,* 154–55; U.S. Department of Commerce, *Census of Agriculture, 1935,* 670–76, 681–91.

33. "Baxter County," Historical Appraisals of Extension Work, 1919–1939, Box 3, Arkansas Cooperative Extension Service Records, UASC.

34. Daniel, *Breaking the Land,* 16; "Baxter County," Historical Appraisals of Extension Work, 1919–1939, Box 3, Arkansas Cooperative Extension Service Records, UASC.

35. *Mountain Echo,* 7 July 1921, 1.

36. Mullins, "History of Sharp County," 72.

37. U.S. Department of Commerce, *Fourteenth Census,* 575–81; U.S. Department of Commerce, *Census of Agriculture, 1935,* 685–91.

38. Charles Johnson et al., *Statistical Atlas of Southern Counties*, 57–69.

39. Conkin, *The New Deal*, 38; Luttrell, *The High Cost of Farm Welfare*, 6–7; Schlesinger, *The Crisis of the Old Order*, 174.

40. *Mountain Echo*, 28 August 1930, 1; 4 September 1930, 1.

41. Luttrell, *The High Cost of Farm Welfare*, 8; Conkin, *The New Deal*, 39.

42. Tom Ross interview, OOHP.

43. Doyle Webb interview, OOHP.

44. *Van Buren County Democrat*, 18 October 1934, 1; 2 August 1934, 1.

45. Minutes of Mortgages and Deeds of Trust, Stone County, Arkansas, H, 67–79; *Melbourne Times*, 5 February 1937, 1.

46. Glenn Johnson, "Agriculture and Industry," in Earl Berry, *History of Marion County*, 313; Evalena Berry, *Time and the River*, 345; McClurkan, *Brief History of Camp Sage*, 41; *Dirt Dauber* (no. 4748), 30 September 1936.

47. Biles, *The South and the New Deal*, 40.

48. "Narrative Report of County Extension Workers—Benton County, 1934," Box 81, "Fulton County, 1934," Box 80, "Newton County, 1934," Box 81, "Izard County, 1934," Box 80, FESRA.

49. "Narrative Report of County Extension Workers—Benton County, 1934," "Boone County," Box 81, FESRA.

50. Biles, *The South and the New Deal*, 40–41; "Narrative Report of County Extension Workers—Cleburne County, 1934," "Izard County, 1934," Box 80, FESRA; U.S. Department of Commerce, *Census of Agriculture, 1935*, 685–91.

51. "Narrative Report of County Extension Workers—Baxter County, 1934," Box 80, FESRA.

52. Frances B. Baldwin, "Benton County Industrial and Commercial," Folder 2, WPA Historical Files, AHC; U.S. Department of Commerce, *Census of Agriculture, 1945*, 35.

53. "Newton County Industrial and Commercial," WPA Historical Files, AHC; U.S. Department of Commerce, *Census of Agriculture, 1945*, 42.

54. Frances B. Baldwin, "Izard County Industrial and Commercial," WPA Historical Files, AHC; U.S. Department of Commerce, *Census of Agriculture, 1945*, 39.

55. "Fulton County," in Narrative Reports of All County Extension Agents and All Extension Home Economists, Arkansas, 1950, Box 2, Arkansas Cooperative Extension Service Records, UASC. See also Chesnutt, "Rural Electrification in Arkansas," and D. Clayton Brown, *Electricity for Rural America*. After passage of the Rural Telephone Act in 1949, the REA, responsible for carrying out the act's provisions, also became influential in the growth of telephone service in rural areas; Hadwiger and Cochran, "Rural Telephones in the United States."

56. Osgood, *Farm Planning in the Eastern Ozarks*, 3, 5–6, 16.

Chapter Six

1. Charles Morrow Wilson, "Hemmed-in Holler," 59.

2. Ibid., 59–61.

3. Allured, "Ozark Women and the Companionate Family," 231.

4. Stewart-Abernathy, *Independent but Not Isolated*, 6, 271, 284, 291.

5. Santeford et al., *Empty Rooms and Broken Dishes*, 91, 101, 103.

6. "Narrative Report of County Extension Workers—Madison County, 1925," "Newton County, 1925," Box 19, FESRA. For a discussion of frontier conditions in south central Missouri in the late 1920s, see Browne, "Some Frontier Conditions in the Hilly Portion of the Ozarks," 181–88.

7. Stephens, "The Case of Missing Folk Music," 59, 61.

8. Charles Morrow Wilson, "Hemmed-in Holler," 68. By the time of Wilson's visits—and certainly by the time post–World War II writers entered the Holler—the southern "Anglo-Saxon purity" of this Newton County hideaway had been somewhat compromised by a wave of newcomers, among them the reclusive father of Kewpie Doll creator Rose O'Neill. In a piece typical of her Ozark writings, Marge Lyon devoted a chapter in her book *Hurrah for Arkansas!* to "Newton County—Land of Unspoiled Beauty." According to Lyon, in this county where "one might expect to find the much-publicized barefoot ignorance," one finds instead "keen reasoning, a delicious sense of independence and some of the most delightful people of all Arkansas." Lyon then proceeded to seek out and describe only fellow newcomers to the region: a former Chicago golf professional and his wife and a former Kansas City hotel operator whose wife once owned a linen shop. Lyon, *Hurrah for Arkansas!*, 228, 230.

9. Rayburn, *The Eureka Springs Story*, 8, 9, 16; Fair, *The North Arkansas Line*, 1–4, 8, 18.

10. Rayburn, *The Eureka Springs Story*, 46; Fair, *The North Arkansas Line*, 31, 195.

11. Evalena Berry, *Sugar Loaf Springs*, 2, 10, 59. The Ozark region contained several other smaller healing-water resort towns, including Ravenden Springs and Siloam Springs.

12. Shiloh Museum, *History of Washington County*, 237, 241.

13. Timely Club, *The Hardy History*, 32, 75–76.

14. Ibid., 77, 81.

15. Snelling, *Coin Harvey*, 1, 5, 7, 9, 11, 12, 13, 15, 17, 18.

16. Ibid., 29, 31, 35, 37–38, 40; Kennan, "The Ozark Trails," 299, 300, 313; Kennan, "Coin Harvey's Pyramid," 132.

17. Fite, *From Vision to Reality*, 1, 4, 5.

18. Ibid., 6, 7; Shipley, "The Pleasures of Prosperity," 102.

19. Fite, *From Vision to Reality*, 8, 10, 11, 15, 17, 18.

20. Ibid., 1, 20; Shipley, "The Pleasures of Prosperity," 127, 103.

21. Shipley, "The Pleasures of Prosperity," 105; Fite, *From Vision to Reality*, 24–25, 46, 49, 52, 53, 57.

22. Fite, *From Vision to Reality*, 13; Nancy Caver, "Roy Ritter," *Arkansas Gazette*, 20 September 1998, 6D.

23. Randolph, *The Ozarks*, 300. For a discussion of the development of and transforming effects of tourism in Taney and Stone Counties, Missouri, see Morrow and Myers-Phinney, *Shepherd of the Hills Country*.

24. Lears, *No Place of Grace*, 74.

25. Harington, *Let Us Build Us a City*, 10.

26. Shi, *The Simple Life*, 189; Walter F. Lackey, *History of Newton County*, 404, 147, 148.

27. Harington, *The Architecture of the Arkansas Ozarks*, 233.

28. Walter F. Lackey, *History of Newton County*, 149, 150. As historian Edgar D. McKinney has illustrated, curiosity was not the sole domain of the tourist. In the *Shepherd of the Hills* country of southwestern Missouri, the same native Ozarkers who were frequently asked to pose for pictures with travelers often hitched up their wagons and ventured to Branson to catch a glimpse of the tourists. McKinney, "Images, Realities, and Cultural Transformation," 287.

29. Lears, *No Place of Grace*, 92.

30. Charles Morrow Wilson, "Ozarkadia," *American Magazine*, January 1934, 59; Simpson, "Otto Ernest Rayburn," 164.

31. Shi, *The Simple Life*, 226–28.

32. Charlie May Simon, "Retreat to the Land: An Experience in Poverty," *Scribner's Magazine*, May 1933, 309–12.

33. Rafferty, "Changing Economy and Landscape," 11; C. Fred Williams, "The Bear State Image," 103; Noland, *Pete Whetstone of Devil's Fork*; T. B. Thorpe, "The Big Bear of Arkansas," in Porter, *Big Bear of Arkansas*, 13–31; Morris, "Opie Read, Arkansas Journalist," 246, 249, 250. Though its origins are unclear, the Arkansas Traveler legend focuses on a backwoods encounter between a cosmopolitan traveler and an Arkansas hill man sometime in the 1830s or 1840s. This actual or fabled encounter, in which the hill man comically matches wits with his more polished visitor, spawned a fiddle tune with dialogue, a famous painting, and a play. See Lankford, "Arkansas Traveller," 16, 18. For an in-depth study of the "Arkansas Traveler" legend and other nineteenth-century Arkansas tales and writings, see Masterson, *Tall Tales of Arkansaw*.

34. Shapiro, *Appalachia on Our Mind*. In their study of the White River country of southwestern Missouri, Lynn Morrow and Linda Myers-Phinney trace the "stereotypical characterization of Ozark natives" back into the 1880s when Missouri journalists from outside the region began to explore peculiar karst features and float the swift waters of the White River and its tributaries. Morrow and Myers-Phinney, *Shepherd of the Hills Country*, 41.

35. Shapiro, *Appalachia on Our Mind*, 119.

36. Whisnant, *Modernizing the Mountaineer*, 8.

37. Beary, *Black Bishop*, 200; Synod of Arkansas, *Minutes of the Seventieth Session*, 296; Britton, *Two Centuries of Methodism in Arkansas*, 193; Rayburn, *Forty Years in the Ozarks*, 46, 49. In addition to the school at Valley Springs, the Methodists established short-lived academies at Imboden and Yellville. All three, which were designed in part to provide students for Hendrix College in Conway, eventually became public schools. The Arkansas Synod of the Presbyterian Church in the United States, or Southern Presbyterian Church, devoted most of its missionary zeal to Caddo Valley Academy in the Ouachita region of southwestern Arkansas.

38. Whisnant, *All That Is Native and Fine*, 13. See also Burnett, with Compton and Little, *When the Presbyterians Came to Kingston*.

39. There were a handful of Ozark-themed novels published before *Shepherd of the Hills*, but Wright's book outsold them all and gave birth to a host of similar romantic works in the following two decades, most of which were rather obscure at the time and are forgotten now. Randolph explored the use of Ozark dialect in the fifteen most

prominent novels dating from 1844 to 1925. Randolph, "The Ozark Dialect in Fiction," 283–89.

40. Morrow and Myers-Phinney, *Shepherd of the Hills Country*, 28, 31. It appears that the *Shepherd of the Hills* phenomenon, based as it was on a particular location in southwestern Missouri, remained for the most part localized to Stone and Taney Counties into the depression era. Nevertheless, it must be viewed as a definite precursor to the barrage of Ozark-themed publications of the pre–World War II decade.

41. The following discussion deals only with works of nonfiction, regardless of their level of romanticism, because my purpose is to relate the common themes found in firsthand, contemporary accounts of the Ozarks. The thorough examination and comparison of novels and fictionalized accounts of the region is a work that would prove invaluable to Ozark studies; unfortunately it does not fall within the scope of this study. Furthermore, the following pages obviously do not include evaluations of all depression-era articles and books about the Ozarks. I have excluded Hogue's *Back Yonder* because it is primarily a memoir concerning Hogue's memories of growing up in the Boston Mountains in the late nineteenth century. His "Ozark People," *Scribner's Magazine*, May 1931, 509–20, was written in the same vein. I have also excluded several excessively romantic and unrealistic pieces, such as "Grandpap's A-makin'," *Atlantic Monthly*, October 1938, 551–52, and R. Havelock-Baile, "A Country Boy Goes Home," *Forum and Century*, February 1940, 81–86.

42. Cratis Dearl Williams, "The Southern Mountaineer in Fact and Fiction," 1358. Not all works on Appalachia in the 1930s displayed a greater emphasis on realism. One popular book, Muriel Early Sheppard's *Cabins in the Laurel*, offered a romantic vision of mountain life by focusing on one uncharacteristically isolated community in western North Carolina. Historian Jane S. Becker recognizes *Cabins in the Laurel* as an example of an emerging trend among travel writers and local colorists who, instead of denying the changes taking place in Appalachia, searched for isolated, anachronistic communities in the mountains. This same movement occurred in the Ozarks, resulting in several studies of Newton County communities such as Hemmed-in Holler. Marguerite Lyon's *Hurrah for Arkansas!* devotes an entire chapter to Newton County. Becker, *Selling Tradition*, 57.

43. Eller, *Miners, Millhands, and Mountaineers*, xix.

44. *Who's Who in America*, 2888. Wilson also tried his hand at Ozark-themed fiction. His best-known novel, the 1930s *Acres of Sky*, Randolph praised as "the best Ozark dialect ever written." Randolph, "Recent Fiction and the Ozark Dialect," 427.

45. Charles Morrow Wilson, "Introduction," in Finger, *Ozark Fantasia*, 2.

46. Finger, *Ozark Fantasia*, 40–41, 37. See also Charles Morrow Wilson, "On an Ozark Store-Porch," *North American Review* 228 (October 1929): 493–98.

47. Charles Morrow Wilson, "Elizabethan America," *Atlantic Monthly*, August 1929, 238, reprinted in McNeil, *Appalachian Images*, 206–14.

48. Charles Morrow Wilson, "Hemmed-in Holler"; Charles Morrow Wilson, "Friendly Days in the Ozarks," *Travel*, March 1933, 18, 19, 21, 45; Charles Morrow Wilson, "Ozarkadia," 58, 59 (quote), 112.

49. June Denby to Otto Ernest Rayburn, 2 April 1941, Box 1, Folder 2, Rayburn Collection, UASC.

50. Cochran, *Vance Randolph*, 17, 42, 48; Cochran and Luster, *For Love and for Money*, 76. See also Kephart, *Our Southern Highlanders*; John C. Campbell, *The Southern Highlander and His Homeland*.

51. Randolph, *The Ozarks*, 16.

52. Ibid., v.

53. Ibid., 21–22. Randolph made his living as a writer; consequently, he produced dozens of articles in both popular magazines and scholarly journals before World War II. Because most of these works dealt with folk tales, songs, and superstitions or with dialect, they are not mentioned here. *The Ozarks: An American Survival of Primitive Society* is Randolph's most thorough examination of depression-era Ozark life and is relied upon here to convey his position in comparison with that of other writers of Ozark subjects. For a complete bibliography of Randolph's work, including dozens of ghostwritten books, see Cochran and Luster, *For Love and for Money*.

54. Randolph, *The Ozarks*, 299; Barker, *Yesterday Today*.

55. William R. Draper, "The Ozarks Go Native," *Outlook*, 10 September 1930, 60, 61.

56. Thomas Hart Benton, "America's Yesterday," *Travel*, July 1934, 9, 8, 45, 46. A scholarly presentation of the crux of Benton's argument appeared in a 1936 *American Journal of Sociology* article by Walter O. Cralle, "Social Change and Isolation in the Ozark Mountain Region of Missouri." Focusing on the Missouri Ozarks, Cralle's work was a rare pre–World War II academic study of modernization in the region. His thesis was that somewhere between the hillbilly stereotype and the progressive rhetoric of the chambers of commerce lay a region in transition. An archaic, rural American culture, protected until recently by isolation, was in the 1930s rapidly giving ground before the onslaught of urban civilization. Among the forces of change Cralle cited were automobiles, highways, radio, newspapers, tourists, extension agents, and movies. "In general, the Ozarks may be accurately considered as an internally marginal subculture area whose essential uniqueness is being rapidly lost under the impact of modern civilization." But, harking back to Johann von Thünen's market accessibility thesis, Cralle noted that "the rate of change is closely correlated with accessibility." Whereas Benton simply predicted the demise of the Ozarks of legend, Cralle realized that the destruction of traditional, subsistence culture had largely been accomplished.

57. Randolph, "Ballad Hunters in North Arkansas," 2, 3, 4; Lankford, "John Quincy Wolf, Jr.," 5; Cochran, "All the Songs," 9. H. M. Beldon conducted most of his folk song gatherings in Missouri.

58. Cochran, "All the Songs," 4 (quote), 6, 7, 8, 9, 13. According to Cochran, the Dusenbury house lacked electricity, forcing Lomax to pick Emma up and drive her into Mena each day for recording. Because Lomax paid her a small fee for singing, Dusenbury insisted on putting in a full day at the "studio." In the evening Lomax drove her back home in time for the nightly milking (p. 4). "Child ballads" refers to the ballads recorded in Harvard professor Francis James Child's *The English and Scottish Popular Ballads*, published between 1882 and 1898.

59. Stephens, "The Case of Missing Folk Music"; McNeil, *Ozark Country*, 129; Lindley, "The Hoss-Hair Pullers and Hill-Billy Quartet," 9–13; McCulloh, "Uncle Absie Morrison's Historical Tunes," 95, 96. See also Malone, *Country Music, USA*, and Mal-

one, *Singing Cowboys and Musical Mountaineers.* Other depression-era and World War II–era Arkansas Ozark musicians who achieved regional or national prominence included Ashley's Melody Men from Marshall, Bill and Toby Baker of Madison County, Pinkley Tomlin from Marion County, and Wayne Raney of Wolf Bayou in Cleburne County. Cochran, *Our Own Sweet Sounds,* 28, 29, 31.

60. Lindley, "Hoss-Hair Pullers and Hill-Billy Quartet," 12. For a discussion of similar radio acts in the Missouri Ozarks, see Edgar D. McKinney, "Images, Realities, and Cultural Transformation," 179–87.

61. Lair, *Outlander's History of Carroll County,* 212–13; Walter F. Lackey, *History of Newton County,* 301; Cochran, *Our Own Sweet Sounds,* 30.

62. Whisnant, *All That Is Native and Fine,* 183, 185; McNeil, *Ozark Country,* 167; Cochran, *Vance Randolph,* 133–35, 140.

63. Johnston, "Searcy County Folk Festival," 100, 101, 109; *Baxter Bulletin,* 8 August 1941, 1; Craig Ogilvie, "Ozark Traditions: Folk Culture, Blanchard Springs Caverns Created Stone County Tourism Industry," *Batesville Guard,* 25 January 1994, 10.

64. Rayburn, *Forty Years in the Ozarks,* 4, 18, 19, 33, 42, 43, 45, 50, 53, 59, 64, 72, 76. See also Simpson, "Otto Ernest Rayburn," 160–79.

65. Charles A. Pearce to Otto Ernest Rayburn, 19 November 1941, Box 1, Folder 2, and Duell, Sloan & Pearce, Inc., "Royalty Statement for *Ozark Country,*" 1 April 1942, Box 1, Folder 4, Rayburn Collection, UASC.

66. Randolph, review of *Ozark Country* by Otto Ernest Rayburn, *Kansas City Star,* 13 December 1941, E14.

67. Erskine Caldwell to Otto Ernest Rayburn, 21 May 1940, 3 May 1940, 9 May 1940, Box 1, Folder 2, Rayburn Collection, UASC.

68. Rayburn, *Ozark Country,* 54.

69. Ibid., 118, 344, 345.

Chapter Seven

1. Doyle Webb interview, OOHP.

2. Ibid.

3. U.S. Department of Commerce, *Census of Agriculture, 1945,* 18–33; U.S. Department of Commerce, *Census of Agriculture, 1954,* 92–97. For a brief overview of developments in southern agriculture since World War II, see Winters, "Agriculture in the Post–World War II South," in Hurt, *The Rural South since World War II,* 8–27. For a discussion of the impact of World War II on the Arkansas homefront, see C. Calvin Smith, *War and Wartime Changes.*

4. U.S. Department of Commerce, *Census of Agriculture, 1945,* 18–33; U.S. Department of Commerce, *Census of Agriculture, 1964,* 320–27.

5. U.S. Department of Commerce, *Census of Agriculture, 1945,* 18–33; "Narrative Report of County Extension Workers—Baxter County, 1942," Box 214, "Stone County, 1942," Box 215, FESRA.

6. Fite, "Recent Progress," 27.

7. Kirby, *Rural Worlds Lost,* xvi.

8. Fite, *Cotton Fields No More,* 184.

9. U.S. Department of Commerce, *Census of Agriculture, 1945,* 34–46; U.S. Department of Commerce, *Census of Agriculture, 1964,* 284–91.

10. Fite, "Recent Progress," 20.

11. "Narrative Report of County Extension Workers—Izard County, 1957," Box 415, FESRA.

12. Fite, *Cotton Fields No More,* 195.

13. *Melbourne Times,* 16 March 1950, 1; "Narrative Report of County Extension Workers—Izard County, 1952," Box 357, "Sharp County, 1952," Box 357, "Cleburne County, 1952," Box 356, "Izard County, 1957," Box 415, FESRA; Vernon Wells interview, OOHP; Wilson Powell, "Cotton Ginning in Independence"; *Cleburne County Times,* 26 April 1962, 1.

14. "Narrative Report of County Extension Workers—Newton County, 1942," "Marion County, 1942," Box 218, FESRA; Burleson, *Treasured Memories of a Beautiful Place,* 118; Glenn Johnson, "Agriculture and Industry," in Earl Berry, *History of Marion County,* 294, 299.

15. "Narrative Report of County Extension Workers—Newton County, 1952," Box 359, "Searcy County, 1942," Box 218, FESRA; Earl Allen, "Flintrock Strawberries," *Progressive Farmer* (Mississippi-Arkansas-Louisiana edition), October 1957, 28, 29, 119.

16. "Narrative Report of County Extension Workers—Izard County, 1955," Box 390, "Searcy County, 1962," Box 464, "Izard County, 1963," Box 470, "Sharp County, 1962," Box 464, FESRA.

17. Chesnutt, "Rural Electrification in Arkansas," 246, 250, 253; AAES and Agricultural Marketing Service, *Prices and Price Indexes,* 45.

18. U.S. Department of Commerce, *Census of Agriculture, 1945,* 96–109; Meenen, *Supply and Utilization of Milk Sold in Arkansas,* 10; U.S. Department of Commerce, *Census of Agriculture, 1954,* 104–9; "Narrative Report of County Extension Workers—Benton County, 1952," Box 358, FESRA.

19. Burleson, *Treasured Memories of a Beautiful Place,* 102–3.

20. Ibid., 103–5.

21. Benson Fox interview, OOHP; Burleson, *Treasured Memories of a Beautiful Place,* 103; *Salem Headlight,* 6 June 1963, 7.

22. U.S. Department of Commerce, *Census of Agriculture, 1945,* 38, 39; Chesnutt, "Rural Electrification in Arkansas," 253; U.S. Department of Commerce, *Census of Agriculture, 1954,* 94; "Narrative Report of County Extension Workers—Izard County, 1942," Box 214, FESRA; "Fulton County," in Narrative Reports of All County Extension Agents and All Extension Home Economists, Arkansas, 1950, Box 2, Arkansas Cooperative Extension Service Records, UASC; *Baxter Bulletin,* 28 June 1940, 7.

23. Vernon Wells interview, OOHP.

24. Kennard Billingsley interview, OOHP.

25. Ibid.; "Narrative Report of County Extension Workers—Izard County, 1955," "Fulton County, 1955," Box 390, FESRA.

26. "Narrative Report of County Extension Workers—Izard County, 1955," Box 390, FESRA; *Salem Headlight,* 23 June 1955, 1; "Narrative Report of County Extension Workers—Fulton County, 1955," Box 390, "Baxter County, 1959," Box 436, "Fulton County, 1957," Box 415, FESRA.

27. "Narrative Report of County Extension Workers—Fulton County, 1957," Box 415, FESRA; Jack Justus, "Quality Dairy Heifers Upgrade Izard's Herds," *Progressive Farmer* (Mississippi-Arkansas-Louisiana edition), May 1957, 165; *Melbourne Times*, 1 February 1962, 1; *Salem Headlight*, 31 July 1958, 1.

28. "Narrative Report of County Extension Workers—Fulton County, 1955," "Izard County, 1955," Box 390, FESRA; U.S. Department of Commerce, *Census of Agriculture, 1964*, 316–19.

29. Zela Rhoads interview, OOHP.

30. "Narrative Report of County Extension Workers—Izard County, 1963," Box 470, FESRA.

31. Doyle Webb interview, Hugh Tanner interview, OOHP; "Narrative Report of County Extension Workers—Izard County, 1962," Box 464, FESRA.

32. Strausberg, *Century of Research*, 141; *Melbourne Times*, 17 May 1962, 1; 2 February 1967, 1; 23 February 1967, 1; 18 January 1968, 1.

33. Vernon Wells interview, Hugh Tanner interview, Kennard Billingsley interview, OOHP.

34. U.S. Department of Commerce, *Census of Agriculture, 1974*, 20, 26, 32, 50, 74, 152, 200, 266, 272, 308, 392, 410, 416, 428, 434; U.S. Department of Commerce, *Census of Agriculture, 1954*, 104.

35. Burleson, *Treasured Memories of a Beautiful Place*, 97, 98; *Baxter Bulletin*, 28 June 1940, 14; Pace, Swope, and Simers, "Mammoth Spring," 35; "Narrative Report of County Extension Workers—Fulton County, 1942," Box 214, FESRA.

36. Strausberg, *From Hills and Hollers*, 21, 35; Shiloh Museum, *History of Washington County*, 315; Schwartz, *Tyson*, 3–4.

37. Schwartz, *Tyson*, 4–5; Shiloh Museum, *History of Washington County*, 315.

38. Strausberg, *From Hills and Hollers*, 46, 47; Schwartz, *Tyson*, 5–6; U.S. Department of Commerce, *Census of Agriculture, 1945*, 96–109.

39. Strausberg, *From Hills and Hollers*, 54; Nancy Caver, "Roy Ritter," *Arkansas Democrat-Gazette*, 20 September 1998, 6D.

40. Schwartz, *Tyson*, 6, 11, 12, 31; Shiloh Museum, *History of Washington County*, 317.

41. Southerland and Henry interview, in *The Poultry Industry in Arkansas*, 369–70; McGinnis, *History of Independence County*, 109.

42. Southerland and Henry interview, in *The Poultry Industry in Arkansas*, 370; "Narrative Report of County Extension Workers—Izard County, 1957," Box 415, FESRA; *Stone County Leader*, 11 February 1960, 1.

43. U.S. Department of Commerce, *Census of Agriculture, 1954*, 110–15; U.S. Department of Commerce, *Census of Agriculture, 1974*, 19–437.

44. Earl F. Crouse, "Smart Broiler Contracts," *Progressive Farmer* (Mississippi-Arkansas-Louisiana edition), May 1957, 40.

45. Schwartz, *Tyson*, 65.

46. Strausberg, *From Hills and Hollers*, 105.

47. AAES and Agricultural Marketing Service, *Prices and Price Indexes*, 43; Ruby Neal Clark et al., *History of Van Buren County*, 49; Kennard Billingsley interview, OOHP.

48. Osgood and White, *Livestock Auctions in Arkansas*, 4; Burleson, *Treasured*

Memories of a Beautiful Place, 124; *Baxter Bulletin*, 26 August 1938, 1. The twelve Ozark livestock auctions in 1940 were located at Gentry, Rogers, Siloam Springs, Fayetteville, Berryville, Harrison, Flippin, Mountain Home, Mountain View, Clinton, Heber Springs, and Batesville. By 1950 the region contained twenty-one auctions, nine of which were located in Benton and Washington Counties. Jackson and Lafferty, *Cattle Sales and Purchases*, 10.

49. Burleson, *Treasured Memories of a Beautiful Place*, 123, 125; Tom Ross interview, OOHP; "Narrative Report of County Extension Workers—Stone County, 1942," Box 215, FESRA.

50. *Baxter Bulletin*, 28 June 1940, 18, 20, 21; 5 April 1940, 1; 12 July 1946, 4.

51. Will Rice, "Grass up There, Ponds down Here—Ozarks," *Progressive Farmer* (Mississippi-Arkansas-Louisiana edition), May 1948, 26.

52. Strausberg, *Century of Research*, 78; C. J. Brown, *Cattle on a Thousand Hills*, 188; Marie L. Lavallard, "Year-Round Grazing in Arkansas," *Progressive Farmer* (Mississippi-Arkansas-Louisiana edition), February 1948, 15.

53. "Narrative Report of County Extension Workers—Izard County, 1957," Box 415, FESRA; Singer, "The Role of Migration in the Socio-Economic Adjustment of Households," 89, 92, 95.

54. *Baxter Bulletin*, 28 June 1940, 16; McLeod, *Centennial Memorial History of Lawrence County*, 144.

55. *Baxter Bulletin*, 28 June 1940, 20; Rice, "Grass up There," 26.

56. Rice, "Grass up There," 14, 16; "Narrative Report of County Extension Workers—Izard County, 1942," Box 214, FESRA; Ruby Neal Clark et al., *History of Van Buren County*, 49.

57. *Baxter Bulletin*, 19 April 1940, 1; Strausberg, *Century of Research*, 141.

58. U.S. Department of Commerce, *Census of Agriculture, 1945*, 96–109; U.S. Department of Commerce, *Census of Agriculture, 1974*, 19–431.

59. U.S. Department of Commerce, *Census of Agriculture, 1974*, 19–431.

60. Wilson and Metzler, *Sickness and Medical Care*, 29. The off-farm occupations of these part-time farmers included teaching, store keeping, cattle dealing, and agricultural processing.

61. Fielder, *Type-of-Farming Areas in Arkansas*, 26; Osgood, *Farm Planning in the Eastern Ozarks*, 27.

62. U.S. Department of Commerce, *Census of Agriculture, 1992*, 162–71. The fifteen-county Ozark region in 1992 accounted for one-half of all dairy product sales in Arkansas, 41 percent of poultry sales, and 43 percent of cattle sales. Six of the top ten Arkansas counties in both dairy production and cattle production were located in the region, four of the leading poultry-producing counties were in the Ozarks, and Washington County led the state in the production of both swine and sheep.

Chapter Eight

1. Lillie Mae Watkins interview, OOHP.
2. Audrey Thompson interview, OOHP.
3. Ibid.

4. Zela Rhoads interview, OOHP.

5. Eula Karr Ferrel interview, OHC; Audrey Thompson, "Picking Cotton in the 'Bottoms,'" 2; L. V. Waddell interview, OOHP.

6. Jesse Oren Austin interview, OHC; John E. Miller interview, OOHP; *Mountain Wave*, 1 August 1947, 2; Percy Copeland interview, Stonewall Treat interview, OHI/OOHO. For a similar examination of seasonal migration from the Missouri Ozarks, see Edgar D. McKinney, "Images, Realities, and Cultural Transformation," 61–63.

7. Benson Fox interview, OOHP; Irene Jackson Hunter interview, OHC; McWilliams, *Ill Fares the Land*, 35.

8. Louie Clark interview, OOHP.

9. *Melbourne Times*, 29 March 1962, 1; Reed, *Faubus*, 36, 61; Billingsley, "Arkansas Picnic in Wenatchee," 36.

10. *Melbourne Times*, 28 February 1952, 1.

11. Earl Berry, *History of Marion County*, 516.

12. "Narrative Report of County Extension Workers—Izard County, 1952," Box 357, FESRA.

13. "Preliminary Overall Economic Development Program for North Central Arkansas," August 1961, Box 4, Folder 1, Rainey Papers, UASC.

14. Doyle Webb interview, OOHP.

15. Ibid.

16. Walter J. Stein, "The 'Okie' as Farm Laborer," in Shideler, *Agriculture in the Development of the West*, 205. See also Stein, *California and the Dust Bowl Migration*.

17. Kennard Billingsley interview, OOHP; *Stone County Leader*, 22 May 1953, 1; *Salem Headlight*, 17 January 1963, 5; 13 June 1963, 3.

18. Fligstein, *Going North*, 18. For discussions of outmigration's potential for the improvement of quality of life, see Kirby, *Rural Worlds Lost*, and Flynt, *Poor but Proud*.

19. Audrey Thompson interview, OOHP.

20. Ann Moser Wilson, *Then and Now*, 34, 37, 40.

21. Ibid., 48, 50, 51, 53, 54, 59.

22. "Retiring in Arkansas," *Arkansas Times* advertising supplement, March 1992, 9.

23. Westphal and Osterhage, *A Fame Not Easily Forgotten*, 214; Rayburn, *The Eureka Springs Story*, 51, 72.

24. Clyde T. Ellis, "The Third District of Arkansas in the South," speech delivered at a Fayetteville banquet, 15 December 1938, Box 6, Folder 5, Series 2, Ellis Papers, UASC; Tom Shiras, *Walking Editor of the Ozarks*, 124.

25. Frances H. Shiras, "Norfork Dam," 151, 153, 156, 157; Messick, *History of Baxter County*, 316, 319, 320, 325; *Baxter Bulletin*, 8 January 1943, 1; Fleming, *The White River of the Ozarks*, 53.

26. "Retiring in Arkansas," 9; Glenn Johnson, "The Bull Shoals Dam," in Earl Berry, *History of Marion County*, 317, 319; Rothrock, "Congressman James William Trimble," 76, 83; Rafferty, *The Ozarks Outdoors*, 96. Although Truman was the first sitting president to visit the region, a young Herbert Hoover had visited the same area as a member of a geological expedition in the late nineteenth century. Table Rock Dam was the third of six proposed dams for the White River drainage area. This southwestern Mis-

souri dam was responsible for much of the early growth of the Branson area. The last dam completed in the region—the final two were eventually canceled—was Beaver Dam near Eureka Springs in Carroll County. Completed in 1966, Beaver Dam formed a reservoir covering 42 square miles and extending into eastern Benton County.

27. Fite, *From Vision to Reality*, 74; Timely Club, *The Hardy History*, 83; Larry Ault, "Retirement Community Pioneer Dies," *Arkansas Democrat-Gazette*, 25 January 1998, 1B, 6B.

28. Fite, *From Vision to Reality*, 74, 75; Ault, "Retirement Community Pioneer Dies," 1B; Timely Club, *The Hardy History*, 83; *Cherokee Villager*, special edition, 1956, 1.

29. Audrey Thompson interview, OOHP.

30. Fite, *From Vision to Reality*, 196, 75; Timely Club, *The Hardy History*, 84; "Narrative Report of County Extension Workers—Sharp County, 1963," Box 470, FESRA.

31. Timely Club, *The Hardy History*, 87, 88, 89.

32. *Horseshoe Progress*, 30 August 1969, 1.

33. Ibid., Winter 1968, 4.

34. Ibid., 19 December 1969, 3; January 1970, 3.

35. Ibid., January 1970, 3; March 1970, 2, 10; 29 June 1970, 4, 5; 26 August 1970, 9; 21 October 1970, 9; 25 November 1970, 11; 16 December 1970, 16, 17. The list of homeowners was compiled using the monthly editions of the *Horseshoe Progress* for 1968 through 1971.

36. Hugh Tanner interview, Audrey Thompson interview, OOHP.

37. Ruby Neal Clark et al., *History of Van Buren County*, 164; Rafferty, *The Ozarks Outdoors*, 100; Louie Clark interview, OOHP.

38. *Arkansas Gazette*, 4 May 1969, 1C; Ruby Neal Clark et al., *History of Van Buren County*, 159–61; Stroud, *The Promise of Paradise*, 125, 127, 129.

39. Fite, *From Vision to Reality*, 76, 77, 79, 80, 81, 83, 84, 85, 86, 87, 89.

40. Ibid., 145, 177. The Cherokee Village Development Company was renamed Cooper Communities, Inc., in 1971 and has since developed three additional retirement communities: Hot Springs Village, Arkansas; Tellico Village, Tennessee; and Savannah Lakes Village, South Carolina.

41. Bern Keating, "Arkansas Retirement: God's Own Country," *50 Plus*, August 1988, 56. For a discussion of similar developments in western North Carolina, see Beaver, *Rural Community in the Appalachian South*.

42. Gary D. Ford, "Away in the Arkansas Ozarks," *Southern Living*, August 1982, 71; Paula Thompson, "Country Dreaming," *Mother Earth News*, September–October 1986, 65, 66, 67. For a discussion of hippie settlements in general, see Shi, *The Simple Life*, and Beaver, *Rural Community in the Appalachian South*, chap. 5.

43. Jeff Matthews interview, OOHP.

44. Goldie Faires Ham Benedict interview, OHC.

45. AAES, *Decline of the Church Serving Farmers*, 16. For a brief overview of religion in the rural South since World War II, see Ted Ownby, "Struggling to Be Old-Fashioned: Evangelical Religion in the Modern Rural South," in Hurt, *The Rural South since World War II*, 122–48.

46. While this statement suggests that the denominational makeup of the Arkansas Ozarks was similar to that of Arkansas as a whole and of the wider South, a closer in-

spection of statistics reveals interesting anomalies within the region. Due to the influence of "dissenting Baptists," in 1926 Southern Baptists accounted for just over one in five religious adherents in the region. On the other hand, members of the nineteenth-century restorationist churches (Churches of Christ and Disciples of Christ) accounted for 23 percent of all Ozark churchgoers, and in the thirteen counties outside Benton and Washington, these "Christians" outnumbered both Southern Baptists and southern Methodists. U.S. Department of Commerce, *Religious Bodies, 1926*, 580–83.

47. U.S. Department of Commerce, *Religious Bodies, 1936*, 122–25.

48. Douglas W. Johnson, Picard, and Quinn, *Churches and Church Membership in the United States, 1971*.

49. Bradley et al., *Churches and Church Membership in the United States, 1990*.

50. No census or survey of religious groups or adherents has ever been, or probably will ever be, totally accurate. In the Ozarks today, many nondenominational community churches still exist, most often in small, isolated settlements miles off the beaten paths in the Boston Mountains or White River Hills. These congregations, along with numerous Pentecostal sects, regularly escape researchers. Other groups simply refuse to participate in censuses.

51. McCuen, *Historical Report of the Secretary of State, 1986*, 385–420, 237. Hammerschmidt's election was not unique in the South in the mid-1960s. Other Upper South states began sending Republicans to Washington and to their state houses. In fact, 1966 also witnessed the election of Republican Winthrop Rockefeller as governor of Arkansas. While scholars, most notably Earl Black and Merle Black, have generally attributed the Republican resurgence to conservative, racist reactions toward the national Democratic Party's role in the civil rights movement, the election of Hammerschmidt probably owed more to the influx of Republican voters in the 1960s. Hammerschmidt's campaign most likely benefited from conservative, populist backlash, even though the region's minuscule black population sheltered it from most of the decade's race-related incidents; still, most Democratic Ozark counties, especially ones with small inmigrant populations, remained solidly in the Democratic fold long after 1966. Interestingly, Hammerschmidt's only close campaign after 1966 occurred in 1974 when he narrowly defeated a young University of Arkansas School of Law professor named Bill Clinton. Earl Black and Merle Black, *Politics and Society in the South*; Wayne Parent and Peter A. Petrakis, "Populism Left and Right: Politics of the Rural South," in Hurt, *The Rural South since World War II*, 149–67.

52. Beulah Billingsley interview, OOHP; Pauline Jackson Thacker interview, OHC; Glenn Hackett interview, OOHP.

53. Glenn Hackett interview, OOHP.

54. *Stone County Leader*, 5 June 1953, 1; Rushing, "Early History of Rural Special School," 28, 29. Rural Special is an official appellation used by the state Department of Education to identify rural consolidated school districts. Violet Hill School, the Izard County school mentioned in the previous paragraph, was, until its consolidation with another local district in 1985, known officially as Rural Special District No. 1. As far as I know, Stone County's Rural Special school district is the only one of the state's districts to retain the name instead of adopting the name of the local village or com-

munity as its unofficial name. Rural Special remains an apt title for the district, one of the most rural and isolated in the state of Arkansas.

55. Kennard Billingsley interview, Glenn Hackett interview, OOHP.

56. Pauline Jackson Thacker interview, OHC.

57. Irene Jackson Hunter interview, Eula Harr Ferrel interview, OHC; Zela Rhoads interview, OOHP.

58. Julius Duscha, "Aid for Our Own Underdeveloped Areas," *Reporter*, 1 February 1962, 37.

59. Singer, "The Role of Migration in the Socio-Economic Adjustment of Households," 19, 70, 66.

60. Pauline Jackson Thacker interview, OHC; Benson Fox interview, Lillie Mae Watkins interview, OOHP.

61. U.S. Department of Commerce, *Census of Agriculture, 1935*, 670–91; Morgan, *Black Hillbillies*, 119–29. Although black outmigration in the post–World War II era coincided with white outmigration and appears to have been economic in nature and free of violence, that was not true of at least one community in the early twentieth century. As Jacqueline Froelich and David Zimmermann discovered, two episodes of racial unrest in 1905 and in 1909 forced the small population of blacks in Harrison to abandon the town. Froelich and Zimmermann, "Total Eclipse," 131–59.

62. Lillie Mae Watkins interview, OOHP; U.S. Department of Commerce, *Census of Agriculture, 1974*, 19–431.

63. Ozarks Regional Commission, *1974 Annual Report*, 2, 12, 25.

64. *Forbes*, 26 October 1987, 324, 333.

65. Strausberg, *From Hills and Hollers*, 201–7.

66. Vance and Scott, *Wal-Mart*, 1, 3, 5. See also Trimble, *Sam Walton*.

67. Vance and Scott, *Wal-Mart*, 9, 11, 13, 14. It should be noted that both Ruskin Heights and St. Robert were not as traditionally small-town as many of Walton's other locations. Ruskin Heights was in an area that would soon be absorbed by Kansas City suburbia, and St. Robert was near the army's burgeoning Fort Leonard Wood.

68. Ibid., 41, 43, 44, 46, 47, 51.

69. Gary Farley, "The Wal-Martization of Rural America and Other Things," *OzarksWatch* 2 (1988): 12.

70. Johnson, *Arkansas in Modern America*, 198.

71. Schwartz, *J. B. Hunt*, 1, 2, 4.

72. Ibid., 5, 11, 19, viii, ix.

73. *Forbes*, 26 April 1993, 313, 312; *Fortune*, 19 April 1993; Strausberg, *From Hills and Hollers*, 201–7; Ralph Desmarais, "The End of the Independent Poultry Growers," in Desmarais and Jeffords, *Uncertain Harvest*, 83. In addition to Tyson, Hudson, and Peterson, northwestern Arkansas served as headquarters for George's (Springdale), Simmons Foods (Siloam Springs), and Hillbilly Smokehouse (Rogers).

Chapter Nine

1. "Biographical Sketches of Harold Sherman," File 3, Box 1 of Series 1—Subseries 1, Sherman Papers, UCAA; Sherman, "They All Come Back," 9–14.

2. "Clowns, monsters, and mama's boys" here refer to three classes of hillbillies that J. W. Williamson identifies as presented in movies, reflecting mainstream culture's ambivalent image of mountaineers. Williamson, *Hillbillyland*, 21, 149, 173.

3. Boorstin, *The Image*, 9.

4. Cratis Dearl Williams, "The Southern Mountaineer in Fact and Fiction," 1525.

5. Frederick Simpich, "Land of a Million Smiles," *National Geographic*, May 1943, 589–623.

6. Rayburn, *Forty Years in the Ozarks*, 82, 79.

7. Vance Randolph to Otto Ernest Rayburn, 5 January 1941, Box 1, Folder 2, Rayburn Collection, UASC.

8. Rayburn, *Forty Years in the Ozarks*, 85; Cochran, *Vance Randolph*, 191. Marge Lyon, Rayburn's fellow Eureka Springs booster, produced in addition to her *Chicago Tribune* articles several romantic books on the Ozarks, including *Take to the Hills: A Chronicle of the Ozarks*. Lyon's *Hurrah for Arkansas!* contains a chapter entitled "Newton County—Land of Unspoiled Beauty," a romantic and laudatory discussion of northern Arkansas's most rugged and picturesque county.

9. Oral Deaton to Rayburn, 19 February 1957, Box 13, Folder 1, Rayburn Collection, UASC.

10. Louisa Comstock, "How to Leave Home and Like It," *House Beautiful*, March 1949, 190.

11. Don Eddy, "Let's Go to the Ozarks," *American Magazine*, March 1954, 40.

12. Henry Bradshaw and Vera Bradshaw, "The Ozarks," *Better Homes and Gardens*, May 1952, 71.

13. Hartzell Spence, "Modern Shepherd of the Hills," *Saturday Evening Post*, 8 November 1952, 130, 132. Richmond was featured in several books and articles on the Ozarks. The practice of concentrating on non-Ozark natives when ostensibly writing about Ozark life was quite common. Marge Lyon especially tended to write about fellow midwesterners transplanted in the northern Arkansas hills. Richmond's "Wilderness Library" eventually grew to several thousand volumes; several nationally prominent individuals, including Eleanor Roosevelt, donated books to the library. Richmond's demise remains a mystery, however. He abruptly left his Newton County cabin and books in the late 1950s and never returned. Faris, *Ozark Log Cabin Folks*, 74, 77.

14. Ben Lucien Burman, "Whittling Capital of America," *Collier's*, 2 September 1955, 55; Charles Morrow Wilson, *The Bodacious Ozarks*, 231.

15. Pearl Anoe, "There's No Place Like the Ozarks," *Americas*, May 1955, 10, 15.

16. Julia McAdoo, "Where the Poor Are Rich," *American Mercury*, September 1955, 86–87, 89.

17. Phil Stong, "The Friendly Ozarks," *Holiday*, August 1951, 91, 92, 96.

18. Vance Randolph, "Ozark Humor," *Rayburn's Ozark Guide*, Autumn 1949, 47; Randolph, "Folklore and Common Sense," 108.

19. Cochran and Luster, *For Love and for Money*, 40, 41.

20. Again, for a complete listing of Randolph's Ozark works, as well as his pseudonymous works on other subjects, see Cochran and Luster, *For Love and for Money*.

21. Lankford, "John Quincy Wolf, Jr.," 5, 7; Fletcher, "The Ozark Folklore Society," 115; Rayburn, "Arkansas Folklore: Its Preservation," 218; Fletcher, *Arkansas*, 313.

22. Rudolph, Carpenter, and Simpson, *Selected Letters of John Gould Fletcher*, xxiv, xxvi; Fletcher, "Education, Past and Present," in Twelve Southerners, *I'll Take My Stand*, 92–121; Tyson, "Folklore in the Life and Work of John Gould Fletcher," 3, 66–67; Fletcher, *Life Is My Song*, 382; Johnson, *Fierce Solitude*, 216.

23. Fletcher, *Arkansas*, 313; Tyson, "Folklore in the Life and Work of John Gould Fletcher," 193, 187, 177, 4.

24. Tyson, "Folklore in the Life and Work of John Gould Fletcher," 183–84.

25. Fletcher, *Arkansas*, 262, 230, 264.

26. Fletcher, *Life Is My Song*, 374–75.

27. Williamson, *Hillbillyland*, 251.

28. Limerick, *Reader's Guide to Periodical Literature: March 1963–February 1965*, 98, 1491, 1390.

29. Singer, "The Role of Migration in the Socio-Economic Adjustment of Households," 155.

30. Jordan and Bender, *Economic Survey of the Ozark Region*, 12, 15; Leo Rainey, "Preliminary Overall Economic Development Program for North Central Arkansas," August 1961, Box 4, Folder 1, Rainey Papers, UASC; *Informer and Newton County Times*, 27 June 1969, 1.

31. Gary D. Ford, "Away in the Arkansas Ozarks," *Southern Living*, August 1982, 68; Messick, *History of Baxter County*, 328.

32. Pitcaithley, "Buffalo River," 188, 189, 191, 192, 193.

33. Ibid., 193–207. See also Compton, *Battle for the Buffalo River*.

34. *Informer and Newton County Times*, 22 March 1968, 2; 26 July 1968, 1.

35. Pitcaithley, "Buffalo River," 207; Larry Isch, "Battle for the Buffalo," *Arkansas Democrat-Gazette*, 11 July 1993, 8C.

36. William Bruce Wheeler and Michael J. McDonald, "The 'New Mission' and the Tellico Project, 1945–1970," in Hargrove and Conkin, *TVA: Fifty Years of Grassroots Bureaucracy*, 167–93.

37. Eddy, "Let's Go to the Ozarks," 95; Comstock, "How to Leave Home and Like It," 191.

38. Rayburn, *The Eureka Springs Story*, 74; Faris, *Ozark Log Cabin Folks*, 66.

39. H. William Moore to Rayburn, 19 January 1950, Box 7, Folder 1, and Evan Booth to Rayburn, 17 February 1957, Folder 12, Box 1, Rayburn Collection, UASC; Rayburn, *Forty Years in the Ozarks*, 89.

40. Jeansonne, *Gerald L. K. Smith*, 2, 11, 188, 189.

41. Ibid., 190–92.

42. Ibid., 193, 196, 199.

43. Ibid., 200, 201.

44. *Stone County Leader*, 8 February 1962, 1.

45. Harold Sherman to Wilbur D. Mills, 15 March 1957, File, Box 1, Subseries 3, Se-

ries 1, Sherman Papers, UCAA. Much of Sherman's later life was devoted to working with the International Research Associates Foundation, an ESP study foundation he established in Little Rock.

46. "Land of the Cross-Bow," undated press release from the Arkansas Publicity and Information Department, Little Rock, File 5, Box 4, Subseries 3, Series 1, Sherman Papers, UCAA.

47. Sherman to Mills, 2 July 1957, File 1, Box 1, Subseries 3, Series 1; brochure for the "1st Annual Field Tournament and Organized Deer Hunt," File 2, Box 4, Subseries 3, Series 1; Sherman to Mills, 15 February 1958, File 1, Box 1; Sherman to Mills, 16 May 1958, File 1, Box 1; Sherman to Mills, 24 December 1958, File 1, Box 1, Sherman Papers, UCAA.

48. Fleming, *The Blanchard Springs Caverns Story*, 3, 35, 42; Sherman to Mills, 18 August 1963, 7 November 1963, File 2, Box 1, Subseries 2, Series 1, Sherman Papers, UCAA.

49. "Preliminary Overall Economic Development Program for North Central Arkansas," August 1961, and Leo Rainey, "Summary of Work in the Five-County Area, July 1, 1961–June 30, 1962," Box 4, Folder 1, Rainey Papers, UASC.

50. Founded in 1929, the Southern Highland Handicraft Guild was a loose federation of craft-producing centers and schools scattered across Appalachia. See Becker, *Selling Tradition*.

51. Untitled and undated bulletin, Box 3, Folder 6, Rainey Papers, UASC; Leo Rainey, "The Arkansas Traveller Folk Theatre," theater handbill (Hardy, Arkansas, 1978), 5, LCA; Rainey to Glen Hinkle, 21 September 1973, Box 11, Folder 1; Rainey, "Summary of Work in the Five-County Area," Box 4, Folder 1; Rainey, untitled bulletin, 5 February 1962, Box 3, Folder 6, Rainey Papers, UASC; "Narrative Report of County Extension Workers—Baxter County, 1962," "Sharp County, 1962," Box 464, FESRA. Historian Jane S. Becker found scant survival of "traditional" mountain crafts in Appalachia as early as the depression. Studying the craft movement through the dialectic of authenticity versus inauthenticity, according to Becker, obscures the dynamic, historical development of the handicraft tradition. "In the end, mountain craft traditions were shaped not only by local culture, but also by reformers from outside the region, by the government, by the marketplace, and by middle-class consumers." Becker, *Selling Tradition*, 6.

52. "Narrative Report of County Extension Workers—Stone County, 1962," Box 464, FESRA; Rainey, untitled bulletin, 5 February 1962 (first quote), Box 3, Folder 6, Rainey Papers, UASC; *Stone County Leader*, 12 April 1962, 1; 18 January 1962, 1; 1 March 1962, 1; 29 March 1962, 1; *Melbourne Times*, 12 April 1962, 1.

53. *Stone County Leader*, 12 February 1959, 1; *Informer and Newton County Times*, 18 June 1965, 1; Rainey to William Shaw, 13 September 1963; "Area Development Council Meeting Minutes," 12 September 1963; Rainey to Extension Agents, 17 December 1963; Rainey, "Accomplishments: Area Craft Program," Box 4, Folder 1, Rainey Papers, UASC.

54. Rainey to Hinkle, 21 September 1973, Box 11, Folder 1, Rainey Papers, UASC; McNeil, *Ozark Country*, 168–69.

55. Lucas, "The Music of Jimmy Driftwood," 27; Robert M. Anderson, "Jimmy

Driftwood: Poet Laureate with a Banjo," *Arkansas Times,* October 1979, 62; Ernie Deane, "Folk Songs Preserve Our Heritage," *Arkansas Gazette,* 28 April 1963, 5E; Robert Cochran, "The Ozark Saga of Singer and Songwriter Jimmy Driftwood," *Gadfly,* May–June 2000, 32.

56. Combs, *A Pickin' and a Grinnin' on the Courthouse Square,* 17–19; Lucas, "The Music of Jimmy Driftwood," 27; Anderson, "Jimmy Driftwood," 60; Cochran, "Ozark Saga," 32.

57. Rainey, Pinkston, and Pinkston, *Songs of the Ozark Folk,* 5; J. D. Stark to John Q. Wolf, 22 July 1952, John Quincy Wolf Jr. Papers, LCA; Thomas BeVier, "When He Says 'Hey, Listen to This,' They Do," *Memphis Commercial Appeal,* 16 May 1971, 2-2. See also Abrahams, *A Singer and Her Songs.*

58. Combs, *A Pickin' and a Grinnin' on the Courthouse Square,* 20–21; *Stone County Leader,* 28 February 1963, 1; 25 April 1963, 1; *Batesville Guard,* 29 March 1963, 1 (quote). For a recent publication on Ozark folk songs, see McNeil, *Southern Mountain Folksongs.*

59. McNeil, *Ozark Country,* 169; Craig Ogilvie, "Ozark Traditions: Folk Culture, Blanchard Springs Caverns Created Stone County Tourism Industry," *Batesville Guard,* 25 January 1994, 10; *Stone County Leader,* 24 April 1975, 2; Leo Rainey interview, OOHP.

60. I refer to the original Arkansas Folk Festival as "pure" and "earnest" even though I am aware that the event represented the commodification of folk culture, which according to sociologist Dean MacCannell inherently rendered the folk arts presented less authentic. But, as sociologist Erik Cohen asserts, commodification "does not necessarily destroy the meaning of cultural products, neither for the locals nor for the tourists, although it may do so under certain conditions." It is my contention that commodification was not completely at odds with the spirit of Ozark tradition and culture. Jimmy Driftwood, after all, had at the behest of fellow Ozarker and folklorist John Quincy Wolf Jr. several years earlier profited from his mastery of and love for folk music, and Rex Harral, an original member of the Ozark Foothills Craft Guild, had begun looking for markets for his creations in the late 1950s. Cohen's further assertion that "the emergence of a tourist market frequently facilitates the preservation of a cultural tradition which would otherwise perish" seems to be especially pertinent to the blossoming 1960s folk culture movement in the Ozarks. Nevertheless, in the Arkansas Ozarks, as we shall see, this preservation has generally been accomplished by non-Ozarkers, which may force a reevaluation or remolding of the debate over authenticity and commodification. MacCannell, "Staged Authenticity," 589–603; Cohen, "Authenticity and Commoditization in Tourism," 383, 382.

61. Kirby, *Rural Worlds Lost,* 80.

62. Fersh and Fersh, *Bessie Moore,* 181; McNeil, *Ozark Country,* 169; Rainey to Hinkle, 21 September 1973, Box 11, Folder 1, Rainey Papers, UASC; *Batesville Guard,* 31 March 1995, 3; Whisnant, *Modernizing the Mountaineer,* 72.

63. *Arkansas Gazette,* 15 October 1963, 1A; Fersh and Fersh, *Bessie Moore,* 181, 178; McNeil, *Ozark Country,* 170.

64. McNeil, *Ozark Country,* 169, 170; Fersh and Fersh, *Bessie Moore,* 179, 178.

65. McNeil, *Ozark Country,* 171; Tebbetts, *Resident and Tourist Perceptions of the*

Ozark Folk Center, 2–3; Rainey to Gerald L. Phillips-Chisholm, 12 September 1973, Box 11, Folder 1, Rainey Papers, UASC; *Stone County Leader*, 29 May 1975, 2.

66. *Spring River Times*, 10 June 1970, 1; John Quincy Wolf Jr. to R. W. Wygle, 19 January 1972, Box 3, Folder 1, Rainey Papers, UASC.

67. Tebbetts, *Resident and Tourist Perceptions of the Ozark Folk Center*, 3–4; *Stone County Leader*, 25 September 1975, 2; 2 October 1975, 1.

68. Stephens, "The Case of the Missing Folk Music," 63, 64. See also Malone, *Singing Cowboys and Musical Mountaineers*.

69. *Stone County Leader*, 18 September 1975, 1.

70. Ibid., 24 April 1975, 1, 2; 22 May 1975, 1.

71. Ibid., 24 April 1975, 2; 22 May 1975, 1, 2; 10 July 1975, 1; 17 July 1975, 1; 24 July 1975, 1; 25 September 1975, 1.

72. Ibid., 29 May 1975, 2.

73. Tebbetts, *Resident and Tourist Perceptions of the Ozark Folk Center*, 3; Rainey, Pinkston, and Pinkston, *Songs of the Ozark Folk*, 35; Rex Harral interview, OOHP. The Ozark Folk Center more closely qualifies as "staged authenticity" than did the original Arkansas Folk Festival. The ethnic authenticity of the center's craftspeople and musicians has grown especially dubious in the past two decades as non-Ozarkers have replaced Ozarkers in the craft booths and on stage (MacCannell, "Staged Authenticity"). Sociologist Regina Bendix found a similar development in the Unspunnen revivals of Interlaken, Switzerland, where "many of the active performers are city dwellers who have taken courses in how to sew folk costumes of their region or sing songs of their folk past" (Bendix, "Tourism and Cultural Displays," 136).

74. Jim Buchanan, "Arkansas College Goes to Heart of Folklore," *Arkansas Gazette*, 29 July 1973, 4E.

75. Fletcher, *Arkansas*, 313; Tyson, "Folklore in the Life and Work of John Gould Fletcher," 182. Judging a performer's reaction to the public display (or commodification) of a traditional, cultural practice is difficult and at best inexact. Obviously, Fletcher's Fayetteville pickers suffered stage fright and uneasiness when faced with the self-consciousness accompanying public performance. The fact that their Saturday sessions were not conducted inside a smokehouse rendered their performance more than a little inauthentic. Nevertheless, as Erik Cohen postulates: "In many situations of commoditization, the performers themselves do not necessarily perceive that such a transformation [of meaning as a cultural product] had in fact occurred" (Cohen, "Authenticity and Commoditization in Tourism," 382). Ultimately, the performer's reaction to commodification probably relies on personality and temperament. As John Quincy Wolf Jr. illustrated, Jimmy Driftwood, Neal Morris, Almeda Riddle, and other prominent Ozark folk singers were natural performers whose delivery changed little from sitting room to stage. According to Wolf, these most renowned and artistically inclined singers were more likely to "adapt the songs to their own artistic judgments and/or permit the songs to evolve into what they [felt] to be more effective works of art" (Wolf, "Folksingers and the Re-creation of Folksong," 111).

76. McNeil, *Ozark Country*, 171; *Stone County Leader*, 31 July 1975, 1.

77. Charles Morrow Wilson, *The Bodacious Ozarks*, 239.

78. Rainey, Pinkston, and Pinkston, *Songs of the Ozark Folk*, 77; brochure for the

"10th Annual Anniversary Meeting of the Greers Ferry Lake and Little Red River Association," 20 January 1976, Folder 14, Box 10, Rainey Papers, UASC; *Cleburne County Times*, 12 October 1972, 1.

79. *Arkansas Gazette*, 20 June 1969, 1B; *Horseshoe Progress*, 30 May 1969, 1; 4 July 1969, 1; 30 August 1969, 1; 29 June 1970, 14; 31 March 1971, 1.

80. Leo Rainey interview, OOHP.

81. *Arkansas Gazette*, 6 January 1967, 1B. A popular depression-era radio and vaudeville comedian from Van Buren, Arkansas, Bob Burns was often criticized for capitalizing on and perpetuating negative hillbilly stereotypes associated with his native state.

82. Harington, *Let Us Build Us a City*, 98.

83. *Arkansas Gazette*, 4 January 1967, 1B; 6 January 1967, 1B.

84. Harington, *Let Us Build Us a City*, 110.

85. *Informer and Newton County Times*, 6 October 1967, 1; 17 May 1968, 1; 24 May 1968, 1; *Arkansas Gazette*, 19 May 1968, 3A.

86. *Arkansas Gazette*, 28 October 1968, 1A, 2A, 6A; 9 January 1969, 1A; 4 May 1969, 10A; Reed, *Faubus*, 329.

87. *Informer and Newton County Times*, 20 June 1969, 1; *Arkansas Gazette*, 2 November 1972, 21A.

88. Silver Dollar City is an Ozark pioneer–themed amusement park near Branson, Missouri. Established in 1960 above Marvel Cave to capitalize on the area's *Shepherd of the Hills* fame and the growing popularity of Lake Taneycomo, Silver Dollar City was, according to founder Mary Herscend's design, to be a midwestern Colonial Williamsburg. At the turn of the twenty-first century, Silver Dollar City was still one of Branson's leading tourist attractions. Rafferty, *The Ozarks*, 216.

89. Keyes and van den Berghe, "Tourism and Re-created Ethnicity," 346.

90. Jim Creighton, "'Tis a Gift to Be Free," *St. Louis Post-Dispatch*, 28 April 1974, 16F.

91. In his study of the Missouri Ozarks, Edgar D. McKinney found a similar development. The success of Harold Bell Wright's *Shepherd of the Hills* brought a degree of tourism-inspired modernization and commercialism to Branson's Taney County that was scarcely experienced in the more agriculturally and economically "progressive" plateau sections of south central Missouri. McKinney, "Images, Realities, and Cultural Transformation," 52–53.

92. Richard Rhodes, "Home to the Ozarks," *Reader's Digest*, November 1981, 156.

93. Mike W. Edwards, "Through Ozark Hills and Hollows," *National Geographic*, November 1970, 656–89.

94. Faris, *Ozark Log Cabin Folks*, viii.

95. Godsey and Godsey, *Ozark Mountain Folk*, 18; Minick and Minick, *Hills of Home*, 7.

96. C. W. Gusewelle, "'A Continuity of Place and Blood': The Seasons of Man in the Ozarks," *American Heritage*, December 1977, 108.

97. Godsey and Godsey, *Ozark Mountain Folk*; Faris, *Ozark Log Cabin Folks*, viii.

98. Minick and Minick, *Hills of Home*.

Conclusion

1. Andrei Codrescu, "Heading for the Hills," *Travel Holiday*, May 1994, 84.
2. Lisa Moore LaRoe, "Ozarks Harmony," *National Geographic*, April 1998, 89.
3. Don Johnson, "Northwest Passage," *Arkansas Democrat-Gazette*, March 23, 1997, 1A; Johnson, *Arkansas in Modern America*, 200–201.
4. Charles Morrow Wilson, *The Bodacious Ozarks*, 231.

BIBLIOGRAPHY

Primary Sources

Manuscript Collections

Arkansas History Commission (AHC), Little Rock, Arkansas
    WPA Federal Writers' Project Files
    WPA Historical Files
Lyon College Archives (LCA), Batesville, Arkansas
    Arkansas Lime Company Records
    George Shelby Kennard Papers
    McGuire Family Papers
    John Q. Wolf Sr. Papers
    John Quincy Wolf Jr. Papers
National Archives and Records Administration, Southwest Region,
    Fort Worth, Texas
    Federal Extension Service Records—Arkansas (FESRA), RG 33
Southern Historical Collection (SHC), University of North Carolina, Chapel Hill
    Fred P. Kealer Papers, microfilm
University of Arkansas Special Collections (UASC), Fayetteville, Arkansas
    Arkansas Cooperative Extension Service Records
    Clyde T. Ellis Papers
    Leo Rainey Papers
    Otto Ernest Rayburn Collection
University of Central Arkansas Archives (UCAA), Conway, Arkansas
    Harold M. Sherman Papers

Published Works

Adams, George I. *Zinc and Lead Deposits of Northern Arkansas.* Washington, D.C.: GPO, 1904.
Arkansas State Gazetteer and Business Directory, 1888–1889. Little Rock: R. L. Polk & Company, 1888.
Arkansas State Gazetteer and Business Directory, 1898–1899. Detroit: R. L. Polk & Company, 1898.

Barker, Catherine S. *Yesterday Today: Life in the Ozarks.* Caldwell, Idaho: Caxton Printers, 1941.

Bradshaw, De Emmett. *My Story: The Autobiography of De Emmett Bradshaw.* Omaha, Nebr.: Omaha Printing Company, 1941.

Burleson, Floyd. *Treasured Memories of a Beautiful Place in the North Arkansas Ozark Hills.* Yellville, Ark.: Carrousel Publishing Company, 1989.

Faris, Paul. *Ozark Log Cabin Folks: The Way They Were.* Little Rock: Rose Publishing Company, 1983.

Faubus, Orval Eugene. *In This Faraway Land.* Conway, Ark.: River Road Press, 1971.

Finger, Charles J. *Ozark Fantasia.* Fayetteville, Ark.: Golden Horseman Press, 1927.

Godsey, Helen, and Townsend Godsey. *Ozark Mountain Folk: These Were the Last.* Branson, Mo.: Ozarks Mountaineer, 1977.

Goodspeed. *The Goodspeed Biographical and Historical Memoirs of Northeastern Arkansas.* Chicago: Goodspeed Publishing Company, 1889.

———. *The Goodspeed Biographical and Historical Memoirs of Northwestern Arkansas.* Chicago: Goodspeed Publishing Company, 1889.

Hogue, Wayman. *Back Yonder: An Ozark Chronicle.* New York: Minton, Balch & Company, 1932.

Jeffery, A. C. *Historical and Biographical Sketches of the Early Settlement of the Valley of White River Together with a History of Izard County.* Richmond, Va.: Jeffery Historical Society, 1973.

Lyon, Marguerite. *Hurrah for Arkansas! From Razorbacks to Diamonds.* Indianapolis: Bobbs-Merrill Company, 1947.

———. *Take to the Hills: A Chronicle of the Ozarks.* New York: Grosset & Dunlap, 1941.

Minick, Roger, and Bob Minick. *Hills of Home: The Rural Ozarks of Arkansas.* San Francisco: Scrimshaw Press, 1975. Reprint, with the title *Hills of Home: The Rural Ozarks,* New York: Ballantine Books, 1976.

Miser, Hugh D. *Manganese Carbonate in the Batesville District of Arkansas.* Washington, D.C.: GPO, 1941.

Noland, C. F. M. *Pete Whetstone of Devil's Fork: Letters to the Spirit of the Times.* Edited by Ted R. Worley and Eugene A. Nolte. Van Buren, Ark.: Press-Argus, 1957.

Page, Tate C. *The Voices of Moccasin Creek.* Point Lookout, Mo.: School of the Ozarks Press, 1972.

Randolph, Vance. *The Ozarks: An American Survival of Primitive Society.* New York: Vanguard Press, 1931.

Rayburn, Otto Ernest. *Ozark Country.* New York: Duell, Sloan and Pearce, 1941.

Schoolcraft, Henry R. *Rude Pursuits and Rugged Peaks: Schoolcraft's Ozark Journal, 1818–1819.* Edited by Milton D. Rafferty. Fayetteville: University of Arkansas Press, 1996. Originally published as *Journal of a Tour into the Interior of Missouri and Arkansaw.* London: Sir Richard Phillips and Company, 1821.

Sheppard, Muriel Early. *Cabins in the Laurel.* Chapel Hill: University of North Carolina Press, 1935.

Wilson, Ann Moser. *Then and Now: A Historical Document.* Arcadia, Calif.: N.p., 1995.

Wilson, Charles Morrow. *The Bodacious Ozarks: True Tales of the Backhills.* New York: Hastings House, 1959.

———. "Hemmed-in Holler." *Review of Reviews and World's Work,* August 1935, 58–62.

Wolf, John Quincy. *Life in the Leatherwoods.* Edited by Gene Hyde and Brooks Blevins. Fayetteville: University of Arkansas Press, 2000.

Womack, J. P. *Reminiscences.* Jonesboro, Ark.: Caleb Watson & Company, 1939.

Statistical Documents

Bradley, Martin B., et al. *Churches and Church Membership in the United States, 1990.* Atlanta: Glenmary Research Center, 1992.

Johnson, Charles, et al., comps. *Statistical Atlas of Southern Counties: Listing and Analysis of Socio-Economic Indices of 1,104 Southern Counties.* Chapel Hill: University of North Carolina Press, 1941.

Johnson, Douglas W., Paul R. Picard, and Bernard Quinn. *Churches and Church Membership in the United States, 1971.* Washington, D.C.: Glenmary Research Center, 1974.

Jordan, Max F., and Lloyd D. Bender. *An Economic Survey of the Ozark Region.* Agricultural Economic Report no. 97. Washington, D.C.: Economic Research Service, USDA, 1966.

McCuen, W. J. *Historical Report of the Secretary of State, 1986.* Edited by Steve Faris. Little Rock: Arkansas Secretary of State, 1986.

Minutes of Mortgages and Deeds of Trust, Stone County, Arkansas. Stone County Courthouse, Mountain View, Arkansas.

Ozarks Regional Commission. *1974 Annual Report.* Washington, D.C., 1974.

Population Schedules of the Seventh Census: Slave Schedules. Arkansas, 1850. Microfilm.

Sistler, Byron, and Barbara Sistler, transcribers and indexers. *1850 Census— Tennessee.* 7 vols. Evanston, Ill.: Byron Sistler & Associates, 1974–76.

Synod of Arkansas of the Presbyterian Church in the United States. *Minutes of the Seventieth Session of the Synod of Arkansas of the Presbyterian Church in the United States.* Little Rock, 1922.

U.S. Department of State. Office of the Census. Agricultural Manuscript Census Schedules. Arkansas, 1850, 1860, 1870, 1880. Microfilm.

———. *Compendium of the Enumeration of the Inhabitants and Statistics of the U.S. Sixth Census.* Washington, D.C.: GPO, 1841.

———. *Seventh Census of the United States, 1850: Agriculture.* Washington, D.C.: GPO, 1853.

U.S. Department of the Interior. Office of the Census. *Eighth Census of the United States, 1860: Agriculture.* Washington, D.C.: GPO, 1864.

———. *Ninth Census of the United States, 1870: Wealth and Industry.* Washington, D.C.: GPO, 1872.

———. *Tenth Census of the United States, 1880: Agriculture.* Washington, D.C.: GPO, 1883.

————. *Eleventh Census of the United States, 1890: Agriculture.* Washington, D.C.: GPO, 1895.

————. *Eleventh Census of the United States, 1890: Population.* Washington, D.C.: GPO, 1895.

————. *Eleventh Census of the United States, 1890: Report on Mineral Industries in the United States.* Washington, D.C.: GPO, 1892.

————. *Twelfth Census of the United States, 1900: Agriculture.* Washington, D.C.: GPO, 1903.

U.S. Department of Commerce. Bureau of the Census. *Fourteenth Census of the United States, 1920: Agriculture.* Washington, D.C.: GPO, 1922.

————. *Religious Bodies, 1926: Summary and Detailed Tables.* Vol. 1. Washington, D.C.: GPO, 1930.

————. *Census of Agriculture, 1935: Reports for States, with Statistics by Counties.* Vol. 1, part 2. Washington, D.C.: GPO, 1936.

————. *Religious Bodies, 1936: Summary and Detailed Tables.* Vol. 1. Washington, D.C.: GPO, 1941.

————. *Census of Agriculture, 1945: Statistics for Counties—Arkansas.* Vol. 1, part 23. Washington, D.C.: GPO, 1946.

————. *Census of Agriculture, 1954: Statistics for Counties—Arkansas.* Vol. 1, part 34. Washington, D.C.: GPO, 1957.

————. *Census of Agriculture, 1964: Statistics for Counties—Arkansas.* Vol. 1, part 34. Washington, D.C.: GPO, 1967.

————. *Census of Agriculture, 1974: State and County Data—Arkansas.* Vol. 1, part 4. Washington, D.C.: GPO, 1977.

————. *Census of Agriculture, 1992: State and County Data—Arkansas.* Vol. 1, part 4. Washington, D.C.: GPO, 1994.

Wright, Harold Bell. *The Shepherd of the Hills.* New York: Grosset & Dunlap, 1907.

Arkansas Agricultural Experiment Station Publications

AAES. *Decline of the Church Serving Farmers.* AAES 56th Annual Report. 1944.

AAES and Agricultural Marketing Service. *Prices and Price Indexes for Arkansas Farm Products, 1910–1959.* No. 627. 1960.

Fielder, V. B. *Type-of-Farming Areas in Arkansas.* No. 555. 1955.

Gow, R. M. *Tick Eradication in Arkansas.* No. 119. 1914.

Jackson, Hilliard, and D. G. Lafferty. *Cattle Sales and Purchases by Arkansas Farmers.* No. 516. 1951.

Meenen, H. J. *Supply and Utilization of Milk Sold in Arkansas.* No. 524. 1952.

Osgood, Otis T. *Farm Planning in the Eastern Ozarks.* No. 435. 1943.

Osgood, Otis T., and John W. White. *Livestock Auctions in Arkansas.* No. 439. 1943.

Tebbetts, Diane O. *Resident and Tourist Perceptions of the Ozark Folk Center.* AAES Special Report no. 24. 1976.

Wilson, Isabella C., and William H. Metzler. *Sickness and Medical Care in an Ozark Area in Arkansas.* No. 353. 1938.

Interviews

ORAL HISTORIES

"Good Times and Sorrow" Oral History Collection (OHC), Shiloh Museum of
    Ozark History, Springdale, Arkansas (Susan Young, interviewer)
    Austin, Jesse Oren. King's River Valley, Arkansas. 23 September 1996.
    Benedict, Goldie Faires Ham. Forum, Arkansas. 7 August 1996.
    Ferrel, Eula Karr. Pettigrew, Arkansas. 11 July 1996.
    Hunter, Irene Jackson. Huntsville, Arkansas. 8 July 1996.
    Thacker, Pauline Jackson. Pettigrew, Arkansas. 11 October 1995.
Ozark Heritage Institute and Ozark Oral History Office (OHI/OOHO), University
    of Central Arkansas, Conway, Arkansas (Vaughn Brewer, interviewer)
    Copeland, Percy, and Ida Griffin. Stone County, Arkansas. Ca. 1979.
    Stevens, Aaron. Stone County, Arkansas. Ca. 1979.
    Treat, Stonewall. Big Flat, Arkansas. Ca. 1979.
Ozark Oral History Project (OOHP), Ozark Cultural Resource Center, Ozark Folk
    Center, Mountain View, Arkansas (conducted by author)
    Billingsley, Beulah. Violet Hill, Arkansas. 29 June 1993.
    Billingsley, Kennard. Violet Hill, Arkansas. 10 November 1997.
    Clark, Louie. Drasco, Arkansas. 7 September 1993.
    Fox, Benson. Leslie, Arkansas. 20 July 1993.
    Garner, Glenna. Williford, Arkansas. 24 August 1993.
    Hackett, Glenn. Shirley, Arkansas. 27 August 1993.
    Harral, Rex. Wilburn, Arkansas. 21 July 1993.
    Matthews, Jeff. Imboden, Arkansas. 24 August 1993.
    Miller, John E. Melbourne, Arkansas. 15 December 1997.
    Rainey, Leo. Batesville, Arkansas. 9 October 1998.
    Rhoads, Zela. Agnos, Arkansas. 2 October 1998.
    Ross, Tom. Mountain View, Arkansas. 8 July 1993.
    Tanner, Hugh. Wiseman, Arkansas. 6 November 1997.
    Thompson, Audrey. Highland, Arkansas. 4 August 1993.
    Waddell, L. V. Imboden, Arkansas. 19 August 1993.
    Watkins, Lillie Mae. Batesville, Arkansas. 12 July 1993.
    Watts, Ray. Calico Rock, Arkansas. 3 August 1993.
    Webb, Doyle. Mount Pleasant, Arkansas. 11 November 1997.
    Wells, Vernon. Horseshoe Bend, Arkansas. 21 November 1997.
Shiloh Museum Oral History Collection (SMOHC), Springdale, Arkansas
    Giffels, Irma. No. 5-93-60-09A. 9 June 1992.

PUBLISHED INTERVIEWS

Southerland, Mrs. J. K., and Mr. and Mrs. Paul Henry. Interview by Franklin Evarts.
    June 1987. Transcribed in *The Poultry Industry in Arkansas: An Oral History.* Vol.
    2. Springdale: Shiloh Museum, 1989.
Thompson, John B. Interview by William David Spier. 12 November 1973. Tran-
    scribed in Spier, "Farming and Mining Experience: Independence County,
    Arkansas, 1900–1925." Ph.D. diss., Washington University, 1974.

Newspapers and Periodicals

American Aberdeen-Angus Herd-Book (Webster City, Iowa)
American Heritage
American Magazine
American Mercury
Americas
Arkansas Democrat-Gazette
Arkansas Gazette
Arkansas Times (magazine)
Arkansas Times (newspaper)
Atlantic Monthly
Batesville Guard
Baxter Bulletin (Mountain Home)
Benton County Democrat
Better Homes and Gardens
Cherokee Villager
Cleburne County Times
Collier's
Daily News (Rogers)
Dirt Dauber (Harrison, Arkansas, CCC camp)
50 Plus
Forbes
Fortune
Forum and Century
Gadfly
Harrison Times
Holiday
Horseshoe Progress
House Beautiful
Informer and Newton County Times (Jasper)
Kansas City Star
Melbourne Clipper
Melbourne Times
Mother Earth News
Mountain Echo (Yellville)
Mountain Wave (Marshall)
National Geographic
North American Review
Outlook
OzarksWatch
Progressive Farmer
Rayburn's Ozark Guide
Reader's Digest
Reporter

Review of Reviews and World's Work
St. Louis Post-Dispatch
Salem Headlight
Saturday Evening Post
Scribner's Magazine
Southern Living
Spring River Times (Hardy)
Stone County Leader (Mountain View)
Travel
Travel Holiday
Van Buren County Democrat

Secondary Sources

Abrahams, Roger D. *A Singer and Her Songs: Almeda Riddle's Book of Ballads.* Baton Rouge: Louisiana State University Press, 1970.

Allured, Janet. "Ozark Women and the Companionate Family in the Arkansas Hills, 1870–1910." *Arkansas Historical Quarterly* 47 (Autumn 1988): 230–56.

Ashcraft, Robert, et al. *Pioneer Faith: The History of Missionary Baptist Associations and Churches in Arkansas from 1818 to 1920.* Malvern: State Association of Missionary Baptist Churches in Arkansas, 1994.

Baker, Russell P. "Jacob Wolf." *Arkansas Historical Quarterly* 37 (Summer 1978): 182–92.

Beary, Michael J. *Black Bishop: Edward T. Demby and the Struggle for Racial Equality in the Episcopal Church.* Studies in Anglican History. Urbana: University of Illinois Press, 2001.

Beaver, Patricia Duane. *Rural Community in the Appalachian South.* Lexington: University Press of Kentucky, 1986.

Becker, Jane S. *Selling Tradition: Appalachia and the Construction of an American Folk, 1930–1940.* Chapel Hill: University of North Carolina Press, 1998.

Bendix, Regina. "Tourism and Cultural Displays: Inventing Traditions for Whom?" *Journal of American Folklore* 102 (1989): 131–46.

Benton County Heritage Committee. *History of Benton County, Arkansas.* Rogers, Ark.: Benton County Heritage Committee, 1991.

Berry, Earl, ed. *History of Marion County.* Little Rock: Marion County Historical Association, 1977.

Berry, Evalena. *Sugar Loaf Springs: Heber's Elegant Watering Place.* Conway, Ark.: River Road Press, 1985.

———. *Time and the River: A History of Cleburne County.* Little Rock: Rose Publishing Company, 1982.

Biles, Roger. *The South and the New Deal.* Lexington: University Press of Kentucky, 1994.

Billingsley, Kirby. "The Arkansas Picnic in Wenatchee, Washington." *Izard County Historian* 15 (July 1984): 36–38.

Black, Earl, and Merle Black. *Politics and Society in the South*. Cambridge: Harvard University Press, 1987.

Black, J. Dickson. *History of Benton County*. Little Rock: N.p., 1975.

Boles, John B. *The Great Revival: Beginnings of the Bible Belt*. Religion in the South. 1972. Reprint, Lexington: University Press of Kentucky, 1996.

Bolton, S. Charles. *Arkansas, 1800–1860: Remote and Restless*. Histories of Arkansas. Fayetteville: University of Arkansas Press, 1998.

Boorstin, Daniel J. *The Image, or What Happened to the American Dream*. New York: Atheneum, 1962.

Britton, Nancy. *Two Centuries of Methodism in Arkansas, 1800–2000*. Little Rock: August House, 2000.

———, ed. "The W. L. McGuire Journals." *Independence County Chronicle* 34 (April–July 1993): 3–38.

Brown, C. J. *Cattle on a Thousand Hills: A History of the Cattle Industry in Arkansas*. Fayetteville: University of Arkansas Press, 1996.

Brown, D. Clayton. *Electricity for Rural America: The Fight for the REA*. Contributions in Economics and Economic History, no. 29. Westport, Conn.: Greenwood Press, 1980.

Browne, W. A. "Some Frontier Conditions in the Hilly Portion of the Ozarks." *Journal of Geography* 28 (May 1929): 181–88.

Burnett, Abby, with Ellen Compton and John D. Little. *When the Presbyterians Came to Kingston: Kingston Community Church, 1917–1951*. Kingston, Ark.: Bradshaw Mountain Publishers, 2000.

Campbell, John C. *The Southern Highlander and His Homeland*. New York: Russell Sage Foundation, 1921.

Campbell, Thomas H., et al. *Arkansas Cumberland Presbyterians, 1812–1984: A People of Faith*. Memphis, Tenn.: Arkansas Synod of the Cumberland Presbyterian Church, 1985.

Chesnutt, E. F. "Rural Electrification in Arkansas, 1935–1940: The Formative Years." *Arkansas Historical Quarterly* 46 (Autumn 1987): 215–60.

Christ, Mark K., ed. *Rugged and Sublime: The Civil War in Arkansas*. Fayetteville: University of Arkansas Press, 1994.

Clark, Ruby Neal, et al. *A History of Van Buren County*. Conway, Ark.: River Road Press, 1976.

Clark, Thomas D. *Pills, Petticoats, and Plows: The Southern Country Store*. Norman: University of Oklahoma Press, 1964.

Cochran, Robert B. "All the Songs in the World: The Story of Emma Dusenbury." *Arkansas Historical Quarterly* 44 (Spring 1985): 3–15.

———. *Our Own Sweet Sounds: A Celebration of Popular Music in Arkansas*. Fayetteville: University of Arkansas Press, 1996.

———. *Vance Randolph: An Ozark Life*. Urbana: University of Illinois Press, 1985.

Cochran, Robert, and Michael Luster. *For Love and for Money: The Writings of Vance Randolph, An Annotated Bibliography*. Batesville: Arkansas College Folklore Archive Publications, 1979.

Cohen, Erik. "Authenticity and Commoditization in Tourism." *Annals of Tourism Research* 15 (1988): 371–86.

Combs, Samm Woolley. *A Pickin' and a Grinnin' on the Courthouse Square: An Ozark Family Album*. Mountain View, Ark.: Decisive Moments Press, 1990.

Compton, Neil. *Battle for the Buffalo River: A Twentieth-Century Conservation Crisis in the Ozarks*. Fayetteville: University of Arkansas Press, 1992.

Conkin, Paul K. *The New Deal*. Arlington Heights, Ill.: AHM Publishing, 1967.

Craig, Marion S., and George E. Lankford. "Letters from a Steamboat Passenger." *Independence County Chronicle* 36 (October 1994–January 1995): 9–24.

Cralle, Walter O. "Social Change and Isolation in the Ozark Mountain Region of Missouri." *American Journal of Sociology* 41 (January 1936): 435–46.

Daniel, Pete. *Breaking the Land: The Transformation of Cotton, Tobacco, and Rice Cultures since 1880*. Urbana: University of Illinois Press, 1985.

Denton, I. *Old Brands and Lost Trails: Arkansas and the Great Cattle Drives*. Fayetteville: University of Arkansas Press, 1991.

Desmarais, Ralph, and Edd Jeffords, eds. *Uncertain Harvest: The Family Farm in Arkansas*. Eureka Springs, Ark.: Ozark Institute, 1980.

Dethloff, Henry C., and Donald H. Dyal. *A Special Kind of Doctor: A History of Veterinary Medicine in Texas*. College Station: Texas A&M University Press, 1991.

Dougan, Michael B. *Arkansas Odyssey*. Little Rock: Rose Publishing Company, 1996.

——. *Confederate Arkansas: The People and Policies of a Frontier State in Wartime*. Tuscaloosa: University of Alabama Press, 1976.

Dunn, Durwood. *Cade's Cove: The Life and Death of a Southern Appalachian Community, 1818–1937*. Knoxville: University of Tennessee Press, 1988.

Eller, Ronald D. *Miners, Millhands, and Mountaineers: The Modernization of the Appalachian South, 1880–1930*. Knoxville: University of Tennessee Press, 1982.

Fair, James R., Jr. "The Batesville White Lime Company." *Independence County Chronicle* 16 (January 1975): 2–14.

——. *The North Arkansas Line: The Story of the Missouri & North Arkansas Railroad*. Berkeley, Calif.: Howell-North Books, 1969.

Fersh, George, and Mildred Fersh. *Bessie Moore: A Biography*. Little Rock: August House, 1986.

Fite, Gilbert C. *Cotton Fields No More: Southern Agriculture, 1865–1980*. Lexington: University Press of Kentucky, 1984.

——. *From Vision to Reality: A History of Bella Vista Village, 1915–1993*. Rogers, Ark.: RoArk Printing, 1993.

——. "Recent Progress in the Mechanization of Cotton Production in the United States." *Agricultural History* 24 (January 1950): 19–28.

Fleming, John. *The Blanchard Springs Caverns Story*. Little Rock: Gallinule Society, 1973.

——. *The White River of the Ozarks: From Saber-Tooth Tigers to Fighting Rainbows*. Conway, Ark.: Gallinule Publishing Company, 1973.

Fletcher, John Gould. *Arkansas*. John Gould Fletcher Series, vol. 3. 1947. Reprint, Fayetteville: University of Arkansas Press, 1989.

——. *Life Is My Song*. New York: Farrar and Rinehart, 1937.

————. "The Ozark Folklore Society." *Arkansas Historical Quarterly* 8 (Winter 1949): 115.

Fligstein, Neil. *Going North: Migration of Blacks and Whites from the South, 1900–1950.* New York: Academic Press, 1981.

Flynt, Wayne. *Poor but Proud: Alabama's Poor Whites.* Tuscaloosa: University of Alabama Press, 1989.

Froelich, Jacqueline, and David Zimmermann. "Total Eclipse: The Destruction of the African American Community of Harrison, Arkansas, in 1905 and 1909." *Arkansas Historical Quarterly* 58 (Summer 1999): 131–59.

Gerlach, Russel L. *Immigrants in the Ozarks: A Study in Ethnic Geography.* University of Missouri Studies, no. 64. Columbia: University of Missouri Press, 1976.

————. "Ulster Influence on Ozark Landscapes." *Mid-America Folklore* 18 (Spring 1990): 34–42.

Griffith, Nancy S. "Michael Shelby Kennard." *Independence County Chronicle* 38 (October 1996–January 1997): 33–52.

Hadwiger, Don F., and Clay Cochran. "Rural Telephones in the United States." *Agricultural History* 58 (July 1984): 221–37.

Hahn, Steven. *The Roots of Southern Populism: The Transformation of the Georgia Upcountry, 1850–1890.* New York: Oxford University Press, 1982.

Handley, Lawrence R. "Settlement across Northern Arkansas as Influenced by the Missouri & North Arkansas Railroad." *Arkansas Historical Quarterly* 33 (Winter 1974): 273–92.

Hanks, Dale. "Mount Olive: Its Rise and Fall." *Izard County Historian* 6 (April 1975): 3–12.

Hargrove, Edwin C., and Paul K. Conkin, eds. *TVA: Fifty Years of Grassroots Bureaucracy.* Urbana: University of Illinois Press, 1983.

Harington, Donald. *The Architecture of the Arkansas Ozarks.* 1975. Reprint, New York: Harcourt Brace Jovanovich, Harvest, 1987.

————. *Let Us Build Us a City: Eleven Lost Towns.* 1986. Reprint, New York: Harcourt Brace Jovanovich, Harvest, 1994.

Harrell, David Edwin, Jr. *Quest for a Christian America: The Disciples of Christ and American Society to 1866.* Nashville, Tenn.: Disciples of Christ Historical Society, 1966.

Harris, Hertie. "History of the Town of Guion." *Izard County Historian* 15 (October 1984): 3–15.

Hill, Samuel S., ed. *Varieties of Southern Religious Experience.* Baton Rouge: Louisiana State University Press, 1988.

Hinson, E. Glenn. *A History of Baptists in Arkansas, 1818–1978.* Little Rock: Arkansas Baptist State Convention, 1979.

Hsiung, David C. *Two Worlds in the Tennessee Mountains: Exploring the Origins of Appalachian Stereotypes.* Lexington: University Press of Kentucky, 1997.

Huddleston, Duane. "The Early Jefferys of North Central Arkansas, 1816–1850." *Izard County Historian* 3 (January 1972): 3–24.

Huddleston, Duane, Sammie Rose, and Pat Wood. *Steamboats and Ferries on White River: A Heritage Revisited.* Conway: University of Central Arkansas Press, 1995.

Hull, Clifton E. *Shortline Railroads of Arkansas*. Norman: University of Oklahoma Press, 1969.

Hurt, R. Douglas, ed. *The Rural South since World War II*. Baton Rouge: Louisiana State University Press, 1998.

Hutson, Cecil Kirk. "Texas Fever in Kansas, 1866–1930." *Agricultural History* 68 (Winter 1994): 74–104.

Ingenthron, Elmo. *Borderland Rebellion: The History of the Civil War on the Missouri-Arkansas Border*. Branson, Mo.: Ozarks Mountaineer, 1980.

———. *Indians of the Ozark Plateau*. Branson, Mo.: Ozarks Mountaineer, 1970.

Jansma, Harriet A. "The Benton County Horticultural Society." *Arkansas Historical Quarterly* 45 (Summer 1986): 126–47.

Jeansonne, Glen. *Gerald L. K. Smith: Minister of Hate*. New Haven: Yale University Press, 1988.

Johnson, Ben F., III. *Arkansas in Modern America, 1930–1999*. Histories of Arkansas. Fayetteville: University of Arkansas Press, 2000.

———. *Fierce Solitude: A Life of John Gould Fletcher*. John Gould Fletcher Series, vol. 6. Fayetteville: University of Arkansas Press, 1994.

Johnston, James J. "Searcy County Folk Festival: 1941." *Mid-America Folklore* 17 (Fall 1989): 100–113.

Jones, Donald R. "The National Forests and Arkansas, 1907–1933." *Ozark Historical Review* 8 (Spring 1979): 1–13.

Keefe, James F., and Lynn Morrow, eds. *The White River Chronicles of S. C. Turnbo: Man and Wildlife on the Ozarks Frontier*. Fayetteville: University of Arkansas Press, 1994.

Kennan, Clara B. "Coin Harvey's Pyramid." *Arkansas Historical Quarterly* 6 (Summer 1947): 132–44.

———. "The Ozark Trails and Arkansas's Pathfinder, Coin Harvey." *Arkansas Historical Quarterly* 7 (Spring 1948): 299–316.

Kennard, George P. "Michael Shelby Kennard." In *Publications of the Arkansas Historical Association*, edited by John Hugh Reynolds, 4:379–85. Conway: Arkansas Historical Association, 1917.

Kephart, Horace. *Our Southern Highlanders*. New York: Outing Publishing Company, 1913.

Keyes, Charles F., and Pierre L. van den Berghe. "Tourism and Re-created Ethnicity." *Annals of Tourism Research* 11 (1984): 343–52.

Kirby, Jack Temple. *Rural Worlds Lost: The American South, 1920–1960*. Baton Rouge: Louisiana State University Press, 1987.

Lackey, Daniel Boone. "Cutting and Floating Red Cedar Logs in North Arkansas." *Arkansas Historical Quarterly* 19 (Winter 1960): 361–70.

Lackey, Walter F. *History of Newton County, Arkansas*. 1950. Reprint, Salem, Mass.: Higginson Book Company, n.d.

Lafferty, Lorenzo Dow, IV. "The Lafferty Family and the Rover." *Izard County Historian* 1 (April 1970): 3–11.

Lair, Jim. *An Outlander's History of Carroll County, Arkansas*. Marceline, Mo.: Walsworth Publishing, 1983.

Lankford, George E. "The Arkansas Traveller: The Making of an Icon." *Mid-America Folklore* 10 (Spring 1982): 16–23.

———. "'Beyond the Pale': Frontier Folk in the Southern Ozarks." In *The Folk: Identity, Landscapes, and Lores*, University of Kansas Publications in Anthropology, no. 17, edited by Robert J. Smith and Jerry Stannard, 53–70. Lawrence: University of Kansas, 1989.

———. "The Cherokee Sojourn in North Arkansas." *Independence County Chronicle* 18 (January 1977): 2–18.

———. "John Quincy Wolf, Jr.: An Appreciation." *Mid-America Folklore* 13 (Winter–Spring 1985): 3–8.

———. "Shawnee Convergence: Immigrant Indians in the Ozarks." *Arkansas Historical Quarterly* 58 (Winter 1999): 390–413.

Lears, T. J. Jackson. *No Place of Grace: Antimodernism and the Transformation of American Culture, 1880–1920.* New York: Pantheon Books, 1981.

Leflar, Robert A. *The First 100 Years: Centennial History of the University of Arkansas.* Fayetteville: University of Arkansas Foundation, 1972.

Lewellen, Jeffrey. "'Sheep amidst the Wolves': Father Bandini and the Colony at Tontitown, 1898–1917." *Arkansas Historical Quarterly* 45 (Spring 1986): 19–40.

Liles, Jim. *Old Folks Talking: Historical Sketches of Boxley Valley, on Buffalo River, a Place of Special Value in the Ozarks of Arkansas.* Harrison, Ark.: Buffalo National River, 1999.

Limerick, Zada, ed. *Reader's Guide to Periodical Literature: March 1963–February 1965.* New York: H. W. Wilson Company, 1965.

Lindley, Helen C. "The Hoss-Hair Pullers and Hill-Billy Quartet." *Izard County Historian* 5 (April 1974): 9–13.

———. "The Watkins Brothers and Wild Haws." *Izard County Historian* 5 (October 1974): 2–21.

Lucas, Ann Davenport. "The Music of Jimmy Driftwood." *Mid-America Folklore* 15 (Spring 1987): 27–41.

Luttrell, Clifton B. *The High Cost of Farm Welfare.* Washington, D.C.: Cato Institute, 1989.

McAllister, Lester G. *Arkansas Disciples: A History of the Christian Church (Disciples of Christ) in Arkansas.* N.p.: Christian Church in Arkansas, 1984.

MacCannell, Dean. "Staged Authenticity: Arrangements of Social Space in Tourist Settings." *American Journal of Sociology* 79 (November 1973): 589–603.

McClurkan, Burney B. *A Brief History of Camp Sage.* Little Rock: Arkansas Highway Transportation Department, 1985.

McCulloh, Judith. "Uncle Absie Morrison's Historical Tunes." *Mid-America Folklore* 3 (Winter 1975): 95–104.

McGinnis, A. C. "Arkansas College, 1872–1972." *Independence County Chronicle* 14 (October 1972): 3–64.

———. *A History of Independence County, Arkansas.* Published as *Independence County Chronicle* 17 (April 1976).

McKinney, Edgar D. "Images, Realities, and Cultural Transformation in the Missouri Ozarks, 1920–1960." Ph.D. diss., University of Missouri, 1990.

McKinney, Gordon B. *Southern Mountain Republicans, 1865–1900: Politics and the Appalachian Community.* Appalachian Echoes. 1978. Reprint, Knoxville: University of Tennessee Press, 1998.

McLeod, Walter B. *Centennial Memorial History of Lawrence County.* Russellville, Ark.: Russellville Printing Company, 1936.

McNeil, W. K. *Ozark Country.* Folklife in the South Series. Jackson: University Press of Mississippi, 1995.

———. *Southern Mountain Folksongs: Traditional Songs from the Appalachians and the Ozarks.* American Folklore Series. Little Rock: August House, 1993.

———, ed. *Appalachian Images in Folk and Popular Culture.* 2d ed. Knoxville: University of Tennessee Press, 1995.

McWilliams, Carey. *Ill Fares the Land: Migrants and Migratory Labor in the United States.* Boston: Little, Brown and Company, 1942.

Malone, Bill C. *Country Music, USA.* Austin: University of Texas Press, 1985.

———. *Singing Cowboys and Musical Mountaineers: Southern Culture and the Roots of Country Music.* Athens: University of Georgia Press, 1993.

Masterson, James R. *Tall Tales of Arkansaw.* Boston: Chapman and Grimes, 1942. Reprint, with the title *Arkansas Folklore: The Arkansas Traveler, Davey Crockett, and Other Legends,* Little Rock: Rose Publishing, 1974.

Messick, Mary Ann. *History of Baxter County, 1873–1973.* Mountain Home, Ark.: Chamber of Commerce, 1973.

Miller, Wilbur R. *Revenuers and Moonshiners: Enforcing Federal Liquor Law in the Mountain South, 1865–1900.* Chapel Hill: University of North Carolina Press, 1991.

Moneyhon, Carl H. *Arkansas and the New South, 1874–1929.* Histories of Arkansas. Fayetteville: University of Arkansas Press, 1997.

———. *The Impact of the Civil War and Reconstruction on Arkansas: Persistence in the Midst of Ruin.* Baton Rouge: Louisiana State University Press, 1994.

Morgan, Gordon D. *Black Hillbillies of the Arkansas Ozarks.* Fayetteville: University of Arkansas Department of Sociology, 1973.

Morris, Robert L. "Opie Read, Arkansas Journalist." *Arkansas Historical Quarterly* 2 (March 1943): 246–54.

Morrow, Lynn, and Linda Myers-Phinney. *Shepherd of the Hills Country: Tourism Transforms the Ozarks, 1880s–1930s.* Fayetteville: University of Arkansas Press, 1999.

Morton, H. D. *A History of the Ozark Division Mountain Mission Schools of the Home Mission Board, Southern Baptist Convention.* Russellville, Ark., 1958.

Mosier, Susan. "The 1922 'Tick War': Dynamite, Barn Burning, and Murder in Independence County." *Independence County Chronicle* 41 (October 1999–January 2000): 3–22.

Mullins, David W. "History of Sharp County, Arkansas." M.A. thesis, University of Colorado, 1934.

Otto, John Solomon. *The Southern Frontiers, 1607–1860: The Agricultural Evolution of the Colonial and Antebellum South.* Contributions in American History, no. 133. Westport, Conn.: Greenwood Press, 1989.

Owsley, Frank L. *Plain Folk of the Old South.* 1949. Reprint, Baton Rouge: Louisiana State University Press, 1982.

Pace, Norma, Audrey Swope, and Jean Simers. "Mammoth Spring: The Head of the River." *Fulton County Chronicle* 1 (Winter 1982): 30–36.

Pitcaithley, Dwight T. "Buffalo River: An Ozark Region from Settlement to National River." Ph.D. diss., Texas Tech University, 1976.

———. "Zinc and Lead Mining along the Buffalo River." *Arkansas Historical Quarterly* 37 (Winter 1978): 293–305.

Porter, William T., ed. *The Big Bear of Arkansas and Other Tales.* 1843. Reprint, New York: AMS Press, 1973.

Powell, Lee Riley. *J. William Fulbright and His Times: A Political Biography.* Memphis: Guild Bindery Press, 1996.

Powell, Wilson. "Cotton Ginning in Independence and Other Hill Counties." *Independence County Chronicle* 9 (April 1968): 24–50.

Pudup, Mary Beth, Dwight B. Billings, and Altina L. Waller, eds. *Appalachia in the Making: The Mountain South in the Nineteenth Century.* Chapel Hill: University of North Carolina Press, 1995.

Rafferty, Milton D. "Changing Economy and Landscape in the Ozark-Ouachita Highland." *Mid-America Folklore* 15 (Spring 1987): 4–20.

———. *The Ozarks: Land and Life.* 1980. Reprint, Fayetteville: University of Arkansas Press, 2001.

———. *The Ozarks Outdoors: A Guide for Fishermen, Hunters, and Tourists.* Norman: University of Oklahoma Press, 1985.

Rainey, Leo, Orilla Pinkston, and Olaf Pinkston. *Songs of the Ozark Folk.* Branson, Mo.: Ozarks Mountaineer, 1972.

Rand, Edward Reed. "Edward Nicholas Rand." *Izard County Historian* 2 (October 1971): 14–20.

Randolph, Vance. "Ballad Hunters in North Arkansas." *Arkansas Historical Quarterly* 7 (Spring 1948): 1–10.

———. "Folklore and Common Sense." *Arkansas Historical Quarterly* 9 (Summer 1950): 108–9.

———. "The Ozark Dialect in Fiction." *American Speech* 2 (March 1927): 283–89.

———. "Recent Fiction and the Ozark Dialect." *American Speech* 6 (August 1931): 425–28.

Rayburn, Otto Ernest. "Arkansas Folklore: Its Preservation." *Arkansas Historical Quarterly* 10 (Summer 1951): 210–20.

———. *The Eureka Springs Story.* 1954. Reprint, Eureka Springs, Ark.: Wheeler Printing, 1982.

———. *Forty Years in the Ozarks: An Autobiography.* 1957. Reprint, Eureka Springs, Ark.: Wheeler Printing, 1983.

Reed, Roy. *Faubus: The Life and Times of an American Prodigal.* Fayetteville: University of Arkansas Press, 1997.

Rothrock, Thomas. "Congressman James William Trimble." *Arkansas Historical Quarterly* 28 (Spring 1969): 76–85.

Rudolph, Leighton, Lucas Carpenter, and Ethel C. Simpson, eds. *Selected Letters of John Gould Fletcher.* John Gould Fletcher Series, vol. 7. Fayetteville: University of Arkansas Press, 1996.

Rushing, Phillip Rodney. "Early History of Rural Special School." *Heritage of Stone* 4 (Fall 1980): 27–30.

Salstrom, Paul. *Appalachia's Path to Dependency: Rethinking a Region's Economic History, 1730–1940.* Lexington: University Press of Kentucky, 1994.

Santeford, Lawrence G., et al. *Empty Rooms and Broken Dishes: Results of Testing Ten Historic Sites in the Sullivan Creek Project Area, Independence and Sharp Counties, Arkansas.* West Fork, Ark.: Spears Professional Environmental & Archeological Research Services, 1993.

Sauer, Carl Ortwin. *The Geography of the Ozark Highland of Missouri.* 1920. Reprint, New York: AMS Press, 1971.

Schlesinger, Arthur M., Jr. *The Crisis of the Old Order.* Boston: Houghton Mifflin, 1957.

Schwartz, Marvin. *J. B. Hunt: The Long Haul to Success.* Fayetteville: University of Arkansas Press, 1992.

———. *Tyson: From Farm to Market.* University of Arkansas Press Series in Business History. Fayetteville: University of Arkansas Press, 1991.

Shaddoxx, Diane Patricia. "Sawmills in the Ozark National Forest of Arkansas." M.A. thesis, University of Arkansas, 1986.

Shapiro, Henry. *Appalachia on Our Mind: The Southern Mountains and Mountaineers in the American Consciousness, 1870–1920.* Chapel Hill: University of North Carolina Press, 1978.

Shea, William L., and Earl J. Hess. *Pea Ridge: Civil War Campaign in the West.* Chapel Hill: University of North Carolina Press, 1992.

Sherman, Harold. "They All Come Back." *Heritage of Stone* 2 (Fall 1978): 9–14.

Shi, David E. *The Simple Life: Plain Living and High Thinking in American Culture.* New York: Oxford University Press, 1985.

Shideler, James H., ed. *Agriculture in the Development of the West.* Washington, D.C.: Agricultural History Society, 1975.

Shiloh Museum. *History of Washington County, Arkansas.* Springdale, Ark.: Shiloh Museum, 1989.

Shinn, Josiah H. *Pioneers and Makers of Arkansas.* Little Rock: Democrat, 1908.

Shipley, Ellen Compton. "'But a Smile Looks Better in Print': The Literary Enterprises of Otto Ernest Rayburn." *Arkansas Libraries* (March 1982): 20–23.

———. "The Pleasures of Prosperity: Bella Vista, Arkansas, 1917–1929." *Arkansas Historical Quarterly* 37 (Summer 1978): 99–129.

Shiras, Frances H. *History of Baxter County.* Mountain Home, Ark., 1939.

———. "Norfork Dam." *Arkansas Historical Quarterly* 4 (Spring 1945): 150–58.

Shiras, Tom. *Walking Editor of the Ozarks.* Mountain Home, Ark.: Shiras Family Print Shop, 1998.

Simpson, Ethel. "Arkansas Lives: The Ozark Quest of Otto Ernest Rayburn." *Arkansas Libraries* 39 (March 1982): 12–19.

———. "Otto Ernest Rayburn, an Early Promoter of the Ozarks." *Arkansas Historical Quarterly* 58 (Summer 1999): 160-79.

Singer, Joseph Frank. "The Role of Migration in the Socio-Economic Adjustment of Households in an Arkansas Ozark Area." Ph.D. diss., University of Arkansas, 1971.

Smith, C. Calvin. *War and Wartime Changes: The Transformation of Arkansas, 1940–1945.* Fayetteville: University of Arkansas Press, 1986.

Smith, John I. *The Courage of a Southern Unionist: A Biography of Isaac Murphy, Governor of Arkansas, 1864–1868.* Little Rock: Rose Publishing, 1979.

———. *Forward from Rebellion: Reconstruction and Revolution in Arkansas, 1868–1874.* Little Rock: Rose Publishing, 1983.

Smith, Ted J. "Slavery in Washington County, Arkansas, 1828–1860." M.A. thesis, University of Arkansas, 1995.

Snelling, Lois. *Coin Harvey, Prophet of Monte Ne.* Point Lookout, Mo.: School of the Ozarks Press, 1973.

Spier, William David. "Farming and Mining Experience: Independence County, Arkansas, 1900–1925." Ph.D. diss., Washington University, 1974.

———. "A Social History of Manganese Mining in the Batesville District of Independence County." *Arkansas Historical Quarterly* 36 (Summer 1977): 130–57.

Stapleton, Isaac. *Moonshiners in Arkansas.* Independence, Mo.: Zion, 1948.

Steele, Philip W., and Steve Cottrell. *Civil War in the Ozarks.* Gretna, La.: Pelican Publishing, 1993.

Stein, Walter J. *California and the Dust Bowl Migration.* Contributions in American History, no. 21. Westport, Conn.: Greenwood Press, 1973.

Stephens, H. Page. "The Case of Missing Folk Music: A Study of Aspects of Musical Life in Stone County, Arkansas, from 1890–1980." *Mid-America Folklore* 10 (Fall–Winter 1982): 58–69.

Stewart-Abernathy, Leslie C. *Independent but Not Isolated: The Archeology of a Late Nineteenth Century Ozark Farmstead.* Project no. 534. Little Rock: Arkansas Archeological Survey, 1983.

Strausberg, Stephen F. *A Century of Research: Centennial History of the Arkansas Agricultural Experiment Station.* Fayetteville: Arkansas Agricultural Experiment Station, 1989.

———. *From Hills and Hollers: Rise of the Poultry Industry in Arkansas.* Fayetteville: Arkansas Agricultural Experiment Station, 1995.

Stroud, Hubert B. *The Promise of Paradise: Recreational and Retirement Communities in the United States since 1950.* Baltimore: Johns Hopkins University Press, 1995.

Taylor, Carl C., et al. *Rural Life in the United States.* New York: Alfred A. Knopf, 1949.

Thompson, Audrey. "Picking Cotton in the 'Bottoms.'" *Sharp County Historical Society Newsletter* (Winter 1996): 2.

Thompson, George H. *Arkansas and Reconstruction: The Influence of Geography, Economics, and Personality.* Port Washington, N.Y.: Kennikat Press, 1976.

Thünen, Johann von. *Von Thünen's Isolated State.* Translated by Carla Wartenberg. Oxford, U.K.: Pergamon Press, 1966.

Timely Club. *The Hardy History.* Hardy, Ark.: Timely Club, 1981.

Trimble, Vance H. *Sam Walton: The Inside Story of America's Richest Man.* New York: Dutton, 1990.

Turner, Frederick Jackson. "The Significance of the Frontier in American History."

In *Annual Report of the American Historical Association for the Year 1893*, 199–227. Washington, D.C., 1894.

Twelve Southerners. *I'll Take My Stand: The South and the Agrarian Tradition*. 1930. Reprint, Baton Rouge: Louisiana State University Press, 1977.

Tyson, Van Allen. "Folklore in the Life and Work of John Gould Fletcher." Ph.D. diss., University of Arkansas, 1981.

Vance, Sandra S., and Roy V. Scott. *Wal-Mart: A History of Sam Walton's Retail Phenomenon*. New York: Twayne, 1994.

Vernon, Walter N. *Methodism in Arkansas, 1816–1976*. Little Rock: Joint Committee for the History of Arkansas Methodism, 1976.

Waller, Altina L. *Feud: Hatfields, McCoys, and Social Change in Appalachia, 1860–1900*. Chapel Hill: University of North Carolina Press, 1988.

Walz, Robert Bradshaw. "Migration into Arkansas, 1834–1880." Ph.D. diss., University of Texas, 1958.

Westphal, June, and Catharine Osterhage. *A Fame Not Easily Forgotten: An Autobiography of Eureka Springs*. Conway, Ark.: River Road Press, 1970.

Whisnant, David E. *All That Is Native and Fine: The Politics of Culture in an American Region*. Chapel Hill: University of North Carolina Press, 1983.

———. *Modernizing the Mountaineer: People, Power, and Planning in Appalachia*. Boone, N.C.: Appalachian Consortium Press, 1980.

Who's Who in America: A Biographical Dictionary of Notable Living Men and Women. Vol. 28. Chicago: Marquis—Who's Who, 1954.

Williams, C. Fred. "The Bear State Image: Arkansas in the Nineteenth Century." *Arkansas Historical Quarterly* 39 (Summer 1980): 99–111.

Williams, Cratis Dearl. "The Southern Mountaineer in Fact and Fiction." Ph.D. diss., New York University, 1961.

Williamson, J. W. *Hillbillyland: What the Movies Did to the Mountains and What the Mountains Did to the Movies*. Chapel Hill: University of North Carolina Press, 1995.

Wolf, John Quincy, Jr. "Folksingers and the Re-creation of Folksong." *Western Folklore* 26 (April 1967): 101–11.

Wood, Becky, and Jim Smith. *The Batesville Manganese District and the Cushman Manganese Mines, 1850–1959*. Cushman, Ark., 1994.

Woods, James M. *Rebellion and Realignment: Arkansas' Road to Secession*. Fayetteville: University of Arkansas Press, 1987.

Woods, Randall Bennett. *Fulbright: A Biography*. New York: Cambridge University Press, 1995.

Worley, Ted R. "Story of an Early Settlement in Central Arkansas." *Arkansas Historical Quarterly* 10 (Summer 1951): 117–37.

INDEX

Adams, John, 16
Adams, Matthew, 16
African Americans: in Ozarks, 77,
211–12, 298 (n. 61)
Agricultural Adjustment Administra-
tion, 113, 114, 117, 121
Agricultural experiment station, 94, 104;
research on fruit raising, 43, 96; eradication of cattle ticks, 95–96; effects
of on poultry industry, 105, 106, 163;
effects of on dairy industry, 118, 160;
effects of on cattle industry, 172–73,
174
Agricultural Wheel, 66, 206
Allured, Janet, 51, 120
Alpena, Ark., 99, 100
Ames, D. D., 44
Anglo-Saxon culture, 3, 223, 226, 243,
287 (n. 8)
Anoe, Pearl, 226
Appalachia, xi, 2, 3, 231, 267; migration
to Ozarks from, 19, 20; industrial
conditions in, 89, 102, 131, 232; economic dependency in, 101, 221, 231,
232, 267; image of, 131–32, 133–34, 135,
221, 222, 227, 231–32, 244, 289 (n. 42);
similarities to Ozarks, 135, 136, 190,
212, 222, 233, 237, 276 (n. 7), 277
(n. 27); folk movement in, 141, 142
Appalachian Regional Commission, 213,
267
Appleby, George and Charles, 99
Apples: production of, 35, 41–44, 96–98,

99; migratory picking of, 92, 147, 184,
185–87
Area Redevelopment Administration,
252
Arkansas, 229, 230
Arkansas, University of, 43, 61, 71, 90,
100, 102, 158, 164, 229, 230, 234, 245,
259, 272
Arkansas College (Batesville), xi, 61, 139,
250, 255, 259
Arkansas College (Fayetteville), 55,
60–61
Arkansas Craft Guild. *See* Ozark
Foothills Craft Guild
Arkansas Department of Parks and
Tourism, 254, 255
Arkansas Folk Festival, 247–52, 266, 302
(n. 60), 303 (n. 73)
Arkansas Industrial University. *See*
Arkansas, University of
Arkansas Nature Conservancy, 235
Arkansas Post, Ark., 27, 49, 52
Arkansas Power and Light Company,
117, 153–54
Arkansas River, 17, 18, 245, 276 (n. 6)
Arkansas Traveler, 130, 288 (n. 33)
Arkansaw Traveller Folk Theatre,
261–62
Ash Flat, Ark., 188
Atkins, Chet, 249
Atkins Pickle Company, 152, 153
Austin, Jesse, 183

Index

Cecil, Solomon, 16

Cedar Grove, Ark., 155

Center Ridge, Ark., 245

Centerton, Ark., 106

Champion Hoss-Hair Pullers and Hill-
Billy Quartet, 140

Cherokees, 13, 15, 17, 18, 52, 277 (n. 19)

Cherokee Village, Ark., 194–95, 261, 296
(n. 40)

Choctaw, Ark., 197

Christ of the Ozarks, 240

Church of Christ. *See* Disciples of Christ

Civilian Conservation Corps, 111, 112,
142, 172, 173, 242

Civil War, 30–31, 49

Clark, Louie, 185, 197

Clarksville, Ark., 154

Clayton, Powell, 74, 123

Cleburne County, Ark., xii, 16, 95, 246,
260, 276 (n. 6), 291 (n. 59); cotton
raising in, 36, 107–8, 114, 151; timber
harvesting in, 76; lumber industry in,
80, 185; dairy farming in, 154; poultry
industry in, 165; outmigration from,
185; retiree settlement in, 197–98; education in, 207

Clinton, Ark., 77, 117, 166, 207, 208, 246

Clinton, Bill, xi, 297 (n. 51)

Cochran, Robert, 219, 290 (n. 58)

Codrescu, Andrei, 271

Coker family, 16, 21, 278 (n. 31)

Colleges and universities. *See* Education: higher

Columbia River valley, 185, 186

Combs, Ark., 91, 92, 132

Compton, Ark., 16

Compton, Neil, 235

ConAgra, 166

Concord, Ark., 165

Contemporary ancestors. *See* Images of
Ozarkers and Ozarks

Conway, Ark., 124, 154, 159

Cooksey, William, 34

Cooper, John A., Sr., 193–95, 197, 198,
296 (n. 40)

Cooperative Extension Service, 96, 100,
102, 103, 104, 107–8, 152, 160, 163, 172,
174, 195, 245, 246, 247

Copeland, Percy, 184

Corn: production of, 21, 22, 23, 24, 26,
28, 35, 101, 113, 173; bartering of, 26;
decline in raising of, 118, 149, 173; migratory harvesting of, 184

Cotton: production of, 22, 24, 25, 26,
32–37, 106–9, 147; price of, 37; migratory picking of, 47, 182, 183, 184; and
educational institutions, 62–63; decline in raising of, 114, 118, 148,
149–51, 212

Country store, 64–65, 201–2

Craighead County, Ark.: picking cotton
in, 183

Cralle, Walter O., 290 (n. 56)

Croker, Ark., 117

Crooked Creek, 54, 81

Crutchfield, Marion, 20

Crystal Hill, Ark., 18, 52

Cumberland Presbyterians, 52, 55–57,
58, 61, 203

Cushman, Ark., 64, 73, 89, 93; as center
of manganese mining district, 83–86

Dairy production: production of butter,
23, 28, 29, 46, 104–5; production of
cream, 103, 104–5, 147, 153, 156; production of milk, 103, 104–5, 147, 153–
62, 294 (n. 62); effects of electricity
on, 117–18, 153–54, 155, 157, 158; mechanization of, 155–56, 159

Daniel, Pete, 108

Dare Mine Hollow, 78

Davey brothers, 186

Davidsonville, Ark., 17

Davis, Goldsmith, 43

Deane, Ernie, 198

Decatur, Ark., 217

Delawares, 14

Denieville, Ark., 89

Denison, W. H., 84

Dipping vats. *See* Cattle: tick fever in

Henderson's Creek, 207

Hendrix College, 288 (n. 37)

Heuston, John, 236

Hidden Creek, 95

Hidden Valley, Ark., 195

Hightower, William, 34

Hillbilly. *See* Images of Ozarkers and Ozarks

Hindsville, Ark., 104, 176

Hogs: raising of, 21, 25, 27, 29, 35, 40, 74, 79, 101; number of, 22, 27, 103, 104; marketing of, 27; cholera in, 94; slaughtering of, 113

Hogue, Wayman, 46, 130, 289 (n. 41)

Hogue family, 47

Holiness movement, 57, 203

Hollister, Lloyd, 250

Holt family, 16

Holway, B. F., 40

Hopkins County, Ky., 19

Horseshoe Bend, Ark., 161, 195–97, 261

Horton, Johnny, 249

Hudson Foods, 217

Hunt, Fanny Watkins, 26

Hunt, J. B., 213, 216

Hunter, Irene Jackson, 184, 210

Huntsville, Ala., 52

Huntsville, Ark., 64, 92, 105, 164, 202, 267

Hutchinson, Tim, 206

Hutchinson Mountain, Ark., 96

Hyde, Robert, 240

Illinois River, 23

Images of Ozarkers and Ozarks: before World War II, 119–20, 122, 130–31, 132, 133–38, 142–44, 288 (n. 34); after World War II, 220–21, 222–33, 237–38, 239, 241, 244, 245, 252, 255–56, 258, 260, 262–70, 271, 273

Imboden, Ark., 54, 173, 288 (n. 37)

Independence County, Ark., xii, 50, 52, 121, 245, 276 (n. 6), 277 (n. 18); tobacco production in, 26; Civil War in, 30; railroad construction in, 81; min-

ing in, 82–86, 88, 89; tick eradication in, 96; poultry industry in, 165–66; livestock raising in, 172; industry in, 217

Indian Territory (Okla.), 14

Iron Mountain & Southern Railroad, 66, 72

Izard County, Ark., xii, 15, 16, 117, 140, 147, 277 (n. 18); settlement in, 20, 24; tobacco production in, 22, 26, 37; agricultural production in, 23, 24, 34, 35, 117; slavery in, 25; cotton production in, 26, 32, 34, 35–36, 37, 107–9, 114, 117, 147, 148, 150, 151; corn production in, 34, 35, 117; livestock raising in, 35, 113, 169, 170, 174–75; education in, 49, 60, 62, 117, 207, 208; religion in, 57; railroad construction in, 81; timber harvesting in, 81, 82, 117; mining in, 82, 88, 89, 117; tick eradication in, 95–96; depression in, 112, 245; dairy farming in, 117, 156–62; truck farming in, 152–53; community life in, 179; outmigration from, 179, 180, 182, 186–87, 188–89; retiree settlement in, 195–97; African Americans in, 211–12

Jackson, Alvah, 123

Jackson, Irene, 184, 210

Jackson, Pauline, 207, 209, 211

Jackson, T. U., 99

Jackson County, Tenn., 20

Jacksonport, Ark., 20, 26

Jacobus, George, 197, 198

Jamestown, Ark., 52

Japton, Ark., 92

Jasper, Ark., 16, 36, 112, 116, 128, 262, 273

Jayhawkers, 31, 206

Jefferson County, Tenn., 52

Jeffery, Daniel, 23

Jeffery, Jehoida, 15, 16, 17, 19, 22, 23

Johnson, Charles, 109

Johnson, John T., 55

Johnson, Ralph, 194, 195

Johnson County, Ark., xii

in, 129; mission activity in, 132–33; part-time farming in, 176; outmigration from, 182, 183, 184

Magnetic Mountain, 240

Mammoth Spring, Ark., 33, 34, 65, 88, 124, 156, 163

Manganese. *See* Mining: manganese

Mankins, Peter, 27

Marble Falls (Wilcockson), Ark., 36, 263, 264, 265

Marion County, Ark., xii, 139, 174, 211, 277 (n. 18), 291 (n. 59); cotton production in, 25, 106, 108; tobacco manufacturing in, 37; timber harvesting in, 74; railroad construction in, 81; mining in, 86–88; depression in, 112; canneries in, 152; truck farming in, 152; dairy farming in, 154–55; outmigration from, 186; dam building in, 193; slavery in, 278 (n. 31)

Marrs, Squire B., 20, 21

Marshall, Ark., 64, 74, 75, 76, 152, 171, 211, 235, 267, 291 (n. 59)

Martin, Colonel Matthew, 82

Matney (trading post owner), 16

Matthews, Jeff, 201

Mays, Ed, 173–74

McAdoo, Julia, 226

McCord, May Kennedy, 141

McCracken, Isaac, 206

McCuistian, Rex, 156

McDaniel, Hugh, 73

McElmurray, Henry, 54

McElmurray, Samuel, 34

McElmurray, Stephen, 28

McGarrah, William, 17, 18, 19

McGarrah family, 21, 22, 277 (n. 23)

McGuire, Will, 30

McIlroy, William, 61

McKinney, Edgar D., 284 (n. 7), 288 (n. 28), 304 (n. 91)

McKinney, George, 103

McNeil, Thomas, 127

McNeil, W. K., 135, 260

McRae, Thomas, 102

Mechanization: effects of on farming, 102, 149, 150

Melbourne, Ark., 37, 64, 85, 156, 161, 166, 174, 201, 211, 267

Memphis, Tenn., 34, 124, 125, 170, 194

Menke, Albert, 43

Methodists, 53, 57, 58, 203, 288 (n. 37), 297 (n. 46)

Michigan: migration to from Ozarks, 185

Migration: from Ozarks, 6, 148, 149, 180, 184, 185, 187–90, 209, 233, 273; to Arkansas, 18; to Ozarks, 19, 20, 23, 24, 29, 233, 273; of midwesterners to Ozarks, 38–39, 96–97, 180, 190–91, 193–200; influence of religion on, 52; influence of on politics, 66; migratory labor from Ozarks, 102, 147, 180–87; from rural communities, 201

Mills, Wilbur D., 242, 243, 244, 253

Mineral water resorts, 123–24

Minick, Bob, 269

Minick, Roger, 269

Mining, 69; lead, 82, 86–87; zinc, 82, 86–88, 116; manganese, 82–86; social effects of, 85–86; marble, 88; silica, 88, 116, 117; limestone, 89

Missionary activity in Ozarks, 117, 132–33

Mississippi County, Ark.: picking cotton in, 183

Missouri: Ozark settlers from, 18

Missouri & North Arkansas Railroad, 74–76, 124, 225, 238, 285 (n. 18); influence of on agriculture, 100, 103, 153

Missouri Pacific Railroad, 82, 140, 170

Mitchell, Merlin, 230

Moccasin Creek, 78

Monte Ne, Ark., 125–26

Moonshining, 45–46

Moore, Bessie, 253

Moore, Willis, 36

Morris, James Corbett. *See* Jimmy Driftwood

Morris, Neal, 248, 303 (n. 75)

Ozark Folksongs, 228
Ozark Foothills Craft Guild, 246, 248,
 249, 251, 252, 265, 302 (n. 60)
Ozarkland, 261
Ozark National Forest, 80, 116, 210, 241,
 251
Ozark Playgrounds Association, 140, 223
Ozark Society, 235–37
Ozarks Regional Commission, 212–13,
 261
Ozark Wildlife Club, 264
Ozone, Ark., 206

Page family, 78
Paragould, Ark., 157
Parma, Ark., 208
Part-time farming, 169, 176–78
Pasadena, Calif., 189
Passion Play, 238, 240, 241
Paysinger, Mildred, 259
Peaches, 98, 99
Pea Ridge, Ark., 59; battle of, 31
Pearson, Ben, 243
Pentecostalism, 203
Penter's Bluff Landing, 82
Peorias, 15
Peterson Industries, 217
Pettibone, Levi, 11, 13
Pettigrew, Ark., 73, 121
Pfeiffer, Ark., 85
Phillips, C. W., 73
Piankashaws, 15
Pindall, Ark., 87
Pinkston, Olaf, 261
Pinkston, Orilla, 261
Pinnacle, Ark., 92
Pittman, Samuel, 40
Pleasant View, Ark., 208
Plumlee, William, 46, 47
Pocahontas, Ark., 154, 201
Poinsett County, Ark.: picking cotton
 in, 183
Poke Bayou, Ark., 15, 17, 21. *See also*
 Batesville, Ark.
Politics: in Ozarks, 66, 205–6

Ponca, Ark., 235
Pope County, Ark., xii, 46, 78
Poplar Bluff, Mo., 75
Porterfield, James, 37
Porterfield, John, 34, 37
Possum Trot, Ark., 188, 189
Potatoes: production of Irish, 23, 28, 45;
 production of sweet, 23, 28, 45
Poteau River, 18
Potosi, Mo., 11, 17
Poultry: farming, 103, 105–6, 148, 162–
 68; processing, 148, 164–66, 210; verti-
 cal integration in, 166–68; influence
 of on economy, 213–14, 216, 298
 (n. 73)
Powell, Laurence, 139, 229
Powell, Robert, 34
Pratt, Bill and Dick, 195
Price, David, 19
Pryor, David, 257
Puddister, Tom, 129
Pyeatts, 52

Rackensac, Inc., 257, 258
Rackensack Folklore Society, 249, 250,
 254–55, 256, 257–58
Rafferty, Milton D., 130, 277 (nn. 14, 23)
Railroads: construction of in Ozarks,
 69; effects of on economy, 69, 71, 93;
 and lumber industry, 72–82; demographic effects of, 77; effects of on
 mining, 84, 87; effects of on agriculture, 93, 94, 104, 153
Rainey, Leo, 245–47, 261
Rand, E. N., 64–65, 66, 67
Randolph, Vance, xi, 1, 128, 132, 135–37,
 139, 141, 143, 220, 223, 227–28, 229, 288
 (n. 39), 290 (n. 53)
Randolph County, Ark., xii, 172, 276
 (n. 6)
Rayburn, Otto Ernest, xi, 129, 142–44,
 191, 220, 223–25, 227, 238, 239, 240
Rayburn's Ozark Guide, 191, 223–24, 227,
 238
Read, Opie, 130

Index   335

Recreation Enterprises, Inc., 262, 263
Reed, John, 15
Religion: in Ozarks, 51–59, 202–4
Republican Party, 205–6, 297 (n. 51)
Resettlement Administration, 112
Retiree settlement in Ozarks, 191,
    193–200; effect of on religious de-
    mography, 203–4
Rhoads, Guy, 159, 175, 210
Rhoads, Zela, 159, 175, 183, 210
Richmond, Ted, 225, 299 (n. 13)
Richwoods, Ark., 13
Riddle, Almeda, 250, 303 (n. 75)
Riggs, Jesse, 34
Rinstein, William, 83
Ritter, Roy, 128, 164, 165
Roasting Ear Creek, 107
Robertson, Alexander Campbell, 140
Robertson, Charles F., 240
Rocky Bayou, 15
Rogers, Ark., 43, 44, 45, 88, 97–98, 115,
    125, 272; dairy industry in, 105; poul-
    try industry in, 165, 217; Wal-Mart
    store in, 214
Roman Catholicism, 203, 204
Roosevelt, Franklin D., 110
Roosevelt, Theodore, 80, 128
Ross, Tom, xii, 81, 171
Rowan County, N.C., 19
Ruddells, Ark., 89
Rural Electrification Administration,
    117, 153–54, 286 (n. 55)
Rural Special School, 208, 297 (n. 54)
Rush, Ark., 87, 88
Rush Creek, 86–88
Rushing, Ark., 208
Rushing, Nat, 103
Russell, James, 43
Rutherford County, N.C., 19

Sage (Nubbin Ridge), Ark., 35, 74, 112
Salem, Ark., 74, 117, 147, 156, 158–59, 160,
    161, 211, 246, 267
Salem (Central) Plateau, 11, 12, 13, 17;
    settlement in, 23, 24, 278 (n. 27); cot-

ton production in, 34, 106–9; timber
    harvesting in, 81; dairy farming in,
    156–62; livestock raising in, 173
Salstrom, Paul, 101, 277 (n. 27), 278
Sandburg, Carl, 138
Sanders, Everette, 245
Sandtown, Ark., 121
Santa Fe Railroad, 73
Sauer, Carl O., 21, 37
Schilling, Ernest (By Golly), 238–39
School consolidation, 207–8
Schoolcraft, Henry Rowe, 11, 12, 13, 15,
    16, 17, 21, 86, 277 (n. 23)
Scotch-Irish settlers, 19, 55, 56
Searcy County, Ark., xii, 64, 106, 140, 211,
    277 (n. 18); hunting and trapping in,
    22; cotton production in, 32, 37, 106,
    107, 109; tobacco production in, 40;
    two-party system in, 66, 206; timber
    harvesting in, 72, 75, 77; folk festival
    in, 141–42, 229; truck farming in, 152,
    153; livestock raising in, 170, 173–74;
    Buffalo River controversy in, 234–37
Searcy County Landowners' Associa-
    tion. See Buffalo River Landowners'
    Association
Seligman, Mo., 73, 123
Sense of place, 187, 188
Shaddox, Bob, 171
Shapiro, Henry, 1, 2, 131, 132
Sharp County, Ark., xii, 88, 95, 121, 245,
    259; cotton production in, 32, 36,
    107–9, 150–51; railroad access in, 34;
    religion in, 57; education in, 60; min-
    ing in, 82, 86; resorts in, 124–25; wa-
    termelon production in, 153; dairy
    farming in, 158; livestock raising in,
    170; outmigration from, 180, 182, 194;
    retiree settlement in, 194–95; domi-
    nance of Democratic Party in, 206;
    tourism in, 262
Shawnee, 14, 15
Sheep: number of, 22, 27; production of,
    23, 27, 40
Shepherd of the Hills, 133, 142, 288

(n. 39), 289 (n. 40), 304 (nn. 88, 91)
Sherman, Harold, 219–20, 242–44, 247
Shiras, Tom, 191
Shirley, Ark., 74, 209
Shirt factories, 211
Siloam Springs, Ark., 105, 287 (n. 11)
Silver Dollar City, 265, 304 (n. 88)
Silver Springs, Ark., 125
Simmons, Tommy, 256, 257
Simon, Charlie May, 129–30, 229, 230
Simon, Howard, 129–30, 229
Simpich, Frederick, 223
Singer, Joseph Frank, 233
Skyland, Ark., 208
Slaves and slavery, 17, 23, 25, 26, 29, 71, 278 (n. 31)
Sloan, Fred, 173
Sloan, Lucien, 173
Sloan, M. F., 173
Smith, E. F., 20
Smith, Gerald L. K., 239–41, 244
Smith, H. Harlin, 140
Smith, Kenneth, 234, 235
Smith, Ted J., 23, 26, 29
Smith-Lever Act, 94
Snow, O. J., 262
Snowball, Ark., 248
Soil Conservation Service, 112, 114, 118, 151, 172, 173
Sorghum, 28, 45, 65, 147, 149, 173
Southerland, Cleo Ferguson, 165
Southerland, J. K., 165–66
Southern Highlands Handicraft Guild, 246, 301 (n. 50)
Spence, Hartzell, 225
Spoke Plant, Ark., 209
Springdale, Ark., 42, 44, 272; shipment of lumber from, 73; shipment of fruit from, 98, 99; dairy industry in, 105; poultry industry in, 105–6, 163–65
Springfield, Mo., 141, 162, 170, 232
Springfield Plain, 11, 13, 92, 206; agriculture in, 22, 31, 96, 109; settlement in, 23, 24, 39, 278 (n. 27); livestock raising in, 27, 104, 172; small grains produc-

tion in, 39, 41; influence of midwesterners in, 39, 96–97; tobacco production in, 40–41; fruit production in, 41–44, 96–99, 100; education in, 61; poultry raising in, 105–6, 166; economic success of, 213, 216, 217, 272
Spring River, 17, 54, 88, 234; floating logs down, 72; tourism on, 124–25; cattle raising in bottoms of, 173; retiree settlement along, 194
St. Francis River, 17
St. James, Ark., 74
St. Joe, Ark., 141
St. Louis, Mo., 27, 210
St. Louis, Arkansas & Texas Railroad, 123
St. Louis, Iron Mountain & Southern Railroad, 34, 73, 81, 86, 87, 89, 93. *See also* Missouri Pacific Railroad
St. Louis & North Arkansas Railroad, 74. *See also* Missouri & North Arkansas Railroad
St. Louis & San Francisco Railroad (Frisco), 279 (n. 6); influence of on fruit industry, 42, 96, 100; influence of on timber and lumber industry, 72–73; influence of on agriculture, 93, 105, 156; role in development of tourism, 124
St. Paul, Ark., 73, 100, 121
Standlee, John, 17
Stay More, Ark., 129
Steamboating, 25, 32, 33, 34
Stein, Walter J., 187
Stephens, H. Page, 122, 139, 255, 256
Stevens, Aaron, 107
Stilley family, 269–70
Stockard, Sallie Walker, 138
Stone, Barton, 55
Stone County, Ark., xii, 13, 14, 95, 220, 241, 267; agriculture in, 35; education in, 60, 208, 297 (n. 54); timber harvesting in, 81; mining in, 82; dairy farming in, 103, 154; cotton production in, 107, 109, 149; depressed con-

ditions in, 112, 233; traditional music in, 122, 139, 255; folk festival in, 142, 247–52; cattle raising in, 171; outmigration from, 186; back-to-the-land movement in, 200, 251; tourism in, 241–47; folk center in, 253–60
Stong, Phil, 226
Strawberries: production of, 44, 98, 99, 100, 152
Strawberry River, 17, 57, 86, 195, 277 (n. 14); floating logs down, 72
Strickland, Stephen, 55
Stuart, Myrtle, 183
Stuttgart, Ark., 216
Sugar Loaf Prairie, 16
Sugar Loaf Springs, Ark., 124. *See also* Heber Springs, Ark.
Sullivan, Emmett, 240
Sullivan Creek, 121
Summers, Ark., 99
Summit Home, Ark., 124. *See also* Winslow, Ark.
Sunnyland, Ark., 208
Swan, William, 35, 64
Sweet Home Baptist Church, 179
Sylamore, Ark., 82, 89, 241, 244

Table Rock Dam, 191
Taney County, Mo., 16
Tanner, Hugh, 160, 161, 175, 197
Tanner, Vera, 197
Tebbetts, Diane O., 255, 258
Tellico Dam, 237
Tennessee: Ozark settlers from, 18, 19, 20
Tennessee Valley Authority, 193, 237
Thacker, Ernest, 209
Thacker, Pauline Jackson, 207, 209, 211
Thomas, Herbert L., Sr., 197
Thompson, Audrey, 181–82, 194, 197
Thompson, Ruth, 197
Thorpe, Thomas Bangs, 130
Timber and lumber industry, 71–82; environmental damage caused by, 79; effects of on livestock raising, 101, 103
Timbo, Ark., 248

Tobacco: production of, 22, 24, 25, 26, 28, 33, 37, 40–41; manufacture of, 22, 26, 37, 40
Tomatoes, 152
Tontitown, Ark., 44
Tourism: in nineteenth century, 123–24; resort communities, 125–28; after World War II, 220, 221–22, 223, 225, 233–48, 261–67; heritage-based, 241–42, 265
Treat, Stonewall, 184
Trimble, James W., 193, 235
Truck farming, 44, 151–53
Truman, Harry S., 193, 295 (n. 26)
Turkey Creek, 208
Turner, Frederick Jackson, 21
Tyson, John, 105, 162, 163–64, 165, 214
Tyson, Van A., 229
Tyson Foods, xi, 165, 213, 217

Union, Ark., 147

Valley Springs, Ark., 132
Van Buren, Ark., 25
Van Buren County, Ark., xii, 17, 80, 95, 206, 246, 260, 276 (n. 6), 277 (n. 18); cotton raising in, 32, 36, 107–8; depression in, 111; poultry industry in, 166; cattle raising in, 169; outmigration from, 180; retiree settlement in, 197–98; education in, 207, 208; African Americans in, 211
Van den Berghe, Pierre L., 266
Van Winkle, Peter, 71, 72
Violet Hill, Ark., 157, 208, 297 (n. 54)

Waddell, L. V., 183
Walker, David, 28
Walker, Wythe, 28
Wal-Mart, xi, 213, 214–16; effect of on rural and small-town businesses, 201, 202, 215
Walton, Sam, 214–16, 298 (n. 67)
Walz, Robert B., 18, 277 (n. 18)
Ward, Loyd, Sr., 125